THE VIDEO PRODUCTION GUIDE

TV 525 lines
30 frames per second

About the Author

Lon McQuillin is a producer, director, and editor of commercials, entertainment programs, and corporate, educational, and industrial programs, with more than 100 production credits to his name. His productions have won major awards at international festivals. His experience with television production dates back to 1967, and his film experience to 1961. He established his own firm, McQ Productions, in San Mateo, California, in 1976.

His writing experience includes more than four years as editor of the International Television News for ITVA, two years as contributing editor for *Video Systems* magazine, and the contribution of numerous articles and columns to various industry publications.

Lon has presented numerous seminars and workshops for ITVA and other organizations. He has given seminars at every Video Expo held in San Francisco to date, and at the Professional Videoshow in Los Angeles. He presents workshops on computer editing in San Francisco and is a faculty member of the College of San Mateo, where he teaches a course in television production.

About the Editor

Charles Bensinger has written 3 major popular how-to video books since 1977 — *The Guide to Videotape Recording, The Home Video Handbook,* and *The Video Guide.* He has also published several articles on the subject. He recently completed editing a new book, *The Video Production Guide.* Mr. Bensinger's extensive experience with video dates back to 1969 when he created instructional workshops in Television for professional advertising and film people in Hollywood, California. In 1972, he founded his own company, INNOVISION VIDEO SERVICES in Santa Barbara, California which specialized in providing editing and in-service training services for schools and institutions. In 1981. Mr. Bensinger moved his video production and writing operations to northern New Mexico where he is currently exploring the "electronic cottage concept" and the applications of small computers and video to self-sufficient rural communities.

THE VIDEO PRODUCTION GUIDE

by

LON B. McQUILLIN

EDITED BY CHARLES BENSINGER

Distributed by
video-info publications
PO Box 2685   Santa Fe, New Mexico 87501

International Standard Book Number: 0-672-22053-9
Library of Congress Catalog Card Number: 82-62200

Illustrated by: *Angela Warneke*

Printed in the United States of America.

PREFACE

Television production is one of the most fascinating, intricate, and demanding activities in which one can become involved. To many, it transcends mere occupation, and becomes a way of life—sometimes to the chagrin of spouses and other family members. It is multifaceted, to the point where the ideal television producer or director would resemble the nine-headed Hydra of Greek mythology: each head would be a specialist in one particular discipline involved in production, while all being embodied in a single person. Those who are new to the field are often over-whelmed by how much there is to learn about the practices of video production. That, however, is just the beginning. Once established in the field, one finds that the learning never stops—it's impossible to ever know everything about production, if only because the technology is constantly changing, dragging the art along with it (or in some cases, the other way around).

There are hundreds of books and magazines available that deal with various aspects of the subject, and, yet, in surveying the offerings I discovered that much of what was available fell into three rather distinct categories: introductions to low-end nonbroadcast equipment; examinations of broadcast equipment; and textbooks based mainly on studio production. There are also many books dealing with one particular aspect of production, such as lighting or sound, and many on the uses of television, but there was almost nothing that covered the entire range of operations involved in creating programs that reflected the realities of how it is done today. A good many of the books available were written ten, or even twenty, years ago, and are now out of date in areas dealing with technical matters. Thus it was that I perceived some gaps in the available literature that I thought would be worth filling, and hence, this effort.

This book provides a broad overview of television production, from the viewpoint of the producer and director. It covers both studio and location production. It deals with multicamera and single-camera production. It starts with pre-production, and takes the reader through the entire process of creating a program, to post-production and distribution. It deals with the technol-ogy (the science) and with the techniques (the art) of making programs. Perhaps most importantly, it is based on the real-life practices, including the nitty-gritty details, of production as you'll find it done by professionals.

There is information for the beginner, usually towards the front of each section, and advanced information for those who have some experience behind them. It is as multileveled and inter-disciplinary as I could make it.

As you'll discover in working your way through the pages, the tone is somewhat personal. What follows is based on my own experiences as a working producer, director and editor, and my goal has been to share as many of the tips and techniques, knowledge and understanding of the medium as I could. A personal approach seemed the best way to communicate with you as directly as possible.

The major nemesis of a book such as this is time, as was indicated above. Books about video technology tend to be outdated even as they roll off the press. While we intend to revise the book as necessary, I also have made a concerted effort to keep the importance of references to specific pieces of equipment to a minimum. While equipment is an important factor, its importance is secondary to the creative and management skills required during production.

A final note with regard to the structure of the book. While each chapter deals with a specific subject or set of subjects, and can be used as a reference on that particular area, the various aspects of production are highly interdependent, each affecting the others. This is the "gestalt" of television production, which you'll find I've dealt with in three chapters which include that word in their titles. (A definition of the word is included in the glossary.) Thus, to a fairly large extent, each chapter builds on information presented in the earlier ones, and the book was really designed to be read from front to back. (Another reason for the personal tone—to help make this a little easier to do.)

Actually, what I've attempted to present here is a miniature course of instruction—a tutorial primer on the basics and not-so-basics of television production. If you first skim the pages to get a feeling for it, and then work your way through from start to finish, you'll get the most out of it.

Welcome to the marvelous field of television production. Welcome to THE VIDEO PRODUCTION GUIDE.

LON McQUILLIN

For Brice.
I wish you could have seen this.

FOREWORD

For some time I have promised my readers a sequel to *The Video Guide*. *The Video Production Guide* is the result. I have concluded that the best way to present the enormously broad range of information dealing with hardware, people, organization, method and material associated with professional video production was to work with a writer who is constantly and currently working in broadcast, pay cable and nonbroadcast television. Author Lon McQuillin has such an involvement.

I felt that the book should immerse the reader in the actual *experience* of video production—the sights, the sounds, the movement of the crew, the conglomeration of equipment, the personal camaraderie, the busyness and tension of the set—all those physical and psychological things that make video and TV the unique personal event that it is.

I have tried to recreate the personal experience of the video production process through careful text editing, selection of photography and artwork, and special attention to the design of the book. It has been my intention also to provide the reader with a kind of personal guide through the often overwhelmingly complex and intimidating process of video production. Thus, my choice of Lon McQuillin as an experienced guide to share his substantial knowledge of all aspects of the video and television process.

It is my hope that we have succeeded in revealing and simplifying hitherto guarded and complex critical information in such a way as to assist the aspiring media producer/director toward a higher level of personal confidence as a result of this text. I would also like to feel that *The Video Production Guide* inspires some of you who experience this text to utilize video and television in a creative and constructive way that may realize some of the enormous positive potential of this great medium.

CHARLES BENSINGER

ACKNOWLEDGEMENTS

Photographic Credits:

Charles Bensinger, Lon McQuillin, Robyn Bensinger & Phelan Productions, John Sundstrom, Hali Paul and Positive Images, *Hour Magazine* (Westinghouse Broadcasting) and the following companies: American Data, Ampex, Amtel, Anton Bauer, Anvil, Arriflex, Arvin/Echo, Asaca, Barco, BTX, Chyron, Cine 60, Cinema Products, CMX, Colortran, Comprehensive Video Supply, Computer Graphic Lab, Convergence Corporation, Crosspoint Latch, Datatron, Digital Video Systems, Dynair Electronics, Grass Valley Group, Hitachi, HME, Ikegami, JVC, Kangaroo Products, Lowel, Lyon Lamb, Microtime, Mole Richardson, NEC America, O'Connor Engineering, Panasonic, Porta Brace, MCI Quantel, Rank Cintel, RCA, Recortec, Sennheiser, Sharp, Shure, Sony, Tektronix, Thompson-CSF, 3-M, Toshiba, Videomedia, and Faroudja Laboratories.

Cartoons by Michael Cockran

The author would like to thank the following organizations and individuals for their assistance in making this book possible. Some of them are seen in photographs, some read various versions of the manuscript and offered their comments and suggestions, and all contributed in one form or another to the success of the project.

Companies & Institutions:

College of San Mateo, KCSM-TV San Mateo, KTEH-TV San Jose, McDonnell/Douglas Electronics Company, One Pass Video, Phoenix Video Center, Positive Video, Recortec Inc., Stanford University Medical Center, and Video By Design.

Individuals:

Al Abrams, Matthew Adams, Agamemnon Andrianos, Tom Balhatchet, Sara Carrigan, John Chapin, Dewey Dellinger, Charles (Curly) Eason, Nick Eldridge, Ashleigh Evans, Sylvia Jacobs, Michael Kelley, Lance Kelson, Ron Litz, Liz Mamorsky, Phil Martino, Mark McCollum, Sid McCollum, Skoog McQuillin, Steve Michelson, P. J. O'Brien, Larry Rief, Peter Schiller, Conrad Slater, Beverly Steele, Bob Sweeney, Peter Thomas, Morrie Treat, Tomas Tucker, Ann Turley, Rod Williams, Jim Wiseman, and Robert Zadek.

Finally, I wish to thank Charles Bensinger, who, in his role as a publisher, made this book possible, and who, in his role as editor, along with his staff, made it much better than it might have been.

The editor would like to thank John Sundstrom, Jan Olsen, Helen Lyons, Hali Paul, Jerry Feldman, Marc Plitt, Eve Muir, and John Rupert for their valuable assistance in editing.

Contents

Part 1
Pre-Production

CHAPTER 1

Program Style

They're out there—millions of them. They may be the most valuable resource of our new age of information. In nearly every place we live and work they sit, waiting for the sizzle of micro-lightning to strike their phosphors and bring to their screens the illusion of life.

Only 40 years ago, they were the stuff of fiction. Television was a dream, a "marvel of the future" to be wondered at. Its power, its influence, could only be the subject of conjecture. Had we known at the beginning what television would become, what would we have done differently? More to the point, now that we begin to understand it, where shall we take it—and have it take us—from here?

We've arrived at a time when video technology is available to almost everyone. Home video systems now being sold in department stores all but match the quality of the large and complicated machines of a mere ten years ago. They far surpass the older equipment in terms of their size, ease of use, and economy. On a higher level, equipment capable of superb performance can now be had for the price of yesterday's "industrial" quality equipment. In short, the most powerful communications system in history has become accessible.

As this has happened, some of its "magic"—born of the mystery of the process—has evaporated. The average person can now begin to see behind the screen; can take part in the process and create his or her own programs rather than simply view those made by others.

So we lose magic in one form, but gain handsomely in the bargain as we learn to be magicians ourselves.

This book is a magician's manual. It guides the reader through the entire process of creating television programming, from pre-production, through production, to post-production, and distribution. It examines the technology involved, along with the practices of applying this technical wizardry in pursuit of the simplest and oldest of human goals: *communication.*

As with any medium, television is only a conduit, a way to get a message from one person to another. The message may be general, or personal, important, or frivolous. It may further the goals of business, education, art, philosophy, health, or government, or it may simply entertain. From a technical viewpoint, the message itself matters not at all; the process of creating and transmitting a message remains essentially the same no matter what the message is. In terms of end results, however, that statement can be turned around completely: it is the message, after all, that the entire paraphernalia has been constructed to transmit.

The point is that it's up to the reader to determine the use to which he or she will put the technology. The purpose of this book is to acquaint the reader with the mechanics, aesthetics, and, to some extent, the psychology of getting the message—whatever it may be—onto the screen.

Without ideas, creativity, and the ability to apply them, the machines are nothing but plastic, metal, and glass, and lifeless—the screens remain dark. But remember that the yin and the yang must fit together as a whole. Without the machines, and the knowledge of how to use them, the message remains a personal possession, in want of a way to make itself seen and heard.

This book, therefore, places equal emphasis on both sides of the equation, in recognition of the fact that television production involves *both* art and science.

For something so familiar and seemingly such an innocuous part of our daily lives, the average person's understanding of the processes by which we interact with television remains almost frightening vague, despite the advances of the last few years. In order to create effective programming, it is first necessary to examine the capabilities and constraints inherent in the system.

The Nature of Television

Video is a medium unlike any other. It is not like film. It is not like slides or stills. It is a medium unto itself, with very different rules and results. It has its own psychology.

Some of the differences are obvious, and are the first things taught to TV Production students, especially those making a transition from film. The most obvious difference is the smaller viewing screen, with its fixed aspect—height-to-width—ratio of 3:4. Television thus depends to a much greater extent than film on close ups. Film has greater resolution than video in that it can store many more picture elements per frame. In terms of bandwidth, film can hold upwards of 30 MHz (30 million cycles) of frequency response, whereas the best NTSC video can handle about 4.2 MHz. High Definition TV will operate in the 30 MHz range, approaching 35mm film resolution.

Videotape usually appears sharper than film on television, and this can be due to several factors—losses during the film-to-tape transfer, high quality video shown along side poor quality film, and the fact that videotape was designed for the pecularities of an electronic color system and film was not. As a result, even though TV's color resolution is far less than film, the overall TV picture appears more accurate. Again, this is because the TV color system can reproduce nearly all of the color spectrum whereas film emulsions are somewhat limited in comparison and cannot be so easily "tuned" like a video camera. Film is almost always at a disadvantage when placed on television.

At this point we should define VIDEO and TELEVISION. These words mean different things to different people, but for our purposes we are defining VIDEO as the technical process of producing tapes and TELEVISION as the end-viewable result, regardless of the method of distribution be it broadcast, cassette, cable, disc, etc. Basically, though, these two words have now become almost interchangeable with the context determining the application. The old lines of division are disappearing, and will do so even more in the future.

Television has very subtle nuances, and they need to be understood by all those who create video programming. To examine these, we need to discuss the way in which the human mind deals with and accepts stimulus from television.

Hypnotism and trance states depend on the ability of the mind to enter what is known as the alpha state. This is characterized by slow, synchronous brainwave activity. This is the basis of meditation, which is akin to common daydreaming. It is now known that the eyes and the brain are directly linked, and that the eyes may indeed be thought of as extensions of the brain. When you read a book, fry an egg, or watch a film projected on a large screen, your eyes move, creating a certain degree of active mental involvement. On the other hand, when you watch television, unless you are watching a video projector, your eyes barely move. This condition of sitting still with your eyes fixed to a small screen is an ideal method for relaxing to an alpha state. If, under these conditions, the programming is dull, the usual result is drowsiness or boredom. This will depend to an extent on other factors, such as how much coffee the viewer has recently had. It's likely that either you or friends of yours have been known to fall asleep in front of the television, thinking that you did so only because it was late and you were tired. There may have been more to it than that.

One answer would thus seem to be keeping the visual stimulus fast-paced and interesting. It's not quite that simple, though, since there is a limit to the rate at which the mind can assimilate information. When you read a book, you can stop and consider a point, or go back and re-read a section. Also, since your eyes move and your hands turn the pages, your mental state of involvement is more active. You have the ability to *participate* in the process of absorbing the information. This is not usually the case with television, since it comes

at its own rate, and the average viewer cannot go back to review something he or she has seen. In order to cope with this rapid rate of information reception, the mind tends to divert the information directly into the subconscious, with the expectation of returning to it later for consideration. Unfortunately, with commercial broadcast television, when one show ends, another begins, and all those ideas and concepts that were stored away remain there—stored away. They're there, working on your thought processes. Of course, you're less than actively aware of them. This is one of the reasons commercials work so well. It's also why many nonbroadcast educational and training programs take time to review and reinforce ideas and information, often including stopping points within the program to allow discussion of the material.

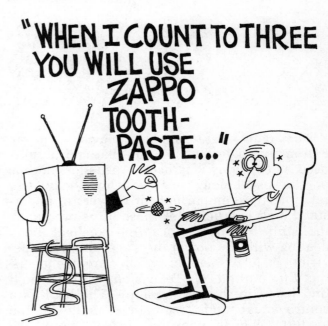

"WHEN I COUNT TO THREE YOU WILL USE ZAPPO TOOTH-PASTE..."

When I'm watching a videotape, I often stop the machine to replay a section because something previous to that section caught my attention and got me thinking, with the result that I missed what followed. Since I watch a lot of taped material, and have developed this habit, I often find that while watching broadcast television, I'll catch myself jumping up to stop the tape—only the tape is back at the station where it's out of my control!

Videotape, and the personal control it gives me, has changed the way in which I watch and react to television. More precisely, videotape allows me to *interact with* television rather than *react to it* or simply absorb it.

The point here is that television is an extremely powerful tool, one that can be misused as easily as it is used. An understanding of the psychology of the television/viewer relationship is important for viewers to understand, and is *crucial* for those of us producing the stuff to understand. An excellent book dealing with the power, use, and abuse of television is Jerry Mander's *Four Arguments for the Elimination of Television*, which you'll find listed in the bibliography. The book is a controversial and fascinating study of the medium and is one that I feel should be required reading for anyone producing video programming.

But getting back to the nature of the television medium, I feel that in order to produce effective programming it is necessary to comprehend the mechanisms by which television works. The viewer constitutes more than half the process. This is an important point: making pretty pictures with nice clean audio means nothing if the content doesn't achieve the desired results. The reverse, of course, is also true: good content presented poorly can lose

its impact. In view of the realities of both viewer expectations and the mechanics of viewer reaction, high production values and technical quality are of crucial importance in getting the message or information across. Sloppy or amateurish production values will turn most viewers off, except in instances where the content is of such high interest that the technical and aesthetic quality can be overlooked. Such instances happen, but they are very rare.

Program Style

There are perhaps dozens of ways to structure a program. Variations in style and format will determine the basic nature and "viewability" of a program. Here's a brief list of some of the available styles:

- In-studio (interviewer/host, talk show/panel discussion, talking head)
- ENG/EFP (Electronic Newsgathering/Electronic Field Production) (talking head/narrator)
- Documentary/Video Verite (Variation of above)
- Single camera or Multiple camera
- Dramatic (includes Comedy)
- Other

The "Other" category is perhaps the largest in terms of use, as it includes combinations and variations of all of the above, in addition to other forms known and unknown. For example, a soft-drink company did a series of training tapes a few years ago that were done in the style of a sportscast. Called something along the lines of *The Bottle-Handling Olympics*, it showed bottle handlers (delivery people) the correct way to handle heavy loads without injury. The program demonstrated its points by depicting an imaginary competition in which points were scored for both speed and safety. Two network-style sportscasters were on hand to commentate on the proceedings. (I've always wondered why that isn't simply "comment.") The show was handsomely done, and evidently very effective.

Of the available program styles, the dramatic and documentary forms tend to draw the viewer more deeply into the program, creating a greater sense of involvement with the information or concepts being presented. As we have seen, TV can allow the programmer to relay the material almost directly into the brain. Again, there does exist an easy opportunity to propagandize the viewer. The subjectivity of the viewer should be taken into consideration by the programmer.

It's not unusual to combine several forms within the same program. For instance, an insurance program I recently completed combined dramatic form for the opening, a documentary form for the introduction, and a talking head that included an interview, for the body of the show.

In instructional TV, the talking head, sometimes known as "Shooting the Wizard," or getting an expert in front of the camera and turning him loose, can be very appropriate to certain shows like those mentioned. In industrial or educational programs there are times when this form can be the most appropriate way to deliver the information.

On the other hand talking heads can be boring unless the talent being used is extraordinary in some way or a particular effect is intended. Sometimes, it's a real challenge to turn out an interesting and informative talking head show. Try to pull out all the stops with lighting, staging, and camerawork in an attempt to at least keep the pacing and the viewer's interest from flagging. Nevertheless, a seemingly uncinematic talking head can be used as an effective and powerful image if used creatively. Your talking head can be made more visual by shooting on location, or using some snazzy camera angles. Almost any variation is preferable to shooting dead-on in a studio, although this too can be a powerful visual statement in a dramatic or documentary production. If a studio is a hard and fast requirement, then include an interesting, but not distracting backdrop, quality lighting, and visually appealing camerawork.

Good lighting greatly enhances program technical quality.

19

Back in the early days of nonbroadcast (closed circuit) television, when studios were run by teachers or corporate training people, they often had loads of black and white equipment dumped on them and were told to make programs. Hundreds of productions were turned out featuring some poor fellow from accounting with a microphone hung around his neck who'd try to explain why this or that form should be properly filled out. The sales force would then be forced to sit down in some starkly lit storage-room-cum-viewing-room to watch, and the only thing that saved many of these programs was the novelty effect ("Hey!—That's old Harry from Accounting!—Look at him sweat!").

The novelty effect, thank Vidicon, is rarely operative now. Audiences today have become much more accustomed to the miracle of videotape, and a show such as the one described would be hooted out of the company, or, more seriously, would be viewed but not absorbed.

Production Values

This brings us to the most important point in this section on program style. No matter what program style you choose, the PRODUCTION VALUES of the show are of critical importance to its effectiveness.

PRODUCTION VALUES is a term used to indicate the overall design, execution, and technical quality of a show. These values are determined by such things as sets, lighting, sound quality, and camera work (including the number of cameras used). For example, a simple two-character play shot on a bare stage with two cameras, would naturally have simple production values. On the other hand, a fully choreographed song and dance routine with twelve dancers and expensive sets, shot with six cameras, would be an example of high production values. Either could be done effectively and well, or done poorly. Production values are thus a matter of style, and are not necessarily a measure of effectiveness. Money plays a big role here also as an adequate budget can allow for hiring of experts and additional and better equipment.

Whether your program is for educational, industrial, training, motivational, sales, or entertainment purposes, your audience is made up of members of the most sophisticated group of viewers in the world—the viewing

An example of high production values.

20

public. The sophistication of your audience is a direct result of network television production values. Despite all the derogatory things that can be said regarding the content or quality of the networks' programming, the production values are almost universally high, and it is this level to which your audience has become accustomed.

Analyze some network programming. One excellent way to do this is to watch some television with the sound turned completely down. The audio carries a great percentage of the stimulus we receive through television, and makes objective analysis of just the visual portion difficult. In dramatic programs, you're likely to find that an edit occurs on the average of every four to six seconds, keeping the visual pacing moving along at a rapid rate. Commercials are the most powerful example of how to use television to rapidly communicate. With the change in recent years in standard advertising spot length from 60 to 30 seconds, visual pacing receives extraordinary attention. The advertiser has only 30 seconds in which to grab viewer attention, entertain, inform, motivate, and, of course, sell.

Commercials in particular demonstrate the effect of money on production values as more money is spent per second than in any other type of TV programming.

SHOOTING RATIOS (the ratio of film or tape shot to the amount actually used) on commercials often run as high as a hundred to one, and a 30-second spot may contain as many as 20 or 30 edits. At the other end of the spectrum you'll also find a beautiful spot comprised of a single shot of a high-steel worker talking about the toughness of his pants as the camera trucks across and zooms, first in and then back out. Of course, 20, 30, or even 40 takes may have been required to get the shot *just* right.

Study commercials with the sound turned off, and you'll be better able to examine the camera and lighting techniques used without the distraction of the audio. If you have a video tape recorder (VTR) available to you, record some commercials and study them with and without the sound. What differences do you find in the overall effect of the spots viewed both ways?

Check the pacing of commercials. With the sound still turned off, time the average scene length. In commercials, the average length of a shot might be as short as two to three seconds. Dramatic programs tend to hold shots a bit longer, but the average shot length still falls somewhere in the neighborhood of six seconds.

Commercials and network TV programming has its characteristic style. Other techniques include very contrary approaches such as the long take, the slow deep focus, the edited montage, etc., that affect the viewer very differently and appeal to other sensibilities.

Study entertainment programming the same way. Examine the visual pacing and variety of shots the director and editor have used. Then look at some films—movies, that is—both those made originally for theatrical release and those made specifically for television. What differences can you see in the styles and production values of the two varieties? You should be able to tell a theatrical movie from a TV movie from the look and feel alone, without having to resort to your *TV Guide*. In movies made for television, the first thing you'll notice is that the pictures fit the screen. Theatrical films are commonly shot in a wide-screen format such as Cinemascope. When shown on television, this results in the edge being cut off. Also, on close examination, the production values will often betray the differences. The budgets for TV movies are usually substantially smaller than those for theatrical releases, and the practiced eye can often determine the difference from the overall texture and craft work of the movie.

Theatrical releases compared to TV movies:

1. More camera angles used.
2. Better lighting—more dramatic and contrasty.
3. Greater audio sweetening.
4. Different picture composition (wider shots work better on the larger theatre screen).
5. Titles and credits are more sophisticated. Composition, size, placement, and order are better.
6. There is more movement within the frame (i.e., dolly moves vs. camera cuts).

Basic Production Guidelines

Let's examine some basic production guidelines. In instructional media, the viewer should know within the first 30 seconds or so what the program is basically about. In general, the main body of information should start within the first minute or two. There are several lines of thought regarding the beginning of a show, as a catchy or dramatic opening can help attract viewer attention. With beauty being in the eye of the beholder, though, what the producer or director may think will be such a great opening—even if it does run three minutes—may only confuse the viewer, who's waiting patiently to find out why he's sitting there.

Program length is also quite important. The optimal running time for instructional media ranges from roughly 10 to 20 minutes, depending on the use and application. Short programs, for uses such as in a classroom, can be very effective. Going 30 minutes is not unusual or necessarily detrimental, but if a program needs to relay, say, 50 minutes worth of information, it might be wise to break the show down into two 25-minute modules. The reasons behind this relate partly to the human absorption capabilities previously discussed and to simple attention span. Remember that commercial broadcast television provides advertising interruptions that are in many ways as helpful to viewers as they are to advertisers (if only as chances to run to the kitchen or bathroom), and that the longest you'll find something running on commercial television without a break is 30 minutes, with the average being 7 to 15 minutes.

With documentaries and entertainment programs, the 20-minute rule is more easily bent or broken without impairing the program's impact or effectiveness.

It's important to note that there are different guidelines for different production styles. While it is generally helpful to be familiar with the established rules of film (video) making, it is possible to some extent to make up your own rules as you go along. Keep in mind, though, that audiences are much more comfortable with the familiar in terms of commonly used formats and program mechanics. They may not understand the vision that exists within your mind, so for better or worse, it is necessary to try to meet the audience on their own ground.

Experimenting With Video

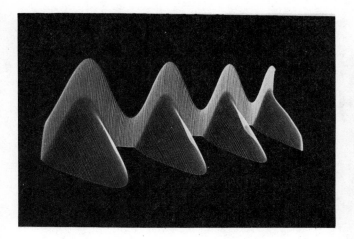

"Time Energy Objects"—1976 by Woody Vasulka

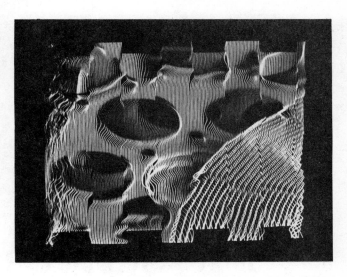

"Sculptures of Tom Price"—1981 by Woody Vasulka

Experimental video deviates from common uses of form, style, and time. Examples can be found in the storefront "video museums" that have struggled along for the past few years in most major cities. Many people find much of this to be deadly dull stuff, but there exists some very impressive video art by video artists Stephen Beck of Berkeley and Ron Hays of Los Angeles who have done some incredible things with their equipment. I suspect that one difference between their work and that of others in the field is that they have a definite concept in mind before they start twisting knobs. They may spend weeks or months trying new techniques and developing new hardware, and will use this period for experimentation. When they are then ready to produce work for public viewing, they are thus able as artists to approach the execution of their concepts with a mastery of their tools.

On the other hand, I recall a "visual essay" displayed at a San Francisco video gallery a few years ago that consisted of a half-hour of the camera being carried up a local mountain under the arm of the "artist." The audio consisted of his huffing and puffing as he climbed. Boy, was it realistic! As a friend who is himself very much into conceptual pieces said: "Hmm ... Must be A R T!"

Experimental video, like any art form, is a highly subjective matter. It would be presumptuous of me to commend my own viewpoint to the reader, as matters of taste are an individual's own choice. Experimental video, though, can serve as an important ground breaking function. Indeed, many of the analog and digital techniques originally developed by independent experimenters in video have since filtered down into more commonly used forms of TV programming, i.e., the computer art and graphics used in commercials and station logos.

Video equipment is now available at dirt-cheap prices, and I would encourage anyone and everyone to try their hand at making videotapes. Experimentation, paying no attention to any established rules, is what develops new concepts and techniques. The ubiquitousness of low-cost equipment permits the production of programming for every taste. There is a great difference, though, between making video on a personal home use level and producing it on a professional level. The two should not be confused, as they sometimes are.

CHAPTER 2

The Script and the Need for Planning

The Need for Planning

It has been said that there are more than ten thousand things that can go wrong with a video production, and that if only a hundred actually do, then the production has been a success. You could not convince me to quarrel with this sentiment. Murphy's Law (If something *can* go wrong, it *will!*) is a tried and true friend (or nemesis, if you will) of the television producer, and it is with the anticipation and circumvention of problems that success in production comes.

This is done during the PRE-PRODUCTION phase, which is when the planning and coordination for an upcoming production are done.

Thorough, careful, painstaking PRE-PRODUCTION PLANNING is an absolutely essential part of the production process. It has only one possible substitute, and that is money. If you don't plan properly ahead of time, then the only way to try to achieve quality in a production is to throw money into it—lots of it. If planning was poor or insufficient, there are many times when even money cannot save a production, except for the ultimate dollar-eater, the reshoot.

Proper planning cannot only prevent the need for spending more than the budget calls for, it can reduce costs in the first place. Good thought and discussion prior to starting a pro-

24

duction can produce a variety of options for achieving a production end.

The old equation "Time = Money" is all too true in the wonderful world of video.

A case in point: I was peripherally involved in a network production for the fall, 1980 season that was shot on location in San Francisco, my home base. The production company had not previously shot in the city, and had failed to send someone up from Los Angeles ahead of time to do a proper job of scouting locations, resources, and people. As a result, most of what got done was accomplished on virtually an emergency basis. Example: For one scene being shot onboard a boat, two simple curtains were needed to hang over a couple of standard-sized portholes. The production company waited until late Saturday afternoon, and then panicked when they realized nobody had done anything about the curtains. Frantic phone calls finally produced someone who was willing to do the job on a rush basis, and when the curtains were finally hung, they had cost nearly $700! This, of course, does not include the cost of time wasted with stars, equipment, and crew all standing idle while the Great Curtain Caper went on.

As we go through the production process, I'll state some basic rules for success, some of which I've developed myself, but most of which I've brazenly stolen from others who have tripped down the same path before. Some, also, are mere common sense that everybody knows, but are somehow enhanced and emphasized through the process of setting them down in type.

McQ's RULE No. 1: Assume that *nothing* has been done!

The first step in starting a production is to evaluate the program needs. A major consideration here is the size of the available budget.

This can be done in two ways: Budgets can define the production, or the production can define the budget. We'll get to this in more detail later.

The next step is to gather together all of the staff members who will be involved in the production, and some of the critical crew members—such as camerapeople, set designers, and others—who will help create, affect, and be affected by the budget. In addition to the producer and the director, staff members attending this meeting might include: The associate producer, the production manager, the operations manager, script writer(s), and others. Principal talent might also be involved at this time, if leading roles have already been cast.

The first meeting will serve primarily to alert everyone that a production is in the works, and to get them thinking in the right directions. The pertinent facts of the production should be run down, and some concept of facilities, crew size, and program content will be discussed. If the budget has already been established, as is often the case, these people should be given a working idea of how much of it they may anticipate being able to play with.

If the script is already available, copies should go to the key people: The director, assistant director, camera people, lighting and audio crew, etc. Copies marked for shooting should go to the creative crew and staff. It is also at this meeting that the job responsibilities will be handed out, at least to the core staff. The primary responsibilities that pertain to pre-production should be established early, even though crew members will be added later. By the time everyone leaves the room, they should have a fair idea of what will be happening, and a time and place, if possible, for the next meeting.

It would be hard to overly stress how important this meeting is for the producer. It serves several purposes, for in addition to what is actually accomplished, it sets a tone of forethought for the entire crew, and for the production itself.

The whole point of starting the planning process as early as possible is to get the production off to a good beginning and avoid surprises later down the line. Keep some sort of

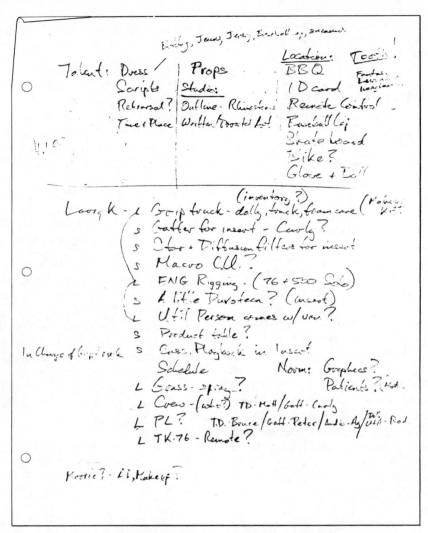

A sample detail sheet from a production notebook.

The producer's notebook contains all the information regarding a production.

notebook with you at all times (well, *almost* all times), so that as things occur to you, you can jot them down. Little details can make all the difference to a production. I keep a three-ring binder in which I stash everything relating to a production—script, budget, all notes of production meetings, etc. For some productions I keep a separate binder, while for others I cordon off a section of my master binder—my *bible*—which contains information and notes on progress of all current projects. My first sheet is a general-notes page that serves to record the details necessary to a production. Often some niggling little detail which could halt the entire production will occur to me at two in the morning, just as I'm ready to wrap up and pack it in for the night. Relying on memory alone can presage disaster, for the thought that occurs just as I'm drifting off to sleep *won't* be there in the morning unless I write it down. By the time the show is in the can and I transfer the entire package of production notes, forms, cue sheets, edit decision list printouts, etc., to a file folder, there are likely to be several if not dozens of detail sheets, presumably with each item checked off as it was taken care of.

The Script

```
"THE HEARTBREAK OF FRECKLES"  #59-12                    Page 7

Establish:

Veranda of Maxwell Manor.
George and Martha are
having their afternoon
tea.                             GEORGE:   TELL ME, MY DEAR, DO YOU

                                           THINK THE COREOPSIS WILL BLOOM

                                           BEFORE THE SNOW THIS YEAR?

Martha glances at George
with a look of great
distaste.                        MARTHA:   (Hesitates)  IF YOU INTEND

                                           TO TALK TO ME IN SUCH A MANNER,

                                           I SEE NO REASON TO CONTINUE

                                           THIS DISCUSSION ANY FURTHER!
CUT TO:

Upstairs, little Freddy
is putting catsup on
Susie's doll.                    FREDDY:   (To himself)  THIS'LL FIX

                                           HER WAGON!
CUT TO:

George is kneeling by
Martha's chair, holding
her hand.                        GEORGE:   DEAREST, I KNOW THAT YOUR

                                           FRECKLES HAVE ALWAYS KEPT US

                                           APART, BUT I THINK I MAY HAVE

                                           FOUND A SOLUTION.
Martha evidences some
skeptisism.                      MARTHA:   REALLY?

George removes a spray
can and masking tape from
his pocket.                      GEORGE:   IT'S REALLY QUITE SIMPLE.

                                           THIS RUSTOLEUM CAN COMPLETELY

                                           HIDE YOUR FRECKLES, SO THAT

                                           NEVER AGAIN WILL YOU BE FACED

                                           WITH LAUGHTER WHEREVER YOU GO.

                  (CONTINUES)
```

A "pseudo-storyboard" television style script, with visual instructions on the left and dialog on the right.

Many times the producer and/or director is handed a script and given the task of turning it into a program. At times there is some flexibility as to how to handle the show, including the power to make changes where necessary, but often the script is iron-clad and must be shot as specified. Commercials and highly technical industrial or training programs often fall into this latter category. Personally, I am sometimes less than comfortable with these situations, especially when there are problems with the writer's vision that will make it hard to translate his ideas to tape. A good writer can be a real pleasure to work with, but there are also those who don't understand the process of creating a program, i.e.—("EXT: CAMERA STARTS WITH VIEW OF EARTH FROM OUTER SPACE. CAMERA MOVES IN ONE CONTINUOUS ZOOM TO ECU OF HENRY's LEFT EYE AS HE WATCHES DIANE APPROACH HIM."). There are those who write in items that would decimate the budget—("CAR CAREENS WILDLY DOWN HILL, DEMOLISHING TWO CADILLAC LIMOS AND A FERRARI"). A script I've just read for a TV movie includes little things that appear innocent, but can be a real bear to achieve—("A DRAGONFLY LANDS ON THE HORSE'S EAR AND HOLDS ON FOR DEAR LIFE AS THE HORSE'S HEAD BOUNCES UP AND DOWN. THIS SHOT IS FROM THE REAR OF THE HORSE'S HEAD WITH THE LITTLE COUNTRY ROAD STRETCHING AHEAD. THE CAMERA SLOWLY PANS UP TO THE TREES TO FOCUS ON A WOODPECKER HAMMERING ON A TREE.").

Obviously, in this last example, the writer is evoking a mood, and he saw the shot clearly when he wrote it. It's a fine shot, too, and would definitely be a dramatic and lovely addition to the show. Logistically, though, it would require cuing the dragonfly and the woodpecker at just the right instant, while shooting from a boom mounted on a camera truck running next to the wagon. The camerawork would tax the abilities of the best cinematographer, and the shot could easily take a full shooting day to get. The budget must reflect such complexity, or the shot must be altered to be more economical.

In the dragonfly/woodpecker case above, the writer in question understands that the mood he's after could be achieved much more simply and inexpensively by breaking the shot down into two or more shots. He is simply telling the director what kind of mood he envisions. There are writers, though, who can cause headaches because they want everything shot to the letter the way it was written.

Such details can almost always be ironed out if the writer is easy to work with, but I find even greater enjoyment in writing the script myself. Obviously, not every producer and/or director is competent at script writing, and it is by no means a job requirement. Combining the roles of writer and director, or writer and producer, though, can be very practical.

The way I approach this combination is to first don my writing hat and determine the essential concept of the show. In an educational or training program, there are certain ideas or bodies of information that are the essence of the program, which have been determined ahead of time by some form of needs assessment. In a dramatic show, there is usually a central story message. This is also usually true in comedies, and even musical variety shows. In other words, clearly defined goals are determined prior to starting on the script. Once these goals have been assessed, I'll let them rattle around in my head for a while to see what happens.

In some cases, it's necessary to put together a TREATMENT or a SYNOPSIS if the project is one that must be sold, either to a programming outlet or to a client. A TREATMENT is a scene-by-scene narrative version of the script which describes the characters, the setting, and the basic plot or information to be presented. It may also include notes to provide details of the intended audience and production techniques to be used. A SYNOPSIS serves similar purposes, being more commonly used for dramatic programs. It is basically a brief, concise description of the story and the characters—enough to give a basic taste of the program.

When I actually start on a corporate or educational script, I'll let everything flow, allowing my thoughts to run wild and including everything I'd *like* to do with the show. After the script is done, I'll then go through it in careful detail to determine its practicality. Often, my wilder flights of fancy can be achieved by changing them just ever so slightly, while other times they're completely out of the question. Of course, I normally won't write in something that I know I'll have to take out later. But when in doubt I'll include an item in the first draft of the script.

I find it important to let the script gather

dust for a day or two after the initial draft is done. These short respites allow me to return to the material with a fresh view, creating a bit more objectivity than if I just hammered away at it straight through. Often, in coming back, I find the entire premise just doesn't work, and will start over from scratch. Even in these instances, though, the first draft has usually been of value. As Thomas Edison said after 9,000 attempts at inventing the light bulb: "I now know 9,000 things that *won't* work."

Once I've got a good script, I then take it to the next step in the pre-production process. If I'm working on contract to a client, then the client or their content expert gets a copy and we go over it together. I help them visualize the program, and, if necessary, explain the whats, whys, and wherefores. If it's an "in-house" project, done independently for some form of distribution, then a copy goes to each member of the production staff, who reads it and cogitates on it a while. We then assemble to talk it over, brainstorm, drink some wine, and see what better ideas may come out of the "script jam-session."

Script format and production scheduling:

Next the script is broken down for shooting. There are a number of ways this can be handled, depending on the nature of the production.

If the production is of moderate scope and the script is simple, straightforward, and/or

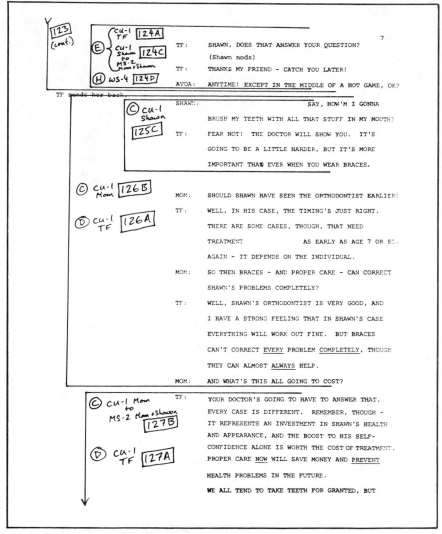

A script marked with scene and shot designations, prior to shooting.

29

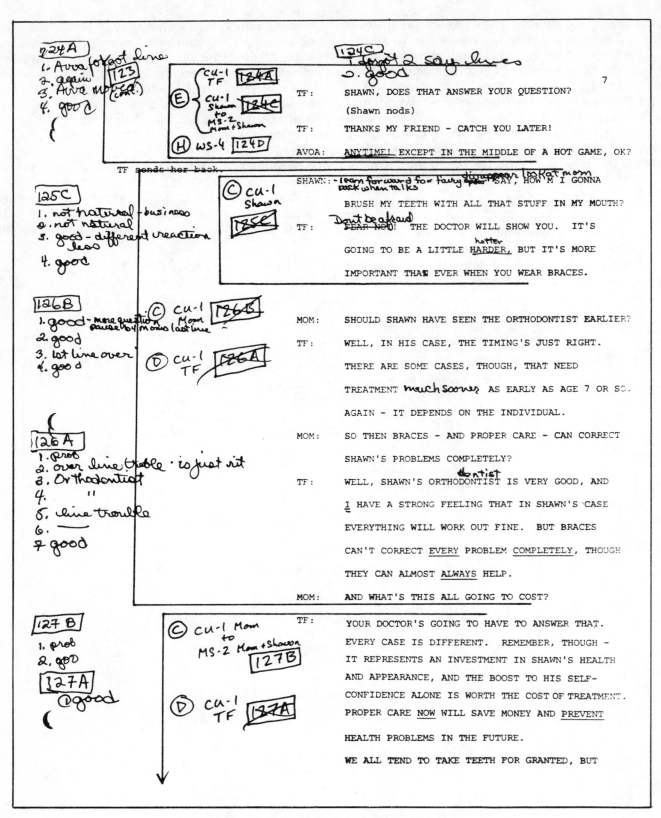

Script after shooting, with script supervisor's notes.

short, I may simply mark an existing copy of the script with scene designations and shots (see illustrations). In single-camera, film-style shooting where the same scene may be shot from several different angles; I use notations to indicate what and where. Accompanying the script is a SHOT LIST, put together in shooting order, that serves as the schedule for each day's shooting. Additionally, I'll sometimes include a PLOT DIAGRAM for each location showing camera position and angle and talent blocking. It's helpful to work these out ahead of time so the crew will know what to expect. With the shot list and plot diagram at the front of their copy of the script, the crew can get the basic setup done for each scene with minimal supervision, leaving me free to fine-tune details prior to rolling tape. On longer or more complex productions, each scene will have its own sheet(s), with adequate white space on

SHOT LIST	#16-01		" "		PAGE 1 OF 2
SET UP	SCENE	PAGE	CHARACTER(S)	SHOT	COMMENTS
A	106A	1	Mom	CU-1	"Dr. Norris...braces"
	108A	1	TF	CU-1	"Who am I?...credentials"
	110A	2	TF	CU-1	"Working day shift...What is it?"
	111A	2	TF	CU-1	"Old days...with care, they can"
	112A	3	TF	CU-1	"Heredity...let me show you"
B	110	2	All	WS-3	Jacket biz
	112	3	All	WS-3	"Long legs...machine, just right"
	113	3	All	WS-3	"More than bite...do just fine"
K	110B	2	Mom	CU-1	"Not sure proves...doing here?"
	112B	3	Mom,Shawn	MS-2	Reactions - heredity speech
C	116B	4	Mom	CU-1	"Temp. problems"; "Mainly heredity?"
	117C	5	Shawn	CU-1	"Hassle...tin grin, stuff like that"
	118C	5	Shawn	CU-1	"How long?", reaction
	120B	6	Mom,Shawn	MCU-2	"Long term"; "Gonna hurt?" Reactions
	125C	7	Shawn	CU-1	"How brush?", reactions
	126B	7	Mom	CU-1	"Seen earlier?"; "Correct?"; "Cost?"
	127B	7	Mom-Mom,Shawn	CU-1 to MS-2	Pan/Zoom out Reactions
	201	-	Mom	CU-1	Reactions
	202	-	Shawn	CU-1	Reactions
	203	-	Mom,Shawn	MS-2	Reactions
D	115A	3-4	TF	CU-1	"For example...irritated easily"
	116A	4	TF	CU-1	Usually opposite...all have effect"
	117A	4-5	TF	MCU-1	"Diagnosis...treatment for you"
	118A	5-6	TF	CU-1	"Kidding...best solution"
	120A	6	TF	CU-1	"Right...work...friend who has"
	126A	7	TF	CU-1	"Fear not...Always help"
	127A	7-8	TF	CU-1	"Doctor answer...a bargain!"
	128A	8	TF	CU-1	"So true...Hm..35?"
	129A	8	TF	CU-1	"Is a gem...Certainly!"

Shot list for same production script.

**Camera plot for same production.
Circled X's are camera positions.
Arrows show camera angle.**

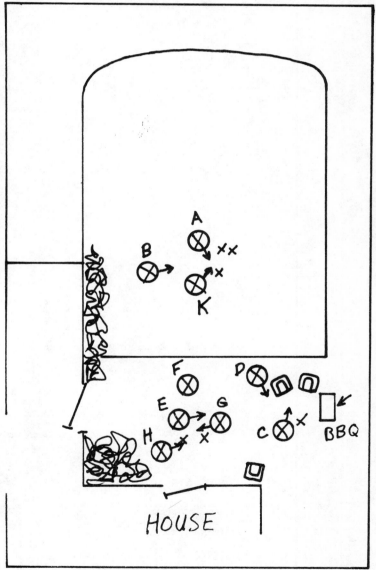

the page for directorial notes (see illustrations). Each sheet may contain anywhere from two or three lines to up to two or three pages of the original script, though the latter is very rare. Some sheets contain no dialog at all.

A critical factor in planning the shooting schedule is to decide how much to attempt in a shooting day. Tremendous problems can be created for the schedule or the budget if the day's shooting schedule is overly ambitious.

Each script is different, of course, but as a general rule, I estimate no more than five pages a day for shooting dialog between two or more characters. I consider a page generally equal to about a minute's running time in the finished show. There have been instances where I've gotten as many as ten pages down in a day, where there was only one location, but this is rather uncommon. You may find a large disparity between my estimate and that of other directors, and differences in style and

McQ Teleproductions SHOOTING SCRIPT Prod. # 59-12 "THE HEARTBREAK OF FRECKLES"	SCENE # 12	Page ___18___ Prod. Day ___9th___ Shoot Date _Wed. 3/24_ Sched. Time __1 PM__

CAMERA		ACTION / DIALOGUE
MASTER SCENE	1	
	2	(GEORGE AND MARTHA ARE HAVING THEIR
Wide angle - favor Martha.	3	AFTERNOON TEA)
	4	GEORGE: Tell me, my dear, do you think
	5	the coreposis will bloom before the
	6	snow this year?
	7	(MARTHA GLANCES AT GEORGE WITH A LOOK
	8	OF GREAT DISTASTE. SHE HESITATES
	9	BEFORE ANSWERING.)
	10	MARTHA: If you intend to talk to me
	11	in such a manner, I see no reason to
	12	continue this discussion any further!
	13	(GEORGE RISES AND MOVES CLOSE TO HER.
	14	HE KNEELS BY HER CHAIR AND TAKES HER
	15	HAND.)
Truck left to favor George.	16	GEORGE: Dearest, I know that your
	17	freckles have always kept us apart, but
	18	I think I may have found a solution.
	19	MARTHA: (Evidencing skeptisism) Really?
	20	(GEORGE TAKES OUT A SPRAY CAN AND SOME
	21	MASKING TAPE FROM HIS POCKET.)
	22	GEORGE: It's really quite simple.

(Continues)

Props & Special Items:	Talent:
Deck chairs. Can of Rustoleum. Masking tape.	George. Martha.

```
McQ Teleproductions          SCENE # 12A & 12B              Page    20
SHOOTING SCRIPT                                         Prod. Day   9th
Prod. # 59-12                                          Shoot Date  Wed.  3/24
"THE HEARTBREAK OF FRECKLES"                           Sched. Time  3 PM
```

CAMERA		ACTION / DIALOGUE
	1	
SCENE 12A	2	Repeat action / dialogue from 12
	3	
Closeups - Martha		
	4	
	5	
SCENE 12B	6	Repeat action / dialogue from 12
	7	
Closeups - George	8	
	9	
	10	
	11	
	12	(CONTINUITY - Watch sun angle for
	13	intercutting with earlier angles.
	14	Full Polaroids to permit cheating
	15	to duplicate shadows.)
	16	
	17	
	18	
	19	
	20	
	21	
	22	

Props & Special Items:	Talent:
Deck chairs. Can of Rustoleum. Masking tape.	George Martha

production standards are major factors. Certainly, I can envision a situation in which one could shoot twenty pages of three-character dialog in a single day, but I suspect I wouldn't want to affix my name as director to the results. Other important factors include talent and casting, and getting the scripts to the talent as early as possible.

It is a fact of production life, often learned through hard experience, that quality production takes *lots of time*. Good programming is the result of craftsmanship, and rushing the job detracts from the final results. This leads us to our next rule.

McQ's RULE No. 2: Exercise *extreme* conservativism in scheduling the production. It is much better to end up on time and under budget.

33

Script vs. the storyboard:

A SCRIPT is comprised of typewritten pages, while a STORYBOARD has pictures on it to describe the shots, usually accompanied by written dialog and instructions for action and BLOCKING (the positioning and movement of actors on the set). Common examples are shown in the illustrations. Storyboards are commonly used in the production of commercials, where they are usually generated by the agency to show the client what the spot will look like when done. Often they are handsomely and expensively produced, with full-color illustrations matted into little cutouts in the shape of a TV screen.

similar technique, known as a PHOTOMATIC, uses still photos of actors or items in place of artwork. Since full animation is not possible, dissolves and cuts simulate the final look, and the finished animatic is then shown to the client, serving as a VIDEO STORYBOARD. This is often done when the art director or account executive knows that the particular client has problems visualizing from a storyboard, or when the account is a major one and all stops are pulled in selling the concept. Animatics and photomatics are also used to test concepts prior to committing to production of the actual commercial. They are shown to test audiences who fill out questionnaires after viewing them.

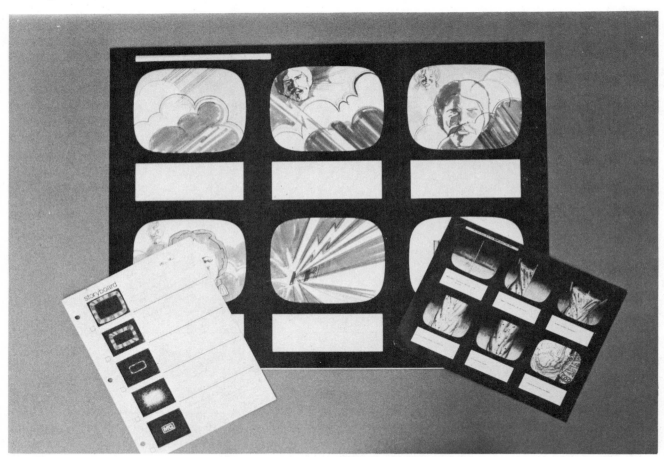

Samples of various types of storyboards.

Some agencies take this a step further by producing what is generally known as an ANIMATIC, a sort of pseudo-animation using storyboard illustrations that are shot and edited to match the soundtrack of the spot. A

At the other end of the spectrum is the script form most often used in dramatic productions. Such scripts may have little more than lines and camera/blocking instructions, and are similar to theatrical scripts. Series pro-

34

ductions are commonly written this way, since the characters, locations, and previously established style of the show are known. Here, the director must work within established guidelines, and is sometimes more of a technician than a creative force. Nonseries productions generally use a simple script that affords the director more latitude to visualize for himself.

In between the two extremes is the QUASI-STORYBOARD, which uses a form that has space at the left for visual content and blocking, and a larger space at the right for dialog and audio information. This form lends itself well to technical or educational scripts, and is commonly used in corporate and industrial video productions.

Whatever form is used, a script or storyboard should clearly define what the video, audio, and characters will be doing at all times. Though you may be directing the program yourself, it's a good idea to write the script as if you were going to hand it over to someone else for shooting.

Make sure that the script does not itself create continuity problems during shooting, that everybody who needs to understand the script has his/her copy well ahead of time, and that all questions or objections have been answered.

The actual form of the script is less important than the fact that it does its job. Find or invent a variation of the above that is appropriate to your program and that you're comfortable with, and you stand a much better chance of going into the shoot properly prepared.

CHAPTER 3

Location and Editing Considerations

Studio vs. Location

Since 1977, there's been a tremendous increase in the availability of lightweight, high-quality portable video equipment. It's now possible to go on location with video nearly as easily as with film. This has released video production from the restricting confines of the studio, and has brought to tape the distinct advantages of producing in the field. Location shooting can be very expensive, and the ability to see immediate results while still set up for a scene, and to shoot an instant retake if necessary, is a marvelous advantage over film, where the results (RUSHES or DAILIES—quickly made prints of the original camera footage) can't be viewed for at least a day.

If a scene calls for a residential location, one need not build a set in the studio; one can go out and find a home and shoot there. There are shows, of course, where the logistics are still easier to manage in a studio, and studio use is by no means a thing of the past. Rather, the producer now has a choice that wasn't previously available.

I said that location shooting can be very expensive. It can, however, be less expensive than studio production. Confused? Stay tuned. Let's look at the two main factors that can help decide the issue: *logistics* and *cost*.

Logistically, studio production can have some distinct advantages, such as control over

36

audio and lighting. A soundproofed stage permits shooting to continue without interruption due to ambient noise levels, which often present considerable problems on location. Location work can be hampered by noise from air traffic, ground traffic, or any number of other noise sources over which the producer has no effective control. This can lead to delays in production, that almost always translate into increased costs. Shooting in a studio eliminates many of these problems.

Studio lighting is much more easily controlled than location lighting. With lighting mounted on overhead pipes and floor stands, there are no unknown variables with which to contend. On location, the weather is a major factor, especially when using reflectors to supplement light. When nature starts to play fast and loose with your lighting, and "God is your gaffer," your choices are limited. About all you can do is grin and bear it and adjust your lighting equipment to maintain a semistable effect as the clouds drift by. Weather itself is the most significant variable, and I've yet to meet a producer with enough clout to order up a change and make it stick. Should your script call for a sunny day, and cloud cover starts at 500 feet and goes up from there, it's hard to find a silver lining. Obviously, studio production avoids these problems.

There are other logistical problems unique to location shooting. Crew meals and comfort facilities must be taken into account. Power is a factor, as very few trees are equipped with three-phase 220-volt outlets. Transportation needs are more demanding, and if the production will take more than a day, shelter will be necessary. These and other factors all must be worked out, especially on a moderate-to-large production, and the price tag is often high.

It would appear, then, that studio work might be cheaper than location production, since the variables are fewer. It is, however, not necessarily so.

The first cost from which one is freed in location work is the cost of the studio itself. Since the location would normally provide the bulk of the "set," staging costs can be less. Real savings can be enjoyed on small-scale productions, or on SECOND UNITS of a larger production. (A SECOND UNIT is a smaller additional crew sent out to shoot secondary or supplemental footage.) If all you need is some portable video equipment, a few pieces of lighting and audio gear, and a two or three-person crew, the mobility, speed, and efficiency of location work can be stunning. The same variables, though, that apply to large location productions also apply to small ones. While a WASH (cancellation) due to weather or other show-stoppers can still happen, it's less expensive when fewer people and pieces of equipment are involved. On balance, then, we could look at it this way: Studio work is more controllable, and thus safer to plan and to budget, while location work can be potentially cheaper but is subject to more hidden pitfalls.

A small crew can work rapidly on location.

38

It goes without saying that many times the script leaves little choice in choosing between shooting in the studio and going on location. All else being equal, such factors as whether a studio is readily and inexpensively available may make the decision for you. If you work for an organization that has an existing studio available, then using the studio may be less costly than scouting a location and going remote.

I, myself, lean slightly toward location production, although I find that the script usually makes my choice. If given a choice, I'll usually go remote. One reason is that REMOTES (productions in the field) can offer more opportunities for FOUND items, such as unusual places, people and props, and it sometimes happens

that some of the nicer elements in a finished show were those that are stumbled across by accident.

Another reason I favor location shooting is my preference for single-camera FILM-STYLE shooting. Generally, single camera shooting is more appropriate in field production, while multiple camera production is more commonly done in the studio. This will be covered in greater detail in *Part 2—Production*.

Location Scouting

The first step in finding a place to shoot is to send out a location scout who is normally one of the production staff. The scout will go out with an understanding of what is needed, a

A mobile 2 person crew.

39

notepad, and usually a Polaroid® camera or (even better) a video portapak.

If, for example, the shoot calls for a new house under construction, the scout will find an area where such activity is going on, perhaps by contacting a builder's association in the area of the search. He will locate possible houses that would seem to fill the bill. He'll check with the contractor to find out what stage of construction the house will be in at the time shooting is scheduled, and will check to see if power will be available at the site. Photos or tape of the house will be taken from all sides and angles to take back to the office. The scout will identify the owner and where he may be contacted. He'll then go on to locate other possibilities in order to provide a variety from which to choose.

Back at the office, the producer and the staff will go over the possibilities, and will eliminate those that have obvious problems. Once the choices are narrowed down to one or two, and preliminary permission has been secured from the owner, a site survey team will be sent out to carry the process to the next step.

The site survey

The survey team normally includes the production manager or operations manager, although the producer, director, associate producer, assistant director, or any number of others might also make the trip. The production manager would be looking at logistics. Will on-site power be adequate, and if not, where can some be located? Where can the cast and crew take meal and bathroom breaks? Can the equipment and support vehicles get in and out without trouble? The director will be looking at backgrounds, camera angles, and light. At what time of day will the action take place? What special problems will need to be solved? The lighting director or gaffer might also come along to determine what special equipment will be needed. Can reflectors handle the requirements, or will supplemental lighting be necessary?

One critical factor that is often overlooked, or to which too little attention is given, is audio. Background noises that seem unnoticeable under normal circumstances can cause terrific problems with sound recording. The low and subtle rushing sound of central air conditioners, for example, is something that most of us are so accustomed to that we usually pay it little heed. The microphones, however, will be very aware of it. It's wise to have the audio engineer along on the survey, but if that's not possible, take careful note of sound yourself. Sit and listen for several minutes. Does traffic noise intrude? Do airplanes fly over often? Are there churchbells chiming on the hour? Sounds such as these that repeat either regularly or at varying times, but that are not constant, can fool you. They can hold up shooting, and over the course of a full day on location can eat into your schedule with big bites. This is why it's important to take time to simply sit and listen for a while.

Time spent for a solid location survey will always pay off in time saved during production. As we've already seen, in production, time is money.

Things To Remember While Scouting
1. Take photos of the site.
2. Locate owner and make arrangements.
3. Do you have adequate power?
4. Know location of fusebox.
5. Do you have food and bathroom facilities?
6. Is the site easily accessible?
7. Will there be lighting problems?
8. Audio: background noises?
9. Any other problems?

Post Considerations

POST-PRODUCTION (editing) must be carefully considered during the pre-production phase. For instance, your choice of mastering format (i.e., QUAD (2-inch), 1-inch, or ¾-inch cassette VTRs) will affect both the production and post-production procedures. The editing style should be considered during pre-production in order to ensure that the production techniques will be compatible with the editing process.

For example: A music program using ¾-inch cassette as the master format might call for stereo audio recording. In such a case, the use of TIME CODE (electronic numerical indexing) as this code normally lives on one of the cassette audio tracks, which in this instance (stereo), both would be in use. Any special effects that are called for in the script should be mapped out during pre-production. If they're not, then editing could provide some unpleasant surprises.

The style of shooting should be decided upon early in the pre-production phase. This will greatly affect the post-production phase. A multicamera shoot that incorporates HOT SWITCHING (making the cuts live through a switcher from multiple cameras onto a single VTR) will have minimal editing requirements whereas the same shoot done with all cameras ISO'D (recording the signal from each camera on a separate ISOlated VTR) will have more extensive editing requirements. Iso shooting simply defers the switching until post-production, on the theory that decisions may then be made with more consideration and at relative leisure. Iso shooting automatically increases post-production costs, and such costs must be figured into the production from the beginning.

Iso shooting can also save the day, i.e., "Car careens wildly down hill demolishing two Cadillac limos and a Ferrari." Clients do not take well to the costs involved in reshooting such events because of a wrong angle or machine malfunction.

Something as mundane as the types of editing facilities available must also be considered at this time. If you're planning to master on the 1-inch format and find that all available 1-inch editing time in the area has been booked for the next six weeks, then it might be worth considering a switch over to quad or another format. One alternative would be to take the editing to a distant facility. Those who have their own facilities may not have this worry. We should all be so fortunate.

There are some other important questions to ask before the production starts:

1. If an OFF-LINE (preliminary) edit is to be done before committing to an ON-LINE (final) edit, how will the WORKPRINTS (working copies) be generated?

2. Will TIME CODE (editing reference numbers) be laid down during original taping, or afterwards?

3. How will titles and credits be created?

4. Will a color camera and/or an INSERT STUDIO (a small studio used to shoot graphics, etc.) be needed during editing?

5. What special duplication or distribution requirements will there be?

6. Will the finished program be transferred to film? If so, there are some special requirements to be kept in mind during the shoot, and a call to the lab might be worthwhile.

If slides will be inserted during the final edit, either as still photos or graphics, there are some important considerations to keep in mind. Television has a fixed ASPECT RATIO (measurement of screen height to width) of 3:4, whereas standard 35mm slides have an aspect ratio of 2:3 (24mm high by 36mm wide). As a result, part of any slide used on television will be lost. Most of the loss is at either side, but there is usually some loss of image at the top and bottom as well. In preparing slides for television, it will be necessary to observe the SAFE ACTION and SAFE TITLE cut-offs for slides.

When shooting stills for television, it's also important to take care with CONTRAST (range of light to dark areas in scene). Video cannot handle as wide a CONTRAST RATIO as film emulsion, and lighting and exposure should be balanced with the capabilities of video in mind.

In *Part 3—Post Production*, the entire process will come together, and we will go into greater detail on these and other questions. If your planning has included editing considerations at every step along the way, the chances are then much better that the show will go together easily and successfully.

CHAPTER 4

Budget

We now arrive at what may be the most critical phase of the entire pre-production process. Budgeting can make or break the production. Whether you're working within an organization or independently, the budget will affect you greatly. Most companies involved in video production have some form of charge-back system to account for production costs, though often a good part of the costs are hidden in a yearly lump-sum *overhead* figure. For the purposes of our discussion, though, we'll deal with the budget as figured for an independent production, since this will allow us to examine the subject under the most stringent circumstances.

Writing a budget for a production is a mixture of science and art. The science involved is making certain that all production requirements are reflected in the budget, and the art deals with predicting what these requirements will be. Some budget items may be predictable. Examples would include equipment rental rates, and crew and talent rates. On the other hand, determining how many days a production will require is basically a matter of experience. Even then, an experienced estimator will have to allow for unknowns such as weather and equipment breakdowns.

Earlier in this section, we discussed the need for an initial pre-production planning meeting, at which a budget discussion was considered optional. The next meeting, though, should be the budget meeting.

These are two primary approaches to establishing a budget, usually determined by the way the production was generated. In the first approach, a program need has been established, and a fixed number of dollars has been allocated for the production. Here the question is: "Can it be done for that amount?" or, more subtly: "What kind of production can be mounted within that figure?" The second approach is more open-ended. Here, a program need has been established, and the question is simply: "How much will it cost?"

The first approach holds more potential for trouble, for if the dollars are fixed, any miscalculation or over-run will spell certain financial disaster. Nor, however, is the second method danger-free. Once you establish a cost figure, the last thing you want to do is go back to your money source, bearing a sheepish grin and asking for more money after you're well into production. It may, in fact, be impossible.

One key to successful budgeting is continuity in writing and tracking the budget for each production. As with almost anything, the more one does it, the better one becomes. The same person who wrote the budget should then track the expenditures, so that when the production is completed and the last bills and invoices are in, a comparison between the original budget and the actual outlay can be made. This is called *job-costing* in bookkeeping.

"How Much Will It Cost?"

In putting together a budget for a production, I first ask the question, "how much will it cost?" Even though I may be dealing with a fixed amount, I ignore that amount, and put the budget together based solely on the script and the way I visualize the program on the screen. This gives me a basic working figure that I can then compare with the amount of money available. I can then adjust my budget figures accordingly.

If my estimate comes in lower than the fixed amount, I then have two options open to me. I can either add production values, which will increase the estimate, or I can happily report to the client/investor/what-have-you that the show won't cost as much as had been thought. A third alternative is to keep this lower estimate to myself, keeping the difference for CONTINGENCY (more on this later).

If everything goes according to plan, and the contingency amount is not used, I then have the very pleasant task of handing over a finished project *and* some change! This has marvelous shock value, and can even provide oneself with a hero image. Of course, if the contingency figure *is* used, which is more often the case, then no one outside the production staff is the wiser, and I've still brought the show in within budget. The point is, that despite all the glamour, bright lights, excitement, etc. ("ho, ho"), involved with production, most production is a *business*, be it for profit or nonprofit. It is subject to the same rules, foibles and politics as any other type of business—if not more so. The independent producer is in essence a contractor, facing many of the same problems and demands as any other.

My basic approach to budgeting is to use a form that prompts me to think of all the different items that might be involved. Until recently, this was a paper form that had a list of normal budget items, a "UNIT" column, a "UNIT COST" column, an "ESTIMATED TOTAL" column, and an "ACTUAL TOTAL" column. "ACTUAL" expenditures are listed in the last column once the production is finished, and are used to provide comparison with the forecast. In addition to being a valuable business record, this last column serves as a guide for future budgeting.

Once the script has been broken down for shooting, and such things as locations, facilities, crew, talent, and other requirements have been determined, the budget can be massaged and refined until it reflects the realities of the production. Several drafts of the budget and/or changes in the script may be necessary before a good balance is reached between production values and costs.

The form illustrated should serve as a starting place for your own form, designed for the particulars of your own situation.

I soon found that as the scope of our productions grew, I needed a form with as many

PRODUCTION BUDGET   Prod.# 232

Teleproduction Services

Program Title: SAMPLE BUDGET
Client: TELECOM   Contact: McQ   Ph: 3/6-/2/t Date: 2-5-81

Function	Est. Units	x	Unit Cost	=	Est. Total	Act. Total
Writer Simon	Flat	x	— /	=	$2,500	$2,500
Producer Lucas	Flat	x	— /	=	$5,000	$5,000
Director Cimino	Flat	x	— /	=	$4,000	$4,000
Staff (Asst. Prod. - O'Brien)	10 days	x	$250/day	=	$2,500	$2,500
Talent (2 on-camera princ.)	5 days	x	700/day	=	$3,500	$4,100
Talent (Extras - 4 ea.)	3	x	400/	=	$1,200	$1,500
Contingency		x	/	=	$5,000	$ —
			Total Above-the-Line -		($23,700)	($19,600)

Production:

	Est. Units	x	Unit Cost	=	Est. Total	Act. Total
Equipment (Camera/VTR)	5 days	x	1,000/day	=	$5,000	$5,000
Location (Studio Rental)	7 days	x	250/day	=	$1,750	$1,750
Graphics (12 pieces art)	12 pc.	x	15/ea.	=	$180	$200
Materials (Tape stock -1")	5 hrs.	x	75/hr.	=	$375	$350
Grip (Truck w/ dolly)	1 day	x	120/day	=	$120	$120
Set (Design + Constr.)	Flat	x	— /	=	$1,000	$925
Lighting (est. 12 instruments)	4 x 12 inst.	x	20/ea.	=	$960	$800
Audio (Eng. w/ wireless (2))	5 days	x	325/day	=	$1,625	$1,500
Crew (5 @ 200/day)	5 days	x	1,000/day	=	$5,000	$6,225
Crew (3 @ 150/day)	5 days	x	450/day	=	$2,250	$2,800
Support Expenses 15 crew x 5 days		x	50/day	=	$3,750	$3,500
Transportation (truck, van, ⟨air⟩ ⟨auto⟩ RT- LAX/SFO)				-	$1,500	$1,725
Expendables	—	x	—	=	$600	$515

Post Production:

	Est. Units	x	Unit Cost	=	Est. Total	Act. Total
Off-Line 3/4 cassette C.T.	80 hrs.	x	25/hr.	=	$2,000	$2,000
On-Line 1" Computer	16 hrs.	x	300/hr.	=	$4,800	$4,500
Add-Ons DUE	3 hrs.	x	175/hr.	=	$525	$700
Workprints 5 windows + code	5 qty.	x	110/ea.	=	$550	$550
Stock 1" B+C (1 hr.) + Prot.	— qty.	x	225/ea.	=	$225	$225
Duplication cassette dubs	5 qty.	x	75/ea.	=	$375	$375
Chyron - credits	1 hr	x	110/hr.	=	$110	$165
B rolls - as needed	—	x	— /	=	$400	$240
		Total Below-the-Line -			($33,095)	($34,165)

TOTAL BUDGET - $56,795 $53,765

Less Contingency - (51,795)
Contingency used (1,970)

A sample budget form, useful for small scale productions.

PROD. # 59-12 (R-2)   "THE HEARTBREAK OF FRECKLES"   1/2/82

CLIENT - H.S. PRODUCTIONS   CONTACT - OTTO FOKUS / 555-7954

```
 ABOVE THE LINE:
PRODUCER:  C.B. DE MERDE  - $ 50000
DIRECTOR:  HARRY FLEX  - $ 25000
ASSOC. PROD.:  TRIXIE LA FLAME - 45 DAYS x $150/DAY =  $ 6750
OFFICE RENT:  PROD. OFFICE - 2 MONTHS x $750/MONTH =   $ 1500
TELEPHONE:     - $ 1000
SCRIPT RIGHTS:     - $ 7500
XEROXES:      - $ 400
TALENT #1:  GEORGE - 20 DAYS x $325/DAY =   $ 6500
TALENT #2:  MARTHA - 15 DAYS x $325/DAY =   $ 4875
TALENT #3:  FREDDY - 45 DAYS x $500/DAY =   $ 22500
EXTRAS:  14 CAMEL DRIVERS  - $ 9875
STUNT, DOUBLES:  STUNT COORDINATOR - 15 DAYS x $250/DAY =   $ 3750
WELFARE, TEACHERS:  WELFARE WORKER - 45 DAYS x $125/DAY =   $ 5625
CAST PAYROLL & FRINGES:     - $ 8550
P & W - AFTRA:     - $ 4275
MUSIC RIGHTS:  SCORING  - $ 5000
TAXES, NON-PAYROLL:  ESTIMATED  - $ 2500
INSURANCE:     - $ 5000
CONTINGENCY:  ESTIMATED  - $ 28000
                              ABOVE-THE-LINE SUBTOTAL -    $ 198,600.00
 PRODUCTION:
CAMERA(S):  HL-79 - 45 DAYS x $500/DAY =   $ 22500
VTR(S):  BVH-500 - 45 DAYS x $500/DAY =   $ 22500
ASST. DIR.:  BOB BULLHORN - 60 DAYS x $250/DAY =   $ 15000
TECH. DIR.:  SCILLIOS SCOPE - 45 DAYS x $200/DAY =   $ 9000
UTILITY:   - 45 DAYS x $150/DAY =   $ 6750
LIGHT EQUIP.:  (ESTIMATED) - 45 DAYS x $75/DAY =   $ 3375
GAFFER:  JUNIOR FRESNEL - 45 DAYS x $225/DAY =   $ 10125
AUDIO ENG.:  MARTY MIX - 45 DAYS x $225/DAY =   $ 10125
GRAPHICS:  OPENING TITLES  - $ 3500
GRIP EQUIP.:  LIGHT/GRIP TRUCK - 6 WEEKS x $320/WEEK =  $ 1920
BOOMS, DOLLIES:  FISHER W/TRACK - 6 WEEKS x $260/WEEK =  $ 1560
LOCATION:  FEES  - $ 750
SUPPORT:  CREW MEALS / ETC.  - $ 2400
PROPS:  AS LISTED  - $ 800
MEDICAL:  REG. NURSE - 30 DAYS x $125/DAY =   $ 3750
MISC. #1:  VEHICLE RENTAL & PREP.  - $ 6000
                              PRODUCTION SUBTOTAL -       $ 120,055.00
 POST PRODUCTION:
OFF-LINE:  CASSETTE - 15 DAYS x $250/DAY =   $ 3750
ON-LINE:  CMX ASSEMBLY - 24 HOURS x $310/HOUR =   $ 7440
CHAR.GEN:  CREDITS  - $ 330
B-ROLLS,ETC.:     - $ 650
B & C STOCK:  EDIT MASTER - 1 EA. x $175/EA. =   $ 175
PROT.MASTER:  ONE COPY - 1 EA. x $150/EA. =   $ 150
AUDIO SWEETEN:  16 TRACK - 48 HOURS x $150/HOUR =   $ 7200
MISC. POST:  OVERTIME  - $ 3000
                              POST-PRODUCTION SUBTOTAL -   $ 22,695.00
                                                        ---------------
        (B-T-L SUB. - $ 142,750.00)     TOTAL BUDGET -     $ 341,350.00
```

A computer budget printout for a medium scale production.

as 12 pages. Though there are numerous such forms available, none were tailored to our specific needs, and I eventually switched to using an Apple II®* computer for budgeting. It is essentially an "electronic form," and is much more flexible. At the time of this writing, the budgeting program included roughly 130 fixed categories, and has provision for a considerable number of special (or "MISC.") items. The computer program can be used by virtually anyone, since it PROMPTS the user by asking questions about the production, performs all the math, gives section totals and descriptions, and the production grand total. Once entered, the data can be filed on a FLOPPY DISK (flexible, circular disk), to be recalled and revised at will, with the revision then stored under a revision number. A hard-copy (meaning a printout or printed copy) can be produced, consisting of from one to as many as four pages, depending on the size of the production. The advantages? This method takes less time, since the computer asks the questions and does the math. Revisions are much faster, since only those items that need changing must be fussed with. The computer then refigures the budget with any changes or additions. It then files the new data along with the original estimate, and then supplies a new hard-copy to add to the job file.

An important advantage of this system is accuracy. Obviously, arithmetic errors are reduced, but this is not what I mean. Since almost every conceivable item that can crop up in a production is part of the programmed query process, it becomes much less likely that important items will be overlooked. Though the program has been thoroughly researched and revised, on each production we still seem to find at least one more item that needs to be incorporated, and the program thus grows constantly. Since the computer came to live with us, we've found it to be a valuable tool for more than just doing budgets. This book, for instance, has been written on the computer using a word-processing software package that speeds the writing process by a factor of three to five. The computer can also be used in its word-processing mode for script writing. A more detailed discussion of our use of the computer and the budgeting program can be found in *Appendix C.*

Whatever the mechanical method used to write a budget, the procedures and final results will be the same. Each section will have a figure established for it, as determined by the producer with the assistance and contribution of the appropriate staff and crew members. A separate meeting, or at least a substantial portion of a pre-production meeting, should be devoted to determining a firm budget figure.

Budgeting Framework

The traditional budgeting framework of the motion picture industry has established what are known as ABOVE-THE-LINE and BELOW-THE-LINE figures. An IN-HOUSE production organization, such as a school or a corporate facility, would probably find the distinctions unnecessary; but for those who may be involved in commercial production, I'll take a moment to explain what the two terms mean.

ABOVE-THE-LINE refers to those costs related to pre-production, staff, and housekeeping functions. These are costs that, with few exceptions, must be paid even if the production were to be cancelled. BELOW-THE-LINE costs relate directly to the production and post-production costs.

The Above-the-Line figure would include: Salaries for the producer, director, associate producer, etc.; program secretaries and production staff; legal fees; writer's salaries; talent fees; office costs (including telephone, rent, copying machines, etc.); music rights and performance costs; payroll taxes, fringes, and artist's pension and welfare payments; and insurance.

The Below-the-Line figures would include: Equipment, technical and support crew (including camera; lighting and sound crew); makeup; costuming; tape stock; vehicle rental (and drivers); security; permits; medical (R.N.s on the set), etc., still photos; gofers; etc.

The process for determining these amounts is fairly straightforward, though the precision with which the job is done is critical. Compli-

---

*Apple II is a registered trademark of Apple Computer, Inc.

cating the matter is the fact that there are some things that simply cannot be predicted ahead of time. For instance, if the entire show will be done in the studio, the budget figure will probably be easier to estimate with a reasonable degree of accuracy, since fewer variables enter into the production itself. If the bulk of the show will be done on location—especially in an outdoor setting—then predictions based on an attitude of "Everything's going to go all right" can breed some mean and nasty surprises that can grow up to bite the hand that feeds the budget.

This brings us to the CONTINGENCY item mentioned earlier, and this can be the most important item in a budget, though it's often the least understood.

A CONTINGENCY figure in your budget simply reflects the fact that video production is a highly complex endeavor that is subject to delays and problems that often cannot be foreseen. Recognizing this, an amount is included that provides for the unknown, so surprises won't be quite so unpleasant.

There are many ways of determining a con-

Off-Line *3/4 cassette C.T.*	**80** hrs. x	**25** /hr. =	$ **2,000**	$ **2,000**
On-Line *1" Computer*	**16** hrs. x	**300** /hr. =	$ **4,800**	$ **4,500**
Add-Ons *DUE*	**3 hrs.** x	**175** /hr. =	$ **525**	$ **700**
Workprints *5 windows + code*	**5** qty. x	**110** /ea. =	$ **550**	$ **550**
Stock *1" B+C (1 hr.) + Prot.*	**—** qty. x	**225** /ea. =	$ **225**	$ **225**
Duplication *cassette dubs*	**5** qty. x	**75** /ea. =	$ **375**	$ **375**
Chyron - credits	**1 hr** x	**110** /hr. =	$ **110**	$ **165**
B rolls - as needed	**—** x	**— /** =	$ **400**	$ **240**
		Total Below-the-Line -	($**33,095**)	($**34,165**)

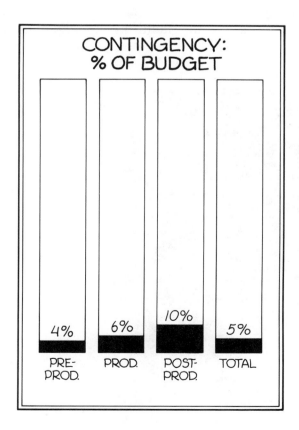

**CONTINGENCY:
% OF BUDGET**

4%   6%   10%   5%

PRE-PROD.   PROD.   POST-PROD.   TOTAL

tingency amount. One is to calculate it as a percentage of the total budget. This percentage will vary with the complexity of the production, and will be influenced by such things as the ratio of studio work to location shooting. Remember, location shooting is subject to more unknowns than studio work. The percentage is also influenced by the experience of the person writing the budget. If this person has been down similar roads many times before, and has a good idea of what to expect, then the contingency figure can be relatively smaller than when embarking into new and different territory.

Each producer also has his or her own idea of a comfortable contingency figure. I would normally set it somewhere in a range of 5% to 20%, depending on the relevant factors. As an example, let me cite an actual budget for a series of four shows with a bottom line in the high six figures. There are three contingency figures within it—one for pre-production, one for production, and one for post-production. The Above-the-line contingency figure is roughly 4% of that section's subtotal, the production figure is about 6%, and the post-production figure is nearly 10% of the post subtotal. My experience with post-production has made me very much aware of how quickly money can be eaten up. In this case, though, the post contingency dollar figure, as opposed to percentage, is the smallest of the lot. Altogether, the three contingency figures total up to almost exactly 5% of the budget.

Normally, all contingency is included in the Above-the-line section of a budget as a single figure. One method is to establish the three separate figures, as mentioned above, and then compile them into a single lump sum shown Above-the-line. Starting with the separate figures helps to increase accuracy.

Budgets for smaller productions would normally include a relatively higher percentage for contingency, since the effect of a $2000 over-run on a $10,000 budget can be far more serious than a $20,000 over-run on a $100,000 budget. The effects of going over budget are not necessarily proportionate as the total amount increases.

This brings us to our third rule.

McQ's RULE No. 3: Always figure you'll spend more than you figured!

Though the producer or the executive producer will bear final responsibility for the budget and the actual expenditures, the job of writing and tracking the budget is often delegated to the associate producer or someone else on the production staff. Proper administration of the budget is plain old time-consuming bookkeeping, and on some larger productions may indeed be turned over to an accountant. If the producer is doing the job right, there won't be time to get bogged down in every last detail of budgeting. Assigning this task to a reliable individual assures that the job will be done properly without distracting from other production matters, and helps to establish one person on the staff as the "budget expert."

Incidentally, the title EXECUTIVE PRODUCER (E.P.) can have several meanings. He may be the in-house budget expert who would actually answer to the producer, or he may be the representative of the money suppliers—backers, distributor, network, etc.—whose job it is to watch over the production and protect the interests behind it. In this second role, the producer answers to the executive producer.

Budgeting is definitely tricky. *It is trouble waiting to happen.* It can cause problems and tension with staff, crew, and clients, and deserves great care and consideration as early in the pre-production process as possible. There is one invariable rule that applies to *all* productions in *all* facilities in *all* circumstances: It is *always* better to come in *under* budget than *over* budget.

CHAPTER 5

The Equipment

Historical Overview

It often seems that many of the people who are fascinated by television and video are as concerned with the equipment itself as they are with what to do with it. I suspect there are an equal number of folks who are horrified at the complexity of all the gizmos and gadgets. Video, to a greater extent than film, is a slave of technology, and this has discouraged many from entering the field. Until very recently, execution of a television program demanded a rather extensive technical background, even if one depended on those hard-core devotees, the Engineers, for the bulk of the technical know-how.

Then along came a new generation of video equipment that, to quote a friend, "any fool can use!" Hallelujah! Television would be freed from the clutches of the networks, and control would be handed to the masses! Soon we'd *all* be making television!

Actually, we should pause here to define some terms and time spans. The first wave of "Everyman" video gear was introduced around 1967, when Sony first started shipping the original CV-series ½-inch black and white reel-to-reel recorders and their companion cameras. The line included something that came to be called a PORTAPAK, that in its first incarnation was an amazing little device that ran on batteries, could be carried over the shoulder,

Old Sony portapak.

and recorded up to 20 minutes of material on a single reel of ½-inch videotape that had to be manually rewound using a little crank that was stored on a clip inside the cover. Everyone was so enchanted with this incredible little device that no apologies were needed for the rather modest picture quality.

Given enough light during shooting, the pictures on the first-generation tape weren't all that bad. After all, the networks were broadcasting shows in black and white, still being in the process of completing the transition to color. These new portapaks seemed to do *almost* everything the big network equipment could do. The system had everything going for it: Small size, light weight, and a low price. Also, low tape costs made using the system far cheaper than film on a per-minute basis.

Portapak in Africa by Joan Logue

Sony originally envisioned the CV-series as a consumer product line (CV = Consumer Video), and the initial sales emphasis took that direction. Systems that incorporated a small TV set and a recorder in the same package were quickly introduced, and walnut-sided models followed for use in the living room. Unfortunately, the public was not particularly interested in recording programs in black and white, having just discovered the wonders of color. The business and educational communities, on the other hand, issued a collective "Ahhh!", and with only slight hesitation, jumped right into the new world of do-it-yourself television.

If the courtship was a whirlwind affair, however, the marriage was often rocky and just as brief.

Teachers often had the new equipment thrust upon them with no real training in its use or potential. They were suddenly confronted with an entirely new and sometimes frightening technology. (After all, you had to thread this fragile little black ribbon through a maze of pins, posts, and blocks; and the Audio Visual Department kept warning you not to touch this strange cylinder or you'd break your heads; and those odd plugs with the bunch of little pins inside kept breaking; and the whole thing's a lot of bother, anyway!) Even if it could be made to work, then what was it supposed to record?

The fact that the equipment was subject to breakdown, as it still is, often resulted in the AV department clamping down on the use of the equipment. At times, a dichotomous situa-

tion arose. The equipment was of no value if it wasn't used, but the AV department didn't want the gear going out because it so often came back inoperable. Though this seems strange, it's true. It's somewhat analogous to the idea of putting tacky plastic covers on a chair to keep it looking good.

1/2-inch non-EIAJ VTR.

Business users had better ideas, but quickly found themselves running up against some inherent limitations. Editing was all but impossible, and copies more than one generation away from the original began to look awfully odd. Interchange between machines was not very dependable. This last problem became even more critical as other manufacturers leapt into the market with systems that *looked* almost like Sony's, but were incompatible. At the peak of the format wars, there were eight or nine different formats, none of which were interchangeable.

In 1969 the EIAJ (Electronic Industries Association of Japan) established the TYPE 1 STANDARD which essentially solved the compatibility problem, and video in business and schools caught on. The consumers, however, stayed away in droves.

EIAJ 1/2-inch VTR.

A better format was needed, and in 1972 Sony again jumped out ahead of the industry by introducing a startling new ¾-inch video-

51

cassette system, called the U-MATIC. The tape was contained inside an easy-to-use cassette the size of a hardbound book, and the unit recorded and played back in full living color! Surely now the revolution had arrived!

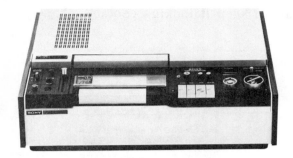

Early U-Matic VCR.

Again, the consumer market was the target, and again, the public responded by staying home. The problem this time was price. Although Sony expected that the prices eventually could be reduced, the world economy at the time was all topsy-turvy, and the lower prices became higher prices as time went by.

But once again, the system was saved by the business and educational sectors. After much grumbling about having to switch to a new format, they embraced the ¾-inch U-Matic system with ill-disguised glee. It did just about everything they wanted. Except edit.

Then, in 1974, Sony again astounded the industry by introducing two devices that opened new dimensions in television: The VO-2850, a videocassette recorder that could actually edit and was accompanied by a simple editing controller; and the VO-3800, a portable, battery-operated color VCR. These two machines sent waves through the television world that are still being felt. The industry sat in awe as CBS used the new technology to cover the Nixon trip to Moscow, and the ENG (Electronic News Gathering) revolution was begun. The consumer, though, felt these technological events only remotely.

Then came the ½-inch Betamax. Challengers came and went until there was VHS (Video Home System); and now VHS and Beta fight for consumer dollars. Although rosy forecasts have now been toned down to more conservative predictions, the "Consumer Video Revolution" is proceeding apace.

We have now reached the age, as predicted, where virtually anybody who can operate a toaster, snapshot camera, and an alarm clock can operate a simple video system that can be bought for under $2000. Such a system includes a color camera and a video recorder, and can make beautiful, exciting, 2-hour programs. Now *anyone* could make television programs!

It's important to note, though, that just having an Instamatic and being able to press the shutter does not necessarily make one a great photographer, except in the strictest dictionary sense, any more than ownership of a pen makes one a great novelist. Likewise, to insert a cassette into a recorder and point the camera in the right direction does not instantly make one into a skilled producer or director.

The enchantment with pictures often tends to overshadow the fact that the average results may leave much to be desired. Viewed alone, the pictures can and often do look quite good,

VO-3800

VHS

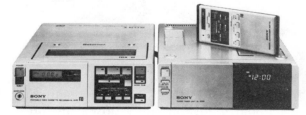

Beta

52

but viewed next to network-quality images, they often fall somewhat short.

Some of this quality difference can certainly be blamed on the equipment itself. It is not reasonable to expect the same performance from a $1000 home video camera as from a $50,000 broadcast unit. However, the quality of today's low cost equipment is sure to improve over the next few years to the point where the home video camera of the mid-Eighties may well approach the quality of its broadcast cousin. Video recorders will also be improved, so it would appear that the disparity between what people see over the air and what they can produce at home will eventually disappear. The reality of the situation, however, isn't quite that simple.

As people started to explore the new video technology, they found that producing high-quality images was not such an easy matter after all. Although basic ½-inch equipment is now relatively inexpensive, small and light-weight enough to be truly portable, the present quality of home systems is good, but not great. Nevertheless, those working with the higher-technology ¾-inch systems often aren't getting significantly better results, either.

Video users are finding that while equipment is important, it's only one part in the pursuit of good program quality. There's a significant difference in quality between ½-inch and ¾-inch cassette recorders using single-tube cameras vs. broadcast rigs using big fancy cameras and recorders; but it's not nearly as significant as the differences in production practices and techniques, including lighting, audio, and engineering.

Broadcast camera.

There was a classic pre-war film in which Mickey Rooney turned to Judy Garland and said: "We could use the old barn, and build a stage, and make some sets, and put on a *show!*" (Or something like that.) Alas, it was only a movie. The sets and lighting and production values that the "kids" came up with in that film could not possibly be the result of bunch of well-meaning young amateurs, although good imagination, creativity, and resourcefulness can produce amazing results in the absence of big budgets.

Standards

Before we can discuss the differences between types of video equipment at various levels of design and cost that are necessary to achieve quality video production, we need to first address the matter of technical standards.

I'll begin by giving a brief definition of what I consider to be BROADCAST STANDARD television, so that we have a mutual understanding of what I mean when I use the oft-abused term. To do so, it will first be necessary to review some of the basics of television technology.

The color television system used in the United States, Canada, Japan, Mexico, and a handful of other countries is known as the NTSC (National Television Standards Committee) system of color transmission. This system was designed to permit compatibility with existing black and white sets already in use at the time color was born.

Because it was a compromise, the NTSC system still leaves much to be desired. Countries that waited to establish color transmission were able to adopt more advanced color standards that differ from ours, since they often had no vast number of black and white sets already in place. The French, for instance, developed a system called SECAM, that they and most of the Communist bloc countries use. The Germans, on the other hand, developed the PAL system, which is not compatible with either NTSC or SECAM. Both PAL and SECAM use a higher number of scan lines which provides higher picture resolution. The PAL system of color encoding also provides somewhat better handling of the color components of the signal.

53

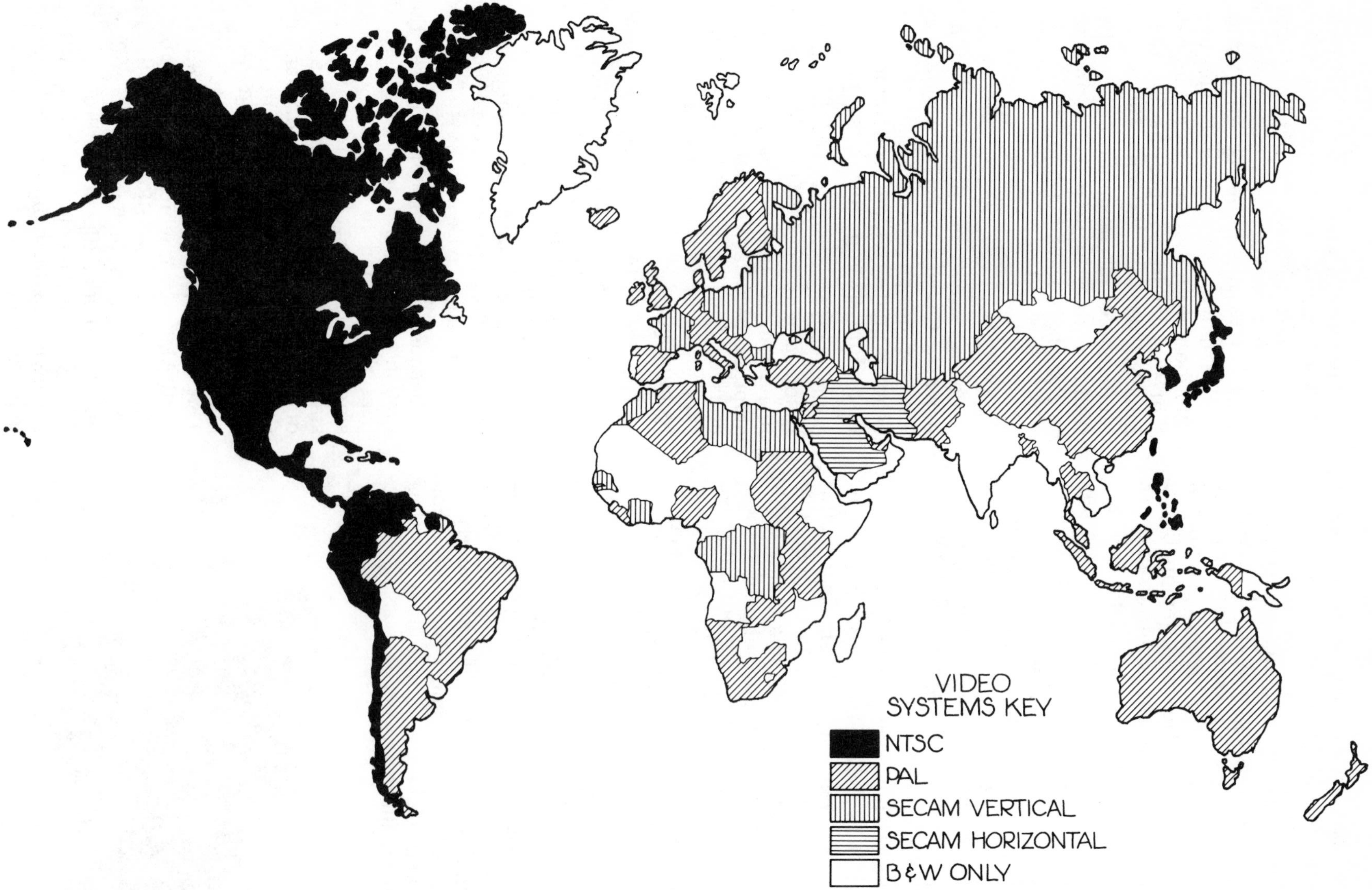

VIDEO
SYSTEMS KEY

NTSC
PAL
SECAM VERTICAL
SECAM HORIZONTAL
B&W ONLY

International Television Standards Chart.

54

Pundits within the industry never tire of the standing joke regarding the true meaning of the three acronyms: NTSC means "Never Twice Same Color"; SECAM stands for "Something Essentially Contrary to American Methods"; while PAL is short for "Peace At Last." I could provide fuel for several dozen barroom brawls by saying that, overall, I feel that PAL is probably the best system currently in use. However, I'll leave it at that and invite those who wish to dispute me to write, and we can argue 'til we're blue in the face.

This brings us (via blue faces—or more appropriately—green and purple faces) back to NTSC color.

It is not my intent to go into deep technical detail on the NTSC encoding process, as there are a number of fine reference books available that do that better. Basically, however, all color television starts the same way. The picture is broken down into the three (ADDITIVE) primary colors of red, green, and blue. In the NTSC system, the color information is then placed on two high-frequency SUBCARRIERS which are transmitted as part of the LUMINANCE (brightness) signal. In essence, this means that the color is transmitted as very fine (high frequency) picture detail. At the receiving end, the tuner senses this high frequency information, and when it finds it, it runs it through a circuit that extracts the color from the luminance. This is why a striped or hounds-tooth fabric sometimes causes flashes of red and blue to appear. The stripes occur at a high enough frequency that the receiver thinks it's seeing color and tries to decode it.

The frequency of the COLOR SUBCARRIER is approximately 3.58 MHz (MHz = MEGAHERTZ, or millions of cycles per second). Actually, the exact subcarrier frequency is 3,579,545 cycles per second. In order to be within FCC specifications for over-the-air transmission, the frequency of the color subcarrier must be accurate to within 10 cycles per second, or 0.00028%.

Transmitting this high frequency signal without loss of quality requires a transmission BANDWIDTH (frequency capacity) of 4.2 MHz. Obviously, there is a lot more involved than I'm willing to get into here, but with this cursory background, I can now define what I consider to be *technical* BROADCAST STANDARDS.

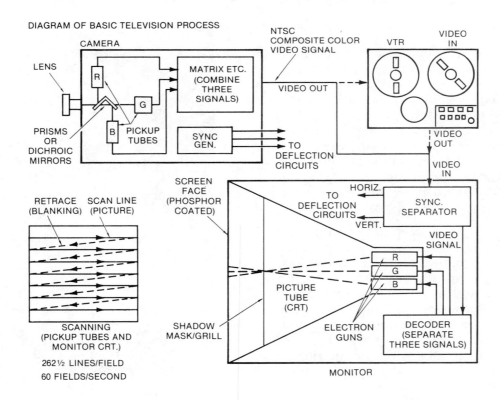

DIAGRAM OF BASIC TELEVISION PROCESS

BROADCAST STANDARD systems are those that provide a full bandwidth, uncompromised signal as the end product, ready to be transmitted over the air; thus implying compliance with all FCC requirements. NON-BROADCAST systems are those that do not meet the above definition.

Understand that the above has been radically simplified. It covers the technical aspects of equipment, and does not involve the aesthetics of what the signal contains. The aesthetics of *broadcast standards* will be discussed later, but are just as important as the technical factors.

Production Values

Earlier, in Chapter 1, *Program Style,* we stressed the importance of high production values. Production values begin with an emphasis on picture quality, as close to broadcast standards as circumstances and resources permit. There are numerous applications of television where nonbroadcast standards are quite acceptable, such as surveillance, home movies, videotaped site surveys, and auditions, but if the purpose is to produce a serious professional program, technical standards are of critical importance.

Of course there are many video users who have no choice in the matter of what equipment they use, and I am *not* saying that quality production is totally impossible with low or middle-range equipment. With *very* careful handling and attention to the details of lighting and engineering, quite acceptable performance can be achieved with modest equipment. Furthermore, certain cameras already approach the quality of today's broadcast units for under $5000, and many who are using the current low cost gear can upgrade.

If you're working in a corporate facility, for instance, and must make use of a single tube camera for your productions, just do the best you can with lighting, staging, and audio, and your production will usually be adequate. On the other hand, if you are contemplating using this type of equipment for a documentary you hope to sell to one of the major networks, or to be distributed on cassette to the population at large, then I *am* trying to—let's say—caution you on standards. You will not be able to squeeze $50,000 pictures out of a $1000 camera, nor 2-inch or 1-inch quality out of a low cost home-type ½-inch VTR.

This book will not spend a great deal of time treating the various pieces of equipment currently on the market. The market changes too rapidly to be kept up with it by anything less ephemeral than a magazine. However, names and model numbers will be mentioned here for purposes of illustration. Now, let's look at some equipment.

Cameras

MINICAMS I find very exciting. These are high-quality, ⅔-INCH-TUBE portable cameras that can be taken out into the field and run on battery power. While not completely matching the better studio units in ultimate picture quality, the best of these designs provide astonishingly good results that rival their studio brethren.

If picture quality were the only factor under consideration, then directors would order up a large studio camera for every production. There are, though, many other factors to be

A single camera "film-style" shoot.

considered, including portability, design, and technical specifications.

Portability means more than just going into the field, since a studio camera can also be trucked out and set up on location. Portability really means that the camera can be hand held, or, even better, placed on a STEADI-CAM, and moved about at will. (The Steadi-cam is a camera stabilizing system that is worn almost like a backpack by the camera operator. It produces dolly-like smoothness in shots requiring vigorous camera movement, even if the operator runs up and down stairs or rides a horse. It will be covered further on, when we get to the section on grip equipment.)

There are creative advantages to portable cameras as well. A small, lightweight camera equipped with a small field viewfinder permits shooting techniques that are more akin to film making than traditional video practice. The intimacy of working close to the camera using an eyepiece-type viewfinder often makes more subtle and precise control of the camera easier.

ENG TV crew.

Minicams provide the handheld portability needed for news, sports and other types of action shooting.

EFP TV crew.

57

Incidentally, the best field viewfinders are those that allow one to see the image from at least a foot away. Many designs require that the operator place his eye virtually right at the eyepiece to see the whole screen, and this is quite bothersome. Sony provided a hinge on their lower-cost models such as the **DXC-1610 & 1640** and the **BVP-200,** so that the eyepiece could be swung up out of the way. The operator could thus directly eyeball the screen, which greatly facilitates shooting from odd angles or positions. Unfortunately, Sony failed to provide this useful feature on their top-of-the-line model, the **BVP-330**. Philips, with their **Video 80** model, didn't take that approach. They almost made up for it by providing a unique and elegantly simple swivel bracket that permits their viewfinder to be rotated to virtually any position. Such human engineer-

ing details are part of the science of ergonometrics—designing with the human body in mind.

"Broadcast" camera specifications:

1. There should be *three camera tubes*—either PLUMBICONS or SATICONS. Plumbicons provide somewhat better control of highlights (bright spots) and lowered lag (image streaking).

2. The camera should employ PRISM OPTICS as opposed to DICHROIC MIRRORS, since prisms generally transmit more light, thereby providing better low-light performance and resolution characteristics than mirrors. Dichroic mirrors can also have alignment problems, whereas prisms are generally more rugged.

3. AUTOMATIC BEAM CONTROL circuitry is necessary—usually called ABC or ABO which helps control LAG and COMET TAILING (streaks that follow highlights when the camera is panned or tilted).

4. Also important is KNEE CONTROL or BLACK STRETCH, which provides control of GAMMA (the response curve of high, middle, and low levels within the picture), which helps out considerably in hard lighting or contrasty situations.

5. Other features would include provision for an optional REMOTE CAMERA CONTROL UNIT (ideally digital, and even better, linked to the camera head via optical fiber), CLIP-ON BATTERIES, and a wide range of lens options and other accessories.

Performance specifications should include 550-700 lines of HORIZONTAL RESOLUTION at center and a SIGNAL-TO-NOISE RATIO of 55+ dB—ideally 57dB or more. A new family of tubes known as DIODE GUN types has recently become available, offering greatly improved operating characteristics. Their resolution is superb, and the tubes are almost totally immune to COMET-TAILING (streaking) and IMAGE BURN-IN.

The features I've described above can be found in cameras starting at about $10-20,000,

Specifications

Rating

1. **Input Signal**
   1) **External Sync Signal:** VBS/BBS 1V(p-p) positive, 75 ohms
   2) **Return Signal:** VBS/VS 1V(p-p) positive, 75 ohms
   3) **Program Audio:** −60 dBm, high impedance
   4) **Tally:** 24V DC or contact closure
   5) **Remote Control:**
2. **Output Signal**
   1) **Composite Signal:** VB/VBS 0.7V/1V(p-p) positive, 75 ohms, 2 outputs
   2) **Monitor Output:** VBS 1V(p-p) positive, 75 ohms, 1 output
   3) **R-G-B Video:** R,G,B 0.7V(p-p) positive, 75 ohms
   4) **Program Audio:** −20 dBm, 600 ohms
   5) **VTR Control:** Start/Stop
   6) **Intercom:** 2-wire system
3. **Pick up Tube:** 2/3 inch Low Capacity Diode gun Plumbicons®
   2/3 inch Diode gun Plumbicons® XQ-2427
   2/3 inch Broadcast Quality Plumbicons® XQ-1427
   2/3 inch Broadcast Quality Saticons® H-8398
4. **Viewfinder:** 1.5-inch high resolution Viewfinder
5. **Filter**

ND	0	0.6	CAP
COLOR	3000°K	4200°K	5600°K

6. **Power:** AC 100V/115V, 50/60 Hz
   DC 12V, 2.5A approx.
7. **Ambient Temperature:** Camera Head −20°C ~ +50°C (−4°F ~ +122°F)
8. **Lens Mount:** Bayonet mount
9. **Weight:** 6.7 Kgs (including 1.5 inch viewfinder)

Performance

1. **Frequency Response:** (100KHz reference)
   1) 50Hz ~ 5.5MHz: +1 dB/−2 dB
   2) Less than 50Hz, and more than 5.5 MHz; falling down (with RETMA standard resolution pattern at 2,000 lux)
2. **Resolution:**
   1) **Center** More than 600 TV lines
   2) **Corners** More than 500 TV lines
3. **Geometric Distortion:**
   Overall picture area Less than 1.5%
4. **Registration:**
   1) **Zone No. 1** Less than 0.1% of the picture height (within circle having a diameter equal to 80% of picture height)
   2) **Zone No. 2** Less than 0.2% of the picture height (within circle having a diameter equal to picture width)
   3) **Zone No. 3** Less than 0.5% of the picture height (outside of Zone No. 2)
5. **Sensitivity:** Standard sensitivity: 2,000 lux, F5
   Mini. illumination: 20 lux. F1.4 (+18 dB Video Gain up)
6. **Signal-to-noise ratio:** 57dB (using Low Capacity Diode gun Plumbicons®, with Gamma, Detail correction all off, Band Width: 4.5 MHz)
7. **Stability:**
   1) **Supply Voltage Fluctuation AC:** ± 5% of rated voltage
   DC: 11 V ~ 16V
   2) **Input Signal Fluctuation** Stable operation in the range of −6 dB ~ + 3 dB.
   3) **Ambient Temperature:** When the ambient temperature varies ± 10°C (± 18°F) of the steup temperature in the range of 0°C ~ 40°C (32°F ~ 104°F), specifications are satisfied without readjustment.

* Plumbicon® Registered Trade Mark of N.V. PHILIPS
* Saticon® Registered Trade Mark of HITACHI LTD.

All specifications are subject to change without prior notice.

Ikegami

Typical camera spec sheet.

though the ones I have in mind run more in the range of $40,000, by the time they are fully loaded with lens, batteries, tubes, power steering, and air conditioning. A random listing of such cameras would include the **Ikegami HL-79**, the **Sony BVP-330**, the **RCA TK-86**, and the **Toshiba PK-39**. All of these, along with others in the same range not listed, are excellent cameras. They are all competitive in terms of options, capabilities, and end results to the point that such minutia as proximity to a service center should be used to make a decision. If, however, I had to make a choice today (late 1982), and plunk down my money for a camera, I'd lean in the direction of the **Ikegami HL-79 D**. The reasons include some of the prettiest pictures I've ever seen from a camera, the comfort of design (despite the fact that the viewfinder doesn't meet my specs), its ruggedness and excellent service access, and Ikegami's fine reputation for quality construction.

Ikegami HL-79D

Sony BVP-330

RCA TK-86

Ikegami ITC-730

Hitachi SK-1

Sony BVP 110

JVC KY-2700A

Overall, careful consideration should be given to the idea of spending $40,000 for *any* camera today, due to the fact that the entire camera industry will go topsy-turvey within the next two or three years as CCD (Charged Coupled Device) cameras begin to appear. (See more on this under *Coming Attractions* later in the *Equipment* section.)

I might also consider a low-cost ($5,000-$10,000) camera for use as a backup and graphics camera, and for use in speculative and personal production. There are a number of cameras currently on the market that provide amazing performance for the dollar, requiring that you know how to treat them. The **JVC KY-1900**, for instance, introduced in 1982, matched the performance of cameras that cost twice as much only a year or so before. In 1981 **Ikegami** introduced their model **ITC-730**, a prism-optic camera with some very impressive features and performance specs, priced at under $10,000. **Sharp** also has their **XC-800** prism camera at roughly $12,000. Almost annually, the entire camera industry goes through changes that bring the cost of quality even lower.

Sony recently introduced a new single-tube camera that verges on challenging the three-tube designs. With claimed resolution of more than 400 lines, and a signal-to-noise ratio well into the 50dB range, the new **BVP-110** represents an interesting development. Weighing less than 8 lbs., and with a price in the range of $12,000-$15,000, it offers the enticing advantages of never needing registration. Designed to be used either as a stand-alone camera, or with the new ½-inch broadcast cassette with built in VCR (as the **BVW-1**—see **Part 4—Future Technology**) the BVP-110 will likely find many advocates for ENG applications.

Sharp XC-800

Choosing a camera:

For commercial work, such as anything done for a client or for public distribution, I usually rent cameras, such as the **Ikegami HL-79 D** or the **RCA TKP-45**. These produce excellent results. The TKP-45 uses 1-inch tubes, which provide superb resolution. I have also had good results with Norelco **(Philips)** Model **PC-70** and the **LDK**-series models **5, 15,** and **25**. All these cameras are in the $35,000 to $100,000 price range.

It is not my intent to disparage anyone's cameras, although I have had experiences ranging from only fair to downright rotten with various camera models. I will not mention them, and wish to make it clear that just because a particular camera is not listed above does not mean it would not belong on the quality list. There are quite a few cameras available, and only one me. Although I have had a wide variety from which to choose, I tend to gravitate to those cameras that give me the results I'm after, and those that do so consistently.

As the list demonstrates, my preference for portable cameras is not absolute. For shots that involve only studio work, a studio camera may be just what's needed, even though portables can be very useful in studio shooting as well. One advantage that many studio cameras have over field units is the relative ease with which extremely LONG-THROW LENSES (e.g., a 45:1 zoom) can be mounted. But, overall, I find portables more flexible because they can be used either in the field or in the studio with relative ease. Mid-priced cameras ($10,000-$25,000) can offer an excellent cost/performance ratio. A case in point would be the **JVC CY-8800**, which has now been discontinued. It represented a breed of cameras that filled the gap between the inexpensive one-tube units at the bottom of the market, and the expensive three-tube designs at the top. The CY-8800 employed dichroic mirrors, and sacrificed service access and sturdiness for the best possible performance for the price. It was an

SHARP

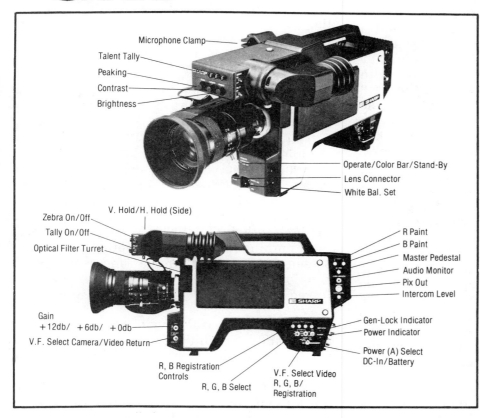
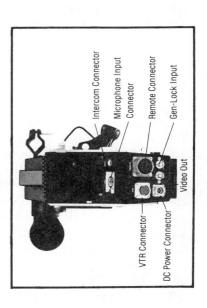

Typical broadcast camera operating controls.

61

excellent value. It does not, however, represent the kind of camera one would use to shoot a national commercial or a program for network or cable.

When one is going for absolute low cost, it is possible to sacrifice certain things to save money. For instance, the relative lack of sensitivity in a lower priced camera will require a higher light level. The lack of easy gamma correction will require a more even spread of light. A lower cost camera will not deliver the same picture quality, but it *will* make pictures—pictures that, with careful work, can be quite pleasing in themselves.

There is a need in the marketplace for low-cost production services, and equipment such as the mid-priced cameras I've discussed is ideal for such purposes. Inventive work, skill, and care can provide very good quality production at a very decent price, and spending time and effort instead of money can often produce excellent results.

Personally, I make every effort to turn out work that is the very best that the state of the art permits. This means I must spend a bit more, though actually, the difference in daily rental between a middle-range camera and a top-of-the-line unit is only perhaps $200 a day. Renting the latter and spending extra money means I can have the best tools available with which to complete the work. If I use the best, and (very important!) use it properly, then the only thing I ever have to apologize for is the state of the art. (Sorry, I can't give you 1000-line resolution today—come back next week.)

At the bottom end of the industrial camera spectrum, we find the single-tube cameras that first became well known in the **Sony DXC-1600** incarnation. Though it wasn't the first of its type on the market, it was perhaps the most revolutionary camera ever to appear. It opened the realm of color teleproduction to what is almost a generation of fledgling videographers. I spent many happy hours behind one of these cumbersome beasts, and it was a remarkable critter. Today, its latest descendant is the **DXC-1800** ($3500), which out-performs the 1600 in nearly every respect, and that, for the money, is a good value.

Similar designs from companies like Panasonic, Hitachi, and JVC compete neck-and-neck. These cameras open color video production to market sectors that would otherwise be excluded. Furthermore, cameras designed for the home video market sell for as low as $500, and do an impressive job, considering their price. I find these very useful for doing site surveys and casting sessions, testing a concept prior to committing to full-scale production, and in general for experimenting to see what kinds of things can be achieved in video. They can be great at parties, and are very simple to operate. They will make you more popular with your friends—maybe even better looking. Some have astonishing low-light capabilities (as well they should, being designed for home use).

For those in education and industry who can afford nothing more expensive, they can be a good way to break into video and do basic productions for in-house use. Beyond this level, however, the more expensive ($10,000-$40,000) cameras are required.

VTRs

Unless the program you're doing will go out live, the chances are that you'll be recording the camera signal on a videotape recorder. Let's take a brief look at video recording—where it's been, and where it is today.

Videotape recording became a practical reality in 1956, when Ampex introduced the first 2-inch QUADRAPLEX (QUAD) machine at that year's NAB (National Association of Broadcasters) convention. CBS was the first to exploit the new technology when, on November 30 of that year, they used videotape to delay *Douglas Edwards and the News* by three hours for replay on the West Coast. Until then, time-zone delays had been accomplished by a method called KINESCOPE recording, which was nothing more than shooting a monitor screen with a film camera, and running the film for playback. The other networks soon followed CBS's lead, and videotape was on its way.

Today there exists a wide range of VTR formats and capabilities. Over the years, machines have been produced using a plethora of tape formats, including ¼-INCH, ½-INCH, ¾-INCH, 1-INCH, and 2-INCH tape. Despite all the formats, there are really only two distinct methods of recording, described by the manner in which the recording heads lay the signal down on the tape.

The original format offered by Ampex used 2-inch tape, and was a TRANSVERSE system, commonly known as QUAD (for quadraplex, meaning four heads). The quad process divides the picture into segments, and the recording heads travel at an angle nearly perpendicular to the direction of tape movement, recording a PACKAGE of roughly 16 lines of the total picture with each pass. During playback, the heads READ each scan in sequence, reassembling the picture for subsequent transmission or re-recording.

The other current method of recording is known as HELICAL SCAN, so called because the heads move across the tape at an acute angle, with the shape of the tape's path similar to the shape of a helix. Whereas transverse

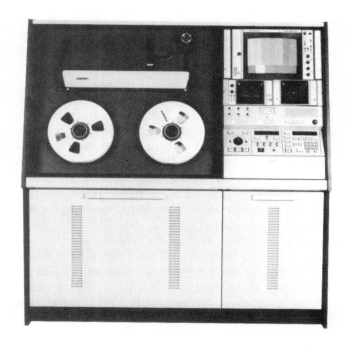

A 2-inch Quad VTR.

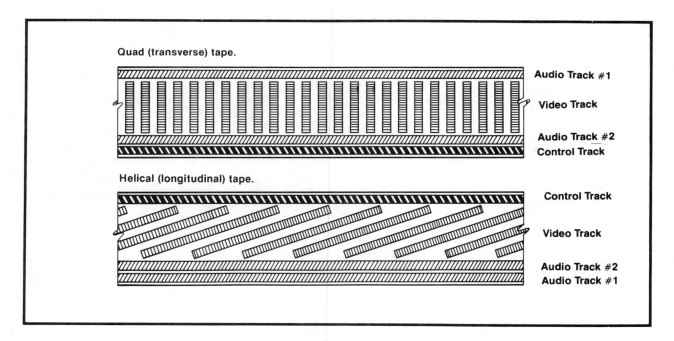

recording is limited mainly to the 2-inch tape width, helical recording has covered the full range of tape widths, from ¼-inch to 2-inch. One company—Asaca of Japan—has had some success with a 1-inch transverse quad format.

Quad VTRs have, until very recently, been the mainstay of broadcasting. Helical VTRs, however, by far outnumber quads, and are the predominant type. Helical machines include EIAJ ½-INCH OPEN REEL, the BETA and VHS ½-INCH CASSETTE, ¾-INCH U-MATIC, 1-INCH TYPES A, B, and C (more on these later), and the IVC 9000 2-inch helical, which is still in use in some studios as an in-house mastering format.

Helical recorders can use a SEGMENTED or NONSEGMENTED FORMAT. The Bosch-Fernseh Type B Design, for instance, is a segmented format, and divides the picture into PACKAGES of lines in a manner similar to quad recording. Most helical VTRs, however, use a nonsegmented format which records a full FIELD (262.5 scanning lines) with each pass of the head. A major advantage to this system is the fact that the picture can be seen in still frame, or at varying speeds in either forward or reverse. The penalty paid for this flexibility is that the required longer tape path results in greater TIME BASE ERRORS (picture instabilities) and more problems with tape guidance and tape stretch and shrinkage. Since 1973, the development and use of DIGITAL TIME BASE CORRECTORS (TBCs) has eased these problems considerably, and permitted broadcast use from these systems. The use of helical formats in broadcasting is now commonplace.

Until about 1978, quad recording was the best standard format available. The very high cost (in the $100,000+ range) put it out of reach of all but broadcasters and major production facilities. About 1978, the new breed of broadcast quality 1-inch VTRs began to appear, culminating in the adoption of the SMPTE (Society of Motion Picture and Television Engineers) standards for the 1-inch formats. Did you notice the "s" at the end of the words standard and format? Not wishing to play favorites and faced with firm commitments by various manufacturers to their individual technologies, SMPTE decided on not just one standard, but *three!* Furthermore, the third of these standards—the much acclaimed TYPE C STANDARD—was provided with options, so that there are "sub-standards" within the standard.

RCA TR-800 Type C System.

Time base corrector.

Type "C" Format

The TH-200A design is based on the SMPTE Type "C" format.

Standard with the TH-200A is a video head system that records video and vertical blanking interval by means of separate heads having identical characteristics. Two record heads are used, one scanning all of the picture information and a part of vertical blanking; the other scanning vertical sync and the remaining part of vertical blanking. Thus all of the information in the waveform is accurately reproduced.

Since all video is derived from a single head, the system is immune to color banding. And the TH-200A offers the further important advantage that all lines of every field are fully reproduced. The entire vertical blanking interval is captured and available for encoding Vertical Interval Reference Signal, Vertical Interval Tests Signal, Vertical Interval Time Code, CEEFAX, or any other special signal required in the future.

The SMPTE Type "C" format offers a high degree of audio reproduction accuracy. Audio tracks have sufficient crosstalk isolation for independent use, permitting high quality stereo programming and second-language transmission via simulcast techniques. The TH-200A has the audio quality required for multiple generations.

With the SMPTE Type "C" format you have the additional advantage of being able to use the address track for time code, cue tone or as a third audio track.

A completely isolated control track prevents crosstalk interference and permits the TH-200A to reach the highest level of performance in 1″ helical scan video tape recorders.

TAPE WRAP CONFIGURATION. Note the location of guides, rollers, and capstans to achieve a gentle, fluid tape path.

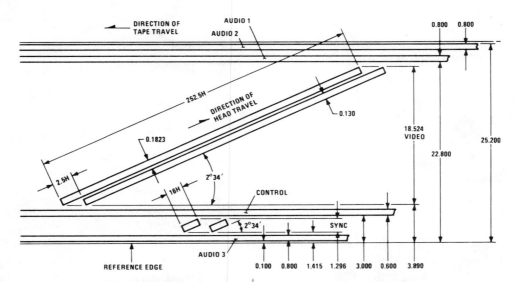

TRACK PATTERN of the TH-200A. Note the 0.8mm width of the two audio tracks, the 0.8mm guardband between them, and the effective isolation of both address track and control track.

65

The TYPE A STANDARD is basically the original Ampex 1-inch format, and the TYPE B STANDARD is essentially the pre-existing Bosch-Fernseh 1-inch segmented format. TYPE C was a compromise between Ampex's format and the newly introduced SONY BVH FORMAT, and was the only *new* format established by SMPTE. While Type B has received wide acceptance in Europe, and has found some adherents in the U.S., the Type C format has been the big winner here, and is the 1-inch format on which we will concentrate.

The networks, stations, and facility houses hailed Type C as the new video messiah, and almost immediately began ordering the machines. The advantages over quad were manifold: The machines sold at perhaps half the price of a quad, tape costs were far lower; portable models were available that could record a full hour of material on battery power in the field, and weighed under 50 pounds, the picture was recognizable at speeds ranging up to 60 times normal, in either forward or reverse, and, astonishingly, the picture quality was potentially better than quad! The fact that a full field was recorded with each pass of the scanner made the Type C format immune to one of quad's worst problems—that of BANDING (color stripes in the picture)—caused by slight differences in EQUALIZATION (electronic adjustment) between the four heads. It also permitted the Type C format to offer some very attractive capabilities, such as still frame and slow motion. Even reverse play is possible with the addition of some video head and TBC options (sometimes called DYNAMIC TRACK-

NEC/3M Type C System

Ampex VPR-80

TYPE C STUDIO VTRS.

Sony BVH-2000 Type C System

66

ING). The variable speed capability eliminated the need for the separate disc recorders that had previously been necessary to achieve these effects.

Type C was just what the industry had been waiting for! King Quad was dead! Long live King C!

Was the industry happy then? Would Type C live and rule forever? Could the search for new and better ways of video recording finally be abandoned? The answer to all of these questions can be summed up in a single word: No.

Problems immediately began to appear with the new Type C format. It quickly developed that interchange between Sony and Ampex machines was not what a standard implies it should be. It was almost as if there were two slightly different standards—one for each manufacturer. Heads spun as other manufacturers threatened to enter the fray. Soon there'd be

Hitachi HR-100 Type C System

Ampex VPR-20B

an Ampex Type C standard, and a Sony Type C standard, and a Hitachi Type C standard, and an NEC Type C standard, and an RCA Type C standard, and so on. What had SMPTE wrought?

Eventually the wrinkles began to be ironed out. The two initial heavies, Ampex and Sony, worked out ways to make their respective machines play each other's tapes, at least most of the time. The later entries into the field—Hitachi, RCA, and NEC—made sure compatibility problems were well in hand before introducing their machines. As more and more facilities took delivery of their 1-inch VTRs and set their engineering departments to work on some of the gremlins, many of the bugs were eliminated, and information was traded within the industry, eventually getting back to the manufacturers.

There are problems that are still inherent in the Type C format. With as many as six video heads hitting the tape with each revolution of the scanner, a percussion effect can result that can ripple its way along the tape. Also, the variable-motion options move some of those heads about with relation to the SCANNER (the drum on which the heads are mounted) in order to provide the still frame and slow motion capabilities. It's thus hard to imagine everything working correctly all the time, even under the best of circumstances. Nevertheless, the Type C format offers some tremendous

Sony BVH-500

Type C Portable VTRs.

67

advantages, and it will serve admirably until the next new format sweeps the industry. When will the next new format appear? What time is it now?

One indication of where VTRs may be headed was provided by a fascinating machine first shown at the 1979 NAB show by **Recortec**, a California company that is best known for its tape evaluators and transport modifications for quad VTRs. Recortec took a standard Sony VO-2860 ¾-inch cassette machine, increased the scanner and tape speeds by three times, installed HIGHBAND (high frequency and wide bandwidth) record electronics, and created a VCR that met or exceeded most quad or 1-inch specs. The primary trade-off of the increased tape speed was a reduction of maximum recording time per cassette to one-third of normal. Good results, though, have been obtained with specially loaded KCA-90 cassettes, providing a 30-minute capacity. The resulting segmentation of the picture by the process has made special treatment of the signal necessary for still framing or slow motion playback. This latter problem is shared with the Type B format and has been solved the same way Bosch addressed the problem: A FRAMESTORE-type TBC (basically a TBC with an extremely wide correction range that can store an entire frame of video) is used to provide still and slow motion capabilities.

The most intriguing thing about the Recortec HBU system is what it portends for the future. The new ½-inch broadcast VTRs recently introduced by Sony, RCA, and Matsushita (Panasonic) may have been inspired by the Recortec machines, and though they are not immediately likely to replace 1-inch VTRs, they certainly will supplement broadcast production.

Choosing a production format:

In deciding on a format for production, one first must determine the desired program standards. For most producers, the choices will come down to three: Quad, 1-inch, or ¾-inch cassette. If the show is to be done to the high-level broadcast standards we defined earlier, then quad or 1-inch would be the choice.

If the program is not intended primarily for broadcast television, then ¾-inch cassette is

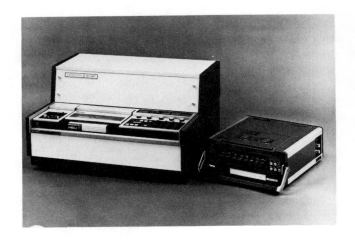

Recortec VTRs.

worth consideration. It certainly costs less to use, though at the expense of some technical quality. Let's examine the inherent limitations of the ¾-inch U-format.

The HEAD-TO-TAPE, or WRITING SPEED of ¾-inch U-format cassette is roughly 404 inches per second (i.p.s.) as opposed to about 1,560 i.p.s. for quad, and about 1000 i.p.s. for 1-inch Type C. This is simply too low to permit DIRECT (unaltered) RECORDING of a full bandwidth signal. To solve this problem, all standard ¾-inch machines employ a color recording system known as HETERODYNE or COLOR UNDER recording. In this system, the color carrier frequency of 3.58 MHz is converted (heterodyned) down to 688 kHz and recorded on the tape. Although the manufacturers coyly mention DIRECT color recording, the fine print reads "direct recording of *converted* color subcarrier." Upon playback, the signal is heterodyned back up to 3.58 MHz by means of some very clever circuitry. The problem lies in the fact that all this fooling around with the color destroys some very precise relationships that existed between the subcarrier frequency and the horizontal scanning line rate frequency of 15.7342 kHz. Originally, the two had an exact mathematical relationship, and the heterodyne system by its very nature changes this. Once lost, this relationship can never be exactly reconstructed. Close, but no cigar.

As a result, the color, and thus the total picture quality of cassette recording, can never match that of true direct high-band recording.

When the tape goes several generations, as is the case during editing, the problems inherent in the cassette format begin to become readily and literally visible.

There are many places in production where the ¾-inch videocassette format is the most appropriate choice. Perhaps the most obvious is in ENG-type work or the production of local documentaries. For hard news, *magazine*-type programs, and for many, if not most, industrial and educational applications, the quality of ¾-inch is quite adequate. The final quality of a production mastered on ¾-inch is further enhanced if the program is edited from the ¾-inch tapes directly to 1-inch. This is a growing trend, and numerous new post-production facilities are springing up around the country based on systems to do just this. The picture quality of ¾-inch cassette at the first generation can be quite good, and begins to suffer mainly when multiple generation copies are made on ¾-inch. By editing directly to 1-inch, the quality is maintained, and several nationally distributed programs, such as the *PM Magazine* show, are mastered almost entirely on ¾-inch.

An alternative to editing from ¾-inch directly to 1-inch is to transfer the ¾-inch material to 1-inch tapes (called BUMPING) prior to editing. The advantages would be a decrease in editing time, since 1-inch is much faster in shuttling and cuing than ¾-inch cassettes, plus higher overall quality. The quality is likely to be higher because, at the time of transfer, levels and color can be closely monitored and adjusted. In the hectic environment of editing, it's all too easy to forget to check levels for each edit. The drawback would be increased cost. The cost of the transfer itself plus the higher cost of editing time would add to the budget.

Some of the primary advantages offered by the ¾-inch format are the small size and weight and the lower cost of the portables. At about half the weight and volume of a 1-inch portable, and about a tenth of the cost, ¾-inch portables make quality location recording possible to many who could never begin to afford 1-inch. As to the deck-type models, they offer the same cost, weight, and size advantages compared to 1-inch.

The three major manufacturers of ¾-inch systems are familiar names: JVC, Panasonic, and Sony, although NEC also makes a system and several manufacturers offer machines made by one of the big three under their own

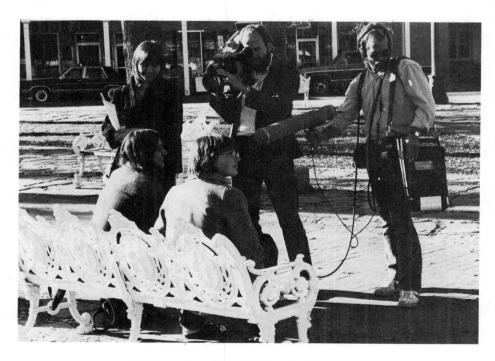

ENG crew shooting magazine style program.

labels. Overall, I'd rate Sony's machines the highest. I say this not without misgivings, for dealing with Sony is often a love/hate affair. Machines from other manufacturers often offer features that Sony does not, but Sony's solid reputation for quality of construction and reliability is the standard of the industry. There have been many times, however, when I've been so angry at Sony that I've hovered on the brink of violence and name-calling. They have a history of leaving out simple features that would have made their machines much more useful, often, it seems, simply to create a demand for the upcoming model.

A case in point, taken from my personal experience, is a pair of VO-2860 editing recorders I purchased a while back. I had the distinct misfortune to buy my machines less than a week before the announcement of the new VO-2860A models, which incorporated a direct-drive head drum, framing servo, and other technical goodies that make the machines much easier to live with. To add insult to injury, I later discovered that the dealership I had purchased them from already had the "A" models in their warehouse (which is part of a separate feud). From experiences like this, on the part of many in the industry, there is an axiom that has developed, which I offer only half kiddingly: Never buy any Sony equipment that doesn't have an "A" suffix on the model number, if not a "B." Based on more than 15 years of dealing with Sony, it's advice that I myself won't forget in the future.

The new generation of Sony VCRs, the VO-5850 and its kin, are fine machines, and represent a major development in 3/4-inch technology. At the broadcast level, the BVU-800 is a quantum leap, handling and performing much like their 1-inch machines, which is to say, superbly. The BVU-820 offers the Dynamic Tracking capabilities (broadcastable still frame, slow motion, reverse play, etc.) of the 1-inch machines, and will provide a tremendous boost to 3/4-inch users. On the portable side, the VO-4800 and its broadcast cousin the BVU-110 are among the best of their kind. The new JVC CR-4700U is also an enticing portable 3/4-inch system and offers the unique feature of *videoconfidence* heads which provide continuous instant playback of the picture while you are recording. The CR-4700U also uses professional broadcast audio connectors and provides a third track for time code.

In most cases, the differences between the Sony VO series (industrial) and the BVU series (broadcast) is in the included features. For example, the VO series machines provide RCA and miniplug audio connectors, while the BVU series uses XLR connectors —the professional standard. The BVU series machines place the head switching point down in the vertical interval, whereas the VO series places it about

A 3/4-inch portable camera and VTR system.

Sony BVU-110

JVC CR-4700

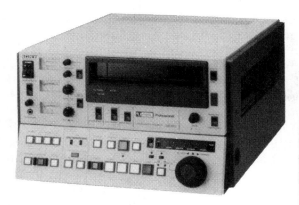

Sony BVU-800

CR-4700 side panel

five-six lines above blanking, at the very bottom of the picture. The BVU machines offer a separate cue channel for recording time code, while the VO units will require the use of an audio channel for time code. In terms of basic picture quality, however, the two types of machines are very close, if not identical. The BVU series was designed, as its name implies, for broadcast uses, and is priced accordingly. For those not working in broadcasting, the VO units are by no means a compromise.

I've spent a fair amount of time on Sony, and as earlier mentioned, I feel that their machines can sometimes be the best overall investment. On the other hand, many users of JVC and Panasonic systems have reported many good experiences over the years with their machines and would make the same decision if they were to buy new equipment. I've found, though, in my visits to many of the major production houses and television stations, that the overwhelming preponderance of 3/4-inch equipment has borne the Sony label, and many engineers tend to agree with my assessment.

Three-quarter inch technology has developed tremendously since the first machines were introduced in the early 1970's, and the quality of performance has improved dramatically since then. Most top-end machines currently available feature a system for dubbing and editing that routes the color signal directly from the heads of the playback machine to the heads of the record machine. This eliminates several steps of SIGNAL PROCESSING, and provides much better MULTIPLE-GENERATION performance than was possible in the past. There is now a new generation of high performance 1/2-inch professional single unit camera/VTR systems which promises increased flexibility for news and documentary productions. This is further discussed in the *Future Technology* section.

My personal preference is the Type C format. Since I contract virtually all of my production and on-line post-production requirements to a single production house, I've had very few interchange problems. I've also taken time to learn the idiosyncrasies of the Type C format (the machines have been **Sony BVH-500s** and **BVH-1000s**), so I've enjoyed excellent results. I find editing on Type C especially pleasurable, as it's very fast and the quality holds up extremely well.

The bottom line with regard to choice of VTRs, then, is rather simple: Choose the best you can afford, whether you're buying or renting. If you're going for the ultimate results this means highband recording. As mentioned, the advantages of the Type C format over quad in terms of cost, size, ease, and speed of use and final results suggest its selection; all else being equal and if you have the budget and availability of equipment facilities.

Three-quarter-inch cassette is very popular for ENG and low-cost production, though its built-in limitations must be considered when choosing a mastering format where top quality is important. So far, we've examined cameras and VTRs, the two basic hardware items common to virtually all video productions. If the camera and VTR can provide excellent quality, then the opportunity is open to do production work of the highest caliber. If, on the other hand, the camera and VTR are not capable of making and saving good, sharp, clean pictures, then the chances are that the production quality will suffer. The quality of the basic video signal is the starting point in production. It would be difficult to place too much emphasis on the importance of starting with a good signal. There will be enough things happening to it as the production moves along that you don't want to *start* with a handicap.

Using Film

While the subject of this book is basically video production, a word here about the use of film would not be out of place. Film still has some advantages over video in certain applications, such as in very adverse lighting conditions, or when extreme mobility is required. Film is the only logical choice when extremes of speed manipulation (slow motion or fast motion) are required. There is also a certain *look* to film—softer, more subtle colors—that is appropriate in certain applications, and which many directors prefer. These advantages will eventually evaporate, though, as video technology matures. Once shot, film can then be transferred to tape for the final edit, and it is possible that film and video might be intermixed. It's important, though, to note that the difference between the two will be obvious.

An ENG crew on location.

Rank-Cintel Flying Spot Scanner.

RCA film chain.

73

The best results I've seen short of 35mm film have been with Eastman Kodak's **7247** 16mm negative stock rated at ASA 100, and transferred to tape via the RANK-CINTEL FLYING SPOT SCANNER, which can work from DIRECT NEGATIVE as well as REVERSAL STOCK. The Rank-Cintel scans the film with an electron beam, unlike a normal film chain in which a projector essentially shoots into a camera. Material shot and transferred in this manner can provide exceptional results, looking almost like 35mm, with almost video-quality color and the look and feel of film.

Kodak now offers a higher speed negative film with a nominal ASA rating of 250. Available in 16mm (#7293) and 35mm (#5293) sizes, this stock can be pushed as high as 1000 ASA or higher, and closely matches the characteristics of the 100 ASA stock, allowing the two to be intercut. This greatly enhances the ability to shoot film in available light.

The **Kodak Video News Films** are reversal type films—yielding a positive, ready-to-project original—and also provide good results, especially for use in extreme low-light conditions.

RCA film transfer color control panel.

CHAPTER 6

People — Staff, Crew, Talent, and Unions

Staff and Crew

Once equipment considerations are set, the primary concern of the producer is the staff and crew. Program production doesn't happen all by itself. Although there are instances where one person **is** the crew, it is very difficult to achieve professional results with such limited resources. In this section, we'll look at the various staff and crew positions and what they entail.

(Going back to our definitions of Above-the-line and Below-the-line, STAFF personnel are usually considered to be those in Above-the-line positions, with CREW being those who fall Below-the-line.)

In discussing personnel, it is important to be aware that there are no hard and fast rules. Job descriptions, functions, and titles are quite variable, and often differ from one facility to the next. Many times the character of the organizational structure (see box) changes from production to production, even within a single facility. The variety of types of facilities and of programs almost ensures that titles and functions will never be delegated the same way twice.

Therefore, this section will provide an overview using definitions that are as close to traditional as they can be. These traditions were established by the motion picture industry, and have been somewhat changed and

ORGANIZATIONAL CHART

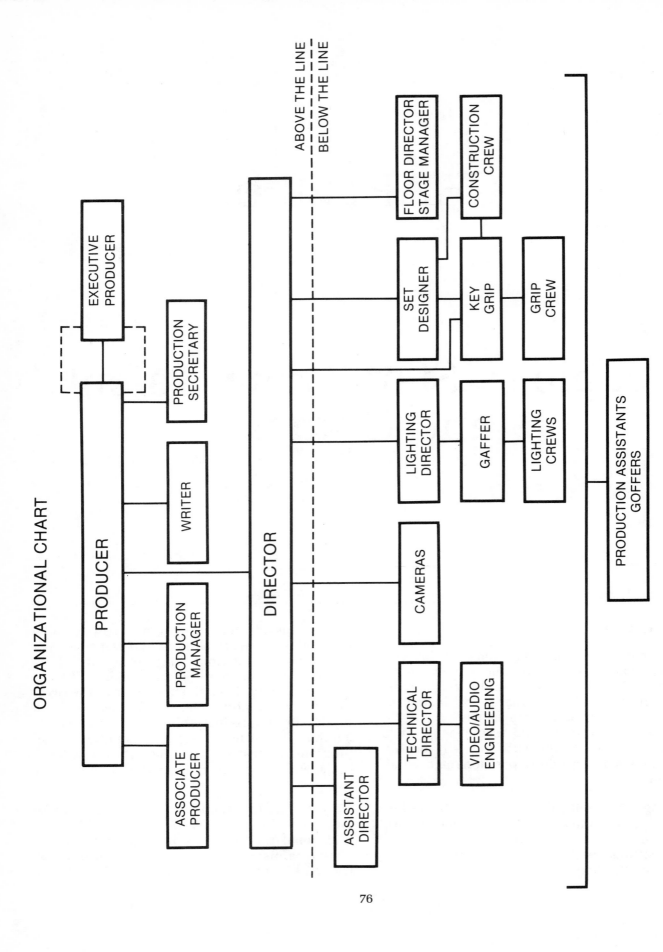

ABOVE THE LINE

BELOW THE LINE

EXECUTIVE PRODUCER

PRODUCER

ASSOCIATE PRODUCER

PRODUCTION MANAGER

WRITER

PRODUCTION SECRETARY

DIRECTOR

ASSISTANT DIRECTOR

TECHNICAL DIRECTOR

VIDEO/AUDIO ENGINEERING

CAMERAS

LIGHTING DIRECTOR

GAFFER

LIGHTING CREWS

SET DESIGNER

KEY GRIP

GRIP CREW

FLOOR DIRECTOR STAGE MANAGER

CONSTRUCTION CREW

PRODUCTION ASSISTANTS GOFFERS

NOTE: The organizational structure is highly variable, depending on the size and nature of the production, and the circumstances. The above is just one example of a common structure.

The Producer.

modified by the different requirements of television. Further discussion of crew positions will be presented in *Part 2—Production*.

Before we begin, it would be worth noting here that there was a time when virtually all major production positions were filled by men. The only roles considered "appropriate" for women were such areas as costuming, makeup, and secretarial positions. Fortunately, this has changed, and there are few if any positions today that are not regularly being filled by women.

Staff:

PRODUCER

Starting at the top, the producer is the person in charge of the entire production, and who bears responsibility for the results.

The producer may answer to an executive producer, to a client, to a department manager, or to himself or herself. In general, though, the only figures higher up the totem pole are the money people.

The producer accepts the credit or blame for the results of the production. He or she does the hiring and firing of the staff, and has the final say in virtually all matters relating to the production.

There is no set requirement for experience or training, and in the strictest sense, anyone who goes to their friendly local photo store and buys a Super-8 camera automatically becomes a producer. In the broadest sense, the title itself is a definition of the job.

The role of the producer is essentially a management function, with the actual work involved being parceled out to the staff and crew.

The producer is most actively involved during the pre-production phase, assembling the staff, working with them, and planning the production. In many respects, a good producer is a kind of "Super Gofer," who assures that all the details of the production fall into proper place. Once production has begun, the producer generally steps back. If the job is properly done, the rest of the staff and crew handles the bulk of the production work, leaving the producer to worry about the bills, schedule, distribution, and any higher-ups who might need coddling. The producer makes sure that his or her people have what they need to do their jobs, and fends off things that could hinder the production. He runs flak for the show, and though he keeps well in touch with how things are progressing and may jump in occasionally to consult, he recognizes that good people work best when given a large degree of freedom. On small productions, especially in in-house facilities, the producer is often the most logical person to make the coffee or tea for everyone. The fact that this may be a rare occurrence does not alter the logic of the philosophy behind the suggestion.

DIRECTOR

The director is the person to whom actual creative control of the show is delegated. The roles of producer and director are often combined, but once a production goes beyond a certain size, it is impossible for one person to handle both roles in a competent manner. In such instances, one method I've used with success has been to retain both titles, and to appoint either a co-producer or an associate producer to take on the operational functions

The Director.

that would normally be handled by the producer. We then get together after hours to go over the progress of the production. There have also been times when I've taken the titles and duties of executive producer and director, appointing someone else as producer. It all depends on the nature and scope of the production.

The director is primarily responsible for the production phase. Though he or she will be very much involved during pre-production, his/her involvement will be mainly in terms of accepting the assignment from the producer and assisting the producer in getting things rolling. Once production starts, though, the director is in charge. The producer still has the ultimate authority, and can jump in at any time, but it is important that the producer respects the chain of command and channels all orders through the director. Going around the director is a guaranteed way to subvert the director's own authority, which can easily upset the smooth operation of the production.

Although the producer may consult with the director in the decisions, it is normally the director who makes out the crew list. In a sense, the director is the top crew member in addition to being a staff member. The director

thus bridges the gap between above-and below-the-line functions. The title of director, then, has several meanings. He or she is responsible for directing the crew in performing their jobs. He is responsible for the presentation of the show. The director must also direct the taping itself. The crew looks to the director for solutions to any troubles or needs they may have. In addition, the director is usually responsible for the technical aspects of the production, and chooses facilities and maintains the technical standards.

The real nut of the director's job is the creative aspect of the production. Although the writer determines the program style and script, the director's job is to turn the script into a visual form. When the cameras are heated up and tape rolls, it is the director who will be the creative force behind the show, and whose vision will determine the way the show is translated from paper to pictures.

The director calls the shots during taping, and in single-camera production often is also

The Director on the set.

78

the DIRECTOR OF PHOTOGRAPHY (D.P.) (okay, Videography), if not the camera operator as well. This is a departure from motion picture production, where union restrictions usually require that the only person to touch the camera be the camera operator, although the D.P. and the director can look through the viewfinder if they promise to be good.

ASSOCIATE PRODUCER (A.P.)

Here things get a bit cloudy. The title of ASSOCIATE PRODUCER, or A.P., can cover a lot of things, and this is good, since flexibility is one of the main requirements of this position. In Lotusland (also known as Hollywood), the duties of the A.P. are fairly closely defined, but elsewhere the definition has a wider range of meaning.

In general, the A.P. serves at the right hand of the producer (that's *at* the right hand, not *as* the right hand), and is assigned a specific set of duties and areas of responsibility. These may include such things as responsibility for

The A.P. Looks over her notes.

keeping track of the budget, locating and arranging for facilities in coordination with the director, keeping the production on schedule, and in general looking for anything that the producer or other staff members might have missed.

The A.P. is not usually considered to be an assistant, but rather, just what the title says—an associate. The job is often a stepping stone for those on the way to becoming a producer, and is an excellent training ground. Conversely, many A.P.s gained their experience as production assistants, or in other lower-level positions.

If filled by the right person, the associate producer position can be of immense value to the producer. It's a demanding job, requiring a person who is both a quick thinker and fast on his or her feet. It's very important that the producer and the associate producer get along, and also helpful if they tend to think along similar lines. In the absence of the producer, the A.P. should be able to step in when decisions are called for and make sure that everything proceeds smoothly.

Other Staff

Depending on the size of the production, there may be any number of other positions and people who are necessary.

WRITER

In most cases a WRITER will be involved in the production. There are times when this is not the case. The writer may just hand over the script and disappear, but usually the writer is involved in the production through to the end. If the show is of an educational or technical nature, the writer assures that the information is not distorted or modified during the translation to tape, whereas in an entertainment project, the writer often takes a less prominent role. It is worth mentioning that it is not unusual for friction to develop between the writer and the director because of the different ways in which the two may visualize the show.

ASSISTANT TO THE PRODUCER

The producer may bring in someone as an assistant, and this position bears the title of

ASSISTANT TO THE PRODUCER. This can be a slightly confusing title, since this position falls below the associate producer in the production hierarchy. The assistant to the producer may indeed answer to both the producer and the associate producer, since in a real sense, he or she works for both.

Moving down the line, there may be one or more PRODUCTION ASSISTANTS (P.A.s). Although they are usually considered to be Below-the-line positions, and will be part of the operating crew during production, they also work for and with Above-the-line people, and are thus included here. Production assistants are also known as GOFERS. (Gofer—n: /fr. slang— "Go for ... (this or that)"/: a person hired in the production of motion picture or television programs to assist in the production by running errands and/or doing any other jobs which will facilitate the completion of the project; alt. spelled GOPHER.)

Others who may be involved according to the needs of the production would include: SCRIPT EDITOR(s); consultants of various stripes; Legal Eagles; secretaries; and others. As already mentioned, each production is different, and the staff needs will make themselves apparent as the pre-production process gets under way.

Crew:

ASSISTANT DIRECTOR (A.D.)

The ASSISTANT DIRECTOR, or A.D., is to the director what the A.P. is to the producer. The A.D. will back up the director in preparing for and executing the production. In instances where a SWITCHED ISO RECORDING (a second recording, simultaneous but separate from the main recording) is done, the A.D. may direct this *second show*. Other duties might include keeping track of TIME CODE (editing logs), crew schedules, 2nd unit operations, supervising setup and STRIKE (teardown), making sure that the SLATE (a board containing production information) is correct and that it's shot at the start of each scene, coordinating still photos and continuity stills, assuring that all cast and crew members necessary for a scene are where they should be, and calling directions on the set as a relay for the director.

The primary function of the A.D., in other words, is to relieve the director from worry about details so that the director can devote full attention to the creative aspects of the show.

TECHNICAL DIRECTOR (T.D.)

This position changes with the production style. In studio operation, the TECHNICAL DIRECTOR, or T.D., is generally the one who actually performs the hands-on operation of the switcher in response to the director's commands. In field production, the T.D. is often in charge of technical facilities, and is responsible for the equipment and its performance. In single camera/VTR shooting, the T.D. may also act as camera shader and tape operator.

PRODUCTION MANAGER

Productions of fairly large scale may require a PRODUCTION MANAGER who handles the over-all coordination of all the various technical and crew elements. In even larger operations, the job may be split between a Production Manager and a PRODUCTION COORDINATOR. The coordinator lets the manager know what needs to be done when, and the manager makes sure it happens.

FLOOR DIRECTOR

The FLOOR DIRECTOR is most commonly found in the studio, though location shots may require a floor director when the director's station is inside a mobile production vehicle. The Floor Director relays directions received over intercom from the director to the crew and talent on the floor (studio or location). He or she acts in the director's place near the cameras while the director is in the control room. The floor director gives camera cues to the talent, and provides warnings or upcoming commercial breaks and other program cues.

STAGE MANAGER

In larger-scale studio productions, or when taping theatrical events, the STAGE MANAGER serves the same function as in legitimate theatre: He or she manages set and prop movements on stage, and makes sure that talent is ready to go on. In some situations, this job is the same as that of Floor Director.

Other crew:

The following is a menu of crew positions that may be used if the production warrants them. On a very large production, most if not all of them would be used, with many requiring more than one person: CAMERA OPERATOR(s), VIDEO SHADER(s) (adjust cameras before and during taping), ASSISTANT CAMERA OPERATOR (A.C.—helps set up camera), FOCUS PULLER (adjusts focus during a shot), TAPE OPERATOR(s), LIGHTING DESIGNER (L.D.), GAFFER (sets up the lighting), BEST BOY (Gaffer's assistant), AUDIO ENGINEER, SET DESIGNER, CARPENTERS, ELECTRICIAN(S), PROPERTY MASTER (in charge of all props), DOLLY/BOOM OPERATOR(s), KEY GRIP (in charge of equipment), GRIP(s), UTILITY PEOPLE, GREENSMAN (landscaping & plants), SCRIPT SUPERVISOR (keeps track of all script changes), CONTINUITY SUPERVISOR, TALENT COORDINATOR, STILL PHOTOGRAPHER, WARDROBE, MAKEUP, HAIRDRESSER, REGISTERED NURSE(S), DRIVERS, PRODUCTION ASSISTANT(S), SECURITY PEOPLE.

As you can see, it can be quite a list, and there are many, many other positions I've not even mentioned. The production will determine who you need. If you're doing a produc-

tion that requires people who are not listed above, the chances are you'll know it, and don't need to be told who they are. At the other end of the scale, the one-man band would have to do everything.

Salaries, day rates, and fringe benefits may consume a large portion of the budget. Overtime and crew support, especially on location, can push the budget even higher. As I mentioned earlier, careful pre-production planning is critical in helping to avoid having any of the above people standing around while the clock is ticking.

Talent

One thing common to virtually all video programs is the fact that people usually appear in them. Whether the show is for training, education, corporate communications, or entertainment, the chances are that someone will be in front of the camera. These people will be the TALENT.

Taking a broad view of television production in general, there are two basic ways in which people will appear: They may appear as themselves, as in an interview or as an instructor in a training program, or they appear as actors, playing some sort of role other than themselves. This latter instance is further broken down into two additional categories: Talent can be either professional or nonprofessional.

In this section, we'll look at the techniques for choosing "real-life" people for on-camera work, and will examine the differences between professional and nonprofessional talent.

Real people:

In using the term REAL PEOPLE, I am not implying that there are some out there who are phony (hmmm . . .), nor am I referring to the NBC show of that name.

Rather, the real people I'm talking about are those who appear on the screen as themselves. Examples would include documentaries; a subject expert ("wizard") in an educational or training program who is there to relay information from within an area of specialization; an executive brought into a corporate employee-relations program for such purposes as explaining management decisions or a new health-benefits package; a doctor making a presentation in a medical program; or a politician appearing on a community-affairs show to explain school funding cutbacks. All of these are examples of real people, appearing as themselves without intent to act out a part.

Despite the fact that these people are not actors, and are not attempting to perform, per se, they do present some of the same problems encountered in using nonprofessional talent. Although they may know their subject matter very well, and do not usually have to memorize lines, they still will be confronting one of the potentially most terrifying beasts in existence—*The Camera.* In *Part 2—Production,* we'll examine some methods that can help people to relax and make a good showing.

There's really not an awful lot that can be said about choosing real people for a show. In most cases, the decision is made by the program itself. There are occasions that permit a choice, however, and common sense is the best guide. For instance, if you're doing a program on the manufacture of integrated circuits, and you have several in-house experts on epitaxial deposition available for the show, talk to each of them and choose the one you suspect would present the information in the most straightforward and understandable manner. If possible, find someone with a sense of humor. This usually indicates a more relaxed nature that will not only help the show itself, but will make production easier. Many people who have not been around television don't understand its detailed, tedious, and stop/start nature, and they tend to get uptight and nervous rather easily. At its worst, this can lead to complete paralysis when the red light goes on.

People with unusually odd appearances are better left off-camera. Such things as a brown wart strategically placed at the end of a nose will surely become the unintended star of the show. As a result, the viewer will absorb little of the topic under discussion. People appearing on camera needn't necessarily be beautiful, but there *are* some obvious things to avoid, if at all possible.

Actors:

I stated earlier that there were two basic types of actors: Professional and nonprofessional. Actually, there is also a third—the amateur, who falls somewhere between professional and nonprofessional, though usually leaning slightly toward the former. Let's start with some definitions.

PROFESSIONALS

Professionals earn their living from acting, or would if there was sufficient work. The fact that a given actor may also work as a waiter or what-have-you does not belie his or her status as a professional. Actors are traditionally often "between engagements," and have to eat like the rest of us. Finding them holding down a part-time job is the norm.

This brings up the matter, however, of hopefuls who consider themselves to be actors, even though the rest of the world has yet to hear the news. How can one determine who is really an actor, and who is simply parading around with the title?

Well, first of all, find out if the individual has actually made any money at the trade.

What experience does he or she have? It's a sad but real fact that the producer views from the upper end the classic "Catch 22" situation. It takes experience to get work, yet working is the only way to get experience.

A talent agency is the best place to start the search for professional talent. These agencies serve as clearing houses, and agents make their living by putting talent and producers together. A good agent will make every attempt not to waste the time of either the talent or the producer. When a connection *is* made, the producer normally pays the agent an amount equal to 10% of the talent's base pay for the effort. The service they provide is usually well worth the cost.

Another method for finding talent is the infamous CATTLE CALL. A cattle call is a description of what occurs when an advertisement is placed in either a trade or general-circulation publication; putting out the word that talent is needed, and usually specifying a time and place for auditions. I shrink in terror at the very thought. Cattle calls are common in theatre, as *Chorus Line* and *All That Jazz* have demonstrated. On occasion they are used in film and television talent searches. They can

serve a purpose, since in rare instances they're the only way to discover new talent with something fresh to offer.

Usually, though, a cattle call is about the most horrendous way possible to waste a lot of people's time. In any major metropolitan area it will ferret out every actor who's hungry for work, and can easily result in hundreds of warm bodies showing up for the auditions. A positive exception to the use of cattle calls is when a large number of extras are needed, as for the scene in your corporate show where the Chairman of the Board is going to part Lake Michigan so that the sales force can cross over unto the Land of Wisconsin.

In smaller cities and towns, a cattle call is likely to bring out every bored housewife and fidgety student who ever dreamed of being a star. It is usually necessary to limit each reading to a few short lines in order to get through the herd. This leaves you numb by the time it's over, often with little more determined than when you started, and the majority of those who showed up leave disappointed and frustrated. For weeks afterwards you'll be getting calls inquiring as to whether casting has been done, unless of course you were crafty enough to list a phony number. Altogether, cattle calls are not a very sensitive way to treat people, or to fill your talent needs. There are a number of better alternatives.

How to choose talent:

The TALENT AGENCY is a much more sensible way to cast roles. The best procedure is to call the agency as soon as your cast requirements are known. Give them a list of characters needed, with a complete description of type, age, appearance, special requirements, etc. If the agency is good and your description is succinct, they'll know their talent well enough to come up with suggestions very quickly. They'll then send you a stack of actors' resumes, along with a stack of photos or COMPS (composite photos, featuring the talent in three or four poses showing different moods and wearing different outfits). Most

A composite shows the talent in various types of dress and different moods.

A resume, usually attached to comp, lists recent experience.

84

agencies also have voice tapes with one to two-minute samples of their clients' capabilities.

What you are producing will determine to a great extent what to look for in talent. On-camera experience is of obvious value, but other factors can enter into the decision as well. For instance, if your script contains a fair amount of dialog, and you want to shoot without using a prompter or cue cards, stage experience can indicate a developed ability to memorize lines. However, be careful of actors with nothing but stage experience. They have been trained to "play to the back of the house"—i.e., to project so that their voice and movements carry throughout the theatre. As a result their movements and voice may be too big for the relatively intimate character of television.

By going through the photos and resumes and listening to the voice tapes, you'll be able to narrow down the possibilities, at which time you'll call the agency and ask them to arrange a reading by the people you've chosen. The reading may be held at your studio, at the agency, or on neutral ground, such as a hotel room. Try to minimize the number of people you'll have read for each part. Five would be ideal, and ten should be about the maximum in most cases. Again, you want to avoid the cattle call syndrome. Most agencies will have no objection to taping the readings, and a portapak is perfect for this. It's usually helpful to have people read against each other in cases where the script involves dialog, as this gives you an idea of how well they might work together. You may ask likely prospects to read several roles, mixing and matching actors to see what chemistry develops. A videotape of the proceedings gives you the ability to study auditions at leisure, shielded from anxious eyes. At the very least, take Polaroid shots of the prospective talent, as you'll find that the composites and glossies provided by the agency may not represent at all what the people look like, especially if their weight, hairstyle, and/or age has changed.

Although you may be able to make a decision on the spot, there is nothing to prevent you from taking a few days to reach one. You may want to ask for additional readings if no one seems right for the part. Though it is sometimes difficult to turn someone down, especially if you know them from a previous production, actors are very accustomed to rejection—it's a regular part of the job.

A note of caution with regard to agencies. It is important to be aware that there are talent agencies and there are MODELING AGENCIES, and the two are not necessarily the same. MODELING AGENCIES may call themselves talent agencies, and even try to promote their people as actors. Their primary business, nevertheless, is supplying models for still photos and commercials, and the fact that someone is attractive, photographs well, and can look super in clothing off the rack does not necessarily mean he or she can act. The photos and composites may look the same, and indeed, many competent actors will list themselves with modeling agencies as well as talent agencies, so be sure to check the resume for actual acting experience. A photo or comp without an accompanying resume can be a sign that the person's acting experience is limited or nonexistent. In such a case, check with the agency.

AMATEURS

An AMATEUR is a person who has dramatic training or experience, but who has not become part of the professional talent pool. This includes drama students and members of little theatre groups and the like. An advantage to amateurs is that they are often available for less money than professionals, but as in anything, you usually get what you pay for. Using these people gives them valuable experience, and they add much to the production. They can, however, also greatly hinder the production.

With care in selection, amateurs can work out very well. The key words here are "care in selection." Since most amateurs have only stage experience, it can be hard to predict how they'll react on camera. In this instance, it is almost a must to tape their readings.

What amateurs may lack in experience, they often make up for in enthusiasm. This can work to your benefit. Also, even though it should not be a part of the final decision-making process, there is an undeniable pleasure in giving an opportunity to an aspiring actor. Furthermore (and this *can* be a factor in deciding), there is some extraordinary talent out there just waiting to be discovered. These "undiscovered gems" could turn out to be great assets to the show. Example: A friend of mine did a human-relations show a few years ago while working as an in-house producer for an electronics firm. The script called for the principal actor to play five different parts, and the task who given to a young, virtually unknown actor/comedian from San Francisco, who did a superb job with the roles. My friend still occasionally shows the outtakes tape from the production, which is in itself hilarious. The actor? Robin Williams, who later went on to fame and fortune in ABC's "Mork and Mindy".

NONPROFESSIONALS

Our last category involves people who are not actors, either professional or amateur, who are chosen to play roles in a program. This is very common in corporate and industrial programs done in-house, where the budgets do not permit the hiring of professionals. Though there is often no other choice, it is unfortunate but true that NONPROFESSIONALS rarely work out very well. They often take inordinate amounts of time to get their performance right, assuming that they ever *do* get it right. More often, what happens is that it takes twice as long to get a performance that's half as good as it should be.

Naturally, nonprofessional actors and "real people" lack familiarity with television production. Even though they enter the studio with good intentions, they are often worn down by the amount of time consumed and the number of retakes necessary to get things right. They usually don't understand that retakes are often necessitated by technical matters, and sometimes tend to blame themselves. They don't understand that single camera shooting may require that the same scene be shot from several angles, with several takes needed at each setup. The acting they see on TV at home looks so *easy*. While a professional is accustomed to repeating lines five, ten, or fifteen times, the nonprofessional can grow impatient or nervous, and the performance, instead of getting tighter with each repetition, gets worse.

This is not to say that there aren't some natural actors hiding out there in the service department, and if you stumble on one of them, put his or her name in your file A.S.A.P. Many corporate facilities that must regularly use employees as talent build up an in-house talent bank, and even go so far as to provide training in acting techniques for their people.

Using nonprofessionals, on an overall basis, however, can be time-consuming and trying to one's patience. The average quality of a nonprofessional's performance is not as good, and this can damage the effectiveness of a program.

Viewers should be able to easily identify with the people they see on the screen, and a poor or unbelievable performance can be worse than no performance at all in terms of end results. In those situations where an actor, rather than a subject expert or "wizard," is called for, professional talent can help to achieve professional results, increasing the chance that the results will be truly effective.

Unions and Guilds

Many producers, especially those in educational and corporate/industrial facilities, will never have to become involved with the production industry unions. In fact, away from the major metropolitan production centers there are often no unions with which to deal.

A nonunion company may also avoid union contact even if it's within the jurisdiction of the unions if they do not need to hire outside people who carry union cards.

For those who do hire union crew members and work in an area within the jurisdiction of local union offices, the unions are a production factor that must be considered. This section will briefly examine these unions, and what it's like to deal with them. If you know you'll never have to deal with unions, please feel free to skip to the next section.

The major unions with which television producers must deal are those that represent craft people and talent. There are also GUILDS, which are slightly different than unions, and represent higher-level staff-type people. Let's run down the list of various unions and guilds.

WGA (Writer's Guild Of America)

The WRITER'S GUILD OF AMERICA (WGA) is the major association of theatrical and broadcast television screenwriters. It is rare to find a WGA member flashing his card outside of network or syndicated television. Although a freelance writer hired to put together a nonbroadcast script may be a member, the chances are that his affiliation will not be a factor in the terms of his employment on such a project. Through a registration program, WGA provides a writer with protection for unsold or speculative scripts. This protection is also available to nonmembers within spe-

cific guidelines. The WGA also sets fixed fees to be received by writers who sell their scripts for broadcast production, and specifies such things as screen credit size and placement, and length of involvement in a project without additional compensation. The WGA is also heavily involved in efforts to gain more recognition for its members.

DGA (Directors's Guild Of America)

Like the WGA, the DIRECTOR'S GUILD OF AMERICA (DGA) represents directors involved in broadcasting, and membership in DGA is rarely a factor in nonbroadcast television. The DGA members receive a specified minimum fee for their work which is determined by the nature and length (RUNNING TIME) of the show in question. Amount of working time allowed for each type of production is also specified. The DGA directors receive at least the minimum amounts called for by their contract, but the sky is the limit at the other end. As is the case with actors, a top director may be paid considerably over scale.

Both WGA and DGA are craft guilds, and are actively involved in training programs for their members. Many DGA members serve an apprenticeship, working their way up as assistant directors before becoming full-fledged directors. The net results of DGA efforts are twofold: they serve to improve the quality and competency of members displaying the DGA banner, and at the same time limit the authorized, "approved" talent pool, thus upping the effective rates.

IATSE (International Alliance of Theatrical and Stage Employees)

The INTERNATIONAL ALLIANCE OF THEATRICAL AND STAGE EMPLOYEES, commonly known as "I.A.", or pronounced "I-AHT-ZEE" has more varieties of locals than you can shake a C-stand at. Just a partial listing would include Film Technicians, Make-up Artists and Hair Stylists, Motion Picture Editors, Motion Picture Set Designers, and Motion Picture First Aid Employees. The list goes on and on, and they're all under the IATSE banner.

The IATSE is the largest "conglomerate" union in the production industry, and locals can be found even in some relatively small towns. Jurisdiction over who can do what is sometimes confusing even to union representatives; though differences between unions seem to be more easily settled than are differences between producers and unions.

Though the name contains the words "theatrical" and "stage," and many of the locals' names have to do with "motion picture," these have been carried over from before the advent of TV. Today, IATSE covers workers in virtually every phase of production, including television. It's not at all unusual to find similar job functions covered by different unions from one geographical area to another, as the one that was established first in a given area usually will have established jurisdiction. Television cameramen, for instance, conceivably can be members of at least three different unions, IATSE, IBEW, or NABET, depending on which union got into what facility or station when. Two overlapping unions sometimes will do battle with each other, and on occasion, members have voted to change affiliation.

IBEW and NABET (The International Brotherhood of Electrical Workers and the National Association of Broadcast Employees and Technicians)

The INTERNATIONAL BROTHERHOOD OF ELECTRICAL WORKERS and the NATIONAL ASSOCIATION OF BROADCAST EMPLOYEES AND TECHNICIANS are good examples of overlapping unions. In San Francisco, for example, employees at different stations are represented by different unions even though they do the same jobs for their respective stations.

The IBEW and NABET are concerned primarily with broadcast stations and larger production houses in major metropolitan areas. Outside the big cities, union penetration is not common, and it's rarely a concern in most educational and industrial studios. The IBEW, like IATSE, covers a wide range of support personnel, such as Electricians, Broadcast TV and Recording Engineers, and even Studio Air Conditioning Engineers.

Television and Radio Artists and the Screen Actors Guild:

The AMERICAN FEDERATION OF TELEVISION AND RADIO ARTISTS (AFTRA) represents performances shot on videotape, while the Screen Actors Guild (SAG) covers performances shot on film. Many, if not most, members of one also belong to the other. In San Francisco, if you call the number for AFTRA or SAG, the answer you'll hear when they pick up the phone is: "Performing Unions." In San Francisco, AFTRA and SAG share offices, and jurisdiction is determined by whether you're shooting on film or on videotape. The Chicago offices of the two are likewise shared, but this is not the case in Los Angeles or New York.

Other Unions

A large broadcast production may require dealing with a variety of other unions. Performing musicians who do not speak or sing on camera are covered by the AMERICAN FEDERATION OF MUSICIANS. Those who sing and act on TV are covered by AFTRA as mentioned above. The SCREEN EXTRAS GUILD covers the nonspeaking multitudes who ride the camel caravans across the desert or try to head the outlaws off at the pass. In Los Angeles, the SCREEN CARTOONISTS GUILD is a Teamsters affiliate. The ORANGUTAN AND GORILLA GUILD (OGG) covers both speaking orangutans and nonspeaking gorillas.

Dealing with the unions:

It's perhaps a part of American tradition that friction occasionally develops between management (the producer) and the unions. Television is no exception. One often hears stories of entire productions being held up because a light needed to be plugged in while the electrician was on a break and no one else was allowed to touch anything electrical. If your situation dictates that you hire union employees, it's important to establish and maintain peaceful relations with the various unions.

If your involvement with unions is optional then the question of whether or not to hire through them is answered by weighing benefits against drawbacks. Overall, the unions and their apprenticeship programs do help to raise the level of competency of their members. As a result, the more competent and experienced people in a field tend to be union members because the union helps them find work and guarantees an established rate of pay.

On the plus side, then, you'll probably find more competent people when you hire through the union. On the minus side, though, if you're accustomed to a loose operation where everyone pitches in and does whatever needs doing without regard to job title, and where overtime is ignored, you're in for a rude awakening the first time you work with a union crew.

The same holds true for the talent unions. True professionals are usually union members. Hiring them means you'll have to sign the AFTRA contract, which binds you to follow the terms of the contract regarding work hours, conditions, pay, etc. Incidentally, the fact that you sign the contract does not prevent you from hiring nonunion actors. If you do, though, you are still bound by the contract terms, and must pay nonunion actors through the union.

The Taft/Hartley form for non union talent.

The AFTRA Network contract runs 63 pages and is only one of several covering different types of productions.

The signatory agreement, to be signed by the producer.

The member report is filled out by talent at the end of the day and submitted to AFTRA.

The pension & welfare (P & W) form, the fee for which is paid by the producer.

The contact is a blanket one with prescribed dates of effectiveness that are renegotiated prior to its expiration (with luck). The union places nonunion actors on what is called a TAFT-HARTLEY FORM, and if they appear on camera again after 30 days from their initial appearance, they must then join the union.

While I must admit that I'm not a big fan of unions in general, I've had very good experiences with AFTRA, and have long been a signator to the AFTRA contracts. I've found the people in the San Francisco office to be very helpful, and they do go to bat for the producer when the talent is at fault just as readily as the other way around.

The Los Angeles area is without doubt the dominion of the production unions, and in no other part of the country do they flex as much muscle. In nonmetropolitan areas, as stated earlier, there are often no union locals to deal with, even if you wanted to. In Los Angeles,

though, very little production goes on that the unions don't know about, or in which they do not become involved. As far as broadcast television production goes, it's truly a union town. Educational and corporate/industrial in-house production is largely exempt, once again.

In certain circumstances your production might be subject to union rules even though you normally have no union involvement. If you were to rent a theatre for a production, for instance, the theatre's employees might be IATSE members. If this were the case, then be aware that many rules and restrictions are negotiable. The shop steward has a certain degree of latitude, as does the head of the local. You may be able to make specific agreements with regard to jurisdiction terms. For example, if you agree to meet a MINIMUM CALL (the minimum number of union members that must be hired before the house can be opened, as specified by the contract signed by the theatre management), the union may then relax restrictions on who can do and touch what.

Above all, if you're in an area where unions exercise strong control, *don't* risk the entire production by getting into a heavy dispute with the union. They can shut you down in a minute. If you're dealing with more than one union and you do get into a hassle, if one goes, the chances are, they'll all go.

Unions have a useful function, and can help both their members and you. On balance, however, if your productions are functioning well without union involvement, why mess with success?

Part 2

Production

CHAPTER 7

Important Production Considerations

Management and Problem Solving

When the production gets under way, it's time for the producer to climb into the back seat and let the director and the crew take the wheel. A smart producer, having made a careful appointment of the director, relaxes operational control and lets his or her people do their jobs.

There'll certainly be enough to occupy the producer's time. While the director's out there playing with the cameras, crew, and talent, the producer and his staff will be following the production along, keeping track of progress, bills, schedules, and the rest.

Earlier I mentioned the concept of the producer being a "Super Gofer." The production phase is when the real gofering starts. Things will go wrong; items and people won't always be where they should, and there will be lots of fires (small disasters) to put out. The staff will be involved in taking care of their own specific details. As well as dealing with these unexpected problems, the producer will be conversing with the people above him, assuring them that everything's just fine, and the show will be done on schedule.

The producer may be involved with more than one production. There may be a subsequent show in a series or an entirely new project underway that may require a fair amount of his time and attention. Companies involved in network series production, or large scale corporate, or educational facilities may have one or more shows in pre-production, one or more in production, and more in post-production—all simultaneously. In addition to this, there will be clearances and script approvals, and in some cases, STANDARDS & PRACTICES people (the network's censors) to deal with, and a myriad of other details to be concerned with.

resembles an enlarged version of the production board. It displays the daily progress of each show as it flows towards completion. A company involved in producing a series of programs will usually require the services of several directors. These directors may be on a "rotating" schedule, whereby one is involved in pre-production, another in production, etc., alternating positions on the schedule. The producer will coordinate with each of them, overseeing the entire production. It is important

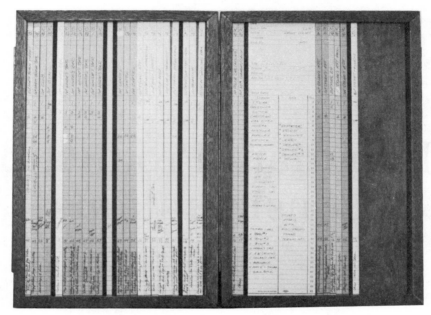

The production board aids in scheduling for maximum efficiency.

Actual production scheduling is often done with the aid of a PRODUCTION BOARD, a device that has been in use for years. It consists of a folder, usually bound in leather or vinyl, that has a space at left for names of talent, extras, vehicles, equipment, etc.—all the various elements that go into the production. Strips of cardboard are color coded to indicate "Day/Night," "Interior/Exterior," "Second Unit," "Inserts," etc., with notations as to who and what will be needed when. These strips are then inserted to the right of item and person entries. The strips provide a visual aid in foreseeing problems and for planning the most efficient use of crew and talent time.

To aid in the operation, a SCHEDULING BOARD of some sort may also be used. This is a large board, often filling an entire wall, that

that the producer keep a wide perspective and let the staff take care of minutia. Producers who have come up through the ranks often find that delegation of responsibility is difficult. Good producers often began their careers worrying about every small detail, and many still love the sleeves-rolled-up, nitty-gritty aspects of production.

Throughout this process, the director and his people will have their hands full. If the pre-production process has been carefully and well thought out and the staff has been functioning smoothly, the director can begin shooting the show with minimal interference from details. The producer and director will confer frequently, making changes here and there as necessary. Time and budget factors will be weighed against aesthetics to achieve the perfect balance of a smooth and good-looking program that comes in on time and within budget. Doing so is very much like walking a tightwire in a stiff breeze.

The production of even a single, simple show is a complex event—one that must be choreographed with as much precision as a ballet. The person who tries to combine the roles of producer and director will really have his or her hands full. A drawback to this dual-role method must always be kept in mind: It's hard, if not impossible, to do two things at once and do them well. This is where a good support staff is essential. The A.P. (Assistant Producer) and the A.D. (Assistant Director) are of the utmost importance here. For instance, if the producer is needed while the dual-role player has the director's hat on, he or she must either break concentration on matters pertinent to directing to attend to production details, or may rely on the A.P. to handle things.

Once you are acting as the director, it's better to let the A.P. take care of most production business. Directing is a full-time chore that requires keen concentration, and stepping out of the role for even a moment is like loosing your place on a page filled with very fine print. A really good A.P. can be worth his or her weight in videotape, and is worthy of respect, if not adoration.

A good associate producer will relieve the producer of the minor (through still important) details of production and will do so without having to be constantly overseen by the producer. The manner of the action is as important as the action itself. A good A.P. is self-motivated not only to solve problems, but to find problems that will need solving. To the producer, it's a real pleasure to have the P.A. report at the end of the day something along the lines of: "I've contracted with the caterer, and the food's all set. The location for Friday didn't have adequate power, so I've rented a generator. By the way, I got a good rate from V.G.S. The permits are taken care of, the Fire Department will have an inspector on site, and we'll have that dolly the director wanted. Anything else?" This is an example of the kind of initiative shown by a good A.P.

The objective is to keep the flow going once it has started. A full-bore production has a lot of momentum, which means that someone had better be looking around the next curve to make certain the way is clear.

As I've said, once shooting begins, there will be dozens or perhaps hundreds of details to attend to. Many will vary according to the nature of the production, while others are common to virtually all productions.

Some of these considerations will include:

- Facilities requests
- Makeup (in proper shades)
- Office and studio supplies
- Props (including replacements for breakables)
- Wardrobe (in correct sizes)
- Forms (releases, AFTRA/SAG member reports)
- Maps (for location shoots)
- Graphics
- Camera filters (other than built-in)
- Travel arrangements
- Call sheets
- Script revisions

Studio production is generally less hectic than remote production, since most of the items needed will be in the studio or close by. Still, there are easily overlooked and obvious items that can bring an entire production to a screeching halt. This is a point worth emphasizing: Even if you stay up late worrying about all the *little* details that are peculiar to a particular production, the chances are that the thing that'll come along to mess you up will be so obvious, so completely ridiculous, that you'll never have thought of it ahead of time. This is not to say, of course, that not-so-obvious items can't provide surprises also.

Example: All the major elements are in place. The cast, set, lights, cameras, crew, and props—all are there and ready to go. You've even remembered that the show calls for a rare stuffed coreopsis bird from South America that is critical to the plot development, even though it only appears in the background of one short scene. You're shooting on a Saturday afternoon, feeling proud that you've been so thoughtful, and sure that everything is going smoothly. That secure feeling alone should be enough to warn you—it's tempting fate. You tell VTR control that you want to ROLL TAPE (start the VTR) in 20 minutes, and to please load up a fresh 60-minute reel. It's only moments later that the tape supervisor comes to you with wonderful news: "Well, I don't know what happened—there were four reels of new stock in there yesterday, but I guess they got sent over to edit for prestriping, cause they're not there now, and damned if I know where we're gonna get tape on a Saturday afternoon." Who ever heard of a studio running out of tape in the middle of a production, for Pete's sake? I have.

Location shooting can be an even jollier exercise in potential for disaster. When you're 18 miles from nowhere, a crucial forgotten item can hold things up very nicely. In addition, there are all those extra factors to contend with in the field that just don't occur in the studio. Here are some important considerations when shooting in the field:

1. *Food* —Cast and crew will have to be fed, and they'll put up with hamburgers from the nearest golden arches for only so long.
2. *Bathrooms* —On "boony" remotes, comfort facilities (this is the polite phrase for toilets) must be arranged. Unless the cast and crew are willing to make use of trees and bushes in the true pioneer spirit, this means bringing in a HONEYWAGON (portable facilities). In any case, it's a civilized thing to do.
3. *Dressing Rooms* —Cast members will need dressing rooms. Motorhomes are ideal for this, and may even be required by the terms of the talent's employment. They are also useful as location offices and for use by the crew on breaks. However, they don't just appear on the scene all by themselves.
4. *Lodging* —Overnight shoots will require sleeping quarters. In a city, hotels are the obvious answer, but on *remote* remotes, other arrangements will have to be made such as tents or mobile homes (RVs).
5. *Power* —Power is a critical factor wherever you're shooting. Most of the new minicam trucks can run on 110 V power, and if their current draw is low, house or office curcuits may be able to handle the load. Beware, though, of power line fluctuations caused by such power suckers as refrigerators or air conditioning kicking on and off which may make available power unusable. The addition of almost any supplemental lighting may necessi-

tate bringing in a generator. GENNIES (generators) run on gas or diesel fuel, which means you'll have to keep a supply line open. Check local gas stations for their locations and hours.

6. *Communication* –Running a remote shoot is in many ways like running a military field campaign, with similarities in logistics and management techniques. Lines of communication must be established and kept operational. Using FM walkie-talkies can be a big help, both in the field and in larger studio situations. Finding a staff or a crew member at a moment's notice is much easier if you can hail them by radio. On extended location productions done in the great outdoors, or in situations that will keep you moving around, a mobile telephone is a must.

The list goes on and on. Mentioning everything that could possibly be required for a production is impossible, due to the endless

A remote shoot.

Spectrum Video remote truck.

variety of types of productions, but in *Appendix A* you'll find a generic checklist that will list at least some of the things that need to be covered. Beyond that, the best thing I can recommend is to get the staff and crew together during pre-production and collectively generate a list. In matters like this, the more minds you have working, the better.

We've already discussed the preparation for a shoot, and now it's time to get into some of the practical techniques for turning out a great end product.

Since we've already looked at equipment choices, we'll assume that standards and production values have been set, gear has been chosen, talent know or are studying their parts, and we're already to begin production. For me, this is the fun part. Even though it involves a lot of hard work, I find the work very satisfying.

Further in this section, we'll break the production elements apart and examine them individually. It's worth remembering that none of these exist in a vacuum (see *Production Gestalt.*) Sets, for instance, will have an effect on lighting, and vice versa. The producer and director must carefully coordinate all the elements both in terms of time and to get the overall effect desired.

As a crew gets *worked in*, and the various members begin to know each other, it is reasonable to assume that they'll evolve into a smooth-running machine. When hiring outside facilities or putting together a freelance crew, it's worthwhile getting people who have previously worked together. A good audio engineer may know of a competent gaffer, who in turn may know of a top dolly grip, and so on. A production will greatly benefit from folks who know each other and can work together well. If you must start from scratch, you can still end up with a good group, but it will take a while longer for the crew to *work in*. If none of the crew knows each other, part of the director's job is to make sure that early problems and frictions are smoothed out, for the best work happens when the crew works like a well-oiled machine. Good management makes for a good production.

Sometimes it happens that a crew doesn't get along together or bears ill feelings towards the director or the production company. It is a sad and somewhat terrifying sight, and such a crew is hard pressed to come up with good results. If this situation goes to the limit and really gets out of hand, it may be wise to halt everything and start over from scratch. It could even be the most sound thing to do financially. A discontented crew can sabotage a production through small and individually meaningless actions, or worse yet, through inactions, so that achieving good results becomes next-to or totally impossible.

On the other hand, as I stated earlier, a crew that gets along well with each other and is motivated to do a good job is one of the most pleasurable experiences to be found in the business.

I recall the feeling I had a few years ago while we were STRIKING (tearing down and packing up) after a three-day shoot in a hotel ballroom we had set up as a studio for a corporate conference. The crew were almost all friends and knew each other's habits and techniques well. We had put in three days of long hours, lugged heavy equipment all over the place, put out truly top-quality work that gave us just the results we were after, and managed to have a lot of fun in the process. I almost always help with the strike and since the show had gone a bit late we didn't have any extra time to remove ourselves and the gear from the location. As I left the control area and entered the "studio" to help, I became a bit overwhelmed by how well the crew had all worked. I went to the back of the raised seating area and sat for a few moments, reflecting on the show I had seen going to tape, and how well the crew had performed. As I sat there watching them tear down the cameras and pack them away, I found myself wearing a big silly grin with a feeling of euphoria that bordered on being sappy. My A.P. caught me at it from across the room and gave me back a grin that told me he knew just how I felt, and that the feeling was shared. Fortunately, I recovered quckly and went to help wrap cable. It

was one of those moments that I'm always grateful to have happen.

The Need To Know

A most important key to the success of a production lies in the ability to hire specialists and give them the freedom to do their thing. Part of the trick here is the ability to recognize who's good, and who's not. In order to make a judgment, I firmly believe that the director and/or producer should have a strong background in all phases of production. A good director should be able to step into any job on the set and at least do a competent job.

In a pinch, I could light a scene and make it look acceptable, SHADE (adjust) a camera, and clean and thread a VTR. I understand the difference between PEAK and AVERAGE metering in audio and am able to record decent sound. In none of these areas am I an expert, although in some I could earn my living if I had to, at least as an assistant.

The point here is that a good director should be able to speak the languages of the specialists he or she will be dealing with and know how to judge when he or she is getting good results, or when the work could be better. I made it a point when I was learning the teleproduction business to give myself a good background in as many areas as I could, and practiced during the early years by hiring on to do each of the production jobs. I've also done little one-man tapes as a way of practicing production techniques. I think it's a good way to learn about production and how to handle your mistakes before you get down to serious business.

While all this would seem to be a fairly logical approach to the production business, it constantly amazes me how few producers and directors bother with any of the production technicalities and practices. In general, I find that directors seem to be less guilty of this than producers. This is probably because a director who doesn't know what he or she's talking about will quickly lose the respect of the crew.

Many producers seem to feel that such details are beneath them, and this attitude is almost traditional in the big-time entertainment fields. In the broadcast industry, producers are not expected or required to have a technical background. This seems to work, at least within the traditional structure.

The traditional structure, however, is already starting to crumble at the corners, and I suspect that the next few years will bring incredible changes in the way television programming is generated. The producer will have a tremendous advantage if he or she knows as much as possible about the actual technicalities of production.

Foremost amongst the advantages is the ability to establish specifications. By this I mean aesthetic specifications, rather than hardware specifications. The producer should logically care more about the show than anyone else. If he doesn't know as much as the crew, in overall terms, then he is limited by what the crew knows, or more to the point, what they are willing to provide. Unless the producer provides extraordinary positive motivation to the director and crew, even the best people are sometimes tempted to take shortcuts here and there. It's human nature to want to take the easier route when faced with a choice. If the producer doesn't know what better results could be achieved, the results he gets will be those he settles for. Let me cite an example from a show I edited for a PBS series:

The program was shot entirely ON REMOTE (on location) using an RCA TK-76 camera and mastered on ¾-inch cassettes that were subsequently BUMPED (transferred) to Type C 1-inch for editing. The producer was the driving force behind the show and stayed closely involved during every phase of the production.

During the edit, I noticed that the VIDEO LEVELS (brightness) varied wildly, and at first thought that the tape operator in the equipment room was adjusting the video levels. It turned out that this was not the case—the operator was not touching the knobs. What had happened was that someone had told the producer to shoot with the camera's auto-iris control turned on, with the result that whenever something moved through the scene or the camera panned, the iris adjusted to the changing brightness.

The producer had no idea that this is *not* the proper use of the AUTO IRIS, and that correcting the error after the fact in post-production would be almost impossible. He had to live with the results in this case, though I seriously doubt he'll ever let this happen again.

This particular producer admitted during conversation that he found "technical stuff" rather boring, and that there were more important things to be concerned with. Unfortunately, the "boring technical stuff" caused some rather distracting visual abberations to become a permanent part of the show. The producer had assumed that the technical people knew what they were doing, and had left such matters up to them.

This can work, however, only if the technical people have proven consistently that they do indeed know what they're doing, and furthermore, that they care about their work. Good intentions by themselves are no more useful than technical know-how is by itself. It takes a combination of the two to turn out top-quality work.

CHAPTER 8

Setting the Scene

The information that follows is not intended to be an in-depth study of each subject area. Each discipline is a complex mixture of science and art that can demand an entire career of study and practice without yielding all its secrets. These disciplines can never be completely mastered, since they change and adapt as technology and program styles evolve. They are somewhat like bottomless holes—the more one learns, the more one finds there is to learn.

The following brief examinations, therefore, are presented in order to provide you with an overview of the subject. Entire textbooks have been devoted to each of them. I would refer you to these for a full expostulation and have presented some suggestions along these lines in the bibliography.

Sets

Sets include existing locations as well as specially constructed scenery built in a studio. In Arizona, there is an entire town—Old Tucson—that is a Western set. Los Angeles boasts a large number of SOUND STAGES (large studios with complete soundproofing) and complete period and neighborhood sets. Universal Studios even gets double duty from them by providing tours for the public.

Many productions can make use of real locations as sets, from streets to offices to

homes, and this can offer some attractive advantages. Costs are almost always lower when an existing location can be used. On the other hand, a private residence, as an example, will not be nearly as well equipped for shooting as will an interior set that has been built in the studio.

Let's first examine the use of existing locations and the special requirements they present before moving on to studio sets.

Location

Once a location has been chosen, as detailed in the pre-production section (Chapter 3), one of the production staff will contact the owner and arrange some form of payment, and get a signed location release. Although it's often possible to secure a location for free, paying at least a nominal fee can be a good idea from a legal standpoint because it helps to codify the agreement. If equipment will be parked in the street—especially if it will block traffic—the city must be contacted and a permit secured. Insurance policies must be checked, to make sure they provide adequate coverage for liability and property damage.

Only when all these details and many others have been attended to can shooting on the site begin.

It may be necessary to make certain changes to the property. Often the owner will agree to these as long as a written guarantee is signed stating that everything will be put back the way it was and any damage repaired. The production company may offer to make improvements or alterations, negotiating with the owner as to whether these are to be removed or left in place. You might be wondering about the need for releases and permits, and I'd answer this by suggesting that common sense is an excellent guide. If you are setting so much as a foot on someone's property, secure their permission. If you are simply driving by, taking shots of a neighborhood without disrupting anyone's life, you may not need to do anything. On the other hand, if you take an establishing shot of the exterior of a house prior to cutting to a studio interior, then the eventual use of the tape becomes the criterion. For an industrial show that will only be seen by employees, a release may not be important, while for a network show that will be seen by anybody and everybody, you'd be well advised to get a release. The same criteria that apply to talent releases apply to locations and personal property (such as a boat). If you single out a person or place in your program, you should get a signed release. If your camera sweeps the skyline of the city, you don't need a release for every person and place in the scene.

Props are counted as part of our discussion of sets. Many locations will require only a minimal number of props, while others will require some help. Lamps, books, planters, and street signs are fairly easy props to manage, but if your scene calls for an above-ground swimming pool, make sure you have enough room and water. Also keep in mind the matter of drainage—that water will have to go somewhere when you're done—and make sure that you have obtained permission from the necessary authorities. Part of the agreement you make with the owner must cover reimbursement for such costs as filling the pool. The unforeseen can be waiting to throw a kink into your plans, too.

A producer I know had to truck in thousands of gallons of water from several hundred miles away to fill a pool during a California drought. It was a good thing that someone on the staff had bothered to check with the city ahead of time regarding restrictions on the use of water so an alternative arrangement could be made.

It is obviously preferable to find a location that is already set up the way you need it, or is close enough so that only minor changes will be necessary. If you must build on location, you then have to contend with a construction job and the further complexities that it can create.

One item that can have grave consequences if overlooked relates to shooting in commercial buildings equipped with sprinkler systems. Television lights can generate a tremendous amount of heat—more than enough to set off automatic sprinklers if placed too close. A producer I know was hit with a double whammy when he obtained permission to shoot in a computer store for a training tape. The first whammy came when the lights set off the sprinkler system. The second was that he carried no production insurance to cover that sort of accident. Thousands of dollars worth of delicate computer equipment was totally destroyed by this "small oversight!"

Many sprinkler systems are designed in such a way that if one sprinkler goes off, the drop in water pressure sets off all the sprinklers in the system. The best protection against such a catastrophe is to exercise extreme care in placing lights, and to stay away from sprinklers. If you must place a light near a sprinkler, then cover the sprinkler with two styrofoam coffee cups taped to the ceiling, a small one inside a large one. Styrofoam is an excellent insulator, and the double-cup system provides excellent protection. Make certain also that the outside cup is flush against the ceiling so that heat doesn't enter despite your precautions.

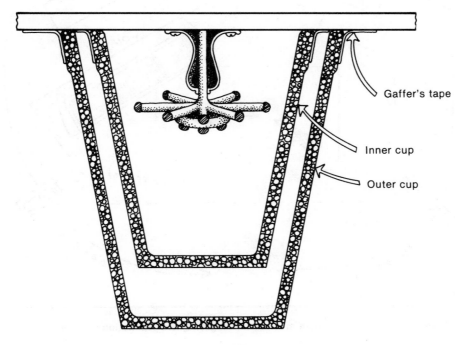

Gaffer's tape

Inner cup

Outer cup

Studio sets:

As I've already mentioned, studio work is made easier by the many resources that are already close at hand. Building a set, or several on the same stage, entails a certain amount of time and expense. Once it is built, however, it is a better environment for production since it was designed and built with the requirements of shooting in mind. It is also available around the clock, and you are free of the worry of disrupting normal activities, which might not be the case on location.

Large production companies or studios usually have a separate department in charge of set design and construction. Smaller operations, however, can also have a need for a set that may often be quite complex. It is possible to get an awful lot for your money in building sets. Luckily the forgiving nature of television allows sets that would appear rather seedy when viewed in the flesh to look just dandy on the screen.

Set construction is an old theatrical art, but techniques and materials have changed—especially in the last ten years or so. Designing an attractive and inexpensive set is not as hard as you might imagine.

The first step is to create a design. Once the set designer has been given the requirements of the show, he will discuss some basic ideas with the producer and director. He will then put together some sketches that indicate what the finished set would look like. The sketches would include a rendering of the overview and might also include a diagram or stage plot similar to an architectural plan. This plot, which shows a top view of the set, would indicate camera positions and capacity for camera movement. Through a series of meetings with the producer, director, lighting director, stage manager, and even the audio engineer, a final design will be chosen.

If the production warrants it, a scale model of the set can be built that will allow study of how lighting and camera positions will work in and around the set.

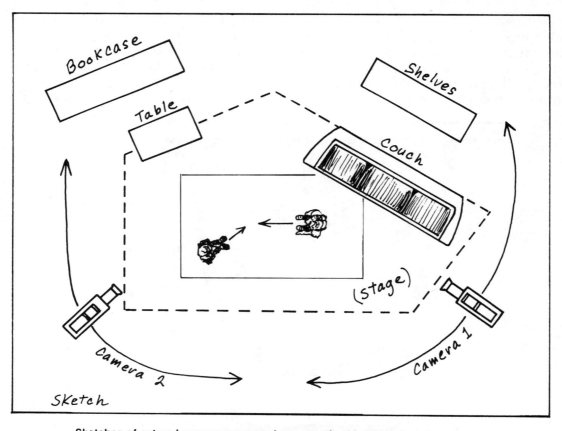

Sketches of set and camera movement can greatly aid production planning.

106

The next step would be to generate a specific set of plans from which the actual construction will be done. These will provide far more detail than the original sketches, and include details of design and engineering.

Construction employs a wide variety of methods and materials. Facilities with scene shops and existing set pieces will have different construction requirements than facilities that offer a large empty space with lights, cable runs, and little else. There are several techniques that can work well in building a set from scratch, depending on your budget.

Most sets are built to *look* good with structural strength provided only where necessary. In the theatre, where set building started, sets are traditionally constructed out of wood and muslin. Long, narrow boards are used to build a frame, on which muslin is then stretched and fastened. The muslin is then SIZED, which involves the application of a kind of glue that causes the cloth to shrink and stiffen when

Flats can be made of simple frames covered with cloth and held up with stage braces.

dry. The surface can then be painted or covered with wallpaper or whatever is necessary to give the desired effect. These pieces are called FLATS, a term used to describe a modular panel that can be combined with others in various ways to comprise a finished set. Although traditionally covered with cloth, they can also be surfaced with plywood, masonite, or any number of other materials. Cloth is most commonly used since it weighs less and costs less, but where rigidity is needed, plywood or masonite would be preferable.

In a facility where large numbers of different shows require a variety of sets, a scene shop builds the set elements as needed. Stair units, risers, wall flats, window and door units, and other types of set pieces are built when needed, and then recycled for subsequent productions. Studios with occasional set needs or small budgets for set construction may elect to rent set elements. However, set rental outside a major production center may be difficult to locate. It might be worthwhile checking with your local civic light opera, the college drama department, your local high school or church, or a little theatre group to see if they could rent or loan you equipment or materials.

Whether your needs are for building up an inventory of set pieces, or creating a set for a single show, there is a marvelous building material that has greatly simplified set design and construction. It is called FOAM CORE, and has uses that extend beyond set construction.

FOAM CORE is a sheet of light plastic foam sandwiched between two sheets of thin white fibreboard. With a thickness of just about $\frac{3}{16}$s of an inch, each standard 4-foot × 8-foot sheet weighs but a few pounds and can be easily cut with a knife. It is fairly tough, easy to handle, and makes a superb building material on the stage.

A set built with foam core requires only a skeletal framework of light lumber (such as 1 × 2s or 1 × 4s). Heavier lumber is used for floors and structural members. The foam core is cut, laid in place, and stapled to the structural members. Final trimming is then done with a knife, seams and edges are sanded and/or taped, and the set is ready to paint. Foam core also has uses in the field. It makes a handy reflector for FILL LIGHTING, as we shall see later. It is wonderful stuff, and if its inventor hasn't received an Oscar or an Emmy, I can't imagine why not.

Other common set construction materials include that old favorite, paper mache, styrofoam, and SEAMLESS BACKGROUND PAPER (large, wide rolls of paper in various colors). A range of colors in seamless is virtually a necessity in the studio, and is well worth a shopping trip to stock up on a variety.

It's also amazing what can be achieved at very little cost by using odd materials and castaways that one wouldn't normally consider for set construction. I once used a background that consisted of two broken old stair units we found in the basement storage area of the theatre in which we were shooting. We propped

Foamcore flats are lightweight, easily cut, and simple to set up.

them up on end to form an entrance upstage center and covered them with sheets of reflective mylar which we allowed to crinkle so that we wouldn't end up with a series of mirrors. The cost was minimal, and the effect was gorgeous. I've also seen a very effective backdrop for a music show that was made by hanging wire between two supports and tossing different colored rolls of paper towels over them, letting the ends sway in the breeze. Combined with some inventive lighting, it was a perfect backdrop for the performers. Furthermore, the entire set was bought at a supermarket for a few dollars. Now *that's* inventive set design!

Studio set design has received less attention lately than it used to, mostly because of the shift towards field production. There are times, though, when using the studio is most appropriate, and an understanding of set design and construction techniques is still important. Remember that television permits you to get away with things that would look awful in real life. Creative set design is a matter not only of aesthetics in concept, but of inventive execution as well. Scrounge for elements without regard to what is normally done. Haunt plastics, used furniture, fabric, and hardware shops in your spare time, and file in the back

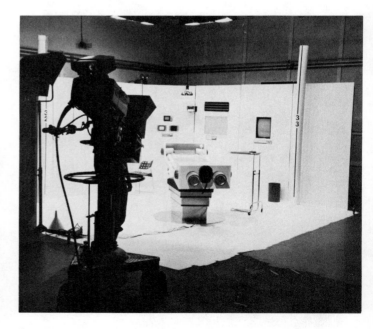

Overview of a set using foamcore flats as shown in previous photo.

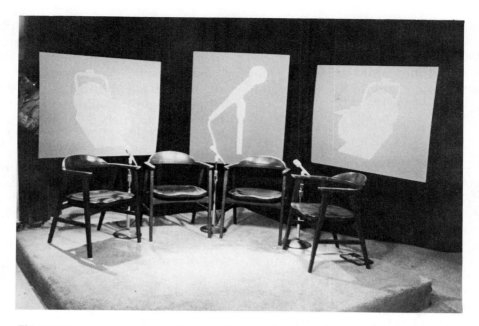

This simple set was made at a total cost of $30 for colored matte board. Panels are suspended with black polyester thread.

Antique stores are good places to find special items.

of your mind (or better, a notebook) things you run across that would be handy in designing or building a future set. You never know when that bowsprit back in the corner of the antique shop at the edge of town will be just what you need to dress your next set.

Lighting

Lighting is not just relevant to pictures; pictures *are* light. This concept has long been understood by still photographers, who have described their work as "painting with light on film," and by cinematographers who also deal with acetate and emulsion. Despite the claims of manufacturers of cameras with good low light level response that their units can shoot in virtual darkness, light is perhaps the single most important ingredient in creating good pictures. Film people have traditionally understood this importance and have invested great amounts of time, money and energy, often with stunning results. Video people, on the other hand, have traditionally accepted, or even encouraged poor lighting techniques. In this chapter we will address some methods of obtaining good results in video production.

Video lighting has traditionally been inferior because early television cameras were complex and unwieldy beasts that required an engineer at the controls and had enormous appetites for light. It was necessary to pump gobs of light into a scene in order to get an acceptable picture.

Further, the ability of television to synchronize several cameras allowed them to shoot a scene from different angles, with the director switching between them in real time. This created a need to light scenes for all of the camera angles at once. The result, generally, was flat, "safe" lighting that served the technical requirements while doing little to enhance the artistry and aesthetics of the images.

I mentioned earlier that I lean towards single-camera FILM-STYLE production. Lighting is a major factor in this preference. Since I only have to deal with one camera angle at a time, the lighting can be tweaked and tuned for that angle without compromise, creating the kind of lighting results that film people take for granted.

This is not without its complications, however. Lighting each angle increases by orders of magnitude the amount of time necessary to shoot a scene. Resetting and reshooting each scene in itself multiplies the time factor, and careful lighting adds another element that resists being rushed. Another matter of importance is LIGHTING CONTINUITY. Just as continuity of action and camera perspective are crucial, so is lighting. The lighting director must understand the scene and design lighting that is optimal to create the desired dramatic effect for each camera angle. When these shots are cut together they should appear to have the same lighting throughout the entire scene. This is not an easy job.

At the opening of this section, I mentioned that the early cameras required lots of light. This is often still the case. While many of the new high-end cameras, especially the ENG/EFP (portable field camera) designs, can operate with very low light levels, the lower cost units such as the one- and two-tube models often require a rather high light level to produce a decent picture. Keep in mind that the ability of a camera to produce a decent picture of a static display is not enough. This is generally what you'll see at the equipment exhibits: The cameras will be shooting lovely models or bowls of flowers, with buckets of light falling on the subjects. Nothing moves. Try moving the cameras, and you'll soon separate the wheat from the chaff. The better cameras simply slide the picture around as you pan, while the lower cost models often produce COMET-TAILS (lasting impressions of highlights in the scene that appear as slowly fading streaks) when panned. In the case of these lower-end units, the old rule still applies: The more light, the merrier.

Even the super-sensitive models, though, need special attention to lighting. A manufacturer may brag about their camera's ability to pick up a black cat in a dark room, but the fact that a camera can provide a recognizable image at only 2 footcandles does not mean that one would actually want to shoot under such conditions. After all, a *recognizable* picture and a *good* picture are not necessarily the same thing.

What, then, is good lighting? Obviously, people have different opinions of what constitutes good lighting. Perhaps the best catch-all definition would be lighting that:

1. Creates or enhances the desired mood or effect.

2. Provides all necessary detail, and, unless done for a particular effect, flatters the subject.

Anything more specific in the way of a definition would have to take the particular circumstances into account. Good lighting can make a picture seem three-dimensional and can take advantage of the sparkle and snap that good equipment is capable of providing. Alternately, special techniques of lighting can give videotape an appearance akin to the soft and gentle colors of film when combined with the proper lens, filter, and setup techniques.

Elaborate sets constructed inside a studio.

It is not my intent to attempt a course of instruction on lighting techniques within these pages. There are a number of fine books available, and numerous expos and conferences provide seminars and workshops on the subject. Some of the best instruction is provided by seminars offered by several major lighting and staging companies. These seminars take place at their own facilities, or can be presented at a client's facility on a custom basis.

Now I'd like to discuss lighting from the perspective of the producer's or director's viewpoint—what they should know about lighting, and how good lighting can be achieved.

Many folks consider lighting to be something done only in the studio. After all, the great outdoors comes with heavenly light as standard equipment. Leaving aside the question of nighttime exteriors, which obviously need human help, this thinking is unilluminated. Lighting outdoors is no less important than lighting indoors—it's just different. Let's examine studio lighting first, and then come back to outdoor lighting.

It takes little exposure to lighting for one to learn that there are two basic kinds of artificial light: HARD LIGHT and SOFT LIGHT. The distinction, greatly simplified, is that HARD LIGHT has a POINT SOURCE (comes from

111

one particular point in space), while SOFT LIGHT has a DIFFUSED SOURCE (does not seem to come from one source). Although a hard light cannot, in practice, have a true point source, since, in theory, any such source would have to be infinitely small it will cast a shadow with a clearly defined edge. Soft light, on the other hand, has a broad or diffused source, and therefore does not cast a clear shadow.

Hard light sources would include spotlights of various types, both INCANDESCENT and QUARTZ, ELIPSOIDAL and FRESNEL instruments, and, of course, direct sunlight. The shadows that are caused by hard light help to define detail, and, in the case of focusing lamps, can throw light over long distances, keeping it concentrated within a certain area.

Soft light sources would include SCOOPS, BROADS, STRIPS, and BANKS. The light they provide helps fill in those shadows mentioned above, lowers contrast, and generally does not travel far.

Three-point lighting:

With regard to lighting techniques, there is a basic, time-proven system known as THREE-POINT LIGHTING. Classic THREE-POINT LIGHTING uses three different lights: KEY, BACK, and FILL. The KEY LIGHT provides the main source of raw illumination and modeling. It provides the feeling of the direction from which the light is coming. The FILL LIGHT provides detail within shadows and softens the impact of the key light, and the BACK LIGHT outlines the subject, providing visual snap that brings the subject out of the background. Additional lights that may also be used include a BACKGROUND LIGHT, which provides a pool of light behind the subject, and an EYELIGHT, which is positioned so that it is reflected in the subject's eyes.

One successful technique is to use a building-block approach that starts with the three classic lights, and adds lights until the desired effect is reached. Care should be taken to avoid over-kill, as a point can be reached where so many lights are filling in the scene so completely that it ends up looking flat and dull. This would take us right back to the kind

Hard light.

Soft light.

112

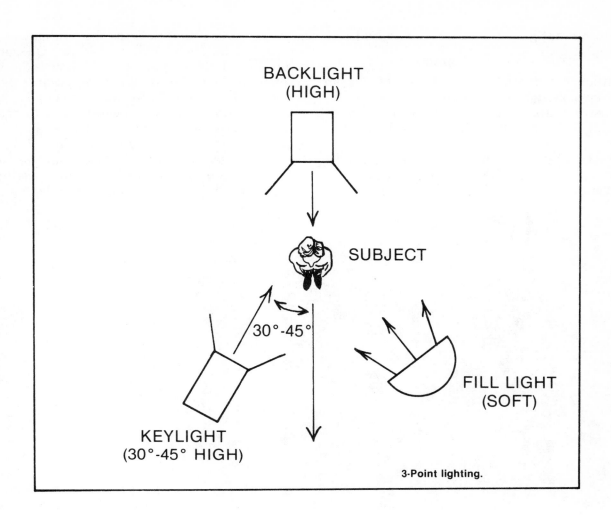

BACKLIGHT
(HIGH)

SUBJECT

30°-45°

KEYLIGHT
(30°-45° HIGH)

FILL LIGHT
(SOFT)

3-Point lighting.

Lighting crew setting lights for a talk show.

113

of lighting that gave television such a bad reputation.

Outdoors, it is often possible to achieve all the necessary lighting without the use of lighting instruments. The tools here are various types of REFLECTORS, FLAGS, and SILKS.

Direct sunlight is not the director's best friend, as you might imagine. The best type of day for outdoor shooting is one with a high, hazy overcast that diffuses the sunlight so that you can barely see your shadow. On such a day, a couple of pieces of foamcore used as reflectors may be all that's necessary to provide a bit of fill light for the subjects. On clear sunny days, there are several ways to reduce the harsh shadows that direct sunlight provides. You can use reflectors to fill in the shadows, facing the subjects so that the sun is behind them and the reflectors are positioned in front. The standard outdoor reflector used

Lighting grip (in hat) aims reflector on outdoor location shoot. Note flag providing shade for camera.

Using reflectors for outside lighting from sun.

114

in film and television production is a 4-feet × 4-feet metallic panel on a gimbal-mounted stand which allows the reflector to pivot and thus be easily adjustable. Various different reflective surfaces are available, from flat and shiny for hard reflection, to pebble-surfaced for diffused reflection. Most reflectors offer a different surface on either side. By using various types of reflecting surfaces, just the right ratio of key to fill can be achieved.

Another method that works well is diffusing the sunlight by the use of a SILK which is a large piece of white fabric suspended overhead to block out direct sunlight. This duplicates the light provided by a heavy haze, and can be further diffused by laying cheesecloth on top of the silk. Silks, which come in various sizes ranging from about 6 feet × 6 feet up to 20 feet × 20 feet, are usually set on stands that allow them to be positioned overhead. Large silks (12

Lighting setup using many small lights.

Lighting setup relying on large key light.

115

feet × 12 feet or 20 feet × 20 feet) will require a two-man crew or larger to keep them under control. Remember, a piece of cloth this large is subject to the same laws of nature that allow sailboats to move about on the water. A large silk, up in the air on its stands, can easily provide enough lift to turn your gaffer into an unwilling hang glider.

The toughest challenge in outdoor lighting is the day that features broken clouds drifting across the sky, creating alternating periods of sunlight and cloud cover. This can be very frustrating, and can create incredible continuity problems. If you have no other choice but to go ahead and shoot, it may be best to go for a total overcast effect, using a silk to create

Use of silks.

FLAGS are dark pieces of cloth stretched over frames or small pieces of black sheet metal that are used to block and control light. Often mounted on flexible arms and on stands, they can also serve to shade the camera from direct sunlight.

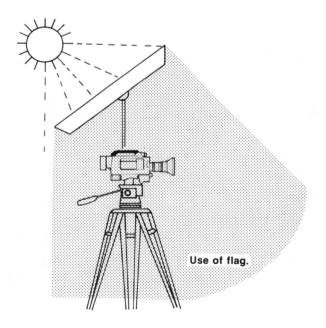

Use of flag.

116

your own clouds when nature's "great silk in the sky" takes a break. Such circumstances provide wonderful opportunities for the gaffer and the grips to show their stuff.

LIGHTING CREW

The lighting crew can take on several forms, depending on the size of the production. On a small production, one person may comprise the entire crew, but on a large production, there may be three, six, or even as many as twenty people involved.

LIGHTING DESIGNER/DIRECTOR (L.D.)

At the top of the hierarchy would be the LIGHTING DESIGNER or DIRECTOR (sometimes called LIGHTING CONSULTANT). This is the person who plans the lighting with regard to positioning, size and type of instruments, and develops the lighting plot. The lighting designer's counterpart in film is the Director of Photography, and both are concerned with the "look" of the pictures.

Gaffer

The GAFFER is the person who is actually in charge of executing the setup of the lighting instruments. Working from the L.D.'s plans, the gaffer directs the lighting crew. If the budget is small, allowing only one person for lighting, an experienced gaffer is the best

choice. A good gaffer can develop a lighting plan, acting as L.D. as well as gaffer.

OTHER LIGHTING CREW MEMBERS

Working for the gaffer as first assistant is the person traditionally known as the BEST BOY. Although the preferred title is now BEST PERSON, the role is the same. The gaffer's crew will also include others known variously as LIGHTING GRIPS or ELECTRICIANS. Large productions will have both, with the grips involved with hanging and adjusting instruments, and the electricians handling power and its routing and control. Some lighting instruments, such as ARC LIGHTS (extremely powerful carbon-arc lamps) and FOLLOW SPOTS (spotlights used to follow a performer) will require a full-time operator for each such instrument. These persons are known as LAMP OPERATORS. Finally, where a generator is required to power the lights, a GENERATOR OPERATOR will be needed.

Color temperature:

When lighting instruments are called for outdoors, the color temperature of the light becomes a factor. The color of light is measured in DEGREES KELVIN. So-called WHITE light is actually made up of light in the full range of the spectrum. The mix of the various colors determines its COLOR TEMPERATURE. Daylight ranges from about 5600 degrees in direct sunlight to about 6200 degrees

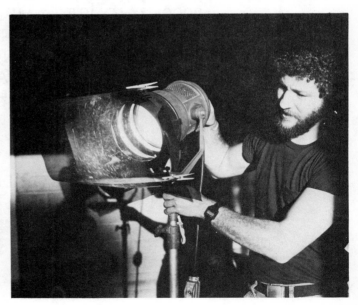

in the shade (where most of the light is coming from the blue sky), and is relatively COOL in tone. Indoor light, as produced by incandescent or quartz lamps, measures at a nominal 3200 degrees (the established standard), and is relatively WARM, or yellow-reddish in color. Standard house lamps may measure as low as 2000 degrees.

Color temperature can be a confusing subject, since light becomes subjectively "warmer" as the degrees Kelvin goes down, and "cooler" as degrees Kelvin goes up. It helps to think of a piece of metal being heated. As the temperature increases, the metal will begin to glow with a *warm* red color. As the temperature increases further, the color changes to yellow and then white. Theoretically, as the temperature gets extremely high, the metal will progressively glow blue, and then move into the ultraviolet range, beyond the visible spectrum. Thus, to recap, warmer light = lower degrees; cooler light = higher degrees. The terms "cool" and "warm" are based on our subjective impressions of color.

Artificial light used out-of-doors, then, must be "cooled" down. This is done by using blue GELS (filters) to "cool" the light to match daylight. There are some lights that are daylight-matched without needing gels.

The reverse can be true when shooting indoors where daylight enters through a window or doorway. In this instance, either the artificial lights must be balanced for daylight, or the daylight must be balanced to mix properly with the artificial sources. This can be accomplished by placing large orange or amber gels over the outside of the windows that will WARM UP (reduce the color temperature) of the daylight to match the artificial lights. NEUTRAL-DENSITY (grey) gels may also be used at the same time to lower the contrast if the windows will appear in the background.

A personal lighting method:

Though it's very tempting to go on and delve further into lighting and its techniques, the

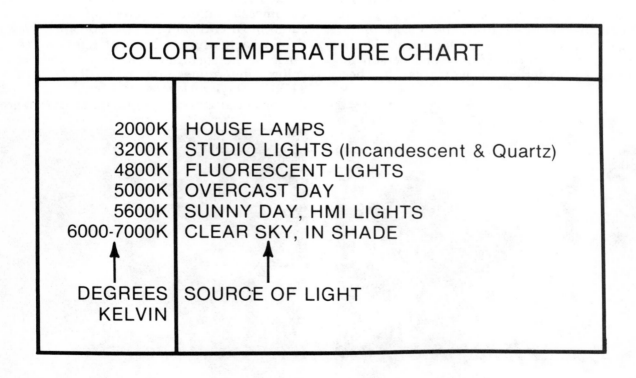

118

subject could fill the balance of this book and then some. Instead, I'd like to explain how I personally handle lighting, since the system I use works well for me.

Putting it simply, the system I use is to hire the best lighting director I can find. I can almost hear you now: "Yeah, that's great if you have the budget for it, but I've got to do it myself!" I sympathize with you. There have been many times when I or one of my crew have had to assume the role of lighting director and gaffer on a production. If you're on your own, I would refer you to one of the books on lighting listed in the bibliography, or suggest you attend a good lighting seminar. The bare basics of lighting—a working understanding that will permit you to do a decent job of it—are not all that hard to learn.

Lighting, is one of the most demanding art forms in television, and an entire career can be spent at it without fully mastering it. Good lighting can look okay, but great lighting will look gorgeous, and will enhance the appearance of the production more than any other single factor. When I have room in my budget for only one specialist, I use the money for a good lighting director (who may also act as gaffer). There is no substitute for a deep understanding of lighting.

For those who are starting out, or who need a lighting package that is easily transportable but effective, I would certainly recommend the lighting kits offered by the various manufacturers. Some of the kits on the market are quite complete, down to a selection of GELS (colored filters), and provide virtually everything one needs to do basic lighting. A good kit would include three, four, or perhaps five instruments, all of which can be focused in some manner; two or three REFLECTORS or UMBRELLAS, which bounce or diffuse light; a full complement of stands, brackets, and holders; and various other accessories such as BARNDOORS which limit the area to be lit, FLAGS and CUTTERS which block light, gels and holders, power cables, adapters, and spare bulbs.

Some examples of the kits available would include the marvelous **Lowell Tota-Lights,** as well as their **Omni-Light** and **D-Head** kits. Tota-Lights are small, thin quartz-type fixtures

omni-kits

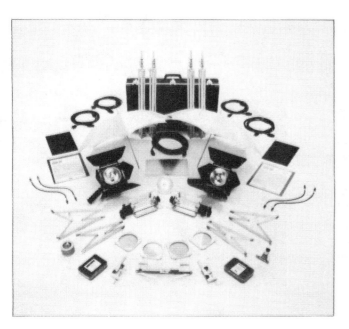

Colortran Pro Lights

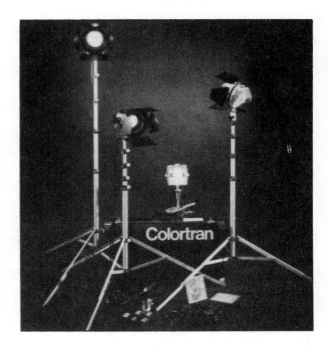

with adjustable panels on both sides that serve either as reflectors for focusing, or as mini barndoors. They fold up into compact little units, and a kit containing three or four lights plus stands, umbrellas, and accessories will fit into a compact and lightweight suitcase. Other, highly flexible kits are available from such manufacturers as **Colortran** and **Smith-Victor**. A large selection of lighting instruments is found in the line offered by **Mole-Richardson**. Mole offers a full range of lights, from the miniature INKY DINKS all the way to large FRESNELS, SCOOPS, and BROADS and they are known for their rugged, dependable design. This also contributes to their only disadvantage: They are quite heavy. A Mole-Richardson lighting kit will probably last longer than you do, but it's not the kind of thing you want to carry for any distance.

There are also collapsible SOFTLIGHTS available that can be packaged in suitcase form. Lowell markets an especially good

tota-kit T1-92

tota-light

omni-light

d light

Quartz-King Dual 550 Mark II

Mini-Pro

120

Molequartz Molepars

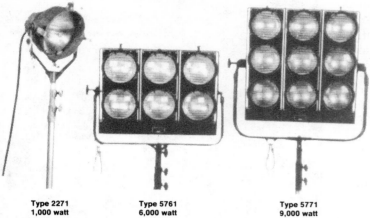

Type 2271
1,000 watt

Type 5761
6,000 watt

Type 5771
9,000 watt

Molequartz Scoops

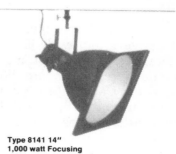

Type 8141 14"
1,000 watt Focusing

Solarspots®

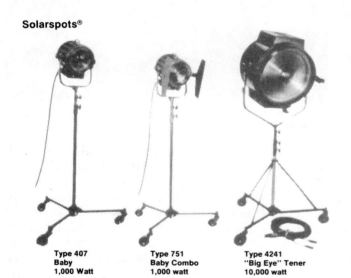

Type 407
Baby
1,000 Watt

Type 751
Baby Combo
1,000 watt

Type 4241
"Big Eye" Tener
10,000 watt

Mole-Richardson Co.

Molequartz Broads

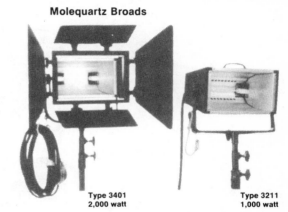

Type 3401
2,000 watt

Type 3211
1,000 watt

Moleffect Equipment

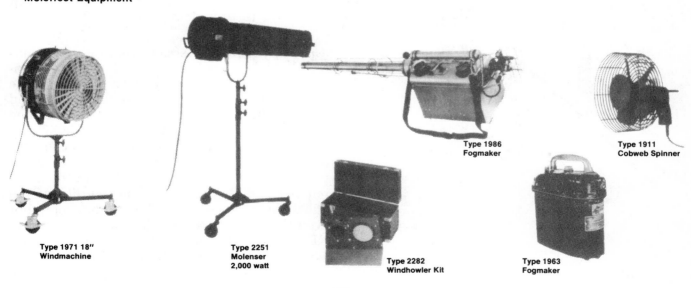

Type 1971 18"
Windmachine

Type 2251
Molenser
2,000 watt

Type 2282
Windhowler Kit

Type 1986
Fogmaker

Type 1911
Cobweb Spinner

Type 1963
Fogmaker

121

design that makes a fine supplement to any basic lighting kit. There are a number of battery-powered lights available for location work, though in my experience, the weight and/or limited capacity of their batteries usually make them a royal pain to use.

For outdoor lighting, a full set of reflectors and silks is very handy. It is also very expensive. A large silk can cost more than $1000. Full, standard reflectors are both costly and bulky, and they absolutely require a truck to carry them around. There are, however some lightweight alternatives available. Once again, Lowell offers a unit called the **Variflector** (a flexible reflector) that can be rolled up and stored in a tube and that can be adjusted by warping to focus light as needed. These are extremely useful, although their light weight can work against them in brisk winds.

In addition to the aforementioned, along with the life-saving foam core, an inexpensive

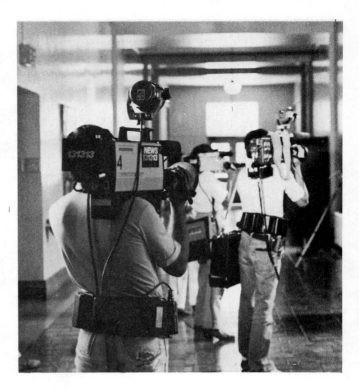

Portable lights.

alternative is aluminum foil. Foil stretched over foam core or everyday cardboard, with some flat and smooth to bounce, and some crinkled to diffuse, will produce cheap but quite utilitarian lighting reflectors. A drawback will be the need to have someone hold them, or provide some sort of rigging to keep them in place. Proper reflectors have stands that permit the light to be aimed easily, and since the boards are double-sided with two different surfaces, it's a simple matter to flip the board to provide a different effect.

While a light meter can be a useful tool, especially if the cameras being used have definite light level requirements, I wouldn't consider one to be absolutely essential. One of the best gaffers I've worked with uses his hand held out in the area he's lighting to determine the light ratio and effect of the various instruments he's using. He does carry a meter, but rarely uses it. The reason is that once you've taken care of providing *enough* light, then the important matter becomes the *quality* of the light. The final judge will be not the meter, nor even the eye, but rather, the camera. Once the L.D. (LIGHTING DIRECTOR) or the gaffer has achieved the results that the director wants, the entire setup is checked on the monitors.

Lowel Variflector.

Reflector and C-Stand.

Cameras see differently than do our eyes, and a careful check of the PROGRAM MONITOR (standard output monitor) and WAVEFORM MONITOR (a test monitor that displays the video signal levels) will tell what, if any, adjustments will be needed. In a sense, the waveform monitor is to television what the light meter is to film.

It's very important to note that each light draws at least 1000 or 1500 watts of power (10 amperes). If you connect more than 2 or 3 lights to one typical household electrical circuit, you will soon blow fuses or trip circuit breakers. Be sure to connect your lights to several different circuits or provide extra power from another source. Also, put your lights on a separate circuit from your VTR, camera, and audio equipment. Remember to bring lots of heavy duty AC extension cords and junction boxes and know where the fuse box or circuit breaker is located. Also bring extra fuses (20 or 30 ampere).

We all know that TV cameras should not be pointed into lights or vice versa, but reflections are also a hazard and can burn the camera tubes as severely. Things like the metal arms of modern chairs can easily reflect enough light to burn the tubes, or at very least, put a SPIKE (a peak highlight) in the picture that can cause all sorts of undesirable effects in the signal. Should you find an offending piece of furniture or other item giving you spectral reflections, it's time to pull out the DULLING SPRAY. Since the can of dulling spray seems always to be empty, or the little nozzle is missing, hair spray makes a very acceptable substitute. Unfortunately, the pre-

sent reign of the "natural look" has made hair spray much less ubiquitous than it once was, creating untold problems for film and television crews out on location.

Lighting is a specialty, and one of the most demanding and intricate skills in television. If you can, hire a specialist in the field. Doing so simply provides better results. Though the same is true in most of the various areas of production, this is as good a place as any to incorporate the thought into another rule.

McQ's RULE No. 4: Let a *specialist* do the job whenever possible.

If you're doing a good job as producer or director, you shouldn't have time to give as much attention to lighting as it deserves. Hire or train a specialist in the field, describe the effect you want, let them do their thing, and then approve or disapprove the results. Sounds simple, doesn't it?

Grip

GRIP is a word with two meanings in film and video. Grips are people on the crew, while grip equipment denotes a wide range of gear used in production, and handled by these people.

Heading the grip crew is the KEY GRIP, who is in charge of any number of other grips. These people are responsible for the RIGGING (setup) of all camera-related paraphernalia, such as tripods, dollies, and booms, and with any special setups required for a scene. Grips are the catch-all workers on the set, and though there are usually distinctions between

the lighting crew and the grip crew, on smaller productions these distinctions are often very blurry.

Grip equipment, as opposed to lighting equipment, primarily has to do with the camera and its support. Camera mounting and movement can be achieved in many different ways, and this section will examine these and other general grip matters.

Camera support:

The standard camera support is, of course, the TRIPOD, though this word covers a lot of ground. Tripods vary in size, construction, and capabilities, and may or may not come equipped with a HEAD (the part on which the

Lightweight Miller fluid head.

camera is mounted). Less expensive units are usually supplied as a single system that includes the legs and the head, but in the range of designs made for professional use, the head is almost always a separate item.

When the camera to be used is one of the new generation minicams, a FLUID HEAD is by far the best method of achieving smooth camera movements. This is a pan/tilt head whose movement is damped by a viscous fluid such as oil to prevent jumps or jerks in the movement. When properly adjusted, it provides a degree of resistance to movement (drag), against which the camera operator works. With a good fluid head it is next to impossible to get a jerky movement. For general-purpose work, it's the best way to achieve professional results.

Nearly all fluid heads offer adjustments for drag in both PANNING (side to side) and TILTING (up and down) movement, in addition to separate locks for pan and tilt. There are fluid heads available with camera weight capacities upwards of 100 pounds. Beyond this weight, other types of camera support are more appropriate.

Though fluid heads are the type most commonly used for small cameras, and are highly versatile, there are times when other types of heads offer a better choice. One of these is the GEARED HEAD. Panning and tilting with a geared head is done by turning cranks, and this method can provide the ultimate in smoothness of movement. They also avoid the problem of backlash. Even the best fluid heads

Heavy O'Connor 50.

124

have a tendency to "settle back" at the end of a move. In some cases this matters little, but in others, such as where precise registration of artwork or ending position of the camera is critical, a geared head is the answer. Using a geared head, however, usually requires the addition of an ASSISTANT CAMERA OPERATOR (A.C.) to operate the head's control.

Larger cameras such as studio units are more comfortable on heads specially designed for them, such as the CRADLE or CAM-LINK heads commonly found on the counter-balanced pedestals that normally reside in the studio.

A pedestal-type design would be the basic studio choice. The larger, more expensive ones will be counter-balanced, so that the camera can be easily raised or lowered. The smaller and less expensive models will have a rack and pinion crank for this purpose. A pedestal type takes up less floor space than does a tripod, and many designs allow the wheels to be locked, or even better, steered, to allow for DOLLYING (moving the camera forwards or backwards) and TRUCKING (moving side-to-side).

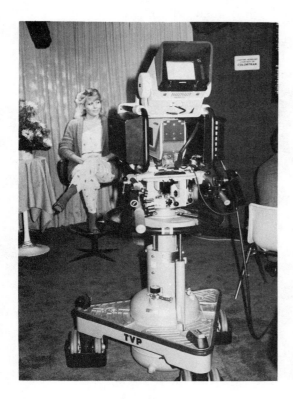

Studio pedestal tripod.

Tripod and spreader.

The other kind of head is the FRICTION HEAD, which is fine for still photographic work, but a very poor choice for television or film. It is virtually impossible to achieve smooth movements with a friction head.

Types of tripod legs:

Once you've chosen a head, you'll need a set of tripod legs on which to mount it. Again, the word *tripod* covers a wide range of options.

In the field, the traditional standby has been the wooden-legged tripod, also known as STICKS. In general, they're lightweight, easy to use, and fairly dependable, although I have seen them snap under a load, in one case sending a lovely Mitchell camera to the repair shop. Today, as a result of space technology spinoffs, there are exotic tripods made of aluminum, magnesium, carbon fiber, and, for all I know, rare molybdenum-titanium alloys. These new designs are dandy, though there is a certain reluctance on the part of veterans to forsake the old sticks that do their voodoo so well.

125

Tripods come in many sizes, with the standards being full size (REGULAR), medium (SAWED OFF), and short (BABY LEGS). For shooting from a very low angle, a device known as a HIGH HAT is used. This is a nonfolding, rigid tripod made of cast aluminum, with a platform height of 6 inches.

Although some tripods have rubber feet either standard or as options, most professional units are equipped with spikes at the feet. When used on a smooth surface such as concrete or linoleum, a device known as a SPREADER is used to keep the legs from spreading too far apart. A POCKET SPREADER can be bought or made from wire or rope, although these will not adjust as quickly or easily as a proper spreader.

Several firms offer a type of device known as a HYDRO-POD, or HYDRO-PED, that is a cross between a pedestal and a tripod. These devices consist of a center pedestal that has legs attached at the bottom and operates with the aid of hydraulic fluid. The unit is held over the place where the camera is to be set up, and a valve is opened. The fluid pressure then lowers the legs until they contact the ground, at which time the valve is closed, locking the legs in place.

One advantage to this type of unit is the speed and ease of setting up and leveling

Various tripods and accessories.

regardless of the terrain, since the pedestal automatically levels itself. Also, these units are more rigid in torsion and bending than conventional tripods, which helps to reduce backlash. Finally, they are true miniatures of studio pedestals, with the better units offering hydraulic counterbalancing and raising and lowering of the camera at adjustable speeds. Their disadvantages are mainly their high cost and considerable weight compared with a simple set of sticks.

In working within the small confines of the television screen, camera movement is one of the best ways to create the illusion of depth and dimension in the picture. DOLLYING IN or OUT of a scene differs from using a ZOOM in that dollying changes the perspective. Since the human eye is not normally equipped with variable focal length capability (aside from any possible mutants out there), we normally change our view by using our own built-in dollies. This sort of movement, applied to camera work, gives a more natural feeling than does a zoom, and, prior to the introduction of zoom lenses, was the only way to vary the shot during a take.

Lending even more to the illusion of depth are movements perpendicular to the camera's shooting axis. These include TRUCKING (side-to-side, as mentioned above), ARCING (moving around the subject in an arc, the center of which is the subject), and PEDESTALING, BOOMING, or CRANING (moving the camera up or down). There are other movements as well, and various movements are often combined during a single shot.

These movements are made possible by mounting the camera on various types of dollies, booms, and cranes. The dolly is perhaps most common outside of the major studios. These devices usually have four sets of wheels, which can be steered in a number of ways: with only the front wheels steered, like a car; or with all four sets of wheels steered, permitting them to CRAB (the dolly can move in any direction while keeping the same orientation to the subject).

The dollies most commonly found in well-equipped studios or equipment rental houses are equipped with small hydraulic or pneumatic booms that offer a limited range of verti-

Hydro-Ped Model 102-B

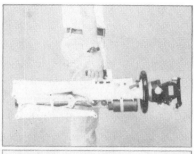

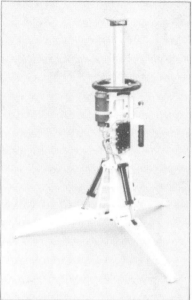

cal camera movement. When large movements are needed, a larger version of essentially the same device—the crane or boom—is used. These may require two or three operators in addition to the camera operator. Some cranes can take the camera from near ground level to 20 feet or more in height in one continuous move.

There are extremely lightweight dollies and cranes available that can be used in areas of poor access or in confined spaces. Quite compact, these units are often collapsible, and can be carried in and set up on location, though this still takes several people. For use on rough terrain, some sort of track will be needed. Dolly track made of pipe permits curving

127

Dollies.

Cranes.

128

movements, although they take time to set up and often cause noise problems by squeaking. When this happens, baby powder sprinkled on the track will usually quiet them down. For straight runs, simple 2 × 12 lumber is easy to obtain and simple to set up.

There are also special dollies designed for working on a product table or with a SNORKLE LENS (periscope lens), that place the camera at the end of a boom arm that swivels on a pedestal. You can rest assured that for whatever need you could possibly imagine, there's a device out there somewhere that someone's built to solve the problem.

If you can't, for one reason or another, get your hands on a proper dolly, there is a way to achieve camera movement without spending a fortune. It's called a WHEELCHAIR. A visit to a local rental shop can provide one at modest cost, and there are even times when a wheelchair can be preferable to a dolly. They are lightweight, easily maneuvered, and most can be collapsed and stowed in the trunk of a car.

A recent innovation in camera mounting is the **Steadicam**® (see Chapter 5), marketed by

Cinema Products, which received a well-deserved Oscar for innovative technical contribution to the industry. This marvelous system is based on an articulated arm that is attached to a body harness worn by the operator. The camera sits on a gimble-mounted platform at the end of the arm. The entire unit is counter-sprung so that the camera effectively has no weight. The resulting camera movements are similar to dolly movements, but the Steadicam allows the operator to walk, run, climb stairs, or even ride a horse with the camera remaining nice and steady at all times.

Similar in purpose, though slightly different in application, is the **Image Stabilizer**, which performs a similar function through the use of gyroscopically-stabilized mirrors. **Arriflex** markets a version of this system, and it eliminates small high-frequency vibrations quite well. An advantage over the Steadicam is that it permits the camera to be held sideways or at any other angle, while the Steadicam makes its living by keeping the camera vertical. The stabilizer is also smaller and lighter, and can be mounted to the front of nearly any lens/camera combination. A disadvantage is that the

The Steadicam®

image stabilizer, in addition to damping out vibrations, will also try to correct pans that are faster than a certain speed (about 4 degrees/second). It also does not damp out gross camera movements. It is ideal, however, for such things as shooting out of a helicopter.

This brings us to some of the more exotic special-purpose camera mounts. Footage shot from airplanes and helicopters usually requires some from of special camera mounting to isolate the camera from vibration. While it is conceivable to hand-hold the camera in these situations, the resulting pictures will tend to be shaky unless the shot is made with a very wide lens. The Image Stabilizer and

Arriflex Image Stabilizer.

Steadicam can both be used in aircraft, although wearing a Steadicam in the tight confines of a small plane or chopper is not an ideal solution. It would be better to mount the Steadicam to the aircraft.

The image stabilizer was designed for precisely this kind of work, and might be a better choice. Another alternative would be to use camera mounts specifically designed for such purposes. These would include the **Tyler** and **Continental** camera mounts. In the larger production centers, it is possible to rent the aircraft and mount from a single source. The system will be set up for the kind of camera you're using when you arrive. You can also often rent the entire package of aircraft, camera, mount, and VTR from a single source.

In the United States, television production jumped right on the zoom lens when it became available, and there has been a strange reticence on the part of many directors to move the camera around. Film people do it all the time, and camera movement is by no means unusual in large television productions. On the smaller scale there seems to be a reluctance to do so that likely stems from the historical unwieldiness of TV cameras. The use of the new small and lightweight cameras makes camera movement much easier to accomplish,

Helicopter mount.

and the techniques that movement facilitates can add tremendously to production values.

Other grip gear:

I find a well-equipped grip truck to be more fun than a candy store, and it's very fortunate that rental is the common mode of obtaining grip equipment. If I had to buy, I'd go broke on an endless series of purchases that would take care of every contingency.

In addition to lighting equipment, already dealt with in brief detail, a good grip truck should contain:

C-STANDS (Century stands, which serve as spare hands for holding or positioning nearly anything), Full, half, and quarter APPLE BOXES (sturdy wooden boxes with no open sides that are used to provide support for such things as leveling dolly track), Wedges, Furniture Pads, Ladders, Stage Jacks, Block and Tackle(s), Ropes, Chairs, Coolers, a Bullhorn, Staple Guns, First Aid Kits, Hoses, Flashlights, Toolkits, Sandbags, Brooms, Dulling Spray, a selection of Spray Paints, A Shovel, an Umbrella, Fire Extinguishers, Folding Tables, Sponges, Can Openers, Gaffer's Tape (lots of that!), other tape of various types and colors, Folding Tables and Table Cloths, Traffic Pylons, Flares, Walkie Talkies, Foamcore, Gels, Window Cleaner, Rags, Kleenex, Marking Pens, C-47s (clothespins), Nails, Tacks, Chalk, Aluminum Foil, Trash Bags, Wire, Paper Cups and Plates, Plastic Forks, Spoons, and Knives, WD-40, Glue, Seamless Background Paper, Black Cloth, Worklights, W-2 and AFTRA forms, and, optionally, a Generator and Mobile Phone.

The above is a *greatly* abbreviated *partial* list, given in no real order, and designed just to provide examples of the kinds of things you'll find in a good grip truck. Also, expendables (foam core, gels, etc.) are mixed into the standard equipment.

Perhaps the best way to examine the kinds of equipment normally provided in a grip truck would be to send for the catalog or information sheet put out by the various companies that rent trucks. Since they do this sort of thing all the time, and have done so for a range of productions that extends far beyond the experience of any one producer or director, the chances are that when you go on location with one of their trucks, you'll find what you need no matter what happens.

BATTERIES

Until fairly recently, nearly all portable cameras were powered from battery belts which were either worn around the waist by the camera operator or hung on the legs of the tripod. With advances in battery design and the increasing reduction of camera power consumption, most of the newer cameras now operate from batteries that are attached to the rear of the camera. This represents a tremendous improvement in operating convenience, as it reduces the forest of cables with which the cameraperson must contend. This is a particular nuisance with hand-held camera work, and in high-mobility tripod situations. Since the camera batteries are a snap-on design, they also can be changed quickly and easily.

The two most common types of batteries used in either belt or rear-mount configurations are nickel-cadmium (nicad) and silver-zinc, with nicads being by far the most predominant. Silver-zinc batteries offer the advantage of much greater power capacity, generally about triple the capacity of nicads. Typical AMP-HOUR (AH) ratings for a nicad battery pack would be 4 AH, whereas a silver-zinc battery would typically be rated at 12 AH, resulting in an increase of operating time with an average camera from 2 hours per battery to 6 hours. The trade-offs, on the other hand, are a much higher initial price tag, and a shorter

Camera mounted battery.

131

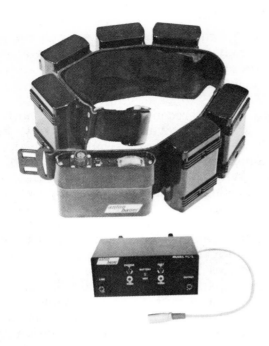

Battery belt.

Equipment that is used in the field needs to be protected against damage, so it's critical to enclose your gear in some sort of a shipping case or carrying case. Odd as it may seem, very little video equipment is supplied with cases. The primary reason is that each user has his or her own idea of how to best protect the equipment, and various users have different needs with regard to shipping.

Hard shell shipping case.

operating life for the battery in terms of how many charges it will take. In general, probably the best choice would be to plan on two or three nicad batteries or battery belts with a charger that can handle at least two belts at a time, rather than spending the money on a single silver battery. This way, one or more can be charging while one is in use.

With regard to chargers, be wary of QUICK CHARGERS. They are rough on batteries and may reduce the battery's life. Quick charging is for emergency situations only, and at all other times, the TRICKLE CHARGE is a better method. There are some chargers available that can work either way.

An important point with nicad batteries is that there is a proper technique for using and charging them, and it requires that the battery be almost fully dissipated before it is recharged. Nicad batteries have what might be called a "memory," and if they are only partially dissipated and then charged, they will eventually "remember" the previous partial drain, and no longer provide full power. In a sense, like an unused muscle, they atrophy, and will provide better service if they are fully exercised.

In the area of shipping cases, there are a number of manufacturers of cases designed especially for video equipment, with **Anvil** and **Thermodyne** among the more prominent. The catalogs of each of these firms list hundreds of different pieces of equipment from dozens of manufacturers, and provide a customized shipping case for each item. In the event that you have a piece of equipment that's either so rare or so old that they don't have a case for it (actually, a rather unlikely occurrence), they can make up a case if supplied the dimensions.

These shipping cases are truly heavy-duty units, designed to protect equipment from damage during commercial shipping. The larger models can in themselves be quite heavy, running as much as 30 or 40 pounds for the empty case. They can also cost as much as $200 to $300, but considering the value of the equipment they protect, they're a cheap form of insurance.

There are also lightweight carrying cases (as opposed to shipping cases) available, designed

132

primarily for ENG and EFP use with portapaks. These cases, commonly made of vinyl or cordova nylon, are offered for most of the ½-inch and ¾-inch portable VCRs and cameras. Although many equipment owners like them, there are also those who prefer to keep their equipment unencumbered and free of a case to provide fast and easy access for tape and battery changes and for maintenance access. Perhaps the best thought-out and best known cases are those made by **K & H Products.** They make the **Porta-Braces** which are units that combine a convertible shoulder strap and backpack style case for the VCR with an arm that extends up and forward to hold the camera. This system also provides for attaching wheels to the frame, turning the whole affair into an equipment cart.

Another highly respected system is the **Kangaroo Pack System,** made by **Kangaroo Products.** It is a highly versatile VTR shoulder type pack with all kinds of pockets, and straps that conveniently hold cables, wireless mikes, and other accessories. Many broadcasters use this pack for their ENG work.

Considering the weight of video equipment, the best means of avoiding back and other injuries is to employ some form of cart or hand truck for moving equipment around. One good choice is a collapsible hand truck that can be folded for storage in a car trunk or a van. On the slightly fancier side, there are specially designed carts, commonly known as "crash carts," that will hold a VTR, AC unit, a monitor, and accessories, and that can be wheeled into place with the equipment connected and ready to be plugged in and used. There are even carts with a built-in camera mount and head, although the prospective buyer should be aware that the heads provided on these units are usually barely adequate, not being of the fluid-head design.

Crash cart.

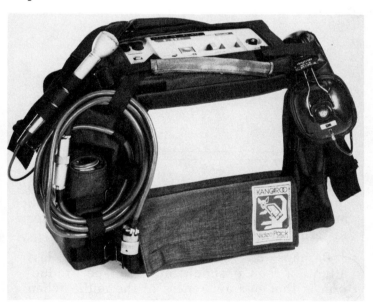

Soft case.

CHAPTER 9

Audio

With all the concentration on making pretty pictures, audio often ends up being the orphan child of television. All too often, the level of sophistication encountered in audio production consists of merely connecting a microphone to the VTR (hoping that it's the right impedance—resistance to alternating current flow), and letting the tape roll.

Consider, however, that the audio portion of many programs is of equal or even greater importance than the video. Far beyond being a simple supplement to the pictures, as much as 75% of the basic information content of a program may be carried in the audio portion.

Even where this is not the case, the audio provides crucial support for the visual content, and the quality of the sound is a major factor in terms of overall production values.

Perhaps one reason audio receives less attention than it should in videotape production is that our awareness of the audio when watching a film or a television program is generally less than is our awareness of the pictures. Anyone with some basic knowledge of production techniques can study the picture and come away with a fairly good idea of at least *what* was done, if not *how* it was done. When audio is done well, however, it should be invisible. If the sound recordist and mixer were striving for realistic sound and did their jobs well, it will not be apparent that there was any undue effort expended on the audio. The sound will simply appear to be natural. Any unusual or unrealistic sound is about your best tip-off that it is not natural.

The final sound in a film or a dramatic television program makes use of techniques that would include such things as DUBBING (adding or changing sounds or dialog) and LOOPING (having actors re-dub their dialog while watching a continuously repeating section of the film). This is done to replace flawed audio, and to add sound effects, such as telephone rings, doors closing, background sounds, etc. (known as FOLEY—rhymes with "holy"); and, of course, recording a music track that will be added during the final MIX-DOWN (mixing of audio tracks).

A complex production may require the eventual use of as many as 48 separate audio tracks, and the use of 16 or 24 tracks is quite common. There are some films, though, that permit analysis of the audio work involved. One difficulty in doing this is that good films suck you in to the point where you're so involved in the story that you quickly forget to be analytical about the audio. Sometimes a second or third viewing can help.

Examples of films that boast some incredibly fine audio work would include *Apocalypse Now*, which features some of the most sophisticated and powerful sound editing in the history of film, and the *Star Wars* sagas, both of which (*Episodes IV* and *V*, to date) are extremely well done in terms of sound effects. It's also interesting to note that all of these employed six-channel DOLBY SOUND, at least for their 70mm releases.

Within the next few years, the establishment of a standard for stereo audio in television broadcasting will leave little room for poor sound in television, but while we wait, there is still no excuse for sound quality that falls short.

Proper audio equipment is available for all levels of production. A microphone *is* all that is required at the most basic level. The trick is in picking the right mike for the right application, and knowing how to use it. Before we examine audio techniques, let's take a moment to examine the equipment.

Types of Microphones

In terms of application there are essentially three basic types of microphones: HARD-WIRED (either placed on the talent, held by the talent, or mounted on a stand in front of the talent), SHOTGUN, and WIRELESS microphones.

The term HARDWIRED means that there is a cable leading from the talent's mike to the recorder or mixer, and the microphone itself may be of many various types. SHOTGUN or BOOM mikes are usually held near the talent, and can be aimed by the sound man or boom operator, who listens on headphones as a guide to positioning. These mikes are usually of the DIRECTIONAL type (picking up sounds mainly from one direction), though again, there are many variations. WIRELESS mikes (also called RF MIKES) are just what the name implies. These are usually either worn or held by the performer, and the signal is transmitted by radio over a short distance to a receiver which is connected to the VTR or mixer.

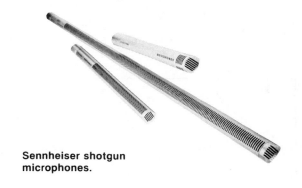

Sennheiser shotgun microphones.

Within these broad classifications there are numerous types of mikes, each type suited to a different purpose. Mikes vary according to their *technical design*—DYNAMIC, CONDENSER, ELECTRET CONDENSER, RIBBON, etc.— and according to their *pickup pattern*—OMNIDIRECTIONAL (picking up sound from all directions), BIDIRECTIONAL (from two directions), CARDIOID (from mainly one direction), and SUPERCARDIOID OR UNIDIRECTIONAL (highly directional, such as shotgun or parabolic designs). Almost all professional audio equipment is of the LOW-IMPEDANCE (low resistance) type, but if you're not sure, it doesn't hurt to check. There are also such things as HIGH-IMPEDANCE mikes, and some equipment requires their use. It's important to make sure your system is consistent and that the mike and input impedances match, or sound quality will suffer.

Hardwired directional microphones.

Lavalier microphone.

Picking the best type of microphone is a matter of examining the requirements of the production. Taping a speaker at a podium could obviously be handled with a mike on a stand at the podium. If the speaker wishes to move about on stage, a LAVALIER MIKE, which is a mike hung on a lanyard or clipped on with a clasp or a pin, may be a better choice.

Hardwired mikes offer several advantages. They provide good consistency of sound and offer simple, reliable operation. Their obvious disadvantage is the necessity to drag a wire around if movement is involved, with the resulting possibility of cable damage.

Of the mikes available for use in television today, perhaps the best-known small hardwired mike is the **Sony ECM-50**, which

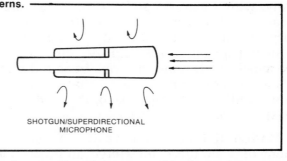

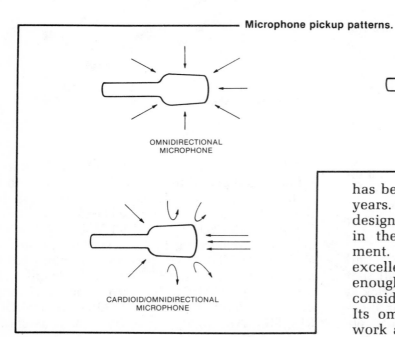

Microphone pickup patterns.

OMNIDIRECTIONAL MICROPHONE

SHOTGUN/SUPERDIRECTIONAL MICROPHONE

CARDIOID/OMNIDIRECTIONAL MICROPHONE

has been offered in several variations over the years. The ECM-50 is an electret condenser design, running off of a small battery that lives in the mike's **XLR**-type connector compartment. It is an omni-directional design with excellent performance quality. It's small enough to be hidden under clothing, and many consider it to be the workhorse of the industry. Its omni-directional design, though, can also work against it, since it will pick up virtually any ambient sounds as well as the subject. Its connecting cable is also somewhat of a mixed blessing. Its small size and good flexibility allows it to be easily concealed, but also makes it more vulnerable to damage. Also, as with any condenser mike, the batteries seem to wait until the "On Air" light is on before failing. For these reasons, it is quite common, and a good practice, to DOUBLE-MIKE the talent (use two microphones), providing backup in the event of a failure.

SHOTGUN mikes provide an excellent alternative for field work, and some provide truly amazing performance. The better designs can literally pluck clean sound out of a noisy environment. Shotgun mikes can be life-savers for field interviews and training tapes done in high-noise environments such as factories.

Use of shotgun microphones.

137

Another use would be for dramatic situations that require a very wide camera angle of view. Since a shotgun mike can pick up sound at a considerable distance, the mike can be off-camera and still pick up dialog between two or more actors. The ultimate in highly directional mikes is the PARABOLIC REFLECTOR, which can turn an ordinary mike into a spy device. By focusing sound picked up over a potentially long distance to a mike placed in the center of the parabola, it offers excellent isolation with a very long reach.

BOOM mikes may be of the shotgun, cardioid, or even omni-directional type, though the latter is not common. Boom mikes are more commonly used in studio production, though

"Fishpole" boom mike.

The audio engineer monitors the sound he's getting from a boom mike on headsets.

their use in the field is not at all unusual. They are mounted on a moveable arm which can range from a full-scale PERAMBULATOR BOOM that has steerable wheels, a seat for the operator, and controls to allow for extending and aiming the mike, down to a hand-held FISHPOLE BOOM. A fishpole is a telescoping tube of light metal or fibreglass that the operator holds just out of camera view. Although not offering much in the way of operational versatility, it is also possible to use an actual fishpole, broomstick, etc., in a pinch.

Boom microphones offer the advantage of being able to pick up the voices of several people simultaneously. This eliminates the need to mix the signals of several mikes together. This can be a double-edged sword, for if the sound levels of the performers differ, the task of re-balancing the sound levels later becomes rather difficult.

WIRELESS mikes have come a long way since they were first introduced, and no longer engender the fear they once did. Their reliabil-

138

ity and quality now let them compete with hardwired mikes in many applications; especially with the introduction of new frequencies and such devices as DIVERSITY ANTENNA SYSTEMS (making use of multiple antennas, thus reducing the chance of hitting a DEAD SPOT—a spot where the signal is weak or where reflections cancel the signal out).

In some applications, wireless mikes have become essential. Extremely long shots are best handled with them. An example is the scene early in *Annie Hall* where you hear Woody Allen and Tony Roberts conversing as they approach from a long block away. The RF mikes allow utmost actor mobility, and the newer designs feature transmitters that are small enough to be easily hidden in almost any clothing (assuming your talent is wearing clothing—a conjecture we'll skip over entirely),

HME wireless microphone.

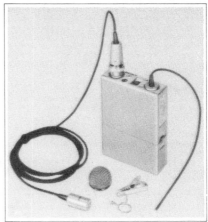

Sony wireless microphone.

Camerman adjusts wireless microphone.

139

Checking wireless microphone system.

For portable use

UHF outdoor use with a portable VTR system

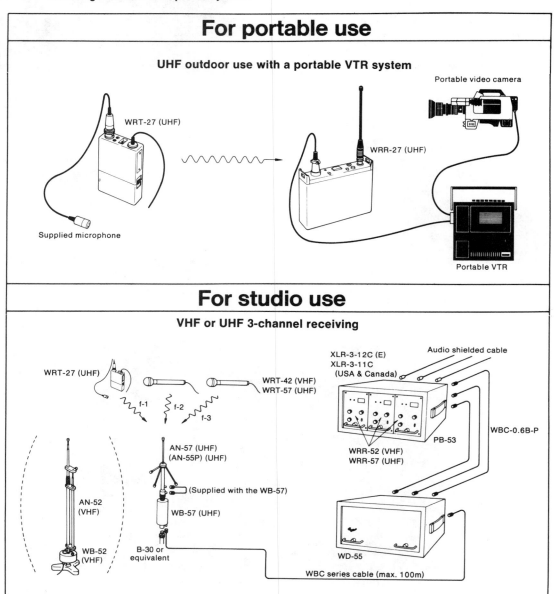

Portable video camera

WRT-27 (UHF)

WRR-27 (UHF)

Supplied microphone

Portable VTR

For studio use

VHF or UHF 3-channel receiving

WRT-27 (UHF)

WRT-42 (VHF)
WRT-57 (UHF)

f-1 f-2 f-3

XLR-3-12C (E)
XLR-3-11C
(USA & Canada)

Audio shielded cable

AN-57 (UHF)
(AN-55P) (UHF)

(Supplied with the WB-57)

AN-52
(VHF)

WB-57 (UHF)

WB-52
(VHF)

B-30 or
equivalent

PB-53

WRR-52 (VHF)
WRR-57 (UHF)

WBC-0.6B-P

WD-55

WBC series cable (max. 100m)

Although wireless mikes are usually hidden, they are also available in hand-held varieties. These units are a boon for circumstances such as active performances in a music or variety show. The best new designs for hand-held mikes are completely self-contained, packing mike, battery, transmitter, and antenna into a single package no larger than a normal hand-held mike. Some VCR carrying cases such as the Kangaroo Bags have convenient pockets designed specifically to hold wireless mikes. This can eliminate the need for an audio person in some cases.

By assigning different frequencies to individual mikes, it is possible to isolate a number of mikes to different mixer or tape input channels. The interference problems that plagued early RF systems have also essentially been eliminated. The cost of these systems is still high compared with standard mikes, but their availability on a rental basis makes it possible to use them on occasions when the job at hand makes them the best choice.

Recording Techniques

While the choice of microphones is important, even more important are the techniques used in recording their signals.

Recording technique starts with mike placement. Nonconcealed mike placement poses few problems. In using more than one mike it's necessary to be concerned with MICROPHONE PHASING. Sound travels in waves, and if two mikes are placed such that one receives the HIGH part of a wave when the second receives the LOW part of the wave, the combined signals are thus 180 degrees apart, or OUT OF PHASE, with the result that they cancel each other out. The resulting sound is thin and lacks dynamic quality. Phase shifting has become very popular in music, where it can be done on purpose with BLACK BOXES built just to achieve that effect, but in normal sound recording it is to be avoided. The effect of PHASE SHIFTS or PHASE CANCELLATION on voices can be quite noticeable and annoying. Furthermore, phasing can also be a problem even with a single mike. Sound that is reflected off a wall, for instance, may arrive at the microphone out of phase with the sound directly received, creating undesirable effects.

If two mikes are used to pick up sound from a single subject, the best technique is to place the mikes close together to prevent phase cancellation. When two or more people are wearing microphones, their positioning becomes important for the same reason. Once they are positioned for good sound without phase cancellation, any change in their positions relative to each other may produce phase-shift effects. This is something the talent should keep in mind, and your audio person will have to watch this. In such instances you might consider using a boom mike, if conditions permit. Remember, though, that even boom mikes are subject to reflection phasing problems.

Another often ignored aspect of sound recording is SOUND PERSPECTIVE. Sound perspective simply means that the sound should match the picture. If the person speaking is seen from a distance, he should sound as if he were far away. If you're shooting a car coming towards and past the camera, you wouldn't expect the sound of the car to remain constant, and the same is true for people and other objects. For an example of poor sound perspective, watch a low-budget foreign film in which the dialog has been dubbed. All too often, the voices retain the same perspective no matter where the actors are or what they're doing.

Closely related to sound perspective is SOUND CONTINUITY. A good example would be dialog between two characters in a production that is shot single-camera film style. If alternating shots are recorded with different mikes or under greatly different conditions, the sound quality will change noticeably between the shots. You may not notice this until the edit, by which time it may be too late to do much about it other than spending a lot of time EQUALIZING (adjusting the tonal quality through what are basically expanded

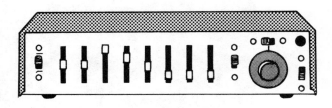

Audio equalizer.

bass/treble controls), or have the dialog looped.

One of the most annoying problems in audio recording is AMBIENT SOUND, which is the general background noise level. In any situation other than an ANECHOIC CHAMBER (a completely sound-deadened room), there will always be noise that is part of the natural background sound. The noise itself is not always the annoying factor, but rather changes in the ambient sound. Consider our example of two-character dialog shot in single-camera style just mentioned. If the first actor's lines were recorded while a plane was passing far overhead (far enough that you went ahead and recorded), and the reverse shots of the other character were recorded after the plane was gone, the result after editing will be a background level that changes abruptly at each edit. There are two possible solutions for this problem. The first is to wait until the plane is gone, and the second is to record some ambient noise that can be added to the mix to even out such changes. Doing both is the best practice.

When working in noisy environments, it's often possible to reduce background sounds with the use of sound blankets. These are usu-ally furniture pads, but a sleeping bag also makes a good sound blanket. Sound blankets can be taped over air conditioning vents, stuffed into transoms, or hung from stands to help block unwanted sounds. They also work wonders on reducing ECHO and LIVENESS in rooms with hard, blank walls.

Odd as it may seem, *totally* clean sound can sound unnatural, and there are times when ambience is added in, if only to enhance the reality of the scene. For instance, if your action takes place on a busy city street, an absence of background noise would seem quite odd. One worthwhile technique is to bring in ambient sound fairly high at the start of a scene to help establish location, and then slowly ease it down to a less obtrusive level. More often than not, though, the problem will be the reduction of background sounds, rather than a lack of them.

Hiding microphones on talent produces another common problem known as clothing rustle. As fabric rubs against the mike, the resulting rustling sound can ruin the audio. There is another similar problem known as the TIN CAN EFFECT, where the rustle comes not from the mike itself, but from clothing rubbing against the hidden mike cable. The sound trav-

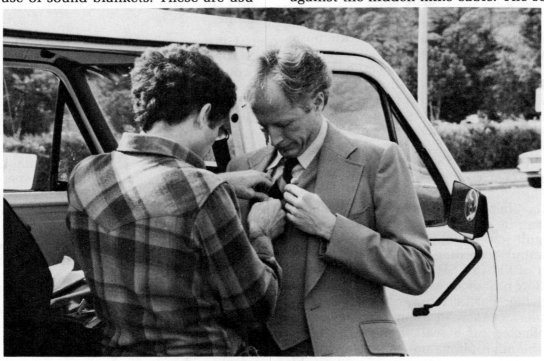

Microphone being hidden on talent.

142

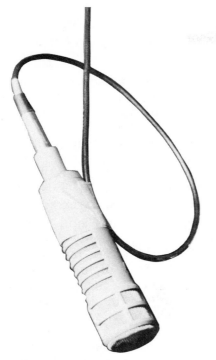

Microphones can be hung overhead to cover a large area.

els up the cable in a manner similar to the old string-and-tin-can telephone, thus the name. Various techniques have been developed to reduce these possibilities, including the placement of small pieces of chamois or silk against the microphone. Small pieces cut from plastic bags can also help prevent these noises, as can tying a very loose knot in the mike cable to prevent clothing noise from traveling up the wire to the mike. Obviously, caution should be exercised in doing this last trick, lest the knot tighten and damage the cable. It should also be mentioned that a wireless mike antenna can also contribute to the tin can effect. The placement of the mike is another factor in reducing clothing noise. When hiding a mike on a woman, placing it in accessories such as a scarf can work well, but be doubly on guard against rustle. Another possibility is clipping it to a bra strap. On men, under the tie is a commonly used spot, but inserting it *into* the knot of the tie can be even better. For open collars, try using a small piece of gaffer's tape to tape the mike to the inside surface of the shirt itself. You'll generally get less noise if the mike rubs against skin than when it rubs against cloth.

Mixers

Audio mixers allow you to combine and mix several sound inputs together. They range in size from little two- or three-input designs with nothing more than simple GAIN (volume) controls all the way up to huge studio systems with as many as 64 inputs, 16 submasters, and

Audio engineer setting levels on portable mixer during location shoot.

143

4 master outputs with complex equalization and effects capabilities for each channel. Choosing the right one for either portable or studio use is a matter of determining the needs that the unit will be required to meet.

Mixers are generally described in terms of the number of inputs and outputs. For example, a 6 × 2 mixer would be one that has six input channels and two output channels, while a 12 × 4 would have twelve input and four output channels. With a fully flexible mixer, any of the input channels can be assigned to any of the output channels, so that, for example, with an 8 × 2 mixer, inputs one through seven could be assigned to output channel one, and input number eight could be assigned to output channel two. Although it might seem that even for stereo production two output channels would be sufficient, there are real advantages to having a least four output channels.

For example, when recording onto two or more video recorders, the opportunity arises to use the audio channels on the additional VTRs to provide greater flexibility for post-production. In shooting a music performance in front of an audience, output channels one and two of the mixer could be used for a basic stereo mix of the music (with, let's say, input channels one through six mixed together), while output channels three and four were used for audience mikes (input channels seven and eight). With the stereo music mix-recorded on the two channels of one VTR, and the audience recorded on the channels of a second VTR, complete flexibility is maintained for post-production, where the final mix of music and audience may be determined. Had the audience been mixed with the music during original taping, there would be little correction possible if the audience turned out to be either too low or too high in relation to the music.

Nagra portable mixer and audio recorder on location.

Shure M267.

Sony MX-P42 portable mixer.

An 18-channel audio board.

For field work, there are numerous options, though battery operation is an obvious must. There are several portable "mini-mixers" available, examples include the **CVMM-15** from Comprehensive Video Supply and the **ENG-1** from **Universal Video,** both of which are battery operated 3 X 1 units measuring about the size of a pocket radio. One of the workhorses of audio has long been the **Shure M-67** mixer, a 4 X 1 unit that has now been replaced in the Shure line by the new **M-267.** These mixers offer the option of battery or AC operation, including automatic switchover to battery power in the event of an AC power loss.

For studio mastering and post-production, the larger mixers offer a higher level of capabilities. Some of the more popular units in small to medium operations are the mixers manufactured by **Teac,** its **Teac/Tascam** subsidiary, and **Yamaha.** Ranging generally from 6 X 2 to 12 X 4 designs, they have decent noise specifications (low noise), a fair range of built-in equalization capabilities, and are easy to learn and use.

At the higher levels, the world of custom audio boards is entered. Most of the really large audio boards are custom designed from a menu of modular elements, although packages representing typical applications are usually available. Some of the better names in the large scale end are **Neve, Ward-Beck, Cetec,** and **Audiotronics,** among many, many others. The audio field is rife with small custom manufacturers, and there are some excellent installations around the country that were built by firms whose names you're unlikely to have ever heard. It's a field that originated early in the century with the advent of radio, and has had ample time to mature.

There are few instances where using a mixer isn't a good idea. If you're shooting ENG style in the field with a single microphone, it may be possible to simply connect the mike to the input on the VTR and have at it, and it's also

145

an acceptable practice when shooting a two-person interview to put a mike on each person and record the signals on the two audio channels of the VTR. Beyond these situations, however, a mixer will be useful, if not necessary.

The normal procedure is to first establish a O VU reference level at both the mixer and the VTR. Some mixers have a test tone generator built in, but when using others, there are small battery operated tone generators available. The tone is used to set the master output(s) at O VU (100 percent modulation) on the mixer's meter and the same on the VTR's meter. Once this is done, all levels can be set at the mixer, and will match at the VTR. Some of this tone should also be recorded along with colorbars at the start of the tape (or at each new setup), to provide a reference signal for post-production.

Getting It on Tape

When it comes to recording the signal on tape, there are a number of ways and means available, and some things to watch in all cases.

A small-budget production will probably benefit from mixing sound in the field, since having all the sound premixed on the tape reduces the need for audio SWEETENING—a subject that will be covered in the post-production section.

In recording audio for television, there are several factors that are often misunderstood. One of the most common errors made by inexperienced producers is the use of AUTOMATIC GAIN CONTROL (AGC) circuits. Automatic gain control may be fine for making notes on an audio cassette recorder, but it has *no* place in serious audio recording. The problem with AGC circuits is simple: They keep the GAIN (input level setting) as high as possible, automatically bringing it down when the level goes too high. This creates two basic problems. First, the AGC circuit will reach out and amplify the background noise between words and sentences, which is quite annoying. The second is that it will take a certain amount of time to react to a loud sound, resulting in too high a level for the first few instants until it brings the volume down.

Automatic gain control can cause problems in your audio that are usually impossible to fix later on during post-production.

Somewhat similar to AGC, though far less dangerous, is the circuit known as a PEAK LIMITER. Whereas AGC "rides" the audio, a PEAK LIMITER has no effect until the input level tries to go too high. If the levels as read on the meters are first set correctly with the peak limiter off, and the limiter is *then* turned on, it will provide protection against the distortion that a momentary peak might cause. The problem with peak limiters is that they *do* clamp down on a momentary peak, and may react slowly in letting go, which produces a dip in the audio level for a few moments after the peak. They also tend to cut down on the dynamic range of the recorded signal, taking some of the sparkle out of the sound. Some limiters are better than others in this regard, and experience with a particular type is the best guide. Though peak limiters can be useful in some instances, in general they cannot take the place of a good audio engineer.

The sense of hearing is far more acute than that of vision. The human ear can distinguish between two different pitches that are only a few cycles apart, and many people can accurately remember a specific pitch. When it comes to sight, our eyes are much more fickle. We're not consciously aware of any difference between daylight and artificial light, even though the two are drastically different, as we saw in the lighting section earlier. Our eyes are relatively forgiving, which is one reason they work so well. What all this means is that most people will notice audio problems such as distortion or abrupt level changes more readily than they will video problems.

While engineering, the audio person doing it becomes what might be called a "thinking AGC circuit." By keeping an eye on the meters, and an ear on the sound itself, the audio person *watches*, *listens*, and *thinks* his way through the audio. Thoughtful reactions mean that a momentary peak that will obviously not recur can be allowed to pass onto tape, while one that will happen again may indicate that the gain should be lowered.

When setting up to record audio, it's important to remember that in the video environ-

The complete audio/video man.

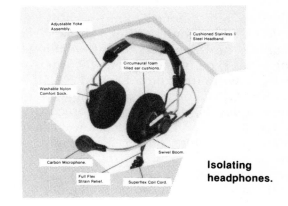

Isolating headphones.

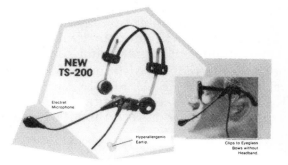

Lightweight headphones.

ment, audio is faced with some unique challenges. Video equipment and lights can create hums and buzzes in the audio, caused by the proximity of audio cables to power cables, poor grounding, or other factors. A final check of the sound should be made with all of the equipment turned on before taping starts. When setting voice levels for performers prior to taping, have them speak in a normal tone of voice, or even better, recite their lines as they will when the taping starts. Nobody ever says "testing" or counts to ten at the same level they'll use when they're "on."

The audio person should monitor the sound with a good set of headphones. There are two reasons *not* to use a speaker, either the one built into some monitors or a separate one: *First,* unless the speaker is of STUDIO MONITOR quality, it won't tell nearly as much about the quality of the sound, including background noise. *Second,* there is a good chance of picking up FEEDBACK that is the screech or whine produced when the mike(s) and the speaker are too close together.

In choosing a set of headphones, there are two basic choices that represent opposite ends of the design spectrum. On one hand are the large, heavy types that block out outside noises (ISOLATING). On the other are the lightweight or even featherweight units that have almost no effect on blocking outside sounds. Both have their place, depending on the situation. The large units provide the best idea of what the actual signal is like, though they're often very uncomfortable to wear for any length of time. The lightweights are comfortable, and are quite capable of excellent sound reproduction, but since they don't block out ambient sounds, it can be hard to tell what's in the signal from what's in the vicinity. However, there are also times when safety or other considerations make the lightweights preferable, since the sound person *can* hear what's happening around him.

It's also very important to select headphones with the proper impedance to match your VTR headphone output impedance. Some VTRs have switchable high and low impedance headphone outputs.

Recording good audio is every bit as much of an art as is good camera work. An experienced audio engineer knows how to "listen

147

like a microphone," knows how different mikes will respond, and can think through the readings on the meters. The first step is knowing what type of meter your recorder or mixer uses. It will either be a PEAK READING or an AVERAGING meter. PEAK meters show the highest levels, and, in proper recording, may move above "0 VU" on occasion without harm. Averaging meters, on the other hand, read the average sound level. Setting levels so that an averaging meter reads at "0 VU" may mean that peaks in the audio go considerably higher than "0 VU" quite often. With such a meter, the best results are obtained when the needle swings up to, and only occasionally past "0 VU." Peak meters will normally swing through a greater number of degrees, and can go a bit higher into the red. It's also important to consider how much HEAD ROOM the VTR or ATR (Audio Tape Recorder) and the particular tape allow. This is a recording level safety margin beyond which distortion will be encountered. Obviously, there's a lot to consider.

Audio, like lighting, is another area where you should consider hiring a professional, or at least acquire some good solid training in audio recording techniques. Decent sound is not terribly hard to obtain, if certain basic rules and techniques are applied. Really *good* sound, however, is the result of expertise. At the very least, audio deserves the full and undivided attention of at least one person who has no other responsibilities on the set. The quality of the audio can make the difference between a show that merely works, and one that comes on like gangbusters.

The sound portion of a show presents as much opportunity for creativity as does the visual portion.

CHAPTER 10

Engineering

It's been my experience that there are two basic types of engineers involved in television.

The first is the type that performs equipment maintenance, and designs special modifications and the like. We might call him an EQUIPMENT MAINTENANCE ENGINEER. The best of these are wizards who often leave me awed by their knowledge of electronics and circuitry. Their efforts, applied to top quality equipment, make beautiful pictures possible.

The second variety is what I would call the PRODUCTION ENGINEER, who may appear under the guise of TECHNICAL DIRECTOR, VIDEO SHADER, or in other roles. These people get the equipment to perform optimally in the studio or in the field, and nurse it along during production.

Although there are a few engineers who are comfortable and competent in either situation, this is not usually the case. Equipment maintenance engineers generally concentrate on the science of television, while production engineers are more involved in the art of making good pictures.

At the risk of overstating a recurring theme, the best results are usually obtained with the aid of a professional.

If you are able to acquire the services of a real-live engineer for your production, you'll first need to determine which variety of engineer you have. This can best be illustrated by example.

You're in the middle of a three-camera shoot with tape and talent rolling, and your video engineer looks up to see that the video level coming from camera three is low. If he's of the maintenance variety, he'll immediately reach over and bring the video level up until he gets a satisfactory waveform display. To him, this will mean having the darkest part of the picture set for 7.5 units, and the brightest part at 100 units, with a nice, full volt from peak to peak.

On the other hand, if he's of the production variety, he'll quickly check the camera's picture monitor to see what the scene is, and whether the picture content calls for a full-volt signal. If his glance at the monitor verifies that the level is too low, he'll check to see if that particular camera is on-line. If it isn't, he'll make a quick adjustment. If it is, he'll then choose between two alternatives. If it's obvious that the director is about to call another shot, he'll wait until the camera is free. If the camera will be on-line for quite a while longer, he'll make a *very slow* adjustment, so that the level change isn't perceptible. He may check with the director in making his decision.

It should be made clear that not every scene should have a full range of signal from TV BLACK to PEAK WHITE. If the scene involves fog, and the desired effect is one of a dull monotone, the levels will likely hover around the 40- to 60-unit level. Although it would be possible to stretch the levels to get more contrast, this may not be what the director wants.

Just as the audio engineer must understand the quality of sound required and must "listen like a microphone," the VIDEO SHADER (who's his counterpart on the video side) must understand the visual quality of the picture that is called for, and must "see like a camera."

A top cinematographer will know the different characteristics of various film emulsions and will pick the one that will provide the results he's after. Likewise, a good engineer will know the response characteristics of the cameras being used and will set them according to the needs of the scene and the production.

Video enjoys a major advantage over film because a good camera can be adjusted to produce a wide variety of results. If a show calls

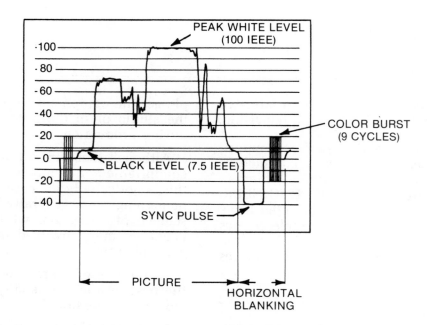

Typical TV signal display on waveform monitor.

for snappy, sparkly pictures with a wide contrast ratio, the engineer can add some ENHANCEMENT (artificial "sharpening" of the image), and adjust GAIN (white level), SETUP (black level), and GAMMA (middle tones/response curve) for maximum contrast. If, on the other hand, the director wants to achieve a film-like look, with it's softer quality and gentler colors, the enhancer gets turned off, and luminance and saturation controls are adjusted for the desired result. A film cinematographer might choose different film stocks for a sunlit scene at the side of a pool and a moody scene by the natural light of a fireplace. In video, though, the same camera and videotape can easily handle both situations, if they're high quality and in the hands of a competent engineer.

It's obvious that the director must be able to communicate his desires clearly with regard to image quality. This is why it's very important for the director to have at least a basic technical background. Of course, it's necessary to know what's possible before specifying requirements.

Obtaining Good Pictures From Your Equipment

Let's examine some of the techniques employed in coaxing good pictures out of production equipment. Most of these techniques relate to the camera, since even the broadcast quad and 1-inch VTRs can generally be set for a proper recording level and left alone.

Auto iris lens.

As mentioned in an earlier section, it's a common misconception that the auto-iris capability (automatic setting of the iris according to light levels) on most newer cameras was designed for use during production. About the only time the auto-iris might be used is in ENG-type (Electronic News Gathering) production, where the picture content may be more important than the picture quality. The auto-iris will react to every change in the scene's overall video level (brightness), reacting either to PEAKS (brightest areas), just as does an audio peak meter to sounds, or to the AVERAGE PICTURE LEVEL (APL), as with an audio averaging meter. As a result, movements within the picture can cause wide and often irreparable variations in the video signal.

The auto-iris can come in handy for field production in the absence of a waveform monitor, where it may be used to let the camera set the video level before tape rolls. The auto-iris is then turned off prior to taping the scene. There may be a few instances where the scene calls for a pan from a light to a dark area, or vice versa, where careful rehearsal might show that the auto-iris will follow the level change smoothly, but these are the exception to the rule. There are also differences from camera to camera. Some auto-iris circuits provide smooth, well-damped adjustments with little or no overshoot, while some seem almost to go into spasms if someone in the scene looks sideways at the camera.

The built-in IMAGE ENHANCERS (circuits that improve image sharpness) found in most of the newer cameras must also be used with caution. These are a big selling feature in the new generation of cameras that use $2/3$-inch (17mm) tubes, and they can, indeed, provide apparent resolution that seems to match that of cameras with larger 1-inch (25mm) or 30mm tubes. Image enhancers work by exaggerating the edges of LEVEL TRANSITION POINTS (transitions between light and dark areas) in the picture, and, in essence, put little SPIKES (peaks) in the video where such transitions appear. This produces apparently sharper edges in the picture.

Unfortunately, these spikes can sometimes become further exaggerated during the post-production process, creating final picture results that can have an almost cartoon-like quality to them.

In general, I prefer to run the enhancer perhaps a quarter-turn up from the lowest possible position, and will often turn it off completely. Enhancement can always be added during post-production, but once it's been recorded into the signal, there's no way on earth to get rid of it. As with so many things, though, there's a trade-off. Adding enhancement in post also adds NOISE which shows up as visual electronic distortion that appears as excess grain in the picture. (The amount of extraneous noise in a picture relative to a pure picture signal is measured in DECIBELS or dBs and is called the SIGNAL TO NOISE RATIO.) (The higher the dB number the better the picture; 54 dB-59 dB is considered very good for cameras, 45 dB is good for VTRs.) Noise is very noticeable when copying ½-inch or ¾-inch tapes. Each successive generation gets noisier and shows more graininess. Probably the best rule of thumb is to add enhancement at the camera until you can just begin to see its effect, and then turn it back down very slightly.

When mastering on cassette, there is a device called "The Image System" (TM) offered by **Faroudja Industries** that can improve picture quality. It works by pre-processing the video prior to recording. During playback, the system corrects several aspects of the signal, improving detail, and reducing noise, ringing, and chroma problems.

Another important camera selling feature is the ability to boost gain. This permits an increase in the camera's effective sensitivity, and some of the better cameras on the market can boost gain as much as 18 dB, which is equal to three extra lens stops (eight times the sensitivity). At the state of the art in 1982, this translated to a minimum illumination specification with 18 dB boost of about 2 footcandles, which is enough to make one's mouth water at the prospects. There is, however, another trade-off.

Depending on the manufacturer's design, the trade-off comes as either increased noise in the picture, or as lowered resolution. Since noise appears mainly as high-frequency information, a filter on the high frequencies can reduce

noise at the expense of ultimate resolution. In balance, my own feeling is that this latter approach is preferable to increased noise.

The best solution is to avoid boosting gain by doing a proper job of lighting in the first place. Aside from scenes such as very wide nighttime exterior shots (as for establishing shots), boosting gain is the lazy way out.

When you get right down to it, the pictures you bring back from a shoot are your stock in trade, and good pictures are always better than bad pictures. Despite all the claims of the manufacturers about how easy their cameras are to use, and what perfect pictures they produce under almost any conditions, it's virtually impossible to produce really excellent results without paying close and careful attention to engineering details.

Earlier, I mentioned the technique of using the auto iris to find levels in the absence of a waveform monitor. I consider this to be a last alternative. Going into the field without a waveform monitor is not a wise practice. In the studio there is no excuse. There are battery-operated units available, and they can more than pay for themselves in terms of improved results. If it's totally impossible to take one along, then the best alternative is to know the camera's characteristics so well that the waveform monitor becomes all but redundant. There is always some sort of level indicator in the viewfinder of the portable cameras and some means of adjusting its threshold level. Most of the better cameras use a system known as ZEBRA, which superimposes a striped pattern over areas of the picture that are brighter than the THRESHOLD LEVEL, which is nominally set at 100 units. This is the most important information you need, since it's generally more damaging to record too high a level than too low a level. A viewfinder level indicator can come close to approximating some of the information a waveform monitor provides.

Using Monitors—WAVEFORM, VECTOR DISPLAY, and PICTURE

The video levels should be adjusted so that PEAK WHITES (the brightest parts of the picture) normally do not exceed 100 units on the

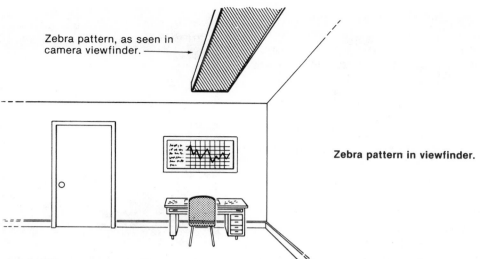

Zebra pattern, as seen in camera viewfinder.

Zebra pattern in viewfinder.

waveform monitor. There are occasions where you may take it higher, but this may cause CLIPPING (the cutting off of any part of the signal that exceeds 100 units) of the HIGH-LIGHTS at some point later down the line. Clipping will remove all detail within the highlights, and the results you obtain will depend on how cleanly your camera and/or VTR accomplish the clipping. Most of the better cameras have an adjustable clip level, whereas most VTRs do not. Some cameras tend to add color impurities in clipped areas, partially a function of the ENCODER (the circuit that takes the three color signals and encodes them into NTSC color). Others produce a clean white clip with smooth edges. In general, if clipping is necessary, it's better to do it purposely in the camera rather than to let it happen on its own later on.

Furthermore, CHROMA (color) levels may, in highly SATURATED (colorful) areas, extend considerably higher than the LUMINANCE (black & white) signal. In such cases, it is permissible to run chroma a bit higher than 100 units, but not much higher. I try to keep all elements of the signal below 105 units, and under no circumstances over 110 units as displayed on the waveform monitor.

Something that requires some discipline is to *always* record COLORBARS—preferably at the beginning of each tape. While many people seem to think that these BARS are for adjusting monitors during viewing, this is not their main purpose. COLORBARS (and an audio test tone) are the references by which the playback video and audio levels will be set up prior to

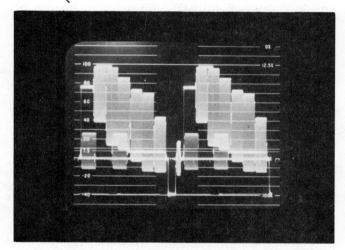

Waveform monitor display of colorbars at "flat" setting.

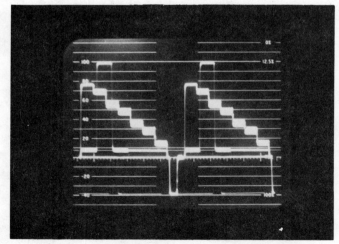

Waveform display of colorbars at IEEE rolloff setting (with chroma removed).

153

editing. They are the only way to get consistent results during post-production and duplication. Without them, finding the proper playback levels, chroma level, etc., becomes a matter of guesswork.

Also, the use of a VECTOR SCOPE will help assure that the correct chroma information is coming out of the camera. A VECTOR SCOPE displays a graphic representation of the colorbar signal, and is a useful engineering tool. It shows both the CHROMA LEVEL (how much color is mixed in with the luminance signal) and the color phasing with reference to a master SYNC GENERATOR or another video source. For instance, it is very important for matching the COLOR PHASE of two or more cameras during multi camera shooting, or of multiple playback sources during editing. We are encroaching now on some rather deep engineering, and could easily take time out to do another book on the nature, care, and feeding of video signals. For those who wish to delve deeper, the books published by **Tektronix** that you'll find listed in the bibliography provide an excellent source of information on the subject.

For practical purposes, and in single-camera shooting situations, the WAVEFORM MONITOR is by far the handiest engineering tool available. The best of these are the Tektronix units, of which the **Model 528** is the most popular, being small, lightweight, and versatile. A very similar unit is offered by **Lenco,** and

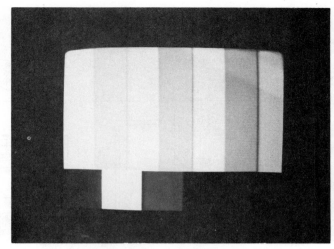

Colorbars as seen on program monitor.

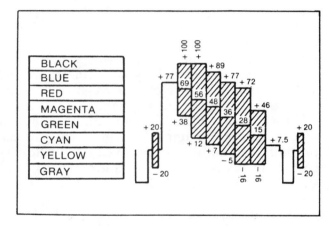

Colorbars and oscilloscope display.

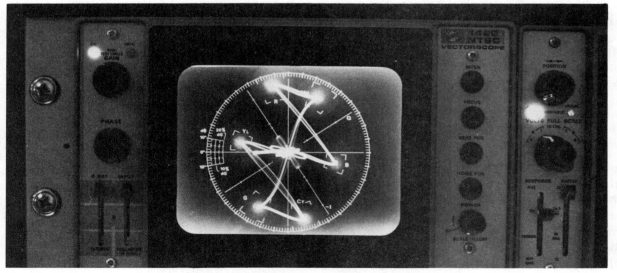

NTSC Vectorscope display.

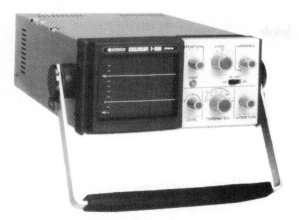

Hitachi portable oscilloscope.

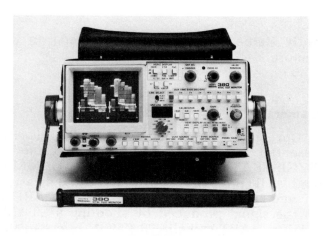

Tektronix 380 NTSC Test Monitor (combination waveform monitor/ vectorscope and oscilloscope).

Hitachi offers a battery-powered oscilloscope that can also function as a waveform monitor. Another alternative at a very reasonable cost is a unit called **The Tweaker,** offered by **Comprehensive Video Supply.** This little box uses any standard monitor to provide both a WAVEFORM SAMPLE (not a full waveform display, but one close enough to be useful) along with a PULSE CROSS DISPLAY. This latter is a special display usually built into higher-level monitors that permits the vertical and horizontal sync pulses to be seen, and is very useful for adjusting SKEW (tape tension) during tape playback. At roughly $500, the Tweaker serves as an excellent "poor man's waveform monitor" as opposed to the $1500 to $5000 cost of a real waveform monitor.

Some common misconceptions regarding PICTURE MONITORS can cause problems. Most color monitors are designed to simply show you a picture, and not to act as references for setting color. In a studio control room, a reference color monitor can be used for this purpose, but only if it has been properly calibrated ahead of time by an engineer and you're familiar with its particular characteristics. A proper reference monitor uses a shadow-mask design with a screen composed of phosphor dots rather than the stripes used by some monitors. This allows the monitor to show picture abberations that are hidden by stripe-phosphor designs. Examples would include units manufactured by **Conrac, Barco, Tektronix, Ikegami,** and others. At this level, the prices run in the $4000-$7000 range, depending on screen size. In field operations where ambient light and its color temperature

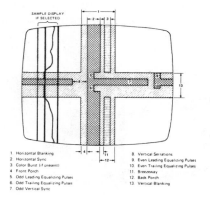

1. Horizontal Blanking
2. Horizontal Sync
3. Color Burst (if present)
4. Front Porch
5. Odd Leading Equalizing Pulses
6. Odd Trailing Equalizing Pulses
7. Odd Vertical Sync
8. Vertical Serrations
9. Even Leading Equalizing Pulses
10. Even Trailing Equalizing Pulses
11. Breezeway
12. Back Porch
13. Vertical Blanking

Pulse cross display

The Tweaker™

often change, it's far more dangerous to use a monitor as any kind of reference other than for focus and framing. It's much better to use a waveform monitor and vectorscope.

The small, battery operated color monitors that many people take into the field can cause real trouble if used as a color reference. DON'T TRUST THEM! They were not designed as color references, and if you set the camera to the monitor, you may be courting disaster.

As much as this may shake your faith, a TRINITRON TUBE, as found in all Sony monitors and receivers and in many other brands that buy tubes from Sony, is just fine for looking at pictures, but is not the best reference unit. Again, for color, a shadow mask design is best, and for stability checks of tape playback, the *least* stable monitor you can find will tell you more about your results. Virtually all units using the Trinitron tube are inher-

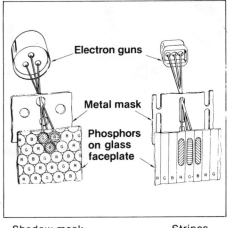

Color monitor picture tubes.

Shadow mask   Stripes

ently stable, and will mask problems in the picture.

Camera Setup

During the setup before taping begins, it's essential to check and adjust the camera's REGISTRATION, and to set BLACK, GAMMA, and WHITE LEVELS. (GAMMA is the measure of mid-range levels, defining the LINEARITY of the signal produced by shooting a STAIR-STEP CHART.) REGISTRATION refers to the alignment together of the red, blue, and green images produced by a 3-tube camera. If the images are not perfectly overlaid on each other, the camera's picture will show red, green, or blue fringes around the objects and will appear to lack clarity. Registration is not a concern with single tube cameras because they

Barco studio monitors.

Sony studio monitors.

JVC portable field monitor.

Various monitors.

have only one tube. Also, cameras in the under $3000 price range generally do not need much or any adjusting other than White Balancing.

Consult the camera manual for proper set-up instructions *only if you feel confident to do this,* or consult an engineer or someone who is very familiar with the camera. Otherwise you risk seriously misadjusting the camera, and it will take a good engineer to realign it. This can be time consuming and *expensive.*

WHITE BALANCE is also set, and on cameras that don't do so automatically, BLACK BALANCE should be set. Any change of light outdoors, including that produced by the sun's position as the day progresses, will necessitate

Stairstep chart

Camera-setup.

157

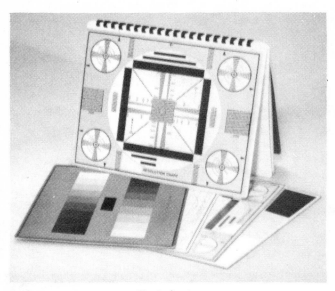

Test charts.

doing another white balance. Though some cameras have a WHITE BALANCE MEMORY that may be fairly reliable, the procedure for the newer cameras is so simple and quick that there is no real reason not to do so whenever appropriate.

The camera should be allowed to warm up for at least an hour prior to rolling tape, since even the best cameras are subject to some amount of drift as they heat up. Obviously, if you're working on battery power this may not be possible. It might be worthwhile in critical productions to hunt up some AC, if only to warm up the camera before going on battery power.

Also, though today's better cameras will hold REGISTRATION between the three tubes very well, it's a good practice to re-register after the camera has been moved or shut down for a while.

Camera Technical Considerations

The growth in the use of portable cameras in the past few years began to increase the incidence of an industry gremlin known as BLANKING WIDTH ERROR. BLANKING is the portion of the video signal during which the beam ends one line or field and makes a dash for the start of the next line or field. The Federal Communications Commission (FCC) has some rather rigid ideas about how wide the horizontal and vertical blanking intervals should be. (Actually, the measurement is one of time, but it's spoken of as width since the measurement is usually made on a waveform monitor where the pulses are viewed and measured in terms of their width on the display.) A fair number of tapes were rejected for OUT-OF-SPEC (did not meet technical standards)

Engineer setting up portable camera on location prior to shooting.

blanking before the FCC relaxed the rule slightly for a grace period during which the manufacturers and engineers could grapple with the problem.

Simply put, the horizontal blanking width should not exceed 11.4 microseconds, and vertical blanking should not exceed 21 lines. In practice, it's good to set for perhaps 10.5 microseconds for the horizontal SPEC (specification), to allow for abberations and growth further down the line. A 21-line vertical spec is workable for mastering, but keep in mind that in both specs, it's easier to enlarge blanking than it is to shrink it once the original material has been shot. Although these specs are important mainly for material that will be broadcast, and are not nearly as critical for other uses, it's still a good practice to adhere to BROADCAST SPECS at all times, as a matter of habit.

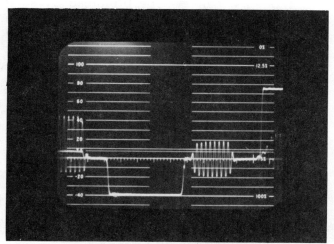

The horizontal blanking interval can be measured using a waveform monitor.

VTR Considerations

With regard to VTRs, the procedures are fairly simple. The heads should be carefully cleaned at the start of each day's production, using head cleaner and chamois cleaning patches or **Tex-wipes.** Actually, if time permits, it's not a bad idea to clean them between reels. The cleaning cassettes that are available for various formats are designed for emergency use only, and should be used very sparingly. They are abrasive and will reduce head life considerably. In very critical productions,

when the highest possible standards are sought or where there is no second chance, it may be worthwhile to use PRE-EVALUATED TAPE, or make a second recording on a backup VTR. Pre-evaluated tape can be purchased from numerous sources, and is accompanied by a test report listing number of dropouts per minute, edge damage, and CALENDARING (uniformity of width) data. It is possible to evaluate tape yourself, but if you don't have a TAPE EVALUATOR (a machine that performs this task) this means recording a signal such as bars on the entire tape, and having someone watch it for problems all the way through. Since the very act of playing it to check it can create tape problems—this is a questionable approach. Tape evaluators can be purchased from a number of companies such as **Chyron, Recortec,** and **Tentel.** (See Manufacturers' Addresses, *Appendix E.*)

Although you can, of course, record over a previously recorded tape, all tape that is being recycled for production should be BULK ERASED (completely erased at one time) prior to use. Again, in critical applications, recycled tape offers dubious (and often false) economy.

Other Technical Considerations

There are thousands of incidentals involved in engineering practices—far too many to fully list here, even if I knew them all, which I don't. Here are a few to consider, however, picked basically at random:

- In running cables, it is important to keep power cables away from audio and video cables. The latter can pick up hum by induction from power cables that cannot be later removed. If it is necessary to cross video or audio cables with power cables, doing so at a 90-degree angle will reduce the chances of picking up hum.

- Recording SMPTE TIME CODE (electronic frame indexing code) in the field is a technique that requires some forethought. Aside from operational considerations that relate to planning for the edit when mastering on cassette, it might be better to record the SMPTE code after the original taping, prior to post. The reason is that the code can bleed through to the other channel, and once in the audio, it's

159

Recortec tape evaluator.

Proper coiling of cables.

very difficult to filter out. This is not the case with the professional or "broadcast" ¾-inch cassette formats which provide a separate channel for time code.

- If you're borrowing power on location, make sure you're not on the same circuit as appliances or equipment that can cause voltage drops as they turn on or off, and which can put spikes on the power line. A voltage regulator can help, and is a good idea in any event. Also, watch out for hum and interference when using dimmers on your lights. Some dimmer designs produce disastrous results when used around video equipment.

- One thing that's hard to avoid in certain circumstances is an effect known as MICROPHONICS. This appears most often when shooting near a loud source of sound, such as in shooting a rock band, though it can also be produced by such things as the hum of the SERVO (zoom motor) of the lens. It results from the mesh inside the camera tubes vibrating at a resonant frequency. This creates HORIZONTAL HUM BARS (horizontal lines that will run through the picture). If they're caused by loud sounds, BLIMPING the camera (covering it with a sound-deadening shroud) may help, but in some cases all you can do is grin and bear it, or move the cameras away from the source of the sound. Cameras with ⅔-inch tubes are less susceptible to this problem, as the

Be prepared for on-location repairs.

160

mesh is smaller than in the bigger tube sizes, and the resonant frequencies are higher.

As I mentioned, these are merely a few examples of the kinds of things one must take into account during production. Before moving on, we should mention one other technique that is valuable in any area of production, but especially in engineering matters. It's so valuable, in fact, that we'll add it to the list:

McQ's RULE NO. 5: Test and double check *EVERYTHING* ahead of time, and then check it again.

Before you roll tape on your masterpiece, make a short test recording that includes shots from all cameras (in multicamera situations) and sound from all microphones; in other words, test the entire system. Then play back the test recording. Once you've seen that playback, you can begin recording with a relatively high level of confidence that you'll actually be getting what you think you are.

CHAPTER 11

Horror Stories

The production was a major corporate communications program—the taping of a management seminar that would be distributed to approximately 26,000 mid-level managers of a major utility to explain the massive reorganization that would be affecting the entire company. It was a two-camera shoot lasting three days, with live switching to a 1-inch master, backed up with alternate shots going to a 3/4-inch cassette. The material would later be edited into a five-part, 2½-hour program for distribution that would be accompanied by study guides and other support material. It was an important production, with most of the company's top brass, from the chairman of the board down to assistant vice presidents,

appearing as speakers. It was being shot before a live audience of mid-level managers, and there would be no second chance in the event something went wrong.

The seminar was being held in a hotel, and our "control room" had been set up in a meeting room across the hall from the main seminar room.

The first day of shooting went very smoothly, and we got a good six hours of tape. On the second day, we had gone through two reels on the 1-inch. (The cassette VTR went on-line during the 1-inch reel changes, which we tried to schedule for times when tapes were being played back for the seminar—these we could

Cameraman shooting cutaways of audience during introductory remarks.

Control room set up for seminar training.

edit directly into our program.) Reel three was threaded up very quickly, and we rolled tape just as the lights in the seminar room came back up and an executive vice president resumed his presentation. I was at my desk in front of the monitors, calling the shots to the cameras and to the T.D. (Technical Director) next to me.

About 15 minutes in, I noticed the T.D. leaning over and listening to the portable 1-inch VTR. Keeping one eye on the monitors, I asked him what was happening. He replied that something sounded wrong. I took over the switcher as he opened the lid of the deck. He was right—something was wrong. It turned out that in hurriedly threading the deck, he had missed a tension arm, and as the tension changed with the amount of tape on the reel, the "odd" noise had grown consistently louder, until finally he had noticed it. It was time for a snap decision.

163

The director checking the errant VTR during the setup day.

We switched the program feed to the cassette unit, and I had him roll back a short way on the 1-inch to check playback tension error on a pulse-cross display and the waveform monitor. The SKEW ERROR (tape tension) shifted considerably on the monitor, but, in both our judgments, was possibly within the reach of a TIME BASE CORRECTOR's ability to compensate. We decided we could salvage, so we rethreaded the machine (correctly this time), rolled into blank tape, and put the 1-inch back on-line. Then we crossed our fingers.

That night we went to the production facility's edit control room and played the tape on the "A" edit playback VTR, which we knew from experience was a bit more forgiving. It didn't come even close to tracking properly. At first look, it appeared we were sunk.

Where there's determination and creative engineering, though, one doesn't give up easily, and we came up with an idea that might possibly work.

We brought the portable VTR into the control room, and duplicated the misthreading as had occurred in the field. The signal was fed through the TBC (Time Base Corrector), and then to a mastering 1-inch VTR. Sure enough, the tension was the same as during recording, and the submaster was recorded cleanly.

When we reached the point at which the error had been found and corrected, we again rethreaded the machine, and continued the dub. The total amount of tape lost from the submaster was about two minutes, and we had cassette backup for that. It turned out that the section lost was not required for the final edit, and to this day (unless they read this and recognize themselves) the client never knew the brief panic we felt in the control room that day. The program came out very well, and ended up testing out with some of the highest results the company had ever achieved.

Three main factors saved what could have been a disastrous situation in this instance: The first was that everybody reacted calmly, and resisted the temptation to tell the client we had to start over—a move that would have created tremendous problems. We still had that option open, of course, and might have ended up using it, but by deferring that decision, we were able to evaluate our position, and come up with a solution.

The second was the cassette backup. Since there is no way ever to be absolutely certain that nothing will go wrong with a master VTR of any format, the use of a backup gave us a major element of protection against just this sort of occurrence. Though the quality would have suffered slightly, with very careful signal processing during transfer to 1-inch, we could

164

intercut material. In fact, there was one segment of importance that did occur during a 1-inch tape change, and the cassette material was used in this manner for about three minutes in the final edited version. By making the switch to cassette at a camera cut, the difference in quality was so slight that it would take an experienced eye knowing what to look for, to see the difference.

The third factor is the excellent quality and capabilities of the 1-inch Type-C format. Its generational loss is such that the SUB-MASTER (copy) made from the troubled tape was nearly indistinguishable from the original.

Ideally, we would have had a second 1-inch machine for backup, and we had suggested this to the client. Their decision to rely on a ¾-inch cassette backup was based on economics, as the additional 1-inch and nearly 20 additional reels of master tape would have added considerably to the budget. That sort of decision is always subjective, but the presence of at least the cassette backup gave us the safety factor we needed, and allowed us to make our decision in a rational state of mind, rather than in total panic.

*   *   *

It was late in 1977 when we were approached by the host of a local talk show and his new-found financial angel. They had been offered a chance to give the show a try-out on a local network affiliate, with the idea that if it took off, the network might be interested. Since his show had appeared only on a small UHF station, this was his chance at the big time. The deal was to produce a pilot independently, which would determine whether or not the show would be purchased. If it was, the show would continue to be produced independently. It was, therefore, a good opportunity for us, in that it could give us an on-going bread-and-butter account, as well as potentially establishing the first commercial network show to originate from San Francisco.

In meeting with the host and his backer, it was decided that to achieve some economy of scale, we'd produce not one, but three shows, putting us ahead if (when?) the show was picked up. There was just one hitch, which we learned during that first meeting: There was a deadline, and all three shows had to be IN THE CAN in thirteen days.

That night we burnt some midnight oil, and by about three in the morning, having worked out a rough production schedule, we decided it could be done, and we so reported back to the client the next morning. It was a decision that I now look back on with a mixture of whimsey and incredulity.

In accordance with the deal that had been struck, we were to provide both total production and creative services. This meant that in addition to lining up location, facilities, and crew, we were to come up with the basic format for the show, design the set, find the music, and book the talent. Since this was a network bid, the local folks who had appeared on the UHF version of the show wouldn't do. We needed real stars, and that meant that with three shows to do on one day, we'd be flying planeloads of talent up from Los Angeles. Our thirteen-day countdown began.

By day T-minus-eleven, our staff had more than quadrupled (not hard, since we keep it small between projects), and included a set designer, lighting designer, audio engineer, camera crew, and several others, including a number of experienced P.A.s (Production Assistants). After examining a number of alternatives, a theatre was chosen as the location. Unfortunately, on the day of taping, a stage show had been scheduled for that night. This meant we'd have to be out—totally clear of the place—by no later than 6:00 PM. Again, though we knew it would be tight, we decided it could be done.

A remote quad production truck was contracted with three studio cameras and one hand-held unit. The final crew was assembled and briefed. While this was happening, we burned up the telephone lines between San Francisco and Los Angeles locating talent. Also, a P.A. was assigned the full-time job of scaring up an audience. Complicating both of these operations was the fact that due to circumstances beyond our control, the taping day would be on a Wednesday, the day before Thanksgiving!

Each of the three shows to be shot that day would feature a rock band. In order to simplify and speed up the otherwise tedious and time-consuming setup procedure, it was decided to have each band go into a recording studio and pretape their music, which would be played back during the show, with them singing live. The one band that was on the road and wouldn't hit town until the day before taping would do a total LIP-SYNC (mime their singing in sync with a playback of their piece).

Each of those thirteen days began at 8:00 AM, and invariably lasted until at least two in the morning. By the time the big day arrived, everything appeared to be in place. The stars had been scheduled to arrive in waves, about two hours before they went on, and a flotilla of limos was standing by to shuttle them back and forth from the airport.

At seven in the morning, we arrived at the theatre and began to set up. Since we could not gain access the day before, we had to set up, shoot our three one-hour shows, and strike—all in eleven hours. The shows were to be shot "live on tape," with no stops or retakes, and we planned to start taping at noon, with a half-hour between shows. This would have us finished by 4:30, in time to strike and clear the theatre. This is how it went:

11:00 AM. Cameras ready, host holding court in makeup, first crisis strikes. One of the guests—scheduled for show number one—has taken ill, and will not be showing up. Quick reshuffle, move major guest from show three to show one, bring in one of our back-up local acts and plug him into show three. First crisis taken care of.

11:30. Hand-held camera develops connector problems—reliability in question. Apply liberal amounts of gaffer's tape to connector, and hope for the best.

12:00. Flight delayed—two guests for first show only now arriving. Rush through makeup. Audience thin—only about 175 people in a theatre that seats 2500. Producer has them all sit together at the front, and instructs them to "clap fast and loud," to sound like there are more people than there actually are.

12:30. Band setup still under way. Some concern as to whether lead singer is drinking, or is he always that way? Lights only now getting final tweaks, and looking good. Tape is racked up. I retreat to the director's position in the truck, and stay in touch with producer by

walkie-talkie. He says we'll be ready to roll in a few minutes.

12:55. I tell engineer to roll tape in bars, and start final countdown. Host is in position for entrance down aisle, music is ready to go, A.D. has his hand on the timer. We go to black, I issue music cue, music starts, fade up on audience, bring up logo, cue announce, and we're on! The hand-held is shooting the host's entrance down the aisle. As he's about half way down, the connector on the hand-held gives up, and picture goes dead. Cut to camera two—we'll cover it with audience or logo or something—worry about it later. Lost about a second's worth of video. Show start is logged at *12:58.*

2 minutes into show. Intro has gone well, cue music for fade to first commercial slug, bring up logo, fade to black. P.L. (Program Line—crew intercom) full of shouted questions, instructions and cues, connector seems to be OK now, time is good, first guest ready at entrance. Initial adrenalin lowering, settling in for next hour.

5 minutes in. First guest on, doing very well. Second guest ready in green room, equipment running smoothly.

14 minutes in. Second guest comes out, takes seat. Despite having been reminded three times, forgets to take mike from arm of chair and clip it on. Brief panic. Floor director jumps up and walks toward guest—cut comes too late, he's on tape. (Saw the same thing happen on Snyder two days before—don't feel so bad.)

23 minutes in. Band is on. Very popular punk rock band—terrible, raunchy, but very tight act. The P.L. is now full of sarcastic remarks. Camera three wonders how little old ladies in audience, bused in from rest home, are taking it (turns out they loved it).

47 minutes in. Guests three and four are on—turns out camera one, the one for guest number four, can't get a good shot from position. We pay for lack of setup and rehearsal. Have to use the hand-held—even braced on edge of stage, shots not awfully steady. Must get a tripod for shows two and three. Band goes on next—where is lead singer? He shows up 15 seconds before they're to go on for second set.

58 minutes in. Host finally sees cue to thank guests and starts to wrap. Takes extra 20 seconds—have to squeeze credits. Music up, roll credits, last credit as second hand approaches 12—fade to black on the button. The first show's finished! Whoops and yells on the P.L., ask tape operator to roll back and check TAIL (end of tape). Signal STUCK (was recorded), tape's OK. I'm going off P.L.—give crew ten minutes, then be back. Despite problems, show looks pretty good, think problems can be fixed, feeling very relieved.

Back in the theatre, though, more crises. Two more stars are missing, and we reshuffle schedule. Even bigger trouble, though. One of the performing union representatives shows up and informs us we're not cleared. Threatens to halt the taping. Show him letter of clearance from union head—he won't believe it (does he think it's a forgery?). Union head is on vacation. Frantic phone calls—takes a half hour to locate him and have him call off his lackey. That problem solved. Famous authoress scheduled for next show has been hitting the booze heavily, is now all but plastered. We have P.A. (Production Assistant) keep an eye on her, and discuss locking up the liquor (was probably a bad idea anyway). Two other guests for that show (bless their hearts) offer to help sober her up. In confusion, never do get the tripod for hand-held—cameraman will get a real workout that day.

The rest of the day was what could only be described as "controlled pandemonium," but somehow we got our three shows on tape. We finished the last show at 5:28—nearly a full hour behind schedule. We then performed what I'm sure was the fastest strike in history, clearing the entire theatre of any trace of our presence in 29 minutes. We were out with only three minutes to spare.

The crew assembled that night to watch cassettes of the shows, and all in all, we were very pleased. Just about everything that could go wrong did, proving beyond a doubt that Murphy's Law had by no means been repealed. The problems I've detailed above were actually just a few of the things that happened.

Looking back, it was probably insane to try to do what we did, but somehow we managed to get three shows on tape that came out better

A hasty production meeting between shows.

167

than many I've seen on the networks. There wasn't a single technical flaw that I haven't seen many times on other shows, and I was very proud of the staff and the crew. They performed some virtual miracles.

The upshot—not to leave you hanging—is that the affiliate looked at the shows, and felt that for a pilot, there were too many flaws. They said they did like the concept, the talent, and the overall production, and that if we could come up with a bit more polished production, they thought we'd have a deal. The first three shows could then be aired at a later date, once the show was established.

Thirty days later—this time after considerably more preparation—we shot four new shows. Our second taping included a full day of setup and rehearsal in a different and much better theatre, a much more elaborate custom-designed set, a live house band instead of pre-recorded theme music, and a turn-away crowd of more than 900 in the audience. To my mind, and almost everyone else's who's seen the tapes, they were every bit as good—if not better—than most of the stuff that comes down the network lines. The guests were better yet, the bands included some top name groups, and the production itself went down very smoothly, and almost on schedule. Everything went as close to the way it should as can possibly be expected, and the shows themselves were fine—with one exception—the one thing I've failed to mention up till now, and the thing that kept the show from selling.

There were good reasons the host had been relegated to the fringes of UHF television. He simply didn't know how to handle himself on camera. It was less apparent when he was in his element, but as the production values of the show around him reached top-quality levels, he increasingly stuck out like a sore thumb. He couldn't control the show. One of our guests—a well-known comedian—virtually took over one entire show, unfortunately doing a better job than our host. This actually happened a couple of times. The host was a nice enough fellow in person, and we had all hoped he would be able to rise to the occasion, but in the end he was simply out of his depth.

The local affiliate finally looked at the new shows and said they thought they looked good,

and that they'd show them to the New York people who were coming in that week. As well as we were able to reconstruct what happened, the New York brass took one look at the host and said, "You've got to be kidding!" and that was that.

It was a marvelous experience, a hell of a lot of fun, and we got some excellent tape that suffers only from the central character. It's been suggested that the seven shows we have still sitting in the can could be syndicated, or that we could do well in the overseas market, but the momentum was lost, and we moved on to new projects. Quite a while later I spoke to the executive producer—the fellow who had put up the backing—and he still thought the shows might have some potential. To protect the names of the innocent (not to mention myself), I'll leave the name of the show unspoken. But if you ever tune in late some night and see a variety/talk show with great guests and production values, and a host that is so weird it looks like he's playing it for camp, it's likely that you're either seeing the results of our efforts . . . or an old, misplaced tape—one that got lost somewhere in the Twilight Zone.

*   *   *

Anyone who has been in the business of television for any length of time has a personal collection of "war stories." It's great fun swapping these, and hearing them serves to illustrate the fact that there is no end to the variety of things that can and do go wrong. A few examples follow.

Back in the early days of live television, a friend was working at a major midwestern station. One of the major auto manufacturers planned a spectacular commerical for their new model year, and a production crew from the station was sent to a nearby Air Force base to shoot the commercial. The big feature that year was the fins on the rear of the car, which were styled after the tail of a jet fighter. The script called for five of the new model cars to be shot while streaking down the runway, with a jet taking off behind them. The camera would be mounted on a separate car running next to the "hero" cars, and by means of camera angles, the cars would actually seem for a while to be out-accelerating the jet. Since the commercial would be transmitted live across the country, the entire operation was rehearsed quite a few times with the jet merely taxiing down the runway but not taking off. The rehearsals went off without a hitch. The fins on the cars were beautifully echoed by the tail of the plane, and the cars looked majestic.

Airtime approached, and everyone took their places and waited for cues. The director was in the truck as the network began the countdown for the switch-over to the feed from location. "3–2–1–GO!" came the signal, and viewers across the land were transported to the runway at the Air Force base. But where there were supposed to be five cars running side by side, there were only two. It turned out that the other three cars had run out of gas due to all the rehearsals, and nobody had thought to check their fuel gauges. "Never mind—we're on, so we'll go with two," came the direction. And the cars did indeed look beautiful, juxtaposed with the fighter. For the actual commercial, though, the pilot of the jet was to complete his take-off, so he did what he was supposed to do next, but which he had not done during the rehearsals: He turned on his afterburners. Now, if you've ever spent any time around an air base, you won't need to be told what a deafening boom afterburners create. A large part of the nation watched as the sound wave hit the camera and the tube in the camera (a large old type known as an IMAGE ORTHICON) cracked before their eyes. It almost looked as if their TV picture tubes had broken. The network quickly switched back to the program, leaving the crew to clean up, replace the tube, and explain in great detail to the powers that be just what had gone wrong and why it really wasn't anybody's fault.

Often these stories are funny, though sometimes only in retrospect. They can serve the purpose, however, of providing some vicarious experiences that may help the reader in future situations.

Another friend was once on location with a production company to shoot an episode for a new network television series. It was an extremely windy day, and in order to continue shooting, they had constructed a large windbreak out of two-by-fours and plywood. Two men were tending the windbreak, which was battened down with sandbags on its stand. They were getting ready to start striking, and had just one last shot to get. The Eclair film camera they were using was equipped with a 400-foot load, more than 350 feet of which had already been shot.

As my friend stood nearby, he looked over just in time to see a strong gust of wind lift the entire windbreak completely off the ground, flip it over on its top end, and bring it down directly on the Eclair, with an accuracy that could not have been better had it been aimed. The Eclair virtually exploded into a thousand pieces, with the film unspooling into pretty streamers that trailed out across the waterfront. It was one of those instances that seems to happen in slow-motion, and, in this case, resulted from the company's desire to save on expenses and skimp a bit on crew. That large a windbreak, just as is the case with a silk, can generate a tremendous amount of lift in winds as strong as we normally expect near the Bay. It should have been heavily secured, and tended by at least four large-sized men, but then, two is less expensive, right?

All this goes to underscore the point that no matter how much you anticipate, there will still be things that happen that cannot be predicted. You try your best to foresee potential problems, and, in doing so, can often prevent at least some of the more obvious ones. For those that happen anyway, the trick is to be able to quickly compensate—to come up with solutions that will allow you to continue with minimum delay.

And of course, as with anything, experience is the best armament. It comes on its own with time, but can be helped along some by talking with others in the industry, and by consulting with people who have been in similar situations before.

CHAPTER 12

Production Gestalt

Producing a television program, as we saw earlier, is much like running a military campaign. Plans must be laid out, forces marshalled, and progress tracked. It's less a series of events than it is a process, and here is where the word "gestalt" comes into play.

According to Webster's, the word is defined as "a structure or configuration of . . . phenomena so integrated as to constitute a functional unit with properties not derivable from its parts in summation." In other words, the parts interrelate and interact so completely that the whole becomes more than their sum. So it is with all the various areas of television production.

The producer's job entails all of the management activities that relate to production. He or she must keep in mind the logistics of the operation, and must coordinate all the various people and elements. He or she must mentally be everywhere at once.

The resources upon which the producer calls are a major factor in obtaining good results. If the producer makes use of experts in each of the individual fields, the chances of success improve dramatically, and the production is much more likely to run smoothly. On a large scale production, the use of specialists will permit the producer to concentrate on the more esoteric aspects of the production, such as dealing with clients, backers, networks, or what-have-you, and with the overall concept of the show. Whether the situation involves an in-house operation for a business or school, a production company developing programming, an independent producer hired for a single project, or a staff producer with full and established resources on which to draw, the responsibilities of the job will be similar.

There is, however, no distinct definition for the functions of producer. Each individual will develop a personal approach, which must often be determined according to the particular circumstances or needs of the production.

Producers working on a smaller scale are often faced with meager resources, and, at the smallest scale, may be required to give a solo performance. In such cases, it is critically important to develop outside resources, which may be nothing more than a list of people who can be called for the purpose of picking their brains. In general, the people in the industry are usually more than willing to share knowledge and information—there's simply too much involved for any one person to be able to know it all. The interchange of ideas and techniques benefits everybody who participates, helping each one to grow in abilities and experience.

The professional associations also can offer substantial assistance. Organizations such as ITVA, IFPA, VPA, AICP, ATAS, SMPTE, and others (See Glossary) were founded with the overall goal of helping with the professional development of their members. The meetings most of them hold provide an opportunity to meet and talk with others in the field—many of whom have had experiences that can help with problems you may be facing. The meetings also serve to present new techniques, ideas, and equipment, and in general keep the membership up to date on developments in the industry.

The professional journals and trade publications are another major source of information, and there are few being published that are not well worth the subscription price. Actually, many of them are distributed free of charge to qualified subscribers. Essentially, a "qualified" subscriber is anyone who may at some point make equipment purchases, thus making themselves attractive to advertisers. A few examples of worthwhile publications would include *BROADCAST ENGINEERING, BROADCAST MANAGEMENT/ENGINEERING, EDUCATIONAL & INDUSTRIAL TELEVISION (EITV), MILLIMETER, ON LOCATION, VIDEO SYSTEMS, VIDEO USER, VIDEOGRAPHY,* and others listed in the bibliography.

It cannot be emphasized too strongly how important it is to solicit the exchange of ideas with staff and crew. The people with whom

you work are the foundation of any success you will have, and the only motive you really need to encourage their involvement is a healthy enlightened self-interest. They do offer alternative viewpoints and diversity of experience, beyond the fact that they're the ones who will do the actual work. Building a team feeling pays off in a multitude of ways, and is perhaps the single most important ingredient in successful production. Remember that they need your support as much as you need theirs.

Quality production requires discipline on everyone's part, but especially on the part of the producer. There will be times when a problem or choice offers several possible solutions, and in the hectic environment of production, it's often tempting to take the easiest route available. These are the times to stop for a moment, and sit back to evaluate just exactly what you're trying to accomplish: Is your goal a quick and painless production—getting the show in the can as swiftly and easily as possible?—or is it the production of a well-crafted program—one that meets the communications needs with style and grace?

The producer, as has already been stated, is the driving force behind the production. The standards the producer sets for the project provide the lead that everyone involved will follow. At all times the producer must try to keep three different viewpoints in mind, balancing them against each other, and against the factors of time and budget.

The first viewpoint is an objective one. All other considerations aside, what is the ideal way to create the most effective, entertaining or otherwise best program, in light of the goals that have been established?

The second viewpoint should be that of the intended audience. A basic part of the gestalt of production is to be able to put one's self in the place of the members of the audience—to envision their wants and perceptions—to meet them on their own ground. Good programming may require the audience to think, feel, or respond or good programming may simply entertain—it all depends on its purpose. But good programming never requires the audience to struggle to be able to understand, appreciate, or absorb the program's content. It's a technical matter, and it's a creative matter. In a real sense, a program is sold to the audience, and no one watching will be interested in shoddy merchandise.

The third viewpoint is a subjective one—that of the producer—and can only be considered once the first two have been taken into account. Once the first two have been recognized, the third then becomes very important. Again, the producer has the final responsibility for a show, and must be happy with the results. Questions of taste, technique, and execution will eventually depend on the producer's vision, and there are times when the producer must ultimately go with a hunch. It's simple: Good producers have good hunches. The process is intuitive, and in the end, there is only so much that can be taught—or learned. There is no dishonor in the fact that some people are simply not cut out to be producers, either for reasons of temperament or aptitude. The only dishonor comes with refusal to recognize this and defer to someone who is better equipped for the job. There are also those, of course, who were all but born for the role, and have a natural talent for it. Personally, I'd rather direct. My own special joy in production is on the creative and aesthetic side, and I'd just as soon leave producing to someone who loves to work on the details. When I do produce it's usually in combination with the role of director. I must admit that there is a pleasure in seeing the entire process through that I miss when someone else is in the producer's chair.

But at the same time, producing steals some energy from the concerns of directing, and I almost always rely on help with the production chores. I think many people in television are frustrated artists, who couldn't paint with oil and canvas, and have turned to painting with ideas and light instead.

CHAPTER 13

Directorial Techniques

Although directing fits within a subset of the various production tasks, it is in itself every bit as complex as the entire production process around it. It requires a mastery of light, optics, sound, composition, acting and actors, electronics, logistics, and psychology and is aided by an understanding of all the various other disciplines involved in production—and especially post-production.

There are a number of different types of directing, and many directors specialize in one particular area. For example, directing sports programs is substantially different from directing drama or comedy, as single-camera directing differs from multicamera work. Sometimes the differences are ones of style,

while in other instances they are merely ones of technology.

Although single-camera production is probably the most popular production technique, there are a considerable number of situations where a multicamera approach to production is the only logical choice. There are also many occasions which permit the techniques of both styles to be combined, and in any event they often overlap.

Television production shares many similarities with film production. The rules of picture composition are essentially the same for still photography, film, and TV. Good composition is always good composition, regardless of the

173

medium in use. At the same time, there are some special requirements that are forced on the television director by the nature of the TV screen itself. Referring back to the section on *Program Style (Chapter 1)*, specifically the small size of the screen and the effect it has on the viewer, along with some technical factors relating to color and the frame rate, both hinder and help the director working with video.

Again, the relatively small size of the normal television screen requires that the director concentrate on closeups more than would be the case when shooting a film for showing in a theatre. This is a limitation. On the other hand, the director working in video has more freedom of camera motion than when working in film. The much faster frame rate (effectively, the 60-per-second field rate, as opposed to film's rate of 24 frames/second) makes rapid pans and other camera movements much smoother in video than on film. Keep in mind that this is true only for *total* video production. Material that is shot on film and then transferred to tape will suffer the same flicker during fast pans that is common to all filmed material.

The differences between single and multi-camera direction should be mainly ones of dealing with the technology, all else being equal. The goal in either case is the same—to create a sequence of images that flows, and imparts the essential information and ideas. Good television need not necessarily be pretty, but it should be powerful, no matter what the content.

The production style for a program will be suggested by the nature of the program itself, or will be decided by the producer and director in the event the choice is open. Once chosen, it is time for the director to plan the approach. Each director has an individual approach and style, and what follows is a very personal and subjective description of my own process. Though I'm sure there are many who may have different ideas, I can say that the techniques described below have worked well for me.

Single Camera

Single camera production affords the director an opportunity that does not exist in multi-

camera situations: The director may choose to operate the camera personally. In the fields of theatrical film and most network entertainment production, this would be an exceedingly rare occurrence, but in television commercials, documentaries, some news, and in many non-broadcast instances, it is by no means uncommon.

I find that I end up doing my own camera work about half the time. There are several reasons for this, and mainly they have to do with my own style of directing.

Whenever possible, I go into a production with very distinct ideas as to how each scene will look. In going over the script ahead of time and breaking it down for shooting, I envision each scene and connect it to the body of the program in my mind's eye. Although there are cases where this is difficult, if not impossible, I generally have at least some idea of what the camera will see. Often, the situation I actu-

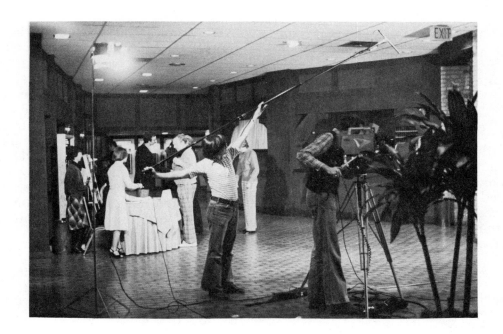

ally encounter ends up being different from what I had envisioned, but the fact that I had a definite intent makes it easier to incorporate changes without violating the concept or continuity. Locations, for example, may present a reality that differs from my expectations. This can, however, work in one's favor, since items or backgrounds will often provide a serendipitous element that could not (or would not) have been planned.

Another reason I like to run camera is that since I usually do have the shots I want firmly in mind, it saves time if I don't have to try to describe each shot to a cameraman. I'm known, I'm afraid, for being rather finicky, and have sometimes found myself restraining my impatience when the cameraman just wasn't getting what I wanted. Finally, on a completely personal level, I simply like getting behind a camera. It gives me a creative outlet of which I've never grown tired.

The instances where I have someone else run camera fall into two basic categories: Where special expertise is needed, such as with a Steadicam, a special crane, a snorkle lens, etc., and in those situations where it's more important that I be watching the monitor. This latter instance would be typified by commercials and productions where very precise camerawork is needed and I need to be watching a monitor. There is only so much one

can tell from a camera's viewfinder, and doing my own camerawork in these instances means stopping to look at each take before I am satisfied.

In setting up to shoot a scene, I go through what might be called a "litany of preparation." It's a mental checklist that makes efficient use of time and helps me get the shot I want.

The *first step* is to check the overall framing, and make sure the subject is displayed to best advantage as called for in the script. This check includes the subject's light, position within the frame, position relative to other picture elements, and continuity—the shot that precedes this one and the one that will follow. If camera movements will be involved, I check starting and ending positions for mechanical correctness first and then for the flow within the move. Depending on the shot, this may include having the talent run through lines and BLOCKING (planning and rehearsing their movements) and, in almost all cases, will involve the gaffer and sound man, who will TWEAK (fine tune) their equipment as we see what we're getting.

Step two repeats the basic process, this time looking at the background and secondary picture elements. Is everything that should show there, and everything that shouldn't show safely out of view? This includes things like booms and their shadows, far-distant objects

175

(the Golden Gate Bridge in a scene that's supposed to take place in Waukeegan), and the little details of the scene (is the colonial settler wearing a digital watch?).

Then comes *step three,* the final COMPOSITION. At this point I do the final framing, striving for an image that will be aesthetically attractive to the eye and that provides the results the shot is supposed to achieve. I should point out that the term "attractive to the eye" is used in a literal sense, and does not necessarily mean pleasing. What I mean by attractive is that it will draw the eye where I want it to go within the frame.

Composition

COMPOSITION is perhaps the most complex and, at the same time, the simplest aspect to making pictures. Done mechanically, it could take hours to properly compose a shot, and, even then, "properly" would still be a subjective judgment. Done by feel, by one who *has* a feeling for composition, it is an effortless and quick process of shot construction.

I find that composition comes easily to me. I was presented with my first camera at about age nine, and was reared in an environment that was conducive to artistic expression. It's something I've always felt was natural. I'm not all that certain it can be taught to someone who hasn't got a feeling for it. There have been a number of sources though from which I've learned some rules that make the processes easier, and the first of these was a little book put out by Eastman Kodak (available at any camera store) called *How to Make Good Pictures.* I have editions of this book dating back to 1936, which was already a 22nd edition. Interestingly enough, the basic suggestions they make haven't changed much over the years. In some ways, I like the early editions more, since photography was not a business of point-the-Instamatic, and the authors spent more time discussing what makes good composition. The newer editions, however, have reduced composition to some easily remembered rules, and these same rules can be found in virtually any textbook on photography, film, or video.

Another excellent reference book, aimed at filmmakers but generally applicable to television, is *The Five Cs of Cinematography.* These are: CAMERA ANGLE, COMPOSITION, CLOSEUPS, CONTINUITY, and CUTTING.

It would be easy to devote an entire book to the subject of composition, and many authors have done so. Herb Zettl's *Sight-Sound-Motion* is one of the basic bibles on which students of television are weaned, and many others that you'll find in the bibliography add to the general fund of knowledge. Although I'll defer to these for the most part, a brief review of a few of the basics of composition can be accommodated.

Pictures work best when they're dynamic, and making them so entails keeping their elements away from the static vertical and horizontal centers of the frame. The simplest way to do this is to divide the frame into thirds, both vertically and horizontally, and place the

main elements where the lines cross. It can also be taken a step further—the "rule of thirds" is a rough approximation of the ancient Greeks' concept of the golden proportion of three to five. They discovered and formalized this ratio, which is drawn from nature (as in the spiral of a conch or snail's shell), and that naturally pleases the eye. It was also a major contributory factor to the birth of their mathematics.

When placing the picture elements at these dynamic points in the frame, the action or subjects would normally WORK (move or direct *their* attention) towards the center. This includes LOOKING SPACE, in the case of a person, and the overall flow of dynamic forces. The best composition creates a triangular energy flow that draws the eye to and around three points, all of which lead back to the center of interest. If the lines do indeed lead back to the center of interest, the picture is reinforced, while if they lead away, the picture is weakened. In any event, placing the subject dead center in the frame creates a sense of stability and boredom, and unless that happens to be the effect you're after, it should be avoided.

It's also important to keep in mind that the eye is naturally attracted to the brightest area within the frame. Actors and other on-camera talent who are told not to wear white because it will cause "technical problems" often do so anyway. I've often suspected that this may be a subconscious attempt to assert their own importance relative to the technology. If you tell these people that they shouldn't wear white because it will lead the viewer's eye away from their face, they then have a positive reason to choose a darker-toned color instead of a negative admonition that gives them an opportunity for self-expressive rebellion.

Television is a two-dimensional medium, so any DEPTH in the picture is an illusion. The creation of an illusion of depth is aided by the use of planes within the image. Foreground and background, when used properly to offset and highlight the main subject, can heighten the illusion, and as we saw when discussing camera support, the use of camera movement—on a dolly, Steadicam, etc.—can also create a strong feeling of depth. Lighting is another major factor in creating a feeling of depth.

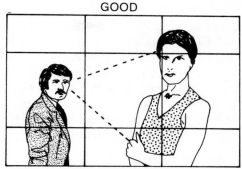

GOOD

POINTS OF INTEREST AT LINES OF INTERSECTION, TRIANGULAR FLOW OF ENERGY.

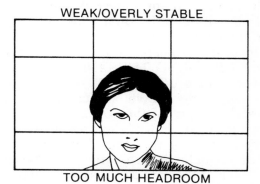

WEAK/OVERLY STABLE

TOO MUCH HEADROOM

GOOD

SUBJECT SLIGHTLY OFF-CENTER LOOKING INTO FRAME

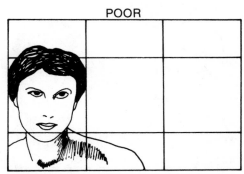

POOR

SUBJECT LACKS "LOOKING SPACE" OR "LEADING SPACE" IN THE CASE OF MOVEMENT.

Continuity

Composition must also take into account the factors of CONTINUITY. It should be obvious that if you have a character running from left to right in one scene, it will confuse the audience if you then cut to a second scene where the action is reversed. Continuity of motion must be kept in mind, and will be further discussed when we get to editing.

The task of keeping track of continuity is aided by the use of an imaginary line that runs along the axis of action. For instance, when shooting dialog between two people, the line would connect them and continue past them. When shooting individual closeups of each actor, the camera must stay on one side of this line in order to keep the continuity of action correct. CROSSING THE LINE, as it is called, will result in a confusion of screen direction. In the example shown subject A is looking towards the right of the screen, and subject B is looking to the left of the screen. As long as this continuity is maintained, the viewer has no trouble believing that they are talking to each other. If the camera crosses the line while shooting the closeups of subject B, however, that person will then appear to be looking towards the right of the screen also, and the continuity of screen direction will have been destroyed. This is also known as the 180 DEGREE RULE, since in such an instance there is a 180-degree arc in which the camera may move while maintaining proper screen continuity.

The illusion of depth can be created by creative use of camera angle and setting.

There is so much more involved in mastering the *Five Cs*, etc., that I'll stop here, and refer you back to other sources of information on that subject before we get in too far.

Single camera production, almost by definition, takes much longer than shooting the same program with multiple cameras. This is both an advantage and a disadvantage.

Using one camera to shoot each separate angle and REACTION SHOT (closeup of a person's reaction) permits one to craft each shot with careful attention to detail, but also means repeating the action over again for each angle, which can wear on both talent and crew.

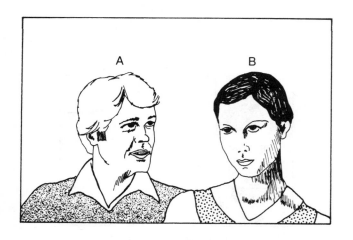

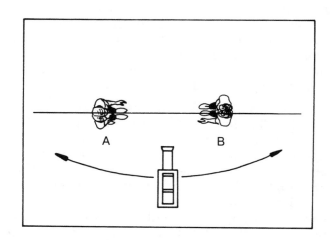

180° RULE

178

It also requires strict attention to action continuity—something that can seriously damage the flow or believability of a scene if it's not handled correctly. For example, if one of the characters ends a scene in the two-shot with his hand shielding his eyes, that action should be matched in any closeups or reaction shots. This is aided by rehearsal, although it's somewhat of a toss-up at times between blocking out every action specifically and striving for natural, unrehearsed movements. Somewhere in between, perhaps, is an area of compromise that will work best overall.

An excellent practice that helps keep track of continuity is the taking of stills at the beginning and end of each scene or shot. On larger productions, there will usually be one person on the set—the continuity person—who will be given a Polaroid® and assigned that specific job. This function can also be combined with that of script supervisor on the set, who will time scenes, make notes, feed lines, and keep track of continuity.

With the capability of videotape to instantly play back, it is always tempting to roll back to a scene and check for continuity. This becomes harder when shooting out of sequence, as is the case more often than not in single camera production. In any event, there is a danger involved in checking a scene. After checking a scene, the tape operator must take extreme care to roll past the last scene on tape, recording the subsequent scene in blank tape. It is all too easy, in the rush of production, to record over a previously recorded scene, and for that reason, I normally try to avoid this practice.

While it is a good practice to check each scene after it has been shot to make sure the scene STUCK (was recorded) to the tape, the best bet is to check just the tail end of the scene, allowing the tape to roll into blank tape before getting ready to record again. If the signal is good at the end of the scene, the chances are that the entire scene was good as well, at least technically. If a video head has clogged, hum has entered the signal, or the machine never went into record, these problems are likely to be evident at the end of the scene, and it won't be necessary to check the entire scene. The one thing that can't be assured in this manner is that there were no large tape DROPOUTS (patches of missing oxide) during the scene. The only way to check for dropouts on critical material is to play back the entire scene.

A trained and experienced tape operator will know these procedures, and will set the counter to zero at the start of each scene or take, permitting the tape to be rolled back if the director wants to see the entire scene. The dual timers provided on some recorders are very useful for this, allowing one timer to keep track of time from the start of the tape, with the other timing each scene.

Since the director may operate the camera in single-camera production, let's take a moment to examine some of the aesthetics of camera work.

Camera Techiques

The camera is the viewer's proxy on the scene, serving as the viewer's window on the action. The viewer, however, has no control over what he sees, and depends entirely on the people behind the camera for visual selection. The director decides *what* the viewer sees, and the camera person (who could be the director) is then responsible for creating the visual image.

Good camera work is normally smooth and even. The exceptions to this would include scenes—generally POINT OF VIEW (POV) shots—that require erratic movements to build tension or to heighten the realism as with a POV shot of a frightened character running for cover.

In operating the camera, it is necessary to analyze the scene with the limitations of the TV format in mind. There's a good reason why directors often carry a viewfinder with them—it allows the scene to be examined the way the camera will see it, divorcing all elements outside the frame.

Camera movements are perhaps the hardest element to master, especially with moving subjects, for here the rules of composition can become quite intricate. In essence, the process of composing is repeated for every frame of the scene. Ideally, any frame selected at random for study should present good composition, and be able to stand on its own. Many still photographers can translate their skills to film or TV camerawork as long as the scene is static, but run into trouble as soon as movement is involved. Part of the reason for this is that it is necessary to think slightly ahead of the movement, and LEAD the subject or action. If a character is to stand up, walk across a room, and sit down, the camera will first lead up to the standing position, starting the pan a bit before the tilt up is finished. The pan will then stop just a hair before the actor's move is complete, so that the actor moves into final position just after the camera has framed for it, completing the composition. This is, of course, a gross simplification of a rather complicated process, but serves to illustrate the concept.

With fully scripted and blocked scenes it's obviously easier to achieve smooth moves than in situations where the movement is impromptu. In the latter instances, the cameraman must learn to read body language and anticipate the talent's movements, taking care to prevent either lag behind the action or overshoot past the end of action. When such an error does occur, it's generally better to resist the temptation to immediately correct, and to combine the correction with another camera move that will mask the correction. A straightforward correction would act as a blunt visual admission that a mistake had been made. If, for instance, your pan overshoots slightly, the error can be hidden by waiting for a moment and then zooming in slightly while panning to reframe. If the combined movements are done smoothly, the end result will appear to be just what you had in mind all along. Helping this is the fact that the audience has no idea what the original intent was, and will often notice nothing wrong with a shot that broke the director's heart.

Each scene will usually be broken down into shots from several angles that will later be put together during the edit. Under normal circumstances, the various angles start with a MASTER SCENE that contains the entire scene from the primary angle or viewpoint. This serves as the reference scene, and all subsequent angles and shots will be matched to this master shot. In two-character dialog, the master scene may be a TWO-SHOT (showing two persons) favoring the principal character, with subsequent shots taken first for closeups of the star, and then for the other player's CLOSEUPS. Although the subsequent shots may run the entire length of the scene, this may not necessarily be the case—a lot depends on how loosely or tightly the script has been broken down.

Once the master scene and closeups have been shot, and if the schedule permits, there may be opportunities to look for some alternate shots. These are opportunities to try some unusual camera angles not originally planned that will afford some additional choices during

Camera movement (pan).

Master scene.

180

Two shot.

Close up.

Safety shot.

editing. This brings up an important point. Tape, being much less expensive per minute than film, makes it both possible and advisable to shoot until you're completely satisfied with a scene, and to spend some footage on safety shots and experimentation. A SAFETY SHOT is one that provides protection in the event that the originally-planned shot doesn't work the way it was supposed to. When in doubt as to whether a shot or angle will intercut correctly with other shots, it's well worthwhile to shoot an alternate that will provide a choice during editing. Considering the cost of going back out to totally reshoot a scene that had some minor, unnoticed, but eventually fatal, flaw, it's far cheaper to record an extra take or two at the time.

Returning to the subject of continuity, remember that in addition to action, screen movement and audio, exterior lighting will also play a part in continuity. As we saw in the section on lighting, such things as a day that varies between sunlight and overcast will present an additional set of continuity problems that must be taken into account. Furthermore, OUT-OF-SEQUENCE SHOOTING means that the changing light during the day must also be considered. If your master scene is shot in the morning and your closeups in the afternoon, the shadows and even the color balance could be noticeably different when the shots are cut together.

Keep in mind also that the camera's viewfinder rarely gives an accurate indication of what will be seen on the screen. Most viewfinders are UNDERSCANNED, and show more around the edges of the scene than will end up on the screen. This can be of help, in that the camera operator can see things entering the scene, but it also means that framing and composition will have to take this into account. It's a good idea, once the camera has been set up, to match and mark frame edges on the viewfinder against the program monitor, and to pay heed to SAFE ACTION AREAS (that part of the viewfinder picture that will actually be seen on the TV set).

Additional factors of continuity and shooting with the edit in mind will be covered as we get further into directorial techniques, so let's now move on to multicamera production.

181

Multicamera

Originally, television production techniques entailed the use of multiple cameras connected to a SWITCHER (a "visual mixer" that allows selection of cameras and other sources) with editing (cuts, dissolves, wipes, etc.) done ON THE FLY—that is, done live by switching in REAL TIME (as it happens) from one camera to another. This routine was established not because it was the best way to produce a program, but because in the early days of television it was the only way, without resorting to film.

Before the advent of videotape, television was strictly a live affair, and what happened in the studio was exactly what the viewer saw at home. When videotape was first introduced, editing technology was so primitive that shooting techniques changed very little. If a program required editing, it was shot on film, edited on film, and usually aired from film.

Even now that videotape editing is commonplace, there are times when the nature of a production dictates the use of multiple cameras and live switching. Examples would include studio interviews, music and variety shows, sports and news shows, and conferences and educational discussions, among others. The use of this technique in dramatic programs is basically limited to the daytime soaps and a few stage-style dramatic presentations.

The fundamental factor in directing a multiple-camera HOT SWITCHED (live switched) shoot is that the editing decisions are made on the spot and in real time, rather than in the relatively calm environment of post-production. While this places more pressure on the director, it also allows a spontaneity that's very hard to duplicate with single-camera techniques. From a more personal perspective, there is a feeling produced in live directing that is highly exhilarating.

Some of the problems inherent in single camera work simply aren't factors in multicamera production. Continuity of action, for instance, pretty much takes care of itself, although continuity of screen movement requires the same amount of care. The latter, however, is strongly influenced by camera positioning.

To keep the visual continuity working properly, the rules concerning "crossing the line" that were discussed earlier must be applied, just as for single-camera production. Again, an imaginary line is drawn along the center of action. If the action were to involve dialog between two characters, the line would be drawn between them, while in a scene involving a moving car, the line would run along the car's direction of movement. As long as all of the cameras stay on one side of the "line" at all times, the visual continuity will normally make sense. Crossing the line will result in a change of screen direction that will confuse the viewer.

In some ways, LIVE DIRECTION (a term that covers both LIVE-ON-TAPE and honest-to-goodness LIVE production) is easier, while in other ways it's harder. It's easier on actors

Multicamera shoot.

The control console in a small multicamera truck.

182

in general, for although they must know all of their lines, as opposed to biting off a chunk at a time, they can go through their entire performance, and often achieve a momentum that never has a chance to build in start/stop production. Live direction is obviously preferable when shooting in front of an audience. It keeps the flow of the program moving. It can be easier on the budget, too, because when you finish shooting, the show may be all but IN THE CAN (finished), while single-camera production is probably less than half done at the end of shooting. This also translates into a potentially shorter schedule.

Live directing can be hard on the director and crew since there is constant time pressure and few opportunities to correct errors. Lighting is more difficult, and the chances are that lighting will be somewhat compromised in order to give decent results at each camera. Of course this depends on the nature of the show. Drama, comedy, and interviews have totally different requirements than rock concerts or conferences.

Under these circumstances, the director no longer has the option of running camera, and must retire to the control room or truck to watch the monitors. Some directors will have a set of monitors set up on the studio floor in order to be near the action. Often this is done during rehearsal, with the actual taping then directed from back in the control room. The director, however, does have the option of doing his or her own switching.

In most situations it is better to have a technical director perform the actual switching, so that the director can concentrate on the monitors and the script. One exception here is when taping music performances, where the director can cut spontaneously, without having a lag from the time he calls a take to the time it actually gets taken. This is not a hard and fast rule, and there are times when the availability of a good TD and the nature of the performance in question make it more appropriate to retain the traditional configuration of having the TD do the switching and the director calling the shots.

If the program requires that effects such as keys or wipes be set up and used live within the show, a TD becomes imperative. If the director tries to do the switching, a lot can happen while he's setting up an effect, and the division of attention between the action, the cameras, and the switcher itself can be catastrophic.

The cameramen in a multicamera production are extensions of the director, and good ones are worth hanging on to. As the camera crew becomes accustomed to each other and to the director, the entire unit should begin to

The director talking with the floor director over the P.L. line.

183

```
     CAMERA 2        SHOT SHEET      #58-03    2/13/82

1 - MS HOST  -  through segment # 1

2 - MS HOST & GUEST  -  talk segment

3 - CU DANCER'S FACE  -  performance

4 - MS HOST  -  throw to break

5 - MS HOST  -  talk

6 - CU BOOK  (be ready!!!)

7 - MS HOST & GUEST

8 - WIDE - FULL SET  -  under credits
```

Shot sheet.

operate like a multilimbed creature, with the director obviously as the head. The style that develops is a team style that changes if any of the team members are replaced.

As with single-camera production, a multi-camera production may be fully scripted, with each camera move fully blocked out ahead of time and usually listed on a SHOT SHEET that is affixed to each of the cameras. It can also be loose, with the director shooting the show as it comes. The latter will require greater coordination, faster response time, and more overall skill on everyone's part than in a carefully rehearsed production. In these instances, there are certain things to keep in mind, and some techniques that can help smooth the process.

Problems To Watch for

Watch out for JUMP CUTS. These can result from cutting from one camera to another while both cameras are identically framed on the subject. Another example would be when shooting three people in an interview situation. If one camera has a two-shot of the person on the left and the one in the middle, and the other camera has a similarly framed two-shot of the person in the middle and the one on the right, cutting between the two cameras will cause the person seated in the middle to jump from one side of the screen to the other. These and other types of jump cuts jar the viewer and should be avoided. Preventing them is a matter of keeping track of the various cameras, and making sure that you have a variety of angles and scenes from which to select.

Often a cameraperson will spot an opportunity for a shot that the director can't see, and the means to handle this will be developed over time between the director and the crew. While it's good to encourage a certain amount of initiative, it's also important to remember that the cameraperson sees only his or her own shot, and will usually not have the overview of the sequence the director may be building. Discipline is of utmost importance, as once the director has lost control (a very dangerous situation), it's often very hard to regain it. Perhaps an example will help illustrate the point.

On a warm summer day in the mid-Seventies, we were taping an outdoor festival of dance, music, and various and sundry acts in an amphitheatre on Mt. Tamalpais in Marin County, California. It was a four-camera shoot, and the show itself was very loosely structured, with the result that we were pretty much "winging it" in terms of production technique. I was in the tape truck directing, and the cameras were spotted around the amphitheatre and stage. The sun was out, it was a beautiful day, and everyone was having a rather good time. As one of the livelier bands performed, the crowd was dancing in the seats, the aisles, and in front of the stage, and quite a few of the generally attractive women in the crowd divested themselves of some of their clothing. I had been giving minimal direction, since the crew and I had done a lot of music taping, and they knew what I would want. Most of my calls were simply to reframe, to avoid shot duplication.

One of the cameramen noticed the new developments, and when I freed him from a shot of the stage, swung over to give me what I guess would be called a COLOR SHOT, which I took. Unfortunately, I made the mistake of offering appreciative comment, and the next thing I knew I had four shots of naked women dancing across the monitors, and no shots of the stage to cut back to. I then made blunder number two: I said "Someone get me a shot of the stage, for Pete's sake!" Can you spot the mistake in this picture? You got it—everyone assumed I meant someone else, and it wasn't until I specified a camera that I got reluctant compliance and a shot of the group on stage we were supposed to be taping.

184

I feel I should note that this was not your normal, serious production, and the tape was for promotional use by the festival organizers. Their only complaint afterwards was that there wasn't more of the crowd and less of the band at that point.

Most productions that are shot multicamera style leave little or no room for this kind of spontaneity, and each shot is generally planned out ahead of time. Here the director will be more concerned with matters of the timing of cuts and with the overall timing of the show. The composition of each shot and the performances of the talent supposedly will have been worked out during rehearsal, and the actual taping may indeed be somewhat anticlimatic once it's under way.

The process of calling the shots to the camera crew can be a point of potential confusion. Although the crew may be good friends, it's still wise to call shots by camera number, both to avoid confusion caused by similar-sounding names (Larry/Mary), and to provide for others on P.L. who may not know the names. Also, it's better to start a call with the camera number—for example: "Camera 2, pull back to a two-shot," as opposed to "Pull back to a two shot, Camera 2," since in the latter example, other cameras may react before hearing the camera number. In actuality, the instructions should be as brief, clear, and concise as possible, and the above call, in it's entirety, would actually be something like: "2, gimme a two-shot . . . Take 2."

Something to stress with each of the camera crew is to make every move smoothly, even when their camera is not ON-LINE (being taken). Aside from rehearsed shows, there are times when a quick and even unforewarned cut may be necessary, and each cameraperson should be prepared to go on-line at any instant. For instance, if you're shooting a conference and a member of the audience suddenly blocks the view of the camera currently on-line, an instantaneous cut to another camera will be necessary.

Sometimes quick action is more important than smooth movement. In cases where you need a shot immediately, the instruction to the camera operator would be to BREAK for the shot, indicating that the normal rule of smooth movement is suspended and you want a different shot *now*. Since the cameraman will have to frame, zoom in, focus, and then compose the shot as called, quick action takes precedence over smooth movement.

This points out the importance of everyone sharing a clear understanding of the directions,

The control area of a multicamera set up on location in a theatre to tape a live performance.

185

and the necessity for standardizing the calls. Although every production team has its differences and special styles, experienced camera operators will be familiar with standard camera directions.

Multicamera production requires more time during setup than does single-camera production, but as mentioned earlier, when tape stops, it's possible to be finished with the show. This process requires coordination of more elements simultaneously, and is a lot like juggling. In the right circumstances, however, multicamera production offers certain creative advantages. Multicamera use is most common in the studio, but is by no means limited to that environment. The logistics of setting up a remote multicamera system on location can be truly mind-boggling, but it may be the most cost-effective way to go in cases where the taping of a "live" or spontaneous event is the task at hand.

There are many differences in technique between single and multicamera production, but the overall goals are the same: the creation of a smooth and interesting program. Although we normally think of multicamera production as being a live, real-time event, it is quite possible to use two or more cameras in film-style production also. We'll explore this later in *Production Methods and Costs*.

Shooting for the Edit

The most frustrating thing an editor can encounter is a lack of sufficient material for a show. Most often, all the scenes will be there, and what's missing is a single variation; a reaction shot or cutaway that could make all the difference in the outcome of the program. A CUTAWAY is a shot that can be used to cover an edit—especially a jump cut. It might be a closeup shot of an interviewee's hands emphasizing a point, a shot of the Eiffel Tower to use while editing a travelog, etc. In addition to providing cover for an edit, cutaways can also act as interesting visuals to help speed up the pacing of a program. Directors with extensive editing experience know this, and will shoot with the edit always in the back of their mind.

Interviews can be ruined by the lack of a cutaway to be used in covering a jump cut. All too often a cutaway ends up being used that

was not really appropriate and doesn't fit in but was the only one available, and consequently sticks out like a sore thumb. REACTION SHOTS—shots of the interviewer nodding at a statement—make excellent cutaways, as virtually all of the major news magazine programs demonstrate. Shoot various reactions when doing these—nodding, smiling, and simple attentive listening. Once the interview is done, you might also take the time to shoot the interviewer asking the questions again. The interviewee need not be present for this. If you plan to do this, make certain you take careful notes on the wording of the questions as they were asked originally, so that the questions match the responses.

If a mistake occurs, when shooting interviews or any other single-camera program that requires a straight-through presentation, and you decide to do a PICKUP shot (picking up at a point just before the mistake occurred, rather than starting over at the beginning), be sure to reframe the shot—either LOOSER (from further away), TIGHTER (closer), or from a different angle—so that when the edit is made it isn't a jump cut. Otherwise, you'll have to depend on a cutaway to cover the cut. For instance, if a performer blows a line while you're on a wide shot, and you decide to do a pickup, reframe to a closeup, and resume. This will permit a smooth edit to be made that will eliminate the error.

Each type of production seems to have its own set of common problems and requirements. In editing original material for documentary production, I've often noticed a tendency to cut shots shorter than they should be. I can only attribute this to some sort of strange time distortion—either the shot seemed longer during shooting than it really was, or it seems shorter during editing than reality proves. I suspect the former is more likely the case. In defense against this, I've developed the habit in this type of shooting of holding the shot for as long as it seems necessary, and then adding a fair amount of extra time, sometimes even doubling the length of the shot. Although it may only pay off one time in ten, it's much easier to take something out during editing than it is to try and figure out how to stretch material when there's not enough available.

We've examined at some length the importance of attention to continuity, and it's during the edit that this attention will pay off. In single camera dramatic production, it helps to imagine that there are multiple cameras on the set, each one positioned where the camera will be when closeups and reactions are shot. This allows the director to block the action so that it will flow properly once all the various elements are brought together.

The director must visualize not only each individual shot, but also the flow of the program in its entirety. Among the notes taken for each scene should be some comments on the pacing—the overall feel and speed of the scene—so that the scenes will cut together well. If, for instance, your principal character has been rushing up a flight of stairs in the previous scene on his way to handle an emergency, it would be silly if he then strolls into the room with a smile, perfectly calm and not breathing hard. In closeups, moods, and facial expressions must be duplicated in alternate shots. Professional talent can be of help here, since trained and experienced actors will automatically keep these factors in mind.

In documentary production, it is sometimes possible to have action or dialog repeated so that another angle can be shot, but often this is not possible. In such instances, the best procedure is to first cover the main action, person, or other point of interest as completely as possible. Then shoot as much cutaway material as possible to use in editing. Obviously, the nature of documentary videography encompasses a huge diversity of subjects and circumstances, making hard and fast rules impossible to establish.

On the technical side, always keep in mind that editing systems require a PREROLL time to allow tapes to LOCK UP prior to reaching the edit point. Since all VTRs require a certain amount of time after they are started before they reach a stable running speed, this preroll time gives them a chance to settle down and be running smoothly and synchronously by the time the edit point is reached. Though some systems may require as little as five seconds to lock, it is a good practice overall to allow at least *15 seconds* of preroll, and ideally *20.*

After 20 seconds the speed will be stable, SERVOS (internal speed controls) will be locked, and the "SPEED" call (meaning that the VTRs are ready) may be given with a comfortable safety margin.

Although it was mentioned during the discussion on engineering, always record at least a minute of colorbars and TEST TONE (audio tone at 0 dB or 100%) at the head of each tape. There are two reasons for doing this: a full minute of bars provides enough time to set up playback levels prior to editing, and it also gets you past the area of high DROPOUTS (oxide flaking off the tape) that is common at the head of tapes.

Any special effects such as graphics to be added during post should be allowed for when shooting. For example, if a speaker's name and title will be KEYED (words matted) over the video when he first appears, the opening shot should be framed so that the words won't appear over his mouth as he's talking.

Often there may be a choice between doing a special effect during original taping or in post-production. The decision comes down to balancing some factors: Doing it in the original taping may cost less, while doing it in post may be safer. An effect added in the original to save money that turns out wrong will end up being far more expensive in the long run, since it will require reshooting. There is, however, a way to have your cake and eat it, too. Shoot the scene two ways—one with and one without the effect in question. You may luck out and get away with the original effect, but you also have a backup in case it doesn't work out and must be redone.

The LOGGING of scenes is a matter of critical importance for those who wish to operate efficiently. TAPE LOGS are notes detailing the scene number, take number, starting and ending point (either by SMPTE code, tape timer, or by counter number), the duration, and notes on the director's initial feelings about the scene's usability and other general comments on the take. A take that is definitely no good will be marked "N.G," while one that the director is happy with will get an asterisk or a star next to it on the log.

VIDEO TAPE LOG   Prod.# _58-02_

M^cQ Teleproduction Services

Program Title: _Video Production Guide_
Client: _Video Info Fairs_   Contact: _Ensinger_   Ph: _460-1146_   Date: _2/12/82_
Director: _McQ_   Camera: _Kelley_   VTR: _see #3_   Audio: _Ag_
Reel# _2_   Aud. Ch.#1: _Boom_   Aud. Ch.#2: _Wireless_

SMPTE	Cntr.	Scene	Take	Description	
2:00:00:00				Bars + Tone	
:5:10:		3	1	Master - Office scene	NG
:8:25:			2	" " " "	⊛
:14:05:		3A	1	CU - Conrad	NG
:17:40:			2	" " "	?? OK
:21:10:			3	" " "	OK
:25:15:		3B	1	CU - Sharon	⊛
:58:00:		6	1	Hallway (Noise)	NG
3:00:20:			2	" "	OK
:2:40:			3	" "	⊛
:28:15:		4	1	Stairway	NG
:32:20:			2	" "	NG
:37:15:			3	" "	NG
:41:40:			4	" "	NG
:46:10:			5	" "	NG
:50:20:			6	" "	?
:55:15:			7	" " (?)	⊛
:59:40:		4A	1	Stairway (Alternate - no boom)	NG
4:04:15:			2	" " "	OK
:19:50:		5	1	Doorway	⊛
:22:30:			2	Doorway	⊛
:42:10:		12	1	Meeting Room (Dolly)	NG
:46:20:			2	" " " "	⊛
:49:50:		12A	1	CU - Lori	NG
:52:15:			2	" " " ? (F.S.)	
:55:35:			3	" " "	⊛
5:20:20:		14	1	Lab - Robin/Nick	NG
:25:30:			2	" " " " "	OK
:29:10:			3	" " " " " "	NG
:36:15:			4	" " " " " (Display)	NG
:41:00:			5	" " " " "	NG

(Continues)

Detailed tape log.

Detailed tape logs save tremendous amounts of time during editing by reducing the time spent in searching for scenes. Another very important practice that goes hand in hand with logging is often forgotten: SLATING each scene.

The SLATE lists:

1. Production number
2. Program title
3. Whether the shot is interior or exterior
4. Reel number
5. Date of taping
6. Air date (if applicable and known)
7. Scene and take number
8. Who's directing and who's on camera
9. What type of sound is being recorded

Sound designations are:

"S.O.T." for sound-on-tape

"SYNC" for separately recorded and synchronized audio

"WILD" for sound recorded separately and not synced

"M.O.S." for silent footage that will have sound added later—the term comes from the bastardized German "Mit Out Sprechen" (without speech).

Sound is usually recorded on the tape along with the video, so it is normally not necessary to use the CLAPSTICK (the hinged stick at the top of a slate that is brought down to produce an audible "clap"). However, if the sound will be stripped off for audio sweetening during editing and SMPTE time code is not being used, or the shoot is an ISO (isolated camera) without DISTRIBUTED SMPTE (identical code sent to all VTRs), it can be of value to use the clapstick to establish a SYNC POINT (starting reference point) for audio and video. SMPTE TIME CODE, which is explained in detail in *Part III, Post-Production*, makes the task of re-syncing video and audio a simple operation.

Recording slate on the tape makes it much easier to find each scene during editing, and eliminates confusion over which TAKE is which. A TAKE is an individual shot of a scene. There may be many takes of the same scene. In the event the director wants to roll right on from one take to the next, as he may when under time pressure or to keep the mood from breaking, there are two alternatives. The first is to put the standard information on the slate, and record it upside down at the end of the take. This is called a TAIL SLATE, and is so indicated by its orientation. The second method, which is faster, though less desirable,

The assistant director stands by with the slate in between takes.

The slate as recorded on tape.

is to record a FINGER SLATE—having someone hold up two fingers, for example, to indicate take two. This type of slate can be all right once in a while, but is harder to see when the tape is searched visually in fast forward or rewind, or at fast play speeds.

189

Incomplete takes should be indicated as such on the log sheet, and false starts that don't warrant logging a new take are indicated by a "F.S." (FALSE START), or something similar.

As each reel is filled and taken off the VTR, the log sheet should go into the box with the tape, and a sticker indicating either "MASTER FOOTAGE," "CAMERA ORIGINAL," or something of the sort should be affixed to both the reel and the box. Cassettes should have the red RECORD-LOCK BUTTON removed, and the tapes should be safely stored out of the way.

Be sure to remove the red button to prevent accidental erasure.

Aside from all the mechanical and procedural practices that should be made a matter of habit, the main thing to emphasize in shooting is that the director must think ahead to the edit, and plan each shot with the edit in mind. The processes of direction and editing are so closely related that they are very hard to separate, and the director who follows through with the edit, or who will edit the show himself, will be unlikely to repeat mistakes very many times. He or she will learn through experience what will and what will not work in the edit. It is no coincidence that many of the better directors began their careers as editors.

Give the editor as much variety as possible when shooting. When in doubt as to how a

scene will work, shoot alternate shots that will provide some options during the edit. A common technique in shooting commercials, where RUNNING TIME (length of the program) is a critical factor, is to shoot the scene with several variations of pacing and overall length, so that when all the scenes are brought together in the edit, the finished spot can be made to fit within its 60, 30, or 10 second space.

While it's tempting to go back and record over takes that are considered to be no good, save them if possible, despite the fact that it may seem a waste of tape. It just may happen that a shot that looked wrong on location is precisely what's needed when it comes time to edit. Even OUTTAKES sometimes fit into the program, as in the case of a show I did where a between-takes laugh by one of the actors that got recorded was *the* perfect cutaway, and was used as a reaction shot. The more material you shoot, the easier it will be for the editor to piece together a smooth final edit.

Shoot some UTILITY FOOTAGE, even though it may not be called for in the script. Utility footage would include some establishing shots, some ART SHOTS, such as out-of-focus footage that might later be used as a background for titles, and any other material that might be handy. By all means, also record some ambient sound at each location. This can be done while shooting a cover or establishing shot and may be a life-saver if it's necessary to edit the audio separately from the video.

In shooting dialog, it pays to overlap lines—extend the scene at the beginning and end for a few lines—just a bit. This is done both to provide options during the edit, and to allow for SPLIT AUDIO/VIDEO EDITS. This technique is also known as SLIPPING the audio or video, and will be covered in the *Post-Production* section. Overlapping lines can also help the talent provide a running start at the scene which in turns helps continuity.

Since single-camera production is more heavily dependent on editing, most of these techniques therefore become especially relevant. Multicamera production, however, can also benefit from the application of some of these techniques, especially if the production is not being shot "live" in a single run-through.

RECAP—List Of Techniques for Shooting for the Edit

1. Shoot sufficient cutaways and utility footage.
2. Reframe for pickup shots.
3. Hold shots a bit longer than may seem necessary.
4. Pay attention to continuity.
5. Allow sufficient preroll time.
6. Record bars and tone at start of tape.
7. Plan ahead for effects and graphics.
8. Log tapes in detail.
9. Record slate at the start of each scene.
10. Overlap lines at start and end of each take.

CHAPTER 14

Production Methods and Costs

Options

There are a number of options available in determining the basic techniques and facilities to be used for a production, depending greatly on the budget and the amount of time available. In examining the options, we'll start with single-camera production, and then move on to multicamera operations.

A major factor in planning a single-camera shoot will be the editing methods that will be used. The first choice would be that of the tape format. If the format chosen for a production is ¾-inch cassette, there will then be a choice in post-production between time code and nontime code editing. Most one-inch and quad production will automatically be edited on a TIME CODE EDITING SYSTEM.

TIME CODE EDITING uses a code that gives each frame of the videotape an individual address, which can then be used to program a computer to perform FRAME-ACCURATE EDITING (edit accuracy to within one frame).

Regardless of the format or editing method chosen, it's usually desirable to generate either a WORKPRINT or a SCRATCH COPY of the original material, which takes the place of the DAILIES or RUSHES used in film. It's a good idea to limit the use of masters as much as possible, and to use them only for the final editing.

A SCRATCH COPY is a duplicate recording of the material, made on a second VTR simultaneously with the master recording. Its main purpose is to provide a viewing copy of the day's shooting that can be watched by the director and perhaps the crew at the end of the day. Although it does not normally receive the attention to engineering detail that the master does, it can also serve as a PROTECTION MASTER in the event there are problems with the master. In some cases, therefore, it may be worthwhile to expend some effort on making it a good copy. Very critical or large-budget productions may record two masters simultaneously, and use one as a daily, or even add a third VTR for scratch copy recording.

In nontime code production, the scratch copy may also serve as the editing workprint if OFF-LINE editing (doing a "rough" edit of the show) will be done prior to the final ON-LINE edit. Otherwise, a copy of the master known as a WORKPRINT will be made for this purpose. Workprints and scratch dubs are usually made on ¾-inch cassette, but the rather recent introduction of decent ½-inch cassette editing equipment makes it a flexible and less expensive alternative choice.

Time code production offers several additional options, and requires that certain decisions be made.

The first is whether to record time code in the field, or later, back in the studio. In part, this decision will be determined by the style of the production.

As mentioned earlier, if the mastering format is ¾-inch cassette, it may be wise to record the time code *after* the original recording—a technique known as POST STRIPING. As mentioned in *Engineering,* time code can leak from its assigned audio channel over to the program audio channel, and once there, it's nearly impossible to remove. One-inch, quad, and the professional ¾-inch VCRs have a separate CUE CHANNEL which eliminates this problem, but there are other factors to consider.

With the start/stop nature of film-style production, if the TIME CODE GENERATOR

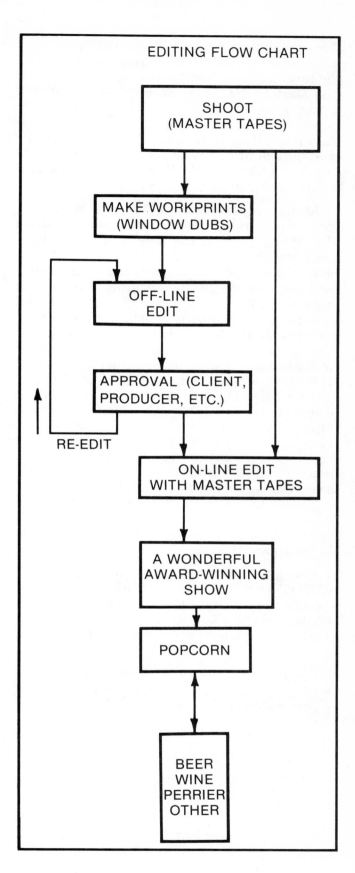

keeps on running between takes, just as a clock would keep counting time, the result will be time code that jumps to a higher number at the start of each new scene. There's nothing necessarily wrong with this, but the jumps in the code caused by stopping the tape can confuse the editing system, with the result that the system will often OVER SHOOT when searching for a particular TIME CODE ADDRESS (frame number).

Most computer editing systems read time code when in fast forward or rewind, and are designed to handle the tape in a semi-intelligent manner. This means that when told to move the tape to a particular time code address, the system will shuttle the tape at high speed in the required direction, and start to slow the tape down as it nears the desired address. If there is a jump in the code just before the address the system is looking for, it will not have started decelerating in time and will thus shoot past the correct location (OVERSHOOT) and then have to reverse direction to go back to the right address. A tape with a large number of short scenes, each of which is accompanied by a jump in time code, can cause the system to spend a large amount of time shuttling back and forth searching for an address. It may not sound like a big deal, but at the high rates charged for computer editing time it can add up to a substantial amount over the course of a long editing session.

One practice that can make the use of NON-CONTINUOUS CODE worthwhile despite the overshoot problem is the use of TIME-OF-DAY CODE (also called REAL TIME or CLOCK TIME code), where the time code generator is synced to time of day, providing a record of progress of the production. This also permits the director, assistant director, and others to make program notes, referring only to their watches, which will match the time code at any particular point. Actually, there are some other factors that complicate the matter further, but for now we'll let it be. We'll examine the intricacies and nature of time code later.

Recording time code on tape in the field during original shooting eliminates the time required to POST-STRIPE (record time code) the tape later, and if your schedule is extremely tight, that may make the decision for you.

One of the main advantages of time code editing is the ability to perform off-line editing on less expensive equipment, thus saving time (and presumably money) during the final on-line edit. In this instance, a ¾-inch or ½-inch cassette workprint is generated with time code that's identical to that on the master, with the code either recorded on an audio channel, keyed into the visible portion of the video (called a WINDOW DUB), or both. Making a window dub requires a device known as a

Portable AMTEL generator/reader.

BTX generator/reader and display.

Time Code Generators.

AMTEL generator/reader, bit encoder, and character generator.

"Window dub" time code.

TIME CODE READER/CHARACTER GENER-ATOR. This unit reads the time code from a master tape, and generates a visual readout of the running code which it then inserts into the picture of a cassette copy as the copy is being made. Each frame of the video thus has a visible address that identifies the time code number of that frame. Since the time code consists of a digital code, the only way to read the code when viewing a tape is to either make a window dub, or use a time code reader/character generator during playback.

On standard ¾-inch cassettes, the time code signal is normally recorded on audio channel 2, with program audio being recorded on audio channel 1. Again, the "professional" ¾-inch machines have a separate channel designed specifically for recording time code, so channel assignments won't be a problem. If you're using standard ¾-inch cassette machines, however, and plan to post-stripe the tape back in the studio, then make sure you record the pro-

gram audio on channel 1. If you record program audio on channel 2, you'll have to redub the audio over to channel 1 to make room for code on channel 2. This technique is called PING-PONGING the audio. It's a practice to be avoided, since it costs time and/or money to perform, and the audio quality will be reduced because the audio will then be a copy of the original audio.

As we've seen, a workprint can be a scratch copy generated in the field during original recording, or it can be made later as a copy of the master. If the latter course is chosen, it may be advantageous to make the workprint at the same time the master tape is being post-striped, accomplishing two tasks simultaneously.

One advantage of using workprints and window dubs rather than a scratch copy made in the field is that they are *exactly* the same as the original material because they are copies of

195

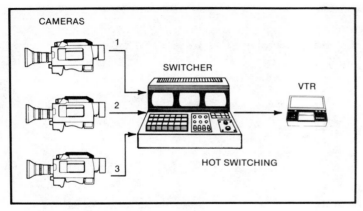

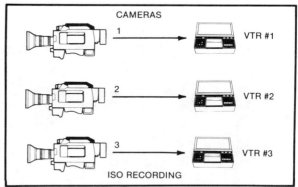

the master. In recording a scratch copy in the field, it is unlikely that the two or more VTRs will be started at precisely the same time, with the result that there will be some differences between the master and the copy. Although the differences are usually minor, they can create problems. You might decide to use a segment after viewing a scratch copy only to find that the piece you want was not recorded on the master.

Multicamera Considerations

Most of the tape format and procedural considerations we've discussed so far apply mainly to single-camera production. Many of them also apply to multicamera production, but there are numerous additional factors to be weighed as well.

Essentially, there are two primary techniques available in multicamera production. The first is live switching onto a master VTR (HOT SWITCHING), and the second is isolated recording of each camera's signal onto its own VTR (ISO RECORDING). There are also a

number of variations on these two basic techniques.

Hot switching to a master VTR offers the time and money saving advantages we've already established: The show may be all but finished at the end of taping. Iso recording, on the other hand, provides a great deal of flexibility in post-production, at the cost of being basically what might be called a "multiple-unit single-camera" technique. Iso tapes must be fully edited, although the editing techniques will be different from those used in editing single-camera material. Programs shot using iso tapes and hot-switched programs that will require editing can both benefit from the recording of a scratch copy or a workprint. In essence, the rule is simple: For any program that will later be edited, a workprint will generally be worthwhile. Workprints are an editing tool, and the format a tape is mastered on and the number of cameras used is immaterial.

Iso recording with multiple cameras offers a large degree of protection from mistakes and flubs, because the switching is deferred until the edit, where decisions may be made at relative leisure. However, two additional factors come into play: *first,* iso recording is generally the most expensive production technique available, because the original taping requires more equipment than usual, *and* full post-production is still necessary. *Second,* since the program is already on a series of tapes, it's too late to make changes in camera moves and the like. If two scenes don't cut together properly, there's little that can be done about it.

trating that he can't call directions to the cameras. For this reason, directing an isoed recording requires a wholly different frame of mind, and the transition from directing live hot switching to directing iso's can be a bit difficult.

There are two techniques, though, that offer an excellent compromise. They are basically two variations on the same theme.

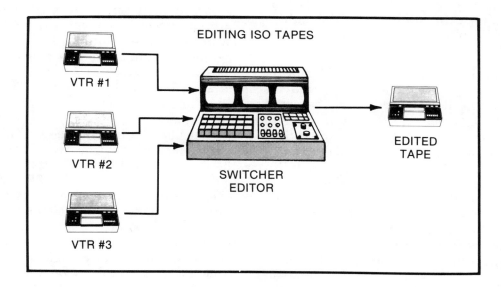

One popular editing technique used on isoed shows is to roll the individual camera tapes in sync, and switch the show as if it were happening live. The director can then change his mind on the choice of which camera's shot is used, but may find it rather frus-

The first is to perform hot switching to a master VTR, and to also iso the signal from each of the cameras. With this method, if the switched master turns out all right, the director is home free, while if there are some flaws to correct, or second thoughts at a later time,

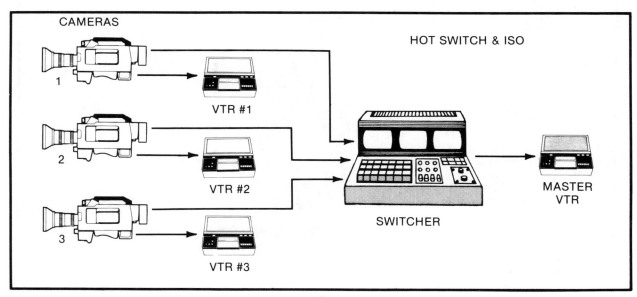

the material, having been recorded iso, is available to make changes. Not only can this method save money, since post-production requirements may be minimal if not nonexistent, but it provides the substantial aesthetic safety factor for critical productions that's afforded by alternate material.

A drawback with this method is the obvious need for several VTRs—a master VTR plus one for each camera, plus any backup VTRs that may be specified. In addition to the equipment, this will require additional videotape and personnel.

One solution is to employ a sort of "hybrid" approach, which is very commonly used on large productions. It involves doing the same hot switch to a master VTR, but instead of isoing each camera's signal to individual VTRs, a separate ISO SWITCH is done to a single secondary VTR by a second director (usually the Assistant Director). The A.D. in this instance would normally be positioned behind the director at a simple CUTS-ONLY SWITCHER (no special effects capability—only camera switches). He would switch to alternate shots while watching what the director is taking. He sometimes works independently, but may also take his cues from the director. This approach reduces both the equipment and the personnel requirements,

and saves a lot of tape that might otherwise not be used in the final edit. Again, the director may walk away at the end of taping with a finished show, but if there are any problems to correct, the switched iso will provide backup material from which to select FIXES (other shots).

On two-camera shoots, there is a related technique available that makes use of the CUT BAR provided on many switchers. This is a button or bar that toggles (switches) the program and preset outputs back and forth. For instance, if camera 1 is selected on the PROGRAM BUSS (row of buttons), and camera 2 on the PRESET BUSS, hitting the cut bar will simultaneously switch camera 2 to program and camera 1 to preset. By repeatedly hitting the cut bar, the two busses will alternate back and forth between the two cameras. Feeding the master VTR from the PROGRAM OUTPUT and the iso VTR from the PRESET OUTPUT gives the result of having *all* material shot by the two cameras on one of the two VTRs. The master has the program as directed, and the iso has the exact opposite shots. The equipment costs for the original shooting will be the same as for a simple two-camera iso plus the cost of the switcher, but there can be a reduction or complete elimination of editing that reduces net costs considerably. (Switcher func-

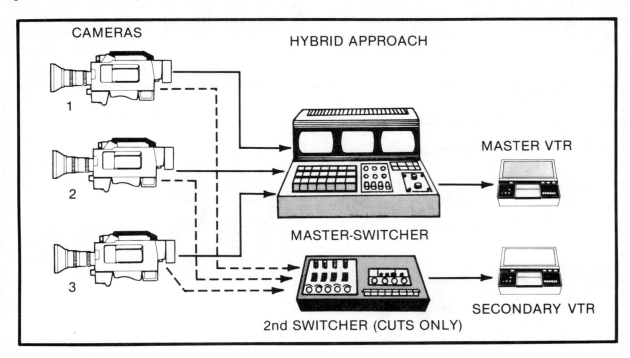

CAMERAS HYBRID APPROACH

1

2

3

MASTER-SWITCHER

MASTER VTR

2nd SWITCHER (CUTS ONLY)

SECONDARY VTR

tions and operations will be examined in more detail in a later section, **Other Equipment.)**

If you intend to shoot fully isoed material and record time code during original taping, there are some definite special requirements. If the time code is to be distributed from a master time code generator, it and all of the cameras must be synchronized in order for the time code to be fully synchronous with each of the tapes. In the studio this is rarely a problem, but on location shoots—especially on battery power—if the code is distributed to VTRs that are recording signals from cameras running on their own sync generators, the code will be NONSYNCHRONOUS with reference to the video, and will make it difficult or impossible for the VTRs to lock up during editing. If this happens, the tapes will have to be recoded in their entirety. The best way to synchronize multiple cameras is to use a MASTER SYNC GENERATOR (a unit that provides sync signals to all equipment) to drive both the cameras and the time code generator, just as is done in the studio.

Selecting the recording technique for a production is a matter of balancing all the various factors of time, budget, facilities available, nature and style of the program, and the personal preferences of the producer and director. Cost is a major consideration, and there are times when a technique that may be more expensive at the head end of the production can save money overall in the long run.

For example, on a three-camera shoot that's been planned for iso recording, the addition of a switcher and additional 1-inch VTR might add $600–$700 to the production cost per day. But, with 1-inch editing time running in the $300/hour range, a live switch could reduce editing time from a complete 8-hour edit to a minor 3-hour repair job, and thus result in a considerable savings despite the extra initial costs.

Application

To help put all of this in perspective, I'll run down some of the techniques I've used that have given a good balance between the ideal and the affordable.

In single-camera production, I usually master on 1-inch, and do not normally record time code in the field. This is because I prefer continuous, unbroken time code, which the

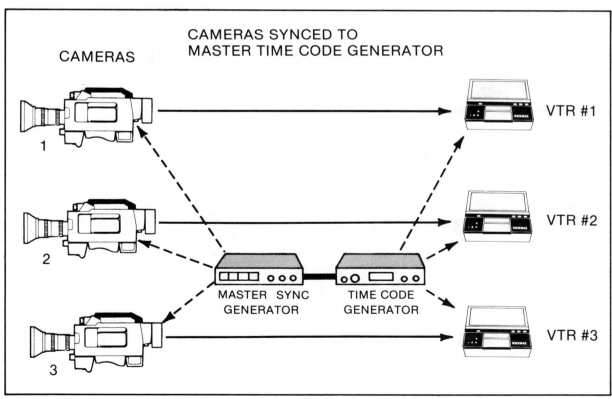

CAMERAS SYNCED TO
MASTER TIME CODE GENERATOR

CAMERAS

1

2

3

MASTER SYNC GENERATOR

TIME CODE GENERATOR

VTR #1

VTR #2

VTR #3

199

off-line editing system I currently use likes much better than code that has large jumps in it. My off-line system uses a simple control track editor, and by using continuous code, the tape timers will keep roughly the same count as the code on the tape, making tape searches faster. If I eventually upgrade to a time code off-line system, I'll probably go to FIELD CODING (placing the time code on the tape while making the original recording), which makes the tape logs made during recording much handier, and POST-LOGGING much less of a chore.

In addition to the master VTR, I usually record a scratch copy on cassette, and prefer to keep the cassette running whenever the camera is on. Although the master may be stopped between takes, the between-takes material has come in handy at times. In some cases the cassette is a ¾-inch unit, while for less critical shoots I may use a Betamax ½-inch cassette

running at the two-hour speed for reasons of economy. There is one minor drawback mentioned earlier, which I feel balances out in the end. Often when I view the scratch copy cassette that was almost always running, I may not know for sure if something that's on the cassette got recorded on the master. There have been several instances when something I dearly hoped was on the master was not.

The cassette scratch copy serves primarily as a daily, and is normally ARCHIVED (permanently stored) after it has served its purpose. At the end of each day's shooting, the master tape is taken back to the studio, and a window dub is made simultaneous to recording code on the master. This workprint will be used first to make up edit tape logs, and subsequently as a workprint to be used in the off-line edit.

In multicamera production, I follow the same practice. Since many such productions are done "live," with time code being recorded in the field, the scratch copy and the master will be identical. Although it would be possi-

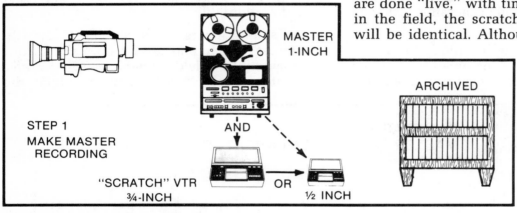

STEP 1
MAKE MASTER
RECORDING

MASTER
1-INCH

AND

"SCRATCH" VTR
¾-INCH

OR

½ INCH

ARCHIVED

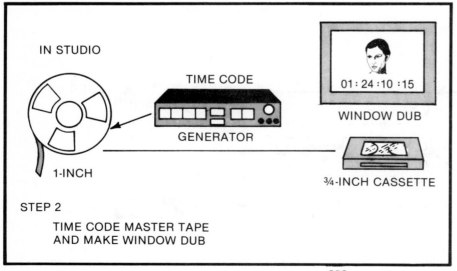

IN STUDIO

TIME CODE

01 : 24 :10 :15

WINDOW DUB

GENERATOR

1-INCH

¾-INCH CASSETTE

STEP 2

TIME CODE MASTER TAPE
AND MAKE WINDOW DUB

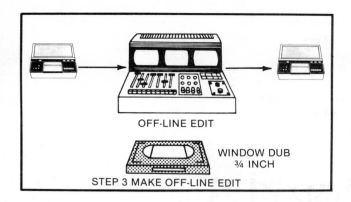

OFF-LINE EDIT

WINDOW DUB
¾ INCH

STEP 3 MAKE OFF-LINE EDIT

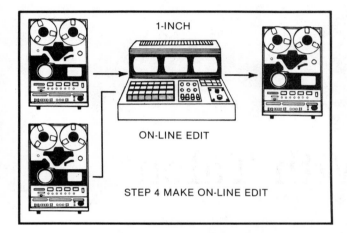

1-INCH

ON-LINE EDIT

STEP 4 MAKE ON-LINE EDIT

ble to use a character generator to make a window dub as the scratch copy, I usually have the window dub made later, back at the studio. This is a good precaution since in addition to serving as a daily, the scratch copy may end up serving as a "last resort" protection master in the event of a disaster with the primary master. If the scratch copy had the code keyed into the video (window dub), it would be unusable as a backup copy.

In multicamera production, I've found it can be very useful to record the P.L. line on the second channel of the scratch copy. Remember, the scratch copy will not be used for editing, since I have a window dub made for that purpose, and thus won't need to have time code on the spare channel. The P.L. recording provides an excellent opportunity to do a postmortem on the production, and to evaluate the crew's responses and coordination. It's a tremendous learning tool, and is often very entertaining. In the *Horror Stories* section, I mentioned the punk rock group we shot, where there were numerous comments made by the crew during taping. All of those comments were saved for posterity on the spare audio channel, and that's the way most of the crew prefers to watch that particular segment—listening to the P.L. instead of the program audio.

One note I'd like to insert with regard to this point: In general, chatter on the P.L. is definitely to be discouraged. It easily and quickly gets out of hand, and is only permissible at all under rare circumstances. When those circumstances occur, it must be understood that a word from the director ends it immediately.

While choosing a cost-effective method of production is important, it's necessary to recognize that any of the particular options may involve hidden costs that may not become apparent until the show goes into post. Any mistakes, errors, or omissions must be caught during production, since the *most expensive technique of all* is going back out to shoot footage that was missed or that came out wrong. The production techniques also must always be designed to protect the original masters, and must include some method that allows viewing the material without using the masters themselves. Thus, I stress the importance of workprints and scratch copies again.

Once again, successful production requires attention to detail, and keeping editing in mind. There are many times when the director will have to make a quick judgment as to whether a piece of tape or a scene is acceptable, or will have to be re-done. Probably the most famous last words that can be uttered by a director are those that have served as the epitaph for many a show: "We'll fix it in post." That phrase is guaranteed to generate snickers among those who've been through the mill, and who have learned the hard way that, usually, the only thing that gets fixed in post is the director's wagon, so to speak.

CHAPTER 15

Working With Talent

Let's assume for this discussion that we're talking about some sort of a "performance," rather than either a documentary type of production or the recording of an event to which the videotaping is incidental. This leaves us with two basic types of situations: the TALENT (actor or actress) may act the part of a character; or the talent may appear as himself, making a presentation specifically to the program audience.

In the first instance, the use of professional actors has much to recommend it. In those cases where this is impossible, though, the director will somehow have to obtain a decent performance without spending inordinate amounts of time and money in the process.

In the section on talent in *Part 1*, we examined some of the ways of securing talent, and it is during production that the director will either enjoy the benefits of good casting or pay for the sins of compromise. Let's further examine some techniques for working with talent, starting with the ideal—working with professionals.

A working professional will generally not waste the director's time. If there are lines to be learned, a true pro will show up knowing them and ready to work. The director's task then becomes one of communicating to the talent the type of delivery and emphasis he wants. If the show is dramatic in nature, the director and actor(s) will have met prior to taping to discuss the character and to build in the actor's mind a feeling for the person he or she is to portray.

One technique I've used with excellent results has been to provide the talent with a biographical background sheet that describes the character as I envision it. A typical background sheet begins with a basic description of the purpose or message of the program. It then specifies the relationship of the particular role to the other characters and the program itself. A brief (fictitious) biography of the character is then provided, including such things as education, past history, and current situation. Next is a personal profile, describing home life, hobbies, reading list, and other incidentals. The character's style of dress and grooming are also detailed. Finally, the character's motivation is examined, and technical notes on the style of delivery are provided.

These background sheets generally fill a single, narrow-margined typewritten page, and are given to the actors along with their copy of the script. Script copies for each of the actors are premarked with their lines and actions highlighted with fluorescent marker, using one color for lines and a second color for action and blocking. I make it clear to the talent that the background sheets are not to be taken as gospel; they are intended merely to describe

my concept of the character. I encourage them to use the sheets as a starting point from which to mold their characters in accordance with their own styles and perceptions.

These background sheets have been a useful tool for me. The process of writing out a character description ahead of time helps me define the role clearly, and provides a "baseline" for the role while still leaving room for the character to evolve. I'll often provide a brief rundown for actors to use during casting sessions, and then expand it into a full background sheet once the roles have been cast. In such cases the casting may influence the final description I write, as I may tailor the characters somewhat to the actors' talents. The response I've had from talent has been excellent. Few of them have ever before encountered the technique, but they have universally appreciated the information. The sheets have given them a solid idea of what is expected from them, rather than their having to guess.

It would be hard to say too many good things about the benefits of rehearsal. Going over characterization and delivery with the talent ahead of time is a tremendously valuable aid to efficient production. Most actors tie their delivery and interpretation to their lines while memorizing them, and if the interpretation they develop is wrong it may be difficult

Talent, writer, and director discuss script changes on location.

Crew prepares talent for shoot.

and time-consuming for them to change it on the set.

One or more rehearsal sessions before the taping can help avoid this problem. Your best bet is to hold a reading as soon as the parts have been cast, to put the actors on the right track. Then, once they're familiar with their lines, hold another rehearsal to fine-tune their interpretation and delivery. At this point, depending on the nature of the program, you may want to work out blocking and BUSI-NESS (also called BIZ)—the small, often unscripted actions that help flesh out the character. In situations where the blocking is relatively simple it may be sufficient to work just on the lines, and to work out blocking during production.

Some actors do not enter their role until the director calls "ACTION!" while others—including those known as METHOD actors—immerse themselves deeply in their role, and may even stay immersed for the length of the production. Though the latter may seem at times almost schizophrenic when they carry it to the extreme, most actors you'll run into will not take their technique quite that far. It is not at all unusual, though, for an actor to try to remain in character between takes.

Some sort of acting background and/or experience can be very helpful to the director. The ability to *show* the talent what you have in mind makes the task of communication easier than trying to explain the concept verbally. This, however, is basically a factor of the director's individual style of directing, and is by no means a requirement.

Professionals are much less likely to be rattled by the need to do numerous takes, and they will understand that things other than their performance can be the cause for retakes. In nondramatic situations such as a technical training program, a pro will accept the need for repetition until all lines and information are correct, and will work with the director until things are right.

Many actors want to know the motivation behind their words and actions, while others simply jump in and do the scene. Again, there are many variations, depending on the actor,

204

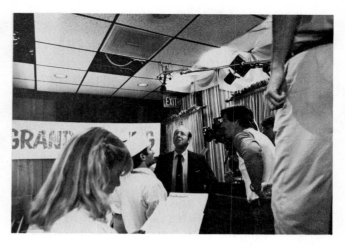

Production in process.

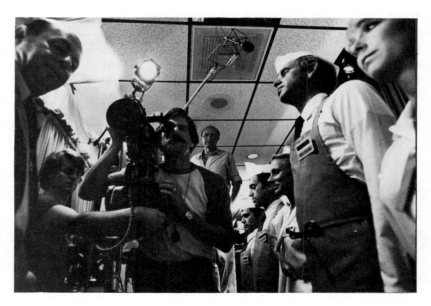

205

the program, and the director, and no two productions are ever quite the same.

In dramatic programs, the things the director should keep in mind are (again) continuity—this time of the actor's performance and characterization—and the interplay and relationships between the various characters. The director has the overview, and will have in mind some distinct personality traits for each of the characters in the script. It is doubtful that these ideas will ever completely match those of the actors, and at times this can lead to conflicts over portrayal. The actor is concerned primarily with his or her own part, and will probably not have as wide a perspective as the director.

We all, of course, have egos of some size or another, but television seems to attract people with strong, if not oversized, self-images. In many ways, this is what makes good production people what they are, but it can also, as we all know, give rise to disagreement. Unfortunately, the two areas where egos seem to be most active are in actors and in directors. The director, however, must be able to rise above such concerns as much as possible, since as the guiding force behind the production, he can ill afford to be petty about personality conflicts.

If such problems arise, the director must do everything possible to smooth the differences, and perhaps compromise on certain items. He must keep in mind that actors are, after all, artists—as much so as are directors, and that they have been known on occasion to raise valid points regarding their characters. In the event of a stalemate—something that should be an exceedingly rare occurrence if the director is doing things right—the director must prevail, even at the expense of losing the actor. Ideally, of course, a less drastic solution will have been reached before things get to such a point.

Nonprofessionals

Working with the nonprofessional can be a completely different experience, possibly one the director wishes never to repeat. This is especially true when such people are required to portray a character—i.e., to act.

It is a plain and simple fact that there are some people who never have, cannot now, and never will be able to act. Dragging an acceptable performance out of them is more than simply time-consuming—it is impossible. If you find yourself faced with this situation, my sincere advice, if you've given it a sporting try, is to find a replacement as graciously and quickly as possible.

There are times, though, when an initial run-through is terrible, but with work, the performance can be improved substantially, and perhaps even made quite good or excellent. The trick is to determine quickly who can work out, and who can't. If in doubt, study the budget and the schedule, and if they tell you that you're over-spent and behind, it may be best to cease flogging the horse, even though it's only ill, and not dead. In a sense, one could consider this to be practicing "triage." Some people will never work out, and should be cut from the team, whereas some are already in good shape, and their problems can be worked out during production. This leaves the middle group on which to concentrate—those who need help, and who will benefit from it. This is where rehearsal becomes critical.

The most common problem with nonprofessionals is their sometimes immobilizing fear of the glassy-eyed beast. If you've been there yourself, you may recall that the first time up, it can, indeed, be an unnerving experience. People tend to think that there are millions of unseen people out there, silently waiting to disapprove their every action. They are afraid of making blunders, or looking foolish, or forgetting their lines, or looking fat, or of any of the other dozens of myths there are about being on television.

There are a number of ways to combat this problem. One very effective approach is to remind your neophyte talent that the normal viewing situation involves one or two people in front of each TV set, and that the crowd they imagine is really only one or two folks at a time. If they think of the camera as a device used to communicate with just those one or two people—almost a one-way picturephone—their fears may be eased considerably. This technique can work in situations ranging from live broadcasting to programs distributed on cassette.

206

Nonprofessional talent may be overwhelmed by the lights and cameras.

If the script calls for your talent to talk directly to the camera, another effective technique is to have them imagine that the camera is a friend of theirs. Alternately, introduce them to the camera operator, and give the two a chance to talk a bit and get acquainted. Then have the talent deliver the lines not to the camera, but to the person behind it.

People who are on a set for the first time, especially in a studio, are often awed and more than a little frightened by all the equipment and activity. Those of us who've been in and around studios for years may find them to be warm and friendly places where magic is made. To a newcomer, though, they can be an all-new and very strange place where everybody seems to be rushing about and shouting, and where nothing seems to make sense. Take some time to show them around, introduce them to the crew, and explain how things work. This can be a great aid in helping them relax. If the fact that everybody seems to be watching them intently when the tape rolls and the TALLY LIGHT (the light that indicates a camera is on-line) comes on makes them nervous or self-conscious, it might be worthwhile

to clear all nonessential personnel from the set. Have the talent relate to a single person, either the cameraman, as mentioned, or maybe a P.A. who can sit near the camera and give them nodding smiles when they need assurance. Having a friendly person with whom to make eye contact and receive assurance can help them immeasurably.

With executives who must pitch to the camera, a little basic psychology can go a long way. Remind them that since the video staff and equipment are at their disposal and are there to make them look good, then for all intents and purposes, the camera is an underling, and should be addressed just the way they'd talk to a subordinate.

An old trick, and one that's quite valid, is to tell the talent that you want to rehearse the scene (or lines) just once, so that everyone can get a feel for how it will go. Almost all non-professionals feel relatively comfortable with this idea, and the trick, of course, is to roll tape even as you fib about your intent. The fact that they're relaxed and secure about not being "on" may make the rehearsal the best delivery they ever give. It's obvious that this trick can't

207

be pulled too many times without losing its effectiveness, but it still can be a workable ruse. It can even at times be your little secret, since they may not recall afterwards what they said or when they said it.

Important Considerations

The individual person in front of the camera will determine for you whether memorization or some form of prompting, either cue cards or a TELEPROMPTER, are more appropriate.

having a P.A. next to the camera. The makeup person is an excellent choice for this role, since they will have a chance to meet and talk with this person anyway. On smaller productions it's often beneficial to combine the roles of makeup and floor director, as this can help set inexperienced talent at ease—they now have a friend nearby.

The only makeup that will normally be required for most nondramatic situations is some powder to keep the nose and forehead from becoming shiny. If an individual has very

Studio camera with teleprompter mounted.

Copy on teleprompter as seen by talent.

Reading naturally from cards or prompters is a learned ability, and it may be better to have them speak off the cuff if they know their material. Sometimes having a card with key phrases or points next to the camera can help keep them on track. An alternative to holding the card next to the camera is to put it on the floor in front of them. With the card so placed, they can appear to be looking down as if in thought, and won't appear to be reading.

Since the director will be well occupied during production, it's good to have one person on the set who acts as liason, guide, and friend to the talent, as in the case mentioned above of

Makeup being applied to talent.

pale skin, a base may be applied to keep the light from penetrating the skin and enhancing small veins and blemishes. Some nonprofessionals react well to the application of makeup, as it acts to assure them they'll look all right on camera. In some cases, the ritual effect alone is worthwhile. Others may feel uncomfortable about having makeup applied. Male business executives in particular sometimes feel that wearing makeup is an affront to their dignity or masculinity. This can present problems, especially since they'll rarely admit that this is the reason. In such cases, you'll have to pull out your old Psychology 101 techniques again. Just tell them that Joe Garagiola and Mike Wallace both wear makeup when they're on camera, and ask them if they want to look like death warmed over in front of the stockholders.

It's a subject of endless debate as to whether it's a good or a bad idea to let the talent see themselves as they appear on camera. In favor of the idea, playing back an early take may demonstrate that they're doing just fine, and help put them at ease. The assumption here, of course, is that they are doing just fine, and not coming off like some backwoods buffoon with a speech impediment. On the other hand, while they may look fine to you, they may be horrified at their appearance or performance. This may be due simply to their unrealistic expectations as to what they thought they'd look and sound like on TV. We all know that our own voices sound odd to us the first time we hear them played back, and that can be one of the factors involved. There's another factor, though, that portrait photographers have long known, yet that few of us in television seem to think of.

When we see ourselves on TV, the image is reversed from the way we see it in the mirror every morning. Since most people part their hair on one side, and since our faces are just slightly asymmetrical, we usually appear odd to ourselves on the screen.

This can cause reactions ranging from amusement, to disappointment, or to downright horror in the case of people who are not used to seeing themselves thus. As a result, the question of whether or not to show them their tape before they're finished remains open, and is a matter that in the end must be played by ear in each individual instance. Generally, with nonprofessionals it's best not to show them the tape until the director has the results he wants, since inexperienced talent can easily block up when confronted with their own appearance. Professionals, on the other hand, are more likely to be able to evaluate their performance, and will fine-tune their delivery by watching and discussing early takes with the director.

Whenever dealing with neophytes, one thing that is definitely not a good idea is to have a monitor placed where they can see it during taping. The attraction of a monitor is positively magnetic, and it will draw their attention away from the camera. The only possible excuse for positioning a monitor where they can see it is when it is necessary to their performance, as when they must point to items that are CHROMAKEYED (electronically inserted) in behind them. This practice itself must be questioned when the talent is new to the process of television.

Lastly, the talent, professional or otherwise, will look to the director as the authority figure, and the respect inherent in the director's position must not be betrayed. In this they are no different from the crew, but the talent's attitudes and responses are much more likely to be visible on the screen. There is nothing wrong with the director's consulting with the talent for ideas and suggestions on how a part should be portrayed. There are some directors who leave characterization almost entirely up to the talent. If the talent asks, "How should I play this line?" the director may validly ask in return, "How do you think you should play it?" as part of the process of developing the character. This process, however, should be an active part of the director's technique, rather than a form of escape from or evasion of responsibility.

The people who get in front of the camera are, after all, only that—people—whether they're a top-name star in a major role, or someone drafted out of the mailroom to explain shipping procedures. The director will find that the conventional wisdom that one draws more flies with honey holds just as true in the matter of getting good performances on videotape. Patience is of utmost importance, and with inexperienced talent, it's far better to lead and coax than to push, shove, and holler. When things go wrong or lines get blown, that's the time for the director to make a joke, break the tension, and assure the talent that the sky ain't about to fall just yet. It seems so obvious, yet it's often forgotten, that relaxed and happy people do a far better job than those under a whip and a deadline. The deadline may be there, but it's sometimes better to not let on that it is.

CHAPTER 16

Direction Gestalt

The director in television has one basic concern that is of foremost importance, and that provides motivation for every action: The Program. At the end of the production process, the director must be able to deliver to the producer a finished tape that accomplishes the given objectives and balances the two major considerations of style and content as originally decided. While an informational program will emphasize content over style, and an entertainment program the opposite, the director must at all times strive to achieve the highest standards with regard to both.

As the cost of basic video equipment reaches ever lower levels, the capability for producing a videotape becomes more common every day. As more people start exercising their newly acquired capability, the field will become increasingly competitive, and the distinctions between good production and mediocre or bad production will come to rely less and less on technical facilities and more on the abilities of the people who use the equipment.

In the midst of this whole process, the director is the single most influential factor in a production. A good director combines the roles and duties of an artist, a technician, and a manager. The person approaching the job must stand ready to be a cheerleader, a nag, an arbitrator, a conductor, and a juggler, and must not only perform all of these roles simultaneously, but perform them capably as well. The essential tools include the script, the talent, the crew, and the equipment, in about equal order of importance. Tying them all together depends on the director's understanding of the *process*—the *gestalt* of production, and a dedication to the program itself. No director can long survive in a vacuum, and the ideas and suggestions of others are tremendously important resources. Whether they come from the crew or talent on the set, or from observing the work of others, a good director will constantly search for better ways to accomplish any given task. It's a process of constantly pushing one's self to new limits, without ever expecting to reach any sort of ultimate achievement. There are no ultimate achievements—there is only constant improvement, or decline.

It's the brand of a good director to never be completely satisfied with a finished program. Even with a program that turned out much better than had been hoped, once there's time to examine it later in detail, there will almost always be room for critical comment over some aspect or another. There may be nothing *wrong* with the program per se, but there are always things that, with benefit of hindsight, could have been done perhaps just a little better. This is a healthy attitude, for it provides a measuring stick by which we can gauge our improvement. Each production offers a tremendous opportunity to learn in the best way possible—by doing, and then evaluating the results.

When I've finished a successful production, I tend to view it with decidedly paradoxical feelings. At the same time, I may be thrilled with the overall results, yet I'll almost wish I could only re-do that one sequence ... or change the lighting in that one scene. It's part of the process of growth, and if the learning takes hold, there will be a steady progression over the years, with better results coming with every new production.

By the time a production is done, there's a good chance I'll be royally sick of it, having eaten, worked, breathed, and slept with it for the duration. Often, one or two viewings are all I can manage before I must put it on the shelf to gather dust for a while. A few weeks or months later, I can then take it down again, and can view it from a fresh perspective that is much more conducive to analysis. The details of the production have by then slipped from my mind, and although the viewing is likely to transport me directly back to the time when it was made, the distance has become great enough that I can view the show with a frame of mind that is much closer to that of the first-time audience. This is when I learn the most about my own strengths and weaknesses.

When I first began working with television and had no idea how much was involved in making not just television, but *good* television, I saw each new project as an exciting challenge. As my experience grew, there came a period when I found myself almost dreading to approach a new project. I knew how much work, how many petty details, would have to be tackled before the show was in the can. Those feelings rarely occur now, or if they do, it's because the show itself is not to my liking. They occur infrequently now mainly because I've fallen in love with the process of production—with taking an idea and turning it into a work that will flash across the screen and affect the people who watch it. I've also learned a secret relating to those programs that still fills me with dread—the ones that are not to my liking. The secret is that those are the very programs that represent the greatest challenge. If you can take a subject that bores you to tears and can do something with it that makes it interesting and creatively pleasing, you've crossed that line that separates professionals from amateurs. Some of my favorite programs sitting on my shelf were just those kinds of shows.

Directing is a truly unique art, for while it's a very personal one, it depends on the interplay and support of a large number of people. In many ways it is one of the most ephemeral of arts because most programs rarely live past a viewing or two. Once a production is finished, the only thing one can do is move on to the next project. The show will have its brief run, and will then retire to a shelf to be forgotten. Great films may live for years, or even indefinitely, but the number of truly immortal television programs can be counted on one or two hands. An occasional "Miracle Worker," or an "Ascent of Man," or an "Autobiography of Miss Jane Pittman" will come along, but most programs quietly fade to black, leading either to the next commercial, or the next program in the training schedule. In our information-hungry society, with it's constant appetite for the *new*, this is to be expected. You can't hang a videotape on the wall for people to look at all the time, and most people won't play a videotape again and again as they may do with a favorite record album. Even programs distributed on cassette or disc have a curious kind of mortality. Although they may continue to find new audiences over the years, each new audience will embrace it, absorb it, and then put it aside.

In this sense, the private nature of television extends past the process of directing, and a director's collected works remain uniquely personal artifacts.

These thoughts may seem somewhat morose, but they are presented for a reason. There comes a point in every director's career when such thoughts may begin to weigh on the mind, and an understanding of their causes can help put the nature of production into perspective. All of the above are true, but there is also a balance—a flip side to the equation—that gives television a life and vitality that is unparalleled.

The director may think of television as an art, and that may be true. But even more than an art, television is a method of communication—the most powerful one ever devised—and this adds a dimension to the director's role and responsibilities that few, if any, endeavors can match. A broadcast TV movie, for instance, may not have the immortal life of a *Citizen Kane*, but it can reach more people in a single night than ever saw *Kane* in the theatre. Direct satellite-to-home broadcasting holds the promise of providing alternative program producers the ability to lash together an "instant network." Satellites, the still-developing cable technology and other new forms of distribution including cassettes and video discs give television enormously exciting and powerful possibilities.

Television, far more so than film, or print, or photographs, or any other medium, is a communications tool which can be put to a wide variety of uses. It can inform, instruct, motivate, sell, and entertain, and can accomplish any and all of these tasks, often all at once, more effectively and efficiently than can any other medium, *if* it's in the hands of someone who understands how to use it.

The director is thus faced with two tasks: *what* to do with that glowing phosphor-coated screen, and, once that's been determined, *how* to make the electrons dance in just the right way.

In the first half of this set of tasks, the director is aided by and will take cues from the writer and producer. They will lay out the groundwork—the concepts to be presented and the resources with which to create the presentation—and the director will then apply the skills of visualization and execution that will meet the objectives that have been set.

As to the *how* side of the job, the director will take charge of and lead the team that does the actual work of turning the concept and the visualization into the pictures and sounds that will eventually reach the TV set.

The three frames of reference—the audience's, the objective as outlined in Chapter 12, and the subjective, must be kept in mind and in balance. In visualizing the show, the director must foresee the way the finished program will look. The script may have flaws or impracticalities which must be smoothed out before shooting starts. One of the tricks to establishing and maintaining the flow of a program is to carefully consider and plan out the transitions between scenes and major portions of the show. We've examined various aspects of continuity, primarily from a somewhat technical point of view. Of equal importance is the continuity of ideas, of consistency of thought, that allows the viewer to flow along with the program and not be jarred, unless that is the desired effect.

It's important to understand the difference between actual reality and television "reality." People, places, and things look substantially different on the screen than they do in real life, and the director must always realize that the appearance of a scene as it actually exists is of minor importance. What *is* important is the way it looks on the screen. This involves a process of working backwards, and designing shots for their effect in an objective, rather than a subjective manner. With practice, the director learns to anticipate and predict the look of the final results, but it's still good to

213

The associate producer, director, and assistant director discussing shots.

remember that it is often necessary to use "phony" techniques—to "cheat"—in order to make things look "real" on the screen.

The cast and crew will respond to good direction, and, conversely, will rebel against poor direction. Not only are a definite vision and firm administration important, but so is an understanding of human relations and basic human nature. A good director knows how to draw the full potential from the crew, and encourages them to grow in their jobs by giving them responsibility and letting them exercise it. Once the job is done, and this is a rule that is all too often violated, the director lets the crew know that their efforts have been appreciated. A "thank you" to the crew costs nothing more than a few minutes of the direc-

tor's time, yet from the evidence of the way many directors work, you'd think it was gold to be hoarded.

Directing involves hard work and long hours, and is definitely not for the weak or lazy. It's just another job, but like any craft, it's one that can be personally very rewarding. Although the directors working in entertainment and commercials get most of the glory and attention, they are far outnumbered by directors working in the more prosaic fields of communications-related television—corporate, industrial, educational, medical, and the like—whose work is most effective when it causes no comment. The director working at that level will understand well what I mean when I call television directing "the private art."

Part 3

Post-Production

CHAPTER 17

Introduction to Editing Systems

The basics of editing are actually quite simple, but the variety of editing systems and the choices of technique and style contrive to make the overall matter of editing quite complex. It's an area fraught with buzz words like "off-line," "on-line," and the ever-popular SMPTE. We've already examined some of these, and in this section we'll further de-mystify these terms and their friends.

Post-production has become increasingly important as single-camera film-style production has become more and more popular, and a solid understanding of editing equipment and procedures is tremendously important. Let's start with some background on videotape editing and its history.

The original method of videotape editing involved the use of razor blades and splicing tape, in much the same manner as audio tape is still edited. Unlike audiotape, videotape had definite places at which a cut had to be made in order to prevent the picture from breaking up at edit points when played back. This meant that it was necessary to determine where one picture ended and the next one began, so that the cut could be made between frames. With film, the frame divisions are easily visible, but with videotape this is not the case. The first problem, therefore, was to find a way to let the editor see what he was doing, and the first solution was the development of a developing solution.

It was found that by suspending microscopic metal particles in a solution of alcohol and painting it on the tape, the particles would align themselves with the tracks on the tape. This left traces on the tape, once the alcohol evaporated, that could be used as a guide for cutting. It was a cumbersome process, to be sure, and provided results that were often less than ideal. In the hands of an experienced cutter, however, the technique could be made to work, and the practice carried through as late as 1967, with the original *Laugh-In* show being edited in just that manner.

A better way to edit was obviously required if videotape was to develop into a practical production tool, and the answer took the form of electronic editing. This is simply the process of copying (rerecording) selected segments from one tape to another, in whatever order is desired. The original tape is not harmed, and can be used at any later time to re-edit the material. In the simplest terms, the edited master that results from an editing session is a copy of the original material, with the unwanted portions left out and, if desired, the order of sequences changed.

The refined abilities of today's editing VTRs have made electronic editing a fast, simple, and accurate operation, and we wouldn't think of actually cutting the tape any more. Even at the lowest level, the ½-inch reel-to-reel black and white recorders offer electronic editing, and this is how all video tape is now edited.

Sony BVE-3000.

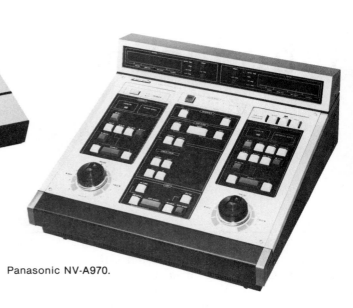

Panasonic NV-A970.

EDITING CONTROLLERS.

Convergence ECS-90.

Editing Methods

At the simplest and least expensive level, an editing system would consist of:

1. A VTR with editing capability and
2. A signal source—either a camera or another VTR.

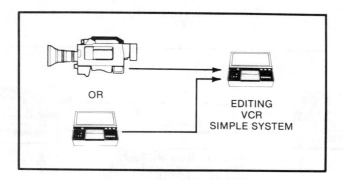

At the upper end of the scale, an editing system could consist of:

1. Numerous playback machines,
2. A computer-based editing controller,
3. Complex switchers with digital effects and color correction capabilities,
4. Multi tracked audio recorders that can be synchronized to the video signal.

Some of the more elaborate facilities have enough equipment to make Houston Control envious.

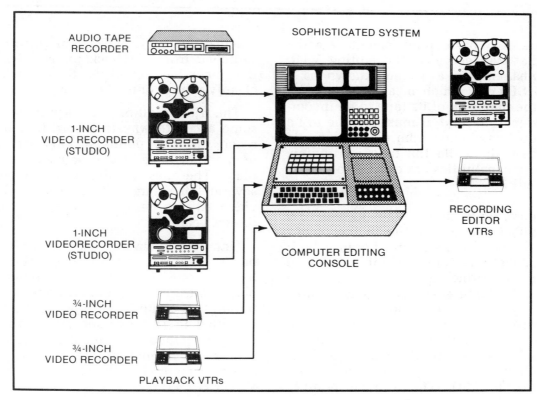

For tape-to-tape editing, which is the most common editing situation, a basic system requires two VTRs, at least one of which has editing capabilities. The original material is played back on one VTR (the PLAYBACK VTR), and the signal from that machine is fed to the video input of the editing VTR (the RECORD VTR).

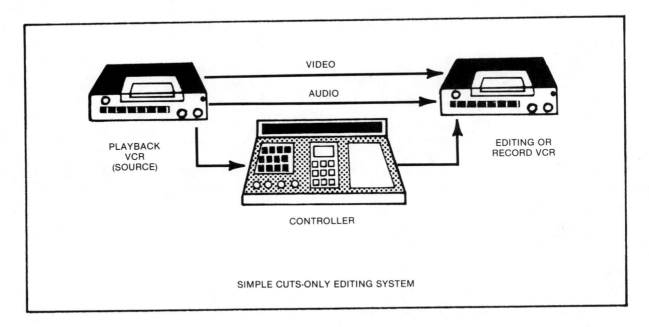

PLAYBACK VCR (SOURCE)

VIDEO

AUDIO

EDITING OR RECORD VCR

CONTROLLER

SIMPLE CUTS-ONLY EDITING SYSTEM

There are two basic requirements for the machine that will serve as the editing VTR: *First*, it must employ a system known as a CAPSTAN SERVO, which means that it synchronizes the playback of its tape to an incoming video signal. *Second*, it must be able to be instantaneously switched from playback mode into record mode while the tape is running. Both of these capabilities are critical to proper videotape editing.

It's not possible to simply start up one VTR in the playback mode and one in the record mode at the start of the scene, because both VTRs will take a certain amount of time to reach their operating speed. The lag time inherent while doing so would create distortions in the picture and sound. Instead, both machines are placed in playback mode at a point ahead of the edit and allowed sufficient time to reach a stable speed. This is the PRE-ROLL TIME mentioned in an earlier section (*Shooting for the Edit*). When the edit point is

reached on both VTRs, the record VTR is switched from playback to record mode, and the incoming signal is thus smoothly and cleanly edited onto the tape.

The trick to all of this, in practice, is to find some accurate way to assure that both VTRs reach the edit points at precisely the right moment, or the edit will be made at the wrong place. The quest for this accuracy has created several fairly large companies specializing in video editing hardware over the past ten or fifteen years.

Once you have at least two VTRs with the basic required capabilities, the question becomes one of how to control them. The simplest controllers are the two hands of an editor, and an awful lot of tape has been and still is edited in this manner. Although there are various methods around designed to aid the process of manual editing, the best and most accurate method is that known as the STOP-WATCH method.

220

The Stopwatch Method—This is a four-step process:

Step 1. Working first with the playback VTR, the editor locates the desired starting edit point on the original (source) tape.

Step 2. He then rewinds the tape and finds an arbitrary reference point on the tape roughly 10–15 seconds ahead of the edit point. This reference point could be a sound or an action. Using a stopwatch, he plays the tape and times the interval from the reference point to the edit point.

Step 3. The tape is then rewound back past the reference point, and the tape is played back again. The stopwatch is started at the reference point, and the tape is paused 5 seconds ahead of the edit point. Thus, if the reference point happened to be 13 seconds ahead of the edit point, he'd pause the tape 8 seconds after the reference point (13 seconds minus 8 seconds leaves a 5 second preroll). These three steps are then repeated for the editing VTR.

Step 4. Once both tapes are paused 5 seconds ahead of the edit point, he starts them simultaneously, and at the precise edit point, 5 seconds later, the editor presses an "EDIT" button on the editing VTR that switches it from playback into record. The 5 seconds for preroll is also an arbitrary number, but most VTRs can lock up and be running stably within that amount of time.

The above process probably sounds more complicated than it is in practice, and with experience, the level of accuracy that can be achieved can be surprisingly high. However, in the long run, it's a time-consuming process, and is, in its own way, almost as cumbersome as cutting the tape manually.

The need for a further editing aid first resulted in the development of systems that could record a tone pulse on an audio channel of the tape. This pulse would be used by a simple controller to switch the editing VTR into the record mode at an accurately established edit point. An OUT-EDIT PULSE could also be recorded, making precise INSERTS (edits into an existing program) possible. It was a tremendous help, but it still was essentially a manual process and did little to aid the real problem, which was synchronization of the two VTRs.

Electronic Editing Systems

In the 1960s, along came a system developed by a company called EECO (Electronic Engineering Company) that recorded an individual address code for every frame of video which permitted automated control and synchronization of VTRs. This system was quite successful, and the technique was subsequently standardized by SMPTE (more on this later).

In the late 60s the EECO system was followed by a machine developed in a joint venture between CBS and Memorex which offered producers much of the flexibility of film editing. This system used computer disks instead of videotape and VTRs to store the video signal, and a LIGHT PEN console at which the editor could make choices and see a rough playback of the edit decisions. No tape was actually used, and no edit master was recorded, the system merely played scenes back in the desired sequence (a paper tape was used to store the information). Once the decisions were made and approved, a computer would use the list of edits that had been generated to CONFORM (execute) or AUTO ASSEMBLE the program, using the master tapes to actually edit the show. This first system was the **CMX-600**, and out of the six ever built, as of 1982, there is only one still in use—in San Francisco. (Time marches on, bringing its changes.)

As small-format nonbroadcast television grew in use and application, the need for an editing aid that could provide speed and accuracy at a reasonable cost became obvious. In the early seventies, systems began to reach the market that were known as CONTROL TRACK editing systems, which went a long way towards answering the need. The control track systems took their name from the fact that the editor would pause both VTRs at the desired edit points and press a CUE button. The electronic controller then ran the tapes backwards and counted CONTROL TRACK PULSES (electronic sprocket holes) from the edit point to a preselected PREROLL or CUE point. It then placed the machines in playback mode, counted down the pulses, and the edit command would automatically be given when the counter reached zero.

221

These systems enjoyed immediate popularity, and companies such as **TRI** (since gone to that great receivership in the sky), **Convergence**, and virtually all of the Japanese VTR manufacturers came out with their own versions. Although the original control track systems were designed for use with older format 1-inch VTRs, they were quickly adapted for use with ¾-inch cassette machines. All of the low-cost (under about $2000) editing controllers currently available use this control track system.

Meanwhile, computer editing took a different direction than had first been envisioned, and all of the systems that were introduced subsequent to the CMX-600 used standard VTRs rather than computer disks. In addition to CMX, now owned by Orrox Corp., such firms as **EECO, Datatron**, and eventually a host of others jumped into the time code editing arena. Their systems all offered compatibility with the defacto CMX edit decision list standard. Some of the more prominent full-scale systems currently marketed include the **Mach I**, the **Epic**, and the **Sony BVE-5000**, among others. Costs run in the $25,000 to $100,000 range.

JVC Videocassette Editing System

CR-5500U Player VTR

CR-8250 Editor VTR

RM-88U Editing Controller

VE-90 Editing Controller

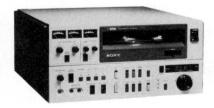

Sony VO-5850

Sony BVE-800

Sony BVU-820

The video producer today is faced with these two basic types of editing systems, and the decision of whether to use a control track system or a time code system will rest on the same basic factors with which we've already become familiar—time, budget, and the nature of the program. The two systems each offer their own set of advantages and requirements, which the producer or director must consider when weighing the choice.

Time code editing systems.

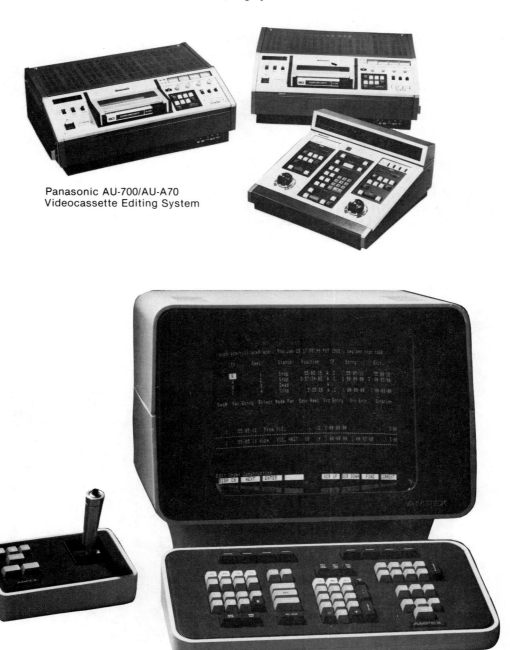

Panasonic AU-700/AU-A70
Videocassette Editing System

Ampex ACE Editing System.

Control Track vs. Time Code Systems

Control track systems are considerably less expensive than are time code systems, both in terms of purchase and rental rates. A basic system, consisting of two ¾-inch cassette VTRs and a controller, would cost roughly $10,000–$15,000, plus monitors and incidentals, and can be rented for as little as $25.00 an hour. They offer the advantage of being able to work with tapes brought straight from the field, with no need to have them time coded, and no special technical requirements beyond clean video and stable sync. Two major factors work against them, however. First, since one control track pulse looks just like the next one to the controller, if the tape slips at all in stopping or starting, or if it stops with a pulse right at the control track head (either of which is easily possible), the controller won't have a clue as to where it *really* is. This translates into an editing inaccuracy of from one to five frames that increases each time an edit is rehearsed. This margin of error is about the same from one system to the next. Putting it simply, control track systems just aren't that accurate.

The second problem follows from this lack of real accuracy. The inability to determine precise frames makes it virtually impossible to roll three machines in sync—let alone two. A two-VTR editing system is limited to making simple CUTS. Special effects such as DISSOLVES, WIPES, or KEYS require the ability to roll three VTRs in precise synchronization (A/B ROLL EDITING). A dissolve, for instance, requires one VTR to play back the DISSOLVE FROM tape, one to play back the DISSOLVE TO tape, plus the record VTR. Control track systems simply don't have the accuracy to reliably synchronize three VTRs to the exact frame, although the editing systems from some manufacturers are capable of making an attempt at it.

There have been a number of schemes developed to get around this accuracy problem, such as altering the control track pulses slightly at regular intervals so that the controller can tell which one is which. The **Z-6** systems marketed by **Videomedia** and the systems from **Cezar International** use this technique. This technique can indeed provide SINGLE FRAME ACCURACY, within certain operational limitations, and has had excellent success. It's a relatively low-cost route to frame-accurate editing.

The best method, however, of obtaining accurate, consistent, and readily repeatable edits is to use an individual frame address that is recorded directly on the tape, and to which a computer can refer in order to synchronize the VTRs. This is, of course, our time code.

A Z-6000 Editor.

SMPTE Time Code Editing

The industry in general adopted a time code standardized by the Society of Motion Picture and Television Engineers called SMPTE (pronounced "Simptee") time code. It is a digital code that assigns each frame a number that breaks down into hours, minutes, seconds, and frames. The code address 01:22:13:24, for instance, would indicate 1 hour, 22 minutes, 13 seconds, and 24 frames. The SMPTE code is recorded directly on the tape, either on an audio channel, or on a separate channel (called the CUE channel) designed especially for it. There are also some systems that insert the code into the video signal during the VERTICAL BLANKING INTERVAL (the blank, unused portion of the signal above the picture area).

Time code in "window".

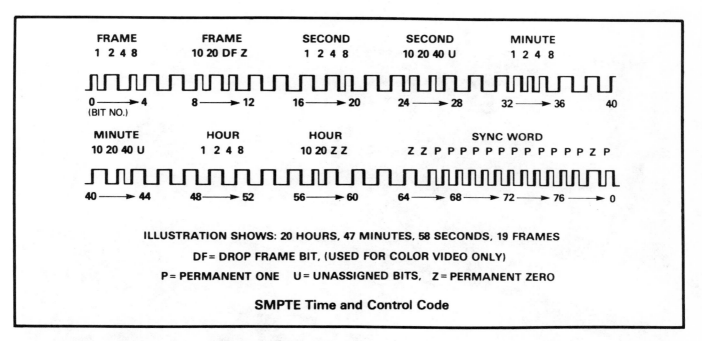

ILLUSTRATION SHOWS: 20 HOURS, 47 MINUTES, 58 SECONDS, 19 FRAMES

DF = DROP FRAME BIT, (USED FOR COLOR VIDEO ONLY)

P = PERMANENT ONE   U = UNASSIGNED BITS,   Z = PERMANENT ZERO

SMPTE Time and Control Code

Actually, there are *two* SMPTE codes, one called DROP FRAME, and the other called NONDROP FRAME. The color television frame rate is not exactly 30 frames per second, but rather approximately 29.97 frames per second, so over the length of a one-hour program, the SMPTE code would be off by 3 seconds and 18 frames compared to actual running time. In many instances this difference might seem trivial, and on such short items as commercials the difference is infinitesimal. In network programming, however, those three seconds in an hour-long show are quite impor-tant, and drop frame code corrects for the error. It does so by dropping two frames every minute except for the tenth minute.

Drop frame code is commonly used in network production, but outside of that field, non-drop code is more commonly used, since it's easier to work with. Getting the editing computer to "understand" that there are time code addresses that simply do not exist, and to do the proper math in figuring duration and such is no easy task; doing the math in one's head while editing is all but impossible.

While the basic requirements for a time code editing system are two VTRs and the controller, the real advantage of time code lies in its ability to accurately synchronize multiple machines. Thus, they're more likely to be found controlling at least two playback VTRs and a record VTR (known as THREE MACHINE EDITING or A/B ROLL EDITING).

Time code systems entail their own trade-off, mainly in terms of cost. Even with cassette-based systems, by the time you add up the computer, the interfaces to control the particular make and model VTRs, at least three VTRs, a switcher, two time base correctors (necessary in order to synchronize playback signals), and other assorted paraphernalia, you're starting to look at some substantial money—about the same amount as a comfortable house or a 50-foot yacht. Start toting up the cost of a full 1-inch or quad system, and the price can quickly go past the million dollar mark.

Because the cost of time code systems is high, most of the systems around belong either to the networks, the stations, or independent production facilities that rent them out on an hourly basis. However, lower cost systems are now becoming available such as the **Convergence ECS-90** for under $20,000; although systems in this price range do not offer anywhere near the full range of capabilities found in the more advanced computer systems.

CMX-340X editing suite.

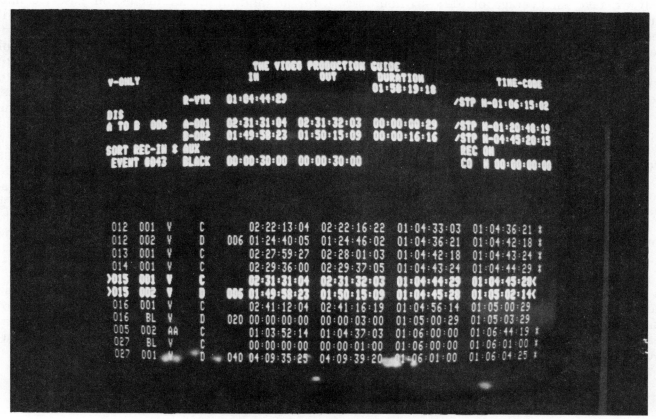

The edit data display screen provided by the CMX-340X.

In operation, time code editing is generally easier and faster than control track editing, since the computer can take over many of the chores. Cuing a tape to a particular time code address, for instance, is done simply by entering the time code into the computer and telling it to "fetch." The computer will read the time code on the tape, and SHUTTLE (move) the tape to the desired point and stop it. Since the time code is a permanent part of the tape, there is never any question of where an address is. In control track editing (which is almost always done on cassette), if a cassette is removed midway through the tape and later reinserted, the reference—either counter or tape timer—is lost, and the tape must be rewound to the beginning in order to reestablish the reference point. It's directly analogous to trying to find a house on a very, very long block. With time code, you have an address, and the search is easy. With control track, you may be looking for "the 18,293rd house down from the corner." If you lose count, you have to start all over again back at the corner.

Comparative Economics of Editing Systems

In nonbroadcast applications, if time code editing has been chosen or is necessary to a production, a possible further choice is whether to select cassette or one of the highband systems as the editing format. Since the 1-inch Type C format is gradually becoming the highband format of choice, let's compare ¾-inch cassette and 1-inch in doing some cost analysis.

At the time of this writing, basic three-machine editing (one record and two playback VTRs) on cassette are priced at between $100 and $150 per hour, varying from one part of the country to another and from one facility to the next. The 1-inch editing is priced from about $250 an hour to $350 an hour, depending again on location, on what additional goodies are included, and on how expensive the woodwork and carpeting in the facility are.

If we take an average of $125 an hour for cassette, and $300 an hour for 1-inch, it would seem at first glance that cassette editing would be considerably cheaper than 1-inch editing, and thus the logical choice for productions with tight budgets. There are, however, additional factors that must be taken into account, and which may make just the opposite true.

First, 1-inch editing obviously offers higher technical quality, and this alone may be enough to make it the initial choice. The question of ultimate cost, however surprising it may be, can make 1-inch editing less expensive in terms of ultimate cost as well! The reason is simple.

Editing on cassette will take *at least* twice as long as editing the same show on 1-inch, in most instances. Unless there is very little material or there are very few edits involved, the search and shuttle time on cassette will be roughly three times longer than on 1-inch. The thread and unthread cycles on cassette add even more time, the previewing sequence still more, with the net result that a half-hour show with, say, 300 edits made from four hours of original tape could take roughly 12 hours to edit on a 1-inch system, and 20 to 30 hours to edit on a cassette system. There are, of course, many variables to be considered, and the newer ¾-inch BVU-800 series from Sony speed editing considerably. But extensive experience with both systems in comparative situations has demonstrated that it is often possible to save money by using the more expensive system. If considering an in-house editing facility, a ¾-inch system would probably be the way to go since it is much cheaper to purchase and much simpler to operate and maintain than 1-inch equipment.

One of the major factors in considering the choice of an editing facility is whether or not an off-line edit will be done prior to the final on-line edit, and this is our next area of examination.

CHAPTER 18

Editing Mechanics

Off-line vs. On-line

These two terms seem to be a source of great confusion, so let's begin by defining them. Put simply, OFF-LINE editing means doing a preliminary rough edit of a production before committing to the final edit. The final edit is called an ON-LINE EDIT and is created after an off-line edit or when only one edited tape is performed to finish the show. The resulting tape is called the EDITED MASTER.

The basic idea of off-line editing is to use a low-cost system using ½-inch or ¾-inch cuts-only equipment to produce a test edit of a production that will be used as a guide in doing

the final edit on a higher level system, such as 1-inch. The system price or hourly rental charge of an off-line system is lower than the cost of an on-line system, so it is possible to take more time with decisions than would be comfortably possible with a clock ticking off expensive minutes. Another reason for doing an off-line edit is to obtain client approvals and SIGN-OFFS (final approvals) before locking the show in final form with an on-line edit.

In a facility working with cassette and a control track system, the only distinction between off-line and on-line editing may be the amount of care taken with technical standards. In some cases when approval is not necessary, it may be decided to go directly on-line and edit the show for keeps.

In time code editing, especially when the on-line format is 1-inch or quad, doing an off-line edit is more often a matter of saving money, and is done to reduce the amount of time spent on the final edit. Off-line time code editing is designed to create two products that will prepare for the on-line edit: An edited rough cut tape that will show how the finished program will look, and an EDIT DECISION LIST (EDL) that contains the information needed by an on-line computer system to perform the final edit. There are several ways in which this edit decision list can be created, depending on the facilities and budget available for post-production.

Cassette editing systems such as the **CMX-50** were originally conceived as off-line systems that would allow the producer and/or director to play with a show to their heart's contents before going on-line with their 2-inch quad masters. In its standard configuration, the CMX-50 is a complete SMPTE time code editing system that uses two ¾-inch cassette units for playback and one for recording. It can perform cuts, dissolves, and a limited number of wipes. While it was originally designed for off-line editing, it can also be used for ¾-inch on-line editing. Other systems that offer this off-line/on-line versatility are marketed by **Convergence, Datatron, United Media,** and **Videomedia,** among others.

Although the rates charged for systems like the CMX-50 are not what most of us would call cheap ($100-$150 an hour), they are indeed lower than the quad or 1-inch systems controlled by higher-level systems such as the **CMX-340.**

One advantage to this type of a system is that at the end of the editing session, the computer will spit out a decision list—usually in the form of a paper punch tape, although sometimes now on a floppy computer disk. This list can then be loaded into an on-line system computer which uses the information contained in the list to perform what is known as an AUTO ASSEMBLE. This means that the on-line computer automatically edits the program from the master tapes, theoretically without human interference.

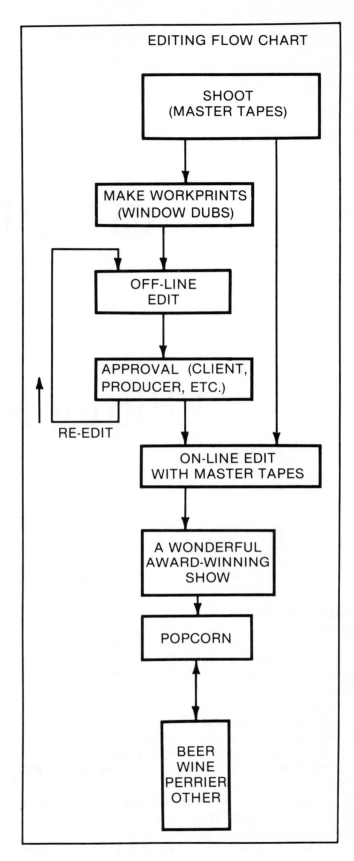

230

Although there are instances where this is done, the concept of a true auto assemble is rarely fully realized. The on-line computer will indeed take the list, and will start assembling the show as the list indicates, but in quality post-production there will be a constant need to carefully adjust video and setup levels, color balance, audio levels, and the like. The chances that the computer can get all the way through an edit with no human intervention are minimal, and the very words "auto assemble" are often taken as a joke and a call for overtime by the crews at post-production houses. Perhaps the greatest value of the EDL is the elimination of the need to reenter the editing numbers by hand for the final edit. Electronic transfer of the edit data saves time, money, and eliminates errors in entering. The

Computer editing system console, including computer keyboard, switcher, digital effects unit, color correctors, monitors, and routing switchers.

format of the edit decision list is a defacto standard originally established by CMX. Most manufacturers of editing systems adopted the CMX format, and virtually all high-level editing systems can use the CMX format to generate or accept the editing information. A sample of the list format would look like this:

```
001 04 B C       04:01:22:13  04:01:27:13  01:00:00:00  01:00:05:00
002 04 B C       04:01:27:13  04:01:27:13  01:00:05:00  01:00:05:00
002 02 B D 030   02:12:18:17  02:12:28:17  01:00:05:00  01:00:15:00
```

The example above shows two edits, also called EVENTS in "computer-editese." You'll notice that event number 2 takes up two lines; we'll get to the reason in a moment. Let's first examine what the various numbers and letters mean.

The far left column lists the EVENT (edit) NUMBER. The sample list starts with event number 1 (001).

The second column lists the SOURCE which could be a VTR or an auxiliary source such as a character generator. Event number 1 used reel number 4, while event number 2 used reel 4 in the first line, and reel 2 in the second line. Other sources would include "AX" for an AUXILIARY source such as colorbars, and "BL" for BLACK.

The third column indicates the EDIT MODE. "B" indicates both video and audio were taken from the source tape, while "V" would indicate VIDEO only, and "A" would indicate AUDIO only.

The fourth column indicates the TYPE OF TRANSITION involved. "C" means the edit is a simple cut, "D" means DISSOLVE, "W" means WIPE, and "K" indicates a KEY or MATTE.

The fifth column is used only when the edit involves a dissolve, wipe, or key, and indicates the DURATION OF THE TRANSITION. The "030" on the second line of event number 2 in the example indicates a 30-frame (1 second) dissolve.

The remaining four columns are the time code numbers for the source and record tapes. These show, in order, the IN (beginning) and OUT (ending) TIME CODE ADDRESSES for the SOURCE TAPE, followed by the IN and OUT TIMES for the RECORD TAPE. The RECORD OUT TIME is actually not needed by the computer, since it can compute this by adding the duration of the edit to the record in time. Some systems, therefore, don't list the record out time, or offer a choice between listing the record out time or the event duration. In either case, the listing is essentially a courtesy, to make the list easier to work with.

You'll notice that in the above example, the reel numbers match the number in the "HOURS" section of the time code. This is not mandatory, but it is helpful to encode the tapes in such a manner. Doing so makes it possible to tell at a glance what reel is involved in an edit. The SMPTE code also includes a provision for what are called USER BITS, which are portions of the code that have been given no specific task. Facilities having a time code generator equipped to program user bits can enter reel numbers, scene numbers, or short descriptions, or anything else they'd like in the user bit sections. This information will be recorded on the tape as a part of the time code. Some editing systems are programmed to read user bits and automatically change the reel numbers as new tapes are loaded, freeing the editor from the task of remembering to do this manually.

The reason event number 2 takes up two lines in the CMX format is that all dissolves and wipes are broken down into two separate actions, beginning with a cut. In the example, event number 1 was a straight cut taken from reel number 4, lasting 5 seconds. The editor then decided to make the next transition a dissolve. The system started by cutting to reel 4 at the exact point where event number 1 ended (called a MATCHED-FRAME EDIT), and then immediately started a 30-frame dissolve to reel 2. Event number 2 then ran for 10 seconds and ended. Of those 10 seconds, the first second included the dissolve from reel 4.

The intricacies of time code editing are far beyond the scope of anything less than a full course of instruction, and we'll not attempt to teach you how to perform computer editing. However, a basic familiarity with the list format is useful.

```
TITLE: SAMPLE EDIT DECISION LIST
FCM: NON-DROP FRAME

001   AX    AA/V   C           00:00:00:00 00:01:00:00 00:58:30:00 00:59:30:00

002   AX    V      C           00:00:00:00 00:00:10:00 00:59:40:00 00:59:50:00

003   BL    B      C           00:00:00:00 00:00:00:00 01:00:00:00 01:00:00:00
003   001   B      D      030  01:23:14:18 01:23:17:18 01:00:00:00 01:00:03:00

004   002   B      C           02:17:22:19 02:17:25:19 01:00:03:00 01:00:06:00
004   002   B      K B         02:17:25:19 02:17:34:04 01:00:06:00 01:00:14:15
004   AX    B      K      030  00:00:00:00 00:00:06:00 01:00:06:00 01:00:12:00

005   007   A2     C           07:53:16:02 07:53:30:17 01:00:00:00 01:00:14:15

006   002   AA/V   C           02:17:34:04 02:17:34:04 01:00:14:15 01:00:14:15
006   005   AA/V   D      030  05:39:11:26 05:39:18:06 01:00:14:15 01:00:20:25

007   005   AA/V   C           05:41:50:13 05:42:17:14 01:00:20:25 01:00:47:26

008   005   AA/V   C           05:42:17:14 05:42:29:14 01:00:47:26 01:00:58:26

009   005   AA/V   C           05:42:29:14 05:42:29:14 01:00:58:26 01:00:58:26
009   005B  AA/V   W014   020  05:45:26:22 05:45:47:26 01:00:58:26 01:01:20:00

010   005B  AA/V   C           05:45:47:26 05:45:47:26 01:01:20:00 01:01:20:00
010   004   AA/V   W114   020  04:19:32:08 04:19:38:23 01:01:20:00 01:01:26:15

011   004   AA/V   C           04:21:33:29 04:21:41:29 01:01:26:15 01:01:34:15

012   004   AA/V   C           04:23:37:05 04:23:48:20 01:01:34:15 01:01:46:00

013   004   V      C           04:25:43:26 04:25:45:26 01:01:32:15 01:01:34:15

014   004   AA/V   C           04:23:48:20 04:23:48:20 01:01:46:00 01:01:46:00
014   002   AA/V   D      015  02:34:19:12 02:34:27:27 01:01:46:00 01:01:54:15

015   002   AA/V   C           02:42:04:18 02:42:20:14 01:01:54:15 01:02:10:11

016   002   AA/V   C           02:45:29:22 02:45:34:26 01:02:10:11 01:02:15:15

017   004   AA     C           04:19:53:02 04:19:56:05 01:02:12:12 01:02:15:15

018   004   AA/V   C           04:19:56:05 04:20:11:11 01:02:15:15 01:02:30:21

019   004B  AA/V   C           04:32:18:28 04:32:21:28 01:02:30:21 01:02:33:21
019   004B  AA/V   K B         04:32:21:28 04:32:28:28 01:02:33:21 01:02:40:21
019   AX    AA/V   K      030  00:00:00:00 00:00:06:00 01:02:33:21 01:02:39:21

020   004B  AA/V   K B         04:32:28:28 04:32:35:28 01:02:40:21 01:02:47:21
020   AX    AA/V   K      030  00:00:00:00 00:00:06:00 01:02:40:21 01:02:46:21

021   004B  AA/V   C           04:32:35:28 04:32:35:28 01:02:47:21 01:02:47:21
021   BL    AA/V   D      030  00:00:00:00 00:00:10:00 01:02:47:21 01:02:57:21
```

A CMX format edit decision list, showing twenty "events." Events will take up one, two or three lines, depending on the type of action they describe.

Edit Decision List Formats

Manufacturers other than CMX now offer alternate list formats, though they also make provisions for their systems to work with the CMX format as well as their own proprietary format. In the strictest sense there is no real standard format—the closest thing to one is the CMX format made popular by the tremendous success of their systems.

The industry in general is under a certain amount of pressure to design a standard EDIT DECISION LIST format that would allow the computer to control level and color correction of the video, audio level, and equalization; along with switcher memory and digital effects systems. The basic problem in developing such a standard is that by the time one is developed, it is already out of date, since new systems and capabilities are continually appearing, and because each of the switcher manufacturers has its own approach to special effects control. Thus it's likely to be a while before we see a standard EDL format with all these provisions.

Facilities that are equipped with their own editing systems, and producers who go outside on quick and simple jobs can probably go directly on-line and save money in the process.

There is no doubt whatsoever, though, that on programs of a complex nature, doing an off-line edit can save money in the long run by speeding the process of assembling the final edited master. The question becomes one of determining the most cost-effective method of producing the edit decision list that is the result of an off-line edit.

Changing Edits and Edit Decision Lists

While the concept of using a computer off-line system is basically valid, there is a hitch caused by one of the basic differences between editing a film workprint and a videotape workprint. Consider a one-hour show with 600 edits that has been through its first CUT (edit). The producer and director screen it, and decide on several changes, all of which come near the middle of the show. The edit decision list can be very easily changed—that's one of the major advantages to computer editing. The editor can REOPEN (recall) an edit, and change its source, duration, or any other parameter. If the length of the edit is altered, the computer will then change the record times of all scenes following the change (called RIPPLING or PULLING UP the list) to correct for the change. On the tape itself, though, it's a very different matter. Each and every edit following the first change will have to be redone, or the result will be a HOLE (blank space), or several holes, somewhere in the show. For instance, if a scene near the middle of the show were shortened, performing the new edit on the tape would leave some of the original edit "hanging out," unless all the following scenes were PULLED UP and re-edited in their new positions.

In film editing it's easy—simply take out the bad scene and replace it with the good one, or splice in or take out a few frames or feet, and go merrily on your way. However, tape doesn't work that way, and it's for this reason that many people who are accustomed to editing film workprints find videotape editing very frustrating.

One obvious solution would be to use the first rough cut as the source tape for a second rough cut, taking the tape DOWN A GENERATION (making a new copy) and re-editing only those scenes that need changing. This can indeed work well, and since the edit is a rough cut, the lowered quality will not normally be a problem. But, there's another hitch, in that the edit decision list—which was the main object of the off-line computer edit—will then consist of *two* lists. The first will be a list of the first cut, and will show all 600 edits, while the second list will show only the changes that have been made. This is further compounded if the show goes through subsequent revisions, as is often the case, and it's entirely possible to end up with an original list, plus three, four, five, or more lists showing changes.

It is conceivable to sit down and manually update the original list to reflect the changes made in subsequent lists, but it's not the kind of task you'd assign to someone you liked, or whose mental health you cared about.

There are special computer programs now available called LIST TRACE, or something similar, that deal with this problem. They do just what their name implies—they trace through all the various Edit Decision Lists of an edited program and compile a single list that includes all changes. Unfortunately, they are rather expensive and require the supervision of an experienced editor. Imagine, just for a moment, how much the computer must do to trace a 600-edit show with five re-edits in drop-frame code. It leaves one with a sense of awe of computers, and of the people who run them.

All this sounds quite complicated, and it is. It also sounds quite expensive, and again, it is. Fortunately, there is a very practical procedure available that can allow for a multigeneration rough-cut and preparation of an edit decision list without costing two arms and a leg. It does, however, have the minor drawback of requiring the final list to be manually entered into the computer used for the on-line edit. This disadvantage, as we shall see shortly, is actually not all that much of a problem.

A Personal Method of Off-line Editing

This is the system I use myself to prepare for on-line editing, and it's one that has worked very well. First, as mentioned earlier, I have WINDOW DUBS made (again, ¾-inch cassette copies of the original footage with the time code visually keyed into the video). These will serve as the source tape for the off-line edit. Using these, I edit the show together on my ¾-inch system into the first rough cut, which is then available for viewing and study. As I make each edit, I note the starting and ending time codes from the source tapes on a standard edit decision list form, thus building a penciled EDL as I go along. All edits in the rough cut itself will be straight cuts. If there are dissolves or other effect transitions in the final edit, the notes will reflect this.

When it comes time to polish and re-edit, I use the first rough cut as the source tape, switching to the original window dubs only when a change is to be made. For instance, if a scene needs to be shortened, I simply edit from the first rough, editing out the unwanted portions. If a scene must be lengthened, I go back

to the original window dub and edit it into the second rough. Then the first rough goes back into the playback VTR, and it continues as the source tape until the next such change.

I'll almost always do at least three rough edits of a show, revising, fine tuning, and polishing a bit more on each version until I'm satisfied. Some shows, however, may go through as many as six, seven, or even more roughs, especially if the client must approve content along the way, and if the production is a complex one.

Using this procedure means that after the first rough cut, the great bulk of a second rough cut will consist of a direct dub from the first rough cut, and a substantial amount of time is saved. Obviously, if the show goes through four or five reworkings, the video will start to get a bit flaky technically, since each new rough cut adds a generation to the video signal. However, it still does its basic job, which is to demonstrate how the pacing and flow of the production will work. If the client must see the final rough (cut) for approval purposes, I may replace really raunchy video by

The author's cuts only 3/4-inch editing system (controller, at right, not visible).

inserting material from the original window dubs, but I generally try to avoid this. For that matter, I am generally somewhat wary of showing rough cuts to clients at all. With clients who are familiar with the process of television, it's relatively safe, since they will easily understand why the rough cut may look awfully weird technically after four or five generations of off-line cassette editing. Inexperienced clients, though, may react with horror, and often no amount of explanation will assure them that the noisy, unstable video with the funny numbers showing, and with cuts where dissolves will be, will turn into a smooth, stable program with sparkly video and clean, clear audio.

Visual time code inserted into vertical interval area, viewed on a pulse cross display.

In situations where I must show such a client a rough cut, there are a few procedures that can help with the problem. One is to have the visual time code compressed and squeezed into the VERTICAL INTERVAL AREA where it won't be visible during normal playback. This requires editing with a PULSE-CROSS MONITOR connected so that the time codes can be read. Secondly, I'll take more time to make sure that each edit is clean and smooth, and will treat the edit as a POLISHED

ROUGH CUT—perhaps including title keys and fades and the like—to provide results that are technically closer to an on-line edit. This, however, is not especially cost-efficient for the client, since it takes considerably longer than simply banging out edits for my own use.

One thing to remember with this technique is that any edit that will take audio from one source and video from another requires special handling. The audio source should be edited first as an audio/video edit because the time code goes with the video not the audio. This procedure is necessary so the time codes can be noted before the video is replaced. The time codes on the edited master of the rough cut are basically the record of the edit decision list. If the video is laid down first and the audio then edited as an audio-only insert, there will be no way to tell from the master what those audio source codes were. Obviously, once the video edit is made, those audio codes will no longer be visible anyway, so it's important to remember to note them before making the video-only edit.

Going On-Line

Once I've got a rough cut with which everyone is happy, I'm ready to go on-line. Armed with the original masters and the edit decision list that I've put together on paper, it becomes a simple matter of entering the codes into the computer and letting the computer do its thing. Here, there are two procedures available.

The first would be to turn off the record function of the computer and load the entire list into memory. With the record function off, the computer enters the edit into the list, but does not make the edit on tape. Once this was done, the record function would then be turned on, and the computer would be told to auto assemble the entire show. This would be very similar to loading the edit from a punch tape generated on an off-line computer editor, and would allow me to go off and have a drink or get into trouble carousing around while the show was being assembled. I'd then walk in when the edit was done and pick up a finished show.

236

The other alternative, and the one that I practice, is to enter the edits one at a time, and have the computer perform them one at a time. This way, if an edit would benefit from being trimmed by a frame or two, or if video or audio levels need tweaking, this can be done while the edit is being made, and the finished show will require no further work. (Besides, this keeps me off the street and out of trouble.)

To speed the process of entering the numbers, have someone read them to the editor, so that he or she won't have to take his eyes from the keyboard. Since I usually operate the computer myself, I bring someone along to feed the numbers to me, and find that this saves a substantial amount of time.

The ideal, of course, would be to find some way to avoid the time spent entering the codes manually, such as by having them entered from a punch tape or floppy disk, but without having to rent a computer off-line system to generate the list. Towards this end, I've written a program for my microcomputer which will store the edit list (instead of manually, on printed EDL forms), and generate a punch tape that can be loaded into the on-line computer. This can save perhaps an hour's time in an average eight-hour edit, which works out to roughly $300 saved at the going rate for each day's editing. You'll find more information on this program in the Appendix on *Computer Use and Application.*

There are now some relatively inexpensive off-line editing systems that use a control track editing controller, and also note SMPTE time codes and generate a punch tape to be subsequently loaded into an on-line system computer. These could be regarded as "hybrids," falling between the basic control track system and systems such as the CMX 50. They don't offer the effects capabilities of the CMX 50, but on the other hand, they're priced considerably lower.

As previously mentioned, if the editing required is fairly simple, such as pasting together segments of a show done with multiple cameras and hot switching, it may be better to go directly on-line. The quality of the 1-inch format in particular is good enough that changes could be made by re-editing the edited master—taking it down a generation in just the

The tape operator helps speed editing by changing tapes and adjusts the VTRs to keep tapes in spec.

same way as in the off-line technique described above—without having any noticeable effect on the video quality.

It is also conceivable that a show can go on-line directly after preparation of a PAPER EDIT, which is a list put together from time codes during viewing sessions, but without actually editing a rough cut. This has the advantage of saving time, and can work well when the director knows exactly how the material will cut together. It does, however, require a fair amount of experience. Scenes don't always cut together the way they were supposed to, and it can be hard to keep track of continuity without actually seeing how the cuts really work.

As with most of the other choices involved in the production process, there is no one simple answer, and all of the factors must be weighed. As a rule of thumb, and leaving aside the producer with in-house facilities, if a program requires a lot of intricate editing and/or must go through several stages of approval prior to doing the final edit, off-line editing will probably save money in the long run.

237

Graphics and Audio for Final Edit

This section applies to on-line editing when it has been preceded by an off-line edit, or is the one and only edit that will be done.

As has already been mentioned, the major distinguishing factor of on-line editing will be the care taken with the process. Again, the most critical factors with which the editor will be concerned will be the continuity, and the pacing and flow of the program. But an equal amount of effort must also be put into the technical quality of each edit. This can be a bit difficult, because while watching either the rehearsal or the playback of an edit for aesthetic considerations, it can be hard to also watch for technical flaws, and vice versa.

Often, when rehearsing a critical edit, I'll run the preview several times—for instance, first for continuity, then for color and video levels, then for audio levels, and then again for over all feel. When watching to get the feel of an edit, I sometimes use an especially long

A title camera mounted on a copy stand.

preroll that makes it easier to establish the flow. Once the edit has been made, I'll then play it back to check for technical quality. On the 1-inch format, this last is important mainly at matched-frame edit points, while on cassette—especially on a control track system—each edit must be checked for technical quality. More on this in the last part of this section.

In film, the final editing (cutting of the negative) is done in the lab, while in tape, the on-line editing room takes the place of the lab. This is why the editor must be part artist and part technician, and must constantly switch back and forth between the roles. The editor is creating the final version of the program, and what's done in the on-line edit will determine what the viewer sees.

Graphics:

The subject of graphics is included under post-production because, in the majority of productions—especially single-camera ones—this is where they are normally inserted into the show. The basic rules, however, would be the same when they are used during a hot-switched multicamera production.

There are two basic types of graphics used in television production: FULL-SCREEN Graphics—paintings, drawings, photographs, etc., and KEYED or SUPERED Graphics—words and titles that are superimposed over other video. In today's environment, keyed graphics come from two primary sources: TITLE CARDS (shot with a title camera), and CHARACTER GENERATORS. There are also graphics that are essentially part of the set, such as the giant weather map used by a station's weather person on the evening news.

A character generator keyboard (Chyron IV).

Full-screen graphics may be used for a variety of purposes. Charts and pies (circular-form charts) may be used to illustrate financial or other information, as for a corporate program; technical drawings for a training program; symbolic drawings to back up a news reader's story; maps to delineate sales effort for a marketing program, etc. Then we have the ANIMATIC (as mentioned earlier in *Chapter 2*), which is a semianimated storyboard most commonly used by ad agencies to demonstrate to a client roughly what the commercial they're pitching will look like. The animatic's kissin' cousin is the PHOTOMATIC (also mentioned in *Chapter 2*) which is a series of still photos edited on tape to serve the same purpose.

Full-screen graphics may come from a variety of sources physically, but the two most common are a separate camera, and a SLIDE CHAIN which is a system (usually a permanent installation) that links a camera optically to one or two slide projectors. The newest technology for storing and recalling graphics is the electronic STILL-STORE, which files graphics as video frames on a computer-type disk for virtually instant, random-access recall. A recent development, one that will certainly expand considerably as computer and memory circuits become more powerful at ever lower cost, is solid-state storage of graphics, where the video is stored on memory chips—providing instant access and requiring no moving parts.

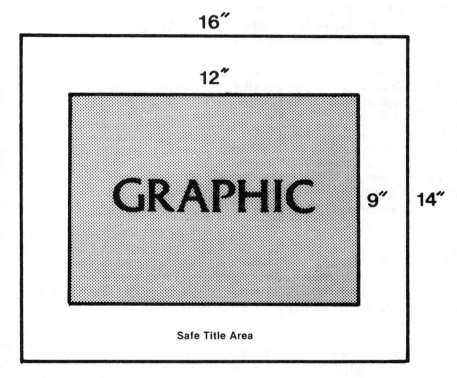

Safe Title Area

No matter how the graphic is produced or stored, it must have been prepared with the television screen in mind. Besides staying within the 3:4 aspect ratio's SAFE TITLE AREA, this dictates the use of strong, bold lines, and the avoidance of very fine detail. Colors can be used to emphasize points, and though most of the receivers in use these days are color ones, in broadcast applications there are still enough people watching in black and white to make it a good practice to check how a graphic looks on a black and white monitor.

Starting late in the 1970s, the use of computer-generated or manipulated graphics began to become common. The advantages are obvious. Graphics can be generated quickly, including animation. Although the cost of these systems is high, the rates charged by the firms that own them and offer their use can be quite reasonable. The disadvantage to many of these is that their graphics almost always *look* like computer graphics, which is to say, the quality is sometimes mediocre, or even "cheap-looking." The state of the art improves daily, though, and some of the work being done at the time of this writing has become very good indeed. The **Aurora Systems, Dubner,** and **MCI/Quantel DPB-7000** systems are examples of advanced computer graphics systems. In the right application, computer graphics can save time and money, and may be worth considering.

With regard to titles and other keyed-over artwork, the same basic factors apply. Character generators offer much quicker generation of graphics, and some of the top-end systems on the market now feature some animation capabilities, taking them beyond the simple character generator level.

A top-quality character generator is an extremely handy tool, and can offer character quality that is quite good. For such things as long credit rolls at the end of a program, they are virtually indispensable. A distinction here is that some character generators may provide good character resolution, but may not provide such features as proportional spacing and ABSOLUTE CENTERING. This means that the characters are arranged in defined columns, so that a line with, say, 14 characters that is followed by a line with 15 characters will have a character on a second line sticking out on one side. With absolute centering, there are no defined columns, and horizontal centering will provide very pleasing results.

The older technique for providing these kinds of graphics—used before character generators were available, and still in use today—is the TITLE CARD. This is shot by a title camera, with the signal being keyed or matted into the picture. Title cameras are usually high-resolution black and white models. The disadvantage to title cards is that they take considerable more time to put together, while on the other hand, they're considerably less expensive. A really high-quality character generator will start at perhaps $10,000–$20,000, and easily move up to $50,000 or more. A good title camera can be had for under $1000, with each title card costing anywhere from 50 cents to $15.00, depending on how it is created. There are character generators available for as little as $1000, but as with most things, you get what you pay for. The quality of the lowest priced units is quite modest. Character generators can sometimes be located for rental, with

Without

With

Absolute centering.

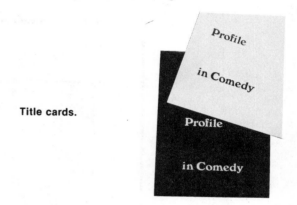

Title cards.

rates ranging from perhaps $50.00 per day for a very basic unit to $500 a day or more for a full-scale system. Be aware that interfacing them to a system may be a fairly complex task which may require some fairly sophisticated technical know-how.

Title cards offer another advantage, however. Well-done title cards will almost always offer higher ultimate quality, as well as completely customized FONTS (typefaces). There are few, if any, character generators available that can do as good a job with spacing and alignment as can a competent graphic artist.

Regardless of how the titles or keys are produced, it's important to keep in mind the requirements and limitations of television when choosing a font. Bolder fonts generally are safer, and many productions stick with SANS-SERIF fonts because of this. SERIF fonts can be very pleasing, but the bolder ones with fairly strong serifs are a safer bet.

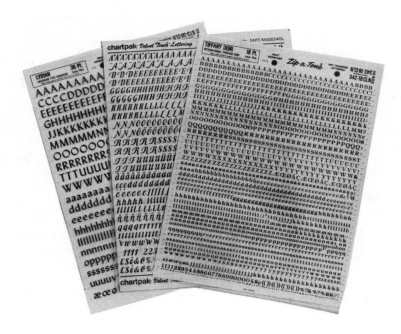

Dry transfer type.

**Helvetica
  Medium**

abcdefghijklmnopqrstuvwxyz
ABCDEFGHIJKLMNOPQRSTUVWXYZ
1234567890 (&.,:;!?'""- _ $¢%/)

Sans-Serif

Windsor

abcdefghijklmnopqrstuvwxyz
ABCDEFGHIJKLMNOPQRSTUVWXYZ
1234567890 (&.,:;!?"-—*$¢%/£#+×=°@)

Serif

Most switchers give better results when keying letters and symbols shot white-on-black than black-on-white because the large white area surrounding black letters tends to cause flare in the lens that reduces resolution. Many graphics cameras provide a negative video function that can reverse artwork for you, but if the camera being used does not, the art must be brought in reversed. Artwork can be made up black-on-white and then photographically reversed, or can be made up directly white-on-black. Having artwork reversed does take longer, but may allow more flexibility and ease of preparation. You will find that the range of "instant lettering" or DRY-TRANSFER letter typefaces is much wider in black characters than in white.

Another factor to consider is the type of keyer that will be used to place the graphics over the video. Digital keyers often have a tendency to produce ragged edges, as when keying in a horizontal line or border that is not quite horizontal with relation to the scan lines. In such an instance, the keyer may start on one line, and switch to another line part way through the graphic. They are also somewhat prone to exhibiting COLOR BEAT (seen as ragged edges on vertical lines) produced by the NTSC system of encoding. ANALOG (also called LINEAR, or SOFT-EDGED) keyers, on the other hand, are a bit less precise, and can thus produce a smoother key with somewhat softer, more natural edges.

The choice between using a character generator and using title cards may be a practical matter. If there are a lot of graphics and/or little time, a character generator is the obvious choice. In news, sports, and other similar types of programs, a character generator may be more than adequate while for a sensitively produced dramatic program with high production standards, it's more likely that some form of custom graphics will add more to the show.

241

Audio treatment

This is one of the least understood and most complex subjects in television, and one that, I'm afraid, we'll be forced to deal with rather lightly. There's so much involved that the subject deserves a separate book of which, fortunately, there are a number of good ones available (see *Bibliography*).

Some shows require little if any special treatment of audio. The audio is edited along with the video, and that is that. At the other end of the scale, some shows require extensive AUDIO SWEETENING—massaging and often completely reworking the sound.

Full audio sweetening is usually accomplished by transferring the sound to a multi-track audio recorder, which can be anything from a four-track up to a 32-track machine, where it is edited and then mixed down for final remarriage to the video. The SMPTE code is normally used to provide a sync reference.

To illustrate by example, a dramatic show might be first edited off-line, with video and audio cut together. Once this has been approved, the on-line edit would be done, where the video is finalized, and the basic dia-log track cut. The dialog track might require relooping of the audio, with the actors coming in to dub over portions that were damaged by background noises or other problems that occurred during the original shooting. The tape then goes to audio sweetening, where the audio would be stripped off and recorded on a track of an audio tape. The procedures can vary widely, and LOOPING (redubbing the voice) may be done after transfer to audiotape—this is just an example of one possible method.

During audio sweetening, any necessary sound effects will be added on separate channels, music will be added, and equalization will be done. Once the producer and others involved are happy with the sound of all the elements, the various tracks will be mixed down to a single channel (more and more often this is now two channels, as stereo television becomes more common, as on tape, videodisc and, soon, broadcasting), and the mix will then be transferred back to the video master.

There are also methods of audio post-production available that can provide a fair amount of flexibility without the heavy expense of a full audio sweetening session.

A computer audio sweetening facility.

242

With 1-inch formats (which provide two audio channels), for instance, one could cut the video and audio together as normal, balancing audio levels along the way to get a good basic and roughly even sound level. The next step would be to TRANSFER (BUMP, or PING-PONG) the sound over to the second channel, this time RIDING (adjusting) the levels to even it out further, and equalizing along the way. Since the two channels are on the same tape, sync will not be a problem.

It may be possible to add sound effects at this point as well, which would come from another VTR or ATR (Audio Tape Recorder) and which would be mixed in with the sound coming off the first channel. The last step would be to bump the audio back to the original channel, this time adding the music track,

or whatever. This obviously means that the audio will have gone several generations, so the quality and signal-to-noise ratio of the VTR become a factor. The 1-inch formats, with their high tape speed and good audio specs, can usually handle that many generations without too much loss, and the present state of television quality makes such a technique acceptable in most cases. If the production were to be SIMULCAST with the audio going out over an FM station, though, or once stereo TV sound is on the air, such practices would probably leave something to be desired. Some facilities are currently using one of the noise-reduction systems, such as **Dolby®** or **DBX®**, for channel-to-channel audio sweetening. This can help, though for music, many audio engineers prefer not to process the audio at all.

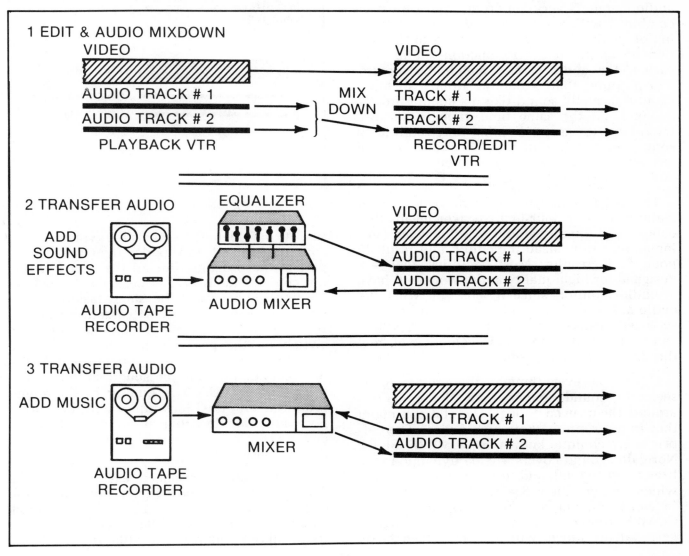

Using the preceding technique on cassette is much harder, since the ultimate audio quality of cassette is not as high, and because the use of SMPTE code normally requires the dedication of one channel to the code itself. Cassette is less often used for broadcast, so the loss in quality may be more acceptable in trade for more sophisticated audio content. If time code is being used and the system requires an audio channel for it, the show should be completely edited and approved before the SMPTE channel is used for audio sweetening. The time code will go away when this is done, erasing any reference that could make a re-edit easier. Also, in this instance the audio work will have to be done on a nontime code system—either on a control track system, or manually.

The ability to "read" and understand the audio meters is very important, but it must be combined with a keen ear and an understanding of sound perspective. Referring to the section on audio in the *Production—Audio* part, earlier, the audio should match the picture, and a sound that is coming from a distance should normally sound like it's coming from a distance. At the same time, though, it's also important to keep in mind any additional sounds or music that will be added, so that any such sounds won't overwhelm the basic audio.

The sad fact that the average television set features a low-fi four-inch speaker means that using a high-quality studio monitor when editing audio can mislead the editor, and result in poor final results. Most facilities that are designed for high quality audio work will have a studio monitor, since it tells you what the audio contains. They will also have a little TV set-sized speaker next to it, however, which can be patched in for final evaluation of how the audio will *really* sound.

Have you ever thought that commercials seem to sound louder than the programs around them, even though the stations claim they're not running them any louder? The culprit is a technique known as COMPRESSION. Normally, sound covers a wide dynamic range from quiet to loud, and in music recording, the wider the dynamic range, the better the sound. In many commercials, however, the sound is COMPRESSED, so that it swings through a very narrow range, with the level then being

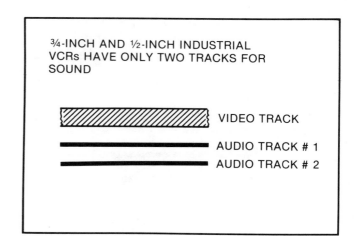

1-INCH AND BROADCAST ¾-INCH VTRs HAVE TWO TRACKS FOR SOUND AND ONE TRACK FOR **SMPTE** TIME CODE

VIDEO TRACK
SMPTE TIME CODE TRACK
AUDIO TRACK # 1
AUDIO TRACK # 2

¾-INCH AND ½-INCH INDUSTRIAL VCRs HAVE ONLY TWO TRACKS FOR SOUND

VIDEO TRACK
AUDIO TRACK # 1
AUDIO TRACK # 2

set at the highest permissible volume. The commercial isn't any louder than the loudest part of the program, but all the sound within the commercial is at this peak level. You can accomplish basically the same task with the peak limiter found on most cassette recorders. If you boost the volume to maximum and then switch on the peak limiter, the limiter will keep the louder parts from going over "0 VU"—in effect compressing the sound so that *everything's* at "0 VU." The quality of the sound produced by this technique will be rather poor, however. In actual production, there are devices that have been designed especially for this purpose.

It takes an experienced ear to achieve a good final sound mix for television, and audio engineers who specialize in TV audio mixing employ practices that differ considerably from those mixing audio for records and the like.

Sound Effects Libraries

There are a large number of sources of sounds and music, the most common of which are the music and sound effects libraries. Though many small-scale studios and independents often grab music from whatever source then can, the rule that applies in *all* cases states that copyrighted audio must be cleared with the copyright holder. If you wish to use commercial recordings in your production, clearance can be obtained through either BMI (Broadcast Music Incorporated) or ASCAP (American Society of Composers, Authors, and Publishers), one of which will have virtually every piece of music registered, and will serve as clearing house for performance rights. It's also possible to go through one of several agencies that perform clearance services. The Harry Fox Agency in New York is the major clearance agency, and can arrange clearance for virtually any music ever recorded.

Music libraries operate in several different ways. Some sell records or tape for a flat price, with the purchaser free to use any of the music contained therein without additional cost. Others sell recordings at a relatively low price, about what a record would cost in a record store, and then charge a NEEDLE DROP fee for every time a cut is used. Rates often vary with the use, and would be higher, for example, on a network program than they would be for an in-house industrial show. There are many different schemes. It is even possible to go to a professional music service that stocks a number of music libraries. They will help you select music or sound effects for a program, charging for their time plus any charges levied by the producer of the particular library involved.

It is also possible, of course, to hire a composer and musicians to put together custom music for a production. Often a struggling young musician can write music, get some friends together, and record really outstanding music, but results and ability obviously vary widely. If you choose this route, make sure the paperwork is all in order to prevent later disputes over rights and payments.

RECORD NO. 13
NEW VISIONS

Comp: Roger Webb PRS
Pub: Unisound Pub. BMI

Side 1

			Tempo
1.	Harry's Angels	2:28	Medium
2.	Open House	2:42	Medium
3.	Dream Machine	3:22	Fast
4.	Jade Pavilion	3:28	Slow
5.	Profiles	3:05	Medium-Fast
6.	Frisbees	2:35	Medium-Fast

Side 2

1.	Disco Fever	2:52	Fast
2.	Insiders	2:18	Slow
3.	Skinny Dip	3:10	Fast
4.	My Camelot	2:52	Slow
5.	Designer Collection	3:11	Fast
6.	Encore	2:15	Slow

Instruments: Full brass with trumpet lead, synthesizer, piano, strings, guitars, female voices, electric bass, and percussion.

Page from music catalog.

Sound effects libraries usually are sold on a flat-price basis, without needle drop charges, and a good library can provide everything from the sound of a hummingbird to a choo-choo train.

The watchword with regard to audio is *CARE*. The time spent on careful attention to the details of sound will pay off in terms of a flawless audio track, which provides critically important support for the video. In the final analysis, there is no substitute for cleanly recorded original audio that is subsequently well edited.

Preparing for the Edit

We've already covered a large part of the preparations for the edit, so this section will clean up a few of the incidentals, and examine a few cost-saving techniques that are available.

Whether an off-line edit will be done first or the show taken directly on-line, and whether SMPTE code is used or control track editing is the choice, the most important factor in speeding the edit will be the preparation of detailed TAPE LOGS. The more information you can list for each scene, the better. For instance, the difference between several takes of the same scene may be very minor, and notes in the log that indicate these differences can save a lot of time during editing. This goes beyond listing *what* a scene or take is, also, since *where* it is located on the tape is equally important information. There's nothing quite as wasteful as spending editing time on searching for a scene on the tape—your logs should have precise notations, either by SMPTE code, by tape timer, or at least by counter number.

MᶜQ TELEPRODUCTIONS

Tape Log & Cue Sheet   PROD. NO. 58-02 PAGE 1/5

DATE 2-25-82 TITLE Video Production Guide CLIENT Biswager REEL # F.M. VTR #

SMPTE CODE ☒   FOOTAGE COUNTER ☐   SCENE LOG ☐   EDIT CUE ☒

SCENE	TAKE	SLATE INFORMATION	SCENE STARTS				SCENE STOPS				REMARKS	CIRCLED TAKE
			HRS.	MINS.	SEC.	FRAME	HRS.	MINS.	SEC.	FRAME		
—	—	Opening title animation	1	00	00	00	1	00	30	00	Animation Reel	
1	4	Sharon enters bldg	1	12	41	15	1	12	45	29	Reel 1	
2	2	Entering Office	1	15	12	19	1	15	19	07	" "	
3	2	Office Master	2	08	27	10	2	08	37	24	Reel 2	
3A	2	CU - Conrad	2	17	52	13	2	17	59	20	" "	
3B	1	CU - Sharon	2	25	35	12	2	25	47	13	" "	
3A	3	CU - Conrad	2	22	05	00	2	22	16	14	" "	
3	2	Master	2	09	13	18	2	09	19	02	" " (extend audio)	2
3B	1	CU - Sharon	2	25	23	14	2	25	25	18	" " (video only)	
3A	3	CU - Conrad	2	23	04	02	2	23	18	05	" "	
3	2	Master - Sharon leaves	2	10	55	12	2	10	59	20	" "	
3A	3	CU - Conrad	2	23	22	12	2	23	29	22	" "	
4	7	Stairway	3	55	17	10	3	55	23	08	" "	
5	1	Doorway	4	19	51	07	4	20	02	13	" "	
6	3	Hallway	3	02	44	12	3	02	53	06	" "	
7	4	Parking lot	7	18	22	16	7	18	41	12	Reel 3	
7A	2	Starting car	7	27	18	13	7	27	23	08	" "	
7B	1	Gary Approaches	7	40	12	05	7	40	19	12	" "	
7B	3	Gary + Sharon Struggle	7	57	35	02	7	57	43	18	" "	

The edit cue sheet lists the time code numbers as determined by the off-line edit and will be used as the guide for on-line editing.

Time coding editing that will involve dissolves and wipes requires that the two scenes involved in the transition be on separate reels and VTRs. If the two scenes are on the same reel of original footage, then at some point a B-ROLL will have to be made. A B-ROLL is a copy of the original material made just for this purpose. If the show will have a lot of such transitions, many of which will be made between scenes on the same reel, it's a good idea to have B-rolls made of all reels, so that the editing session won't have to stop each time a dissolve is required while a B-roll of the scene is made. If there are few such transitions, or if most of the scenes to be used in this manner are on separate reels (as would normally be the case with isoed footage), then it may be possible to make up selective B-rolls on WORKTAPE only as needed.

Whether all material will have B-rolls generated or only a few scenes will require B-rolls, many post-production houses will rent tape for this use, either for the day, or for a short period of a week to a month. The same is often true for worktapes or workprints—many houses will rent used tape stock for use as workprints, to be returned and erased, or billed out at a lower rate than new stock should you decide to keep it.

If the edit will require the use of special audio sources—either narration, music, or sound effects—it might be a good idea to transfer them to videotape before going in to edit. Although it's possible to roll playback of reel-to-reel audio tape accurately enough to edit, it takes additional time, and is likely to be less accurate than if the audio can be taken from a videotape under system control. In doing so, make sure that a video signal (black or colorbars) and time code are recorded along with the audio, to provide sync references for the system. If the editing systems being used can control an audio recorder, then this step may be unnecessary.

Graphic Materials

All graphic materials that will be needed should be prepared ahead of time, and be ready for use during the edit. If the graphics consist of black and white art to be keyed into the picture with a title camera, the artwork itself will be sufficient, but you should check

ahead of time as to technical requirements. Some cameras can reverse black-on-white art, but if not, the art should be prepared REVERSED (white on black). With color camera art, it may be wise to prerecord the graphics on tape, and use the tape as one of the edit source tapes. Time spent fussing with the camera in an INSERT STUDIO (a small studio near the editing suite designed for shooting titles and small product shots, etc.) during the edit is billed at the same rate as the edit time itself.

When using a character generator, some houses charge a flat fee, while others charge an hourly fee as used. In the latter case, schedule some programming time—usually a lower rate—before the edit, to get the graphics loaded into the generator's memory. If possible, record all the C.G. (Character Generator) graphics on tape, to avoid any additional charges for the generator during the edit. In either case, check and verify spelling of names and other graphic information *before* the edit starts—it's amazing how often people wait until the edit before checking on such matters, and everything but the clock stops while they check.

Proper Preparation Saves Money

If someone else will be operating the editing system for you, as is most often the case, find time to sit down with them before the session to go over the program. If possible, furnish them with a copy of the script and, ideally, the tape logs far enough ahead of time so that they can get some idea of what will be happening. Better yet, let them spend some time with the raw footage to familiarize themselves with the material. This will save time and money in editing. It should be noted, that at many post-production houses the editors will have neither the time nor the inclination to do this. Many such staff editors act more as extensions of the machine, and the first time you'll see them is when you sit down to start editing. With editors on your own staff, or with a freelance editor you bring in to edit a show, however, these opportunities exist and can offer benefits that will appear in the finished program.

Whether you have a chance to work with the editor ahead of time or not, be sure you know exactly what you want when you go on-line. If you don't, then that's another occasion to consider an off-line edit first. Of course, if you've got lots of money to spend on outside editing, by all means play to your heart's content. The facility you use makes its money on an hourly basis, and the only complaint they'd be likely to raise would be that their other clients need the time.

There are many shows that require the effects capabilities of a computer editing system—dissolves, wipes, keys, and such—only for a few transitions, with all the rest being simple cuts. In such an instance, you might consider splitting the edit job between two facilities or systems. This entails doing *just* the special effects (the scene leading to the effect, the effect itself, and the scene that follows) onto a SUB MASTER, which then becomes one of the source tapes for editing on a lower-cost system. For example, if you have a ¾-inch cuts-only system at your disposal, but have three places in the show where dissolves are needed, it's possible to rent a few hours on a three-machine computer editing system to put together sub masters using worktape stock that contain just those effects. With these in hand, go back to the cuts-only system and edit the show using the sub masters where the effects are needed. This technique can be used for titles, CHROMAKEYS (electronic mattes), digital effects, and the like as well.

Although most of the preceding rules apply primarily to the use of outside facilities, where time equates directly to cost, they hold true for in-house facilities as well. Any company or institution that has invested in an expensive computer editing system will have (or should have) enough work to keep it busy most of the time. The time you spend editing your tapes is valuable time during which others can't use the equipment. In fact, the same can be true of very small facilities: access to a simple two-machine cassette control-track system is just as valuable in proportion, especially if it's the only means available for editing.

CHAPTER 19

Editing Techniques and Style

Style and Aesthetics

Pace and timing are what editing is basically all about. There's a feel for both of these elements that a good editor develops that is essential to achieving a flow in a program. There is absolutely no substitute for practice, and there's nothing that makes the job easier than a good editing system.

Experienced editors become a part of the editing system, and in a real sense "play" the system like a musical instrument. A full-bore computer editing system with all the bells and whistles is a tremendously complicated device, and the editor should be able to play it with the same proficiency as a skilled pianist, with-

out stopping to think about how to make it work. During a rather lengthy edit one night at a Bay Area post-production house, one of my associates got curious, and counted the buttons on the editing console. They totaled 1,426, and that was a relatively simple system. A really well-equipped system console is roughly equivalent to the flight deck of a 747, and, to the uninitiated, can be just as confusing. Once the functions are learned, though, they're actually rather simple. The real trick is mastering the interaction of the various peripherals and accessories with which a particular system is equipped.

I've edited on systems ranging from two VTRs and a stopwatch to a full-scale computer

Editing suite of a 1-inch facility.

system as previously described, and the irony is that the bigger and more sophisticated the system gets, the faster and easier editing becomes. At present, the ultimate experience in terms of on-line editing is a system comprised of Type C 1-inch recorders under computer control. There is no comparison with any other system, and after using one, going back to lesser systems—especially cassette—is a frustrating experience. The best word to describe these systems would be "sweet."

One factor in editing of which the editor must keep aware is that most shows are put together in little pieces. Since the average edit would run perhaps six seconds, this matter of editing in little chunks can make it hard to keep a feeling for the overall pacing of a show. The way to combat this is to stop every once in a while, and go back a few minutes to watch and re-establish a feel for the pacing of a show. Often an interruption, such as a phone call or a reel change, can throw the editor off. Finding and correcting a change in the pacing is best accomplished before you're too far past it, where a little change could mean a lot of work.

Editing is very similar to switching a live show from multiple cameras, but without the benefits (or, of course, the drawbacks) of work-

The equipment room with three 1-inch VTRs.

250

ing in real time. The editor, in essence, constructs not only the show, but actually constructs what might be called NEW REAL TIME during the process of editing. This adds a dimension to editing that distinguishes it from directing, and in some ways makes it a more demanding task. Overall, it's possible that because of this, it would be easier to make a transition from editing to directing than it would to go the reverse route.

The editor, just as the director, must combine the roles of artist and technician. Video and audio levels must be matched; color correction levels set, if necessary; glitches at edit points watched for and smoothed out; all at the same time that the editor is making creative decisions that will affect the flow of the show. Add to that the fact that the nature of time code editing requires the editor to constantly shuffle numbers around mentally, and that the numbers consist of groups in BASE 30 (frames), BASE 60 (seconds and minutes), and BASE 24 (hours), and the level of mental acuity required for editing becomes quite literally mind-boggling. This is why many full-time editors give the impression of constantly being on amphetamines or on a manic caffeine rush. They rarely are—it's just a natural result of their work. I have surprised store clerks by adding the price of all the items and figuring the tax and total in my head faster than they can work the cash register, having the check written to the exact amount before they've gotten their total. They simply don't know that I've just walked out of a 12-hour editing session, and that the foregoing is a trivial exercise compared with thinking in SMPTE code.

Flow And Continuity

The flow and continuity of a production are the primary concerns of the editor. The best editing is virtually invisible to the viewer, who ideally is not even remotely aware that any editing has taken place. Television suspends reality, and draws the viewer into what happens on the screen. Any edit that disrupts the continuity of the show, or of which the viewer is consciously aware, will shatter this suspension of reality. An edit may be bad due to a technical factor—a jump in the picture, or some other sort of glitch—or it may be bad due to a flaw in the visual or aural continuity. One

of the general rules that the editor tries to follow is to cut on action, such as a hand movement or a character's act of sitting down. If the action does not continue smoothly through the edit, it will be noticeable. Odd as it may seem, this does not always mean that a frame-by-frame analysis of the tape would show an exact match in the action. Sometimes the edit works better if a few frames are cut, and the action shortened. Other times the opposite is true. There are also times when an exact match of action *is* necessary. All of this depends on quite a few different variables, and the editor will end up being guided by the *feel* of the edit—the way it works best. Those systems that allow for accurate preview and TRIMMING (shortening, lengthening, or moving) of the edit, including all time code systems, make this job of determining the right spot for critical edits much easier.

As the editor fine-tunes an edit, he may become so involved—so close to the edit—that objectivity becomes difficult. Remember, there's a substantial difference in the way an edit will be seen by someone who doesn't know it's coming than by someone who has tried it ten different ways and knows the material. It's often a good idea, after a critical edit is made, to snatch someone out of the hallway to watch it and give his or her reaction. It's for this same reason that editing by one's self may not be the best of ideas. Several viewpoints other than the editor's own are very useful when deciding whether an edit works or not, and often a totally uninvolved person is the best choice. The director, for instance, should take an active part in editorial decisions, but is also very close to the show—sometimes too close. When in doubt about an edit, some on-the-spot testing can be of great help.

It's my considered opinion that the director of a production definitely belongs in the editing room while the show is being put together. In certain situations, the director will have other projects pressing hard on available time, and cannot stay constantly in the editing suite. In these instances, it is possible to check on the on-going progress of the edit—something that works best when an off-line edit will be done. There are some directors who prefer to turn the job over to an editor whom they know well, and whose work has pleased them in the past. There is a good argument that can be made for this practice, since the completely different viewpoint of the editor may at times produce aesthetic enhancements from the director's material of which the director himself might not have thought.

Still, the director is the one who visualized the show in the first place, and while some would take exception, I would suggest that involvement on the part of the director is a sound practice. It's also quite possible, of course, that the director has no choice but to do the editing personally.

In instances where the director and an editor are working together for the first time, something that should be coordinated as early as possible is the syntax used to describe the desired action or results. For instance, if the director says, "I want that edit moved back", the editor can interpret this to mean a number of distinctly different things. First, on which tape should the edit be moved? The editor would probably assume this means on the record VTR, although the director could mean the source VTR. Second, what is "back"? Does that mean back on the tape to a later time code address, or back towards the beginning, to an earlier address? An editor at a post-production house works with a different person every day, and many of them either state their wants in their own way, or don't know what they're talking about in the first place. Getting this syntax straight is important, and while it will eventually be ironed out as the two get to know each other, it can be beneficial to establish terminology ahead of time.

Let's close this section by repeating a now familiar theme. If the director is working with an editor, rather than doing the editing himself, the editor represents a substantial and important resource. Full-time editors especially gain tremendous amounts of experience during their careers, and can offer suggestions that will aid and improve the show, if given a bit of encouragement to do so. If they meet any resistance to their comments and suggestions, they'll likely withdraw into the machine, and will from then on simply follow orders—in the worst cases doing so even though they know a mistake is being made. Smile at the editor. Maybe take him or her to lunch. The editor is one of the most important folks involved in a

production, and with luck, will take just as much pride in the results as any other person involved in the project.

Since editing is perhaps the most mysterious part of the production process, it's here that we'll add one more to our list of rules. This applies, to any aspect of production, and to any person from the producer on down who's involved:

McQ's RULE #6: The *only* stupid question is the one that isn't asked.

If you don't understand what's happening, or what the editor (or anyone else) is talking about, *ask for enlightenment!* This business is filled with jargon, and each of the disciplines within it has its own language. It *never* pays to hide embarrassment over a lack of comprehension by letting something slide so that you won't apear less than all-knowing. Besides that, most people like to show off their knowledge, and will be flattered at the chance to demonstrate their expertise. It's why they're there in the first place, isn't it?

Insert vs. Assemble Editing

On the technical side of editing, there are a number of important choices to be made with regard to the various techniques involved. The first of these is the matter of insert vs. assemble editing, a question that pertains mainly to cassette editing.

To review for a moment the distinctions between the two modes, in assemble editing, when the VTR reaches the edit point, it goes into *full record*, laying down new control track pulses, video, and audio signals. Any signals already on the tape will be erased and replaced with the new information. This permits assemble editing to be performed onto a completely blank tape, once the first scene has been laid down in straightforward record mode.

In insert editing, the original control track is left completely alone, and is *never* recorded over. The editor may choose to record just new video, just new audio, or video and audio that will replace any such information already on the tape. This requires that there *must* be something already recorded on the tape—a video signal and control track pulses—for the entire length of the tape over which new material will be edited.

Insert editing was originally developed as a way of changing material on a previously recorded or edited tape. Since the control track pulses are not re-recorded, the new video signal will remain synchronous with the original material. Thus, when the editor CUTS OUT of the insert mode, the end of the new material will flow smoothly into the original signal that follows because the original control track pulses are used. In assemble editing this is not possible for two reasons: new control track pulses are recorded, and though they would probably be very close to SYNCHRONOUS (matching) with the original pulses, in video, close is not enough. Even the slightest drift from the original CONTROL TRACK RATE (drift which is guaranteed to occur) would pro-

duce a bad edit (GLITCH) at the out point, if such a thing were even possible.

It's not possible, however, for the second reason: when the assemble mode is initiated, a full-width erase head positioned ahead of the recording heads is turned on, and cleans all existing material from the tape. If it were possible to cut out of the assemble mode, there would be a section of tape that had already passed the full-width erase head, but that had not reached the record heads. The result during playback would be a large disturbance caused by the fact that a substantial chunk of material just wasn't there any more.

The main question, then, is when to use the assemble mode and when to use the insert mode. It's simple. Insert editing is *always* recommended over assemble editing. Well, *almost* always.

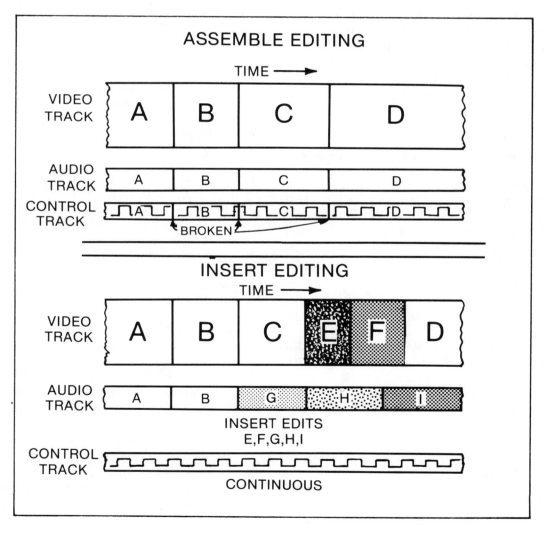

253

The drawback to insert editing is that there must always be STABLE (continuous) control track, and ideally video, on a tape before it can be used for editing. In cases where a change is to be made on a tape that has already been recorded or edited, this is not a problem. When getting ready to start a new edit, though, it will be necessary to record a signal for the length of the program to be edited—ideally over the entire length of the tape. This is normally done by connecting a source of COLOR BLACK (a black signal with COLOR BURST, also known as CRYSTAL BLACK) to the video input of the VTR, and recording it for the length of the tape. The source can be a test signal generator, a switcher, or a camera—any stable source of a video signal will do. In fact, the signal need not necessarily be black. In a pinch, an off-air broadcast TV signal could be used. This would ideally be a strong, clear one from a local independent station. Network stations switch between local and network programming, and are often not too neat about their switching. Black is much preferred, however, for a number of technical reasons. Put simply, using black generally results in a cleaner signal after editing.

Why go to all this additional time and effort, when assemble editing would let you drop in a blank tape and rip away at it? The answer is that editing in the insert mode produces a more stable tape, since the original control track, laid down all at once from a stable source, provides the basic reference during playback. Assemble editing results in slight changes in the rate of the control track at each edit point that are unavoidable, and that produce detrimental TIME BASE ERRORS (instabilities in tape timing).

In control track editing, without the use of a TIME BASE CORRECTOR (TBC), the stability of the signal within each assemble edit is especially vulnerable. This is because the time base errors of the signal coming from the playback VTR will be recorded into the record tape which will introduce further errors when it is played back. The use of a TBC will eliminate this problem. Insert editing, without a TBC, will reduce the significance of the problem, while insert editing with a TBC is perhaps the best choice of all.

Assemble editing is not entirely without its uses, though. Where speed is of the essence, and where technical quality can be less than exact, assemble editing may be appropriate. For instance: I collect commercials (selectively—only the best in terms of concept or execution), along with little oddities and visual snacks that show up now and again over the air. Since most of these pop up on tapes I've recorded for later viewing, as when I'm not home to watch, they will be on one of my "recycle" reels that I use for TIME-SHIFT (playback later) purposes. When I find something I want to keep, I edit it it onto a "collection" tape. For this sort of purpose, assemble editing is adequate, and saves time.

Ninety-nine and 44/100 of all time code editing is done in the insert mode. There are some time code systems available that permit assemble editing, and that edit new code along with the video, audio, and control track at each edit (a technique known as JAM-SYNCING the code), but this produces the same stability problems that are part and parcel of assemble editing in any format. About the only situations in which time code assemble editing might be used would be in some electronic news gathering activities.

For broadcast and other applications that require high technical standards, *all* time code editing is done in the insert mode. In preparing a tape for time code editing, time code is recorded along with the color black signal, and tapes thus prepared are generally known as B & C stock—tape prepared with black and code. The common practice is to prepare tapes ahead of time, usually during off-peak hours, that will be ready for use when someone wants to edit. These tapes normally have time code that starts at 00:58:00:00. This gives the editor space to lay down some colorbars and test tone—usually from 00:58:30:00 to 00:59:30:00, which is followed by 30 seconds of BLACK (space for slate and countdown cue leader) prior to the start of the program, which is at 01:00:00:00. Starting the program at an even number makes it easier to keep track of running time, although the hours number may be other than one at program start. For instance, a series production may use a time code hours number that corresponds to the show number. Show start is rarely zero hours even, since time code generators are 24-hour systems, and such a practice would involve starting code at 23:58:00:00. The ROLL-OVER from 23:59:59:29 hours to 00:00:00:00 hours can confuse the computer.

Entering Edit Points

Time code systems usually offer two basic ways of entering an edit point into the system. The first is ON THE FLY, where the editor watches the tape in playback and hits a "MARK IN" or "MARK OUT" button at the desired edit point. The second is by means of KEYBOARD ENTRY, where the editor hits "SET IN" or "SET OUT," and then manually enters the time code, which obviously must have been predetermined. It is possible to enter a time code by marking a point from a tape that is stopped in pause, but there is a strong possiblity the code will be wrong. This is because, as the tape was coming to a stop, it may well have been moving so slowly that the last few frames of code were garbled. The computer won't know this, however, and will happily report a spurious code. Some of the newer systems make special provisions for entering a time code from a paused tape, while the use of vertical interval time code solves the problem, as it was designed to do.

Control track systems also commonly offer two methods of edit point entry. The original systems and many of the lower-priced units available today determine the edit point by having the editor pause both tapes where the edit is to be made, whereupon they automatically roll back by a predetermined amount to establish the preroll point. Newer designs, mostly at a bit higher prices, offer the ability to mark the edit on the fly, as in time code systems. All time code systems, and some of the fancier control track systems, also allow the editor to select and determine an out-edit point for insert editing. This is a very desirable feature, and is one that is not offered on the simplest and least expensive controllers.

Marking edits on the fly is a much more accurate way to achieve precise edits than pausing the tape. Bringing the tape to a halt, even by ROCKING THE REELS back and forth to find the edit point, destroys any real sense of pace and timing, and makes it much more desirable to rehearse the edit before committing to it. On a control track system, though, rehearsal will reduce the accuracy of the edit, as we saw in a previous section.

Some of the basic techniques used in editing are made easier by the capabilities of a computer editing system. Examples would include SPLITTING EDITS and BACKTIMING edits.

SPLIT EDITS are what the name implies: During a single pass of the tape, the audio and video are edited at different points. For exam-

Time code edit display.

255

ple, the new audio might be brought in a second before the video, providing a change of pace from simple simultaneous cuts. A computer editing system with this capability simplifies the process considerably. Split edits can certainly be accomplished without this built-in capability, but will require two passes of the tape, and may involve some mental juggling of time codes or frame count.

BACKTIMING is the technique of determining where a scene must end, and subtracting the time available for the scene to determine the starting point of the edit. Again, it can be done on any editing system, but time code makes it easier, and by doing the math, a computer can make it a very simple process. An example of an application of the process of backtiming an edit would be where a sound track being added has a certain element that must occur at a definite point well into a scene. The length of time from the start of the video portion to the point at which the element must be heard is noted; the exact point of the sound element on its reel is noted; and the first figure (duration) is subtracted from the second (a code address) to determine the in-edit point on the sound tape. Both tapes can be rolled in sync, and the element will be matched to the video at exactly the right point.

Editing Iso Material

In *Chapter 14,* we discussed how productions shot with signals from the various cameras each recorded on their own VTR (isoed) require complete post-production. The normal procedure involves playing back each of the tapes on a separate machine and in sync with each other, feeding the signals to a switcher,

and switching the program as if it were live. This is usually done with a computer editing system, and it's a relatively expensive proposition, since there must be a playback machine for each camera's tape. If there were four cameras, there will have to be four playback VTRs plus the record VTR, for a total of five. Most new computer editing systems can roll as many machines in sync as you wish, though some are limited to two playback VTRs and one record VTR. Thus, virtually any three-machine computer system can handle a two-camera iso edit, but may or may not be able to handle additional tapes.

Editing iso tapes on a control track system with only two machines is generally considered to be a difficult or nearly impossible task. In theory, when editing a two-camera iso one could put one iso tape in the record VTR and the other in the playback VTR, sync the two tapes together, and simply cut in and out while the two tapes ran through the entire show. There is, however, a problem with this. Since iso editing is essentially the same as live switching, it's necessary to be able to see both tapes in playback in order to "call the shots." The problem is that once you've cut into the tape on the record VTR, you can't see the material that's being replaced with the other VTR's signal. This inability to see both shots at all times makes it difficult to know when to cut back out of the tape in the record VTR. This is why most two-camera iso edits are done on a system with two playback VTRs.

There is a way to work with a two-machine control track editing system, however it does require a third VTR during the preparatory stage and the ability to sync a camera to tape

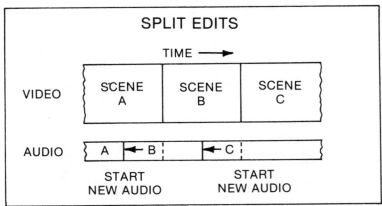

playback. The required equipment would be three VTRs, at least one of which is a capstan-servo model, a camera that can be GENLOCKED (synchronized) to tape playback, and two monitors. The procedure will sound complicated, and there are a number of steps required, but it actually is rather simple once you understand how it works. It entails the preparation of a CUE tape that will be used to perform the final edit. In going through the process, we'll look at a simple two-camera production that has created two iso tapes.

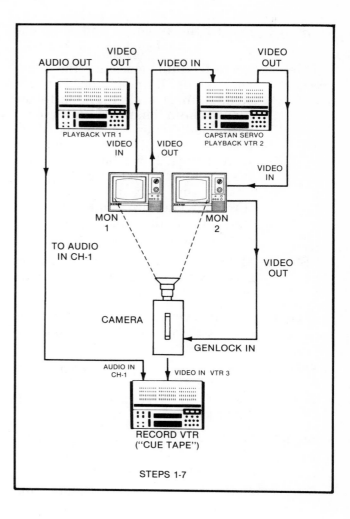

Step 1: Place the tape with the signal from camera 1 in a playback VTR. This VTR need not be a capstan-servo design.

Step 2: Feed the output of this VTR to a monitor and then loop it out to the input of a second VTR. This second VTR must be a capstan-servoed unit so that it will sync to the first VTR.

Step 3: The tape with the signal from camera 2 is placed into this second VTR.

Step 4: Feed the second VTR's output to a second monitor placed next to the first, and then loop it out to provide a sync signal for the camera. If the camera has GENLOCK capability, the signal can be fed directly to the camera's genlock input—otherwise a genlock sync generator must be used to drive the camera. The camera output is fed to the third VTR. (A genlock device allows a camera or a VTR to be slaved to another camera or VTR.)

Step 5: Set the camera up to shoot the two side-by-side monitors, with the one on the left showing the camera 1 tape, and the one on the right showing the camera 2 tape.

Step 6: Play the two original tapes back in sync and record the picture from the camera on the third VTR. The end result will be a new tape that shows both camera pictures as if you were looking at two camera monitors.

Step 7: Record the program audio on one audio channel of this cue tape.

Step 8: Record editing cues on the other channel of the cue tape. For this step, connect a microphone to the blank audio channel, and record verbal edit cues by means of an audio insert edit. This can be done in real time. If a mistake is made, it's a simple matter to go back and change any cue. In essence, the director's cues are being given during post-production, rather than during the original taping.

Step 9: Make a dub of the original camera 2 tape with the program audio on one of the audio channels.

Step 10: Edit the verbal edit cues from the cue tape onto the other audio channel of the camera 2 dub.

Step 11: Load this tape into the record VTR of a standard control track editing system to serve as the BASE TRACK.

Step 12: Load the camera 1 original into the playback VTR, and the tapes are then ready for editing.

Step 13: Sync the two tapes together, and set the record VTR for video-only insert mode.

Step 14: The editor listens to the editing cues from the cue channel of the camera 2 tape, and simply cuts into and out of the camera 2 tape in reaction to the cues. The show is edited in real time.

There are a couple of drawbacks to this system. First, the editor still cannot see the camera 2 picture during inserts of the picture from camera 1. For this reason, the verbal edit cues must be very precisely timed and spoken. Also, if the editor misses a cue during the actual edit, it's very difficult to stop the tapes, go back a bit, and re-synchronize them. There is also no way to perform dissolves between tapes, or other effect transitions.

On the other hand, the equipment required for this technique is common to even very

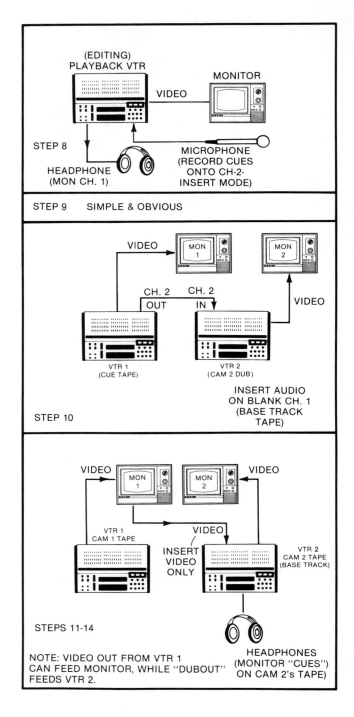

258

small facilities, and the procedure can save considerable money compared with using a full computer editing system. The video quality is not compromised, since the resulting tape is only one generation removed from the masters. With additional equipment, it's possible to prepare a cue tape with up to four different iso signals. Beyond that number, each of the pictures on the cue tape will be rather small and hard to see. Also, the final edit would require several passes, using the camera 4 tape, for instance, as the base track, and inserting camera 3's picture on the first pass, camera 2's on the second, and camera 1's on a third pass. This is not unworkable, but it does become complicated.

I used the technique described above to edit a two-camera talk show, with excellent results. The show was a pilot, and the budget was microscopic. The show was recorded with three VTRs—one taping a live switch of the show, with the other two recording the signals directly from the two cameras. The technique was described earlier—if all had gone well, the live switch would have been fine, but if there were problems with the switch, the isos would serve as protection. As it turned out, there were problems. Just before taping, one of the cameras developed an intermittent genlock problem, and the first ten minutes of the live switch featured a roll in the picture at every camera cut. The errant camera finally settled down and behaved, but if it hadn't been for the iso backup tapes, there would have been nothing we could have done about the bad cuts at the start of the tape.

I re-edited the entire show from the iso tapes, and was able to improve the pacing of the show in the process. The fact that I had done a live switch during taping meant that the camera directions were basically good, and that I had a good shot on one of the tapes at all times.

This is also a good example of figuring out cost-saving techniques using minimal resources. In video production, there are often two ways to do things: the conventional, accepted way, and the way you contrive to get something done. Combine technical know-how with creative problem solving, and you can often achieve amazing results with modest means.

Glitches, Gremlins, and Gizmos

Editing can be a terribly frustrating experience for those without the special patience it requires. Although the operation of virtually any automatic editing system—control track or computer—has been made fairly easy, actually getting the machines to do their jobs well is a wholly different matter.

Videotape recorders are electromechanical devices that attempt to record and reproduce a signal that requires incredible accuracy and stability. To put it simply, a perfect recording and playback is, by definition, totally impossible. The nature of the beast is that there are always some errors, and the trick to quality production is to keep these errors to a minimum. Peripheral machinery is available to help, but it will, in the end, come down to the care taken by the editors and engineers that will determine the quality of the results.

Wrong field edits:

Regardless of tape format, although most commonly seen on cassette, there is a nasty gremlin lurking always nearby called a WHIP EDIT. The worst case of this happens when the editing system tries to edit from an evenly numbered field to another evenly numbered one (or an odd to an odd). The result will be at least a half-line displacement in the video that usually appears as a WHIP or a FLAGGING of the picture at the top of the screen. The newer and better ¾-inch machines and virtually all broadcast formats have FRAMING circuits that prevent this from happening, but many of the existing VTRs around—such as the Sony 2850s and early 2860s that are the workhorses of the cassette segment of the industry—will quite happily make field mis-framed edits (whip edits). If the system being used does not automatically take care of framing, the only way to get a good clean edit will be to check each one and re-do it if necessary. Since the chances are exactly 50/50, this can be a royal pain.

Whip edits can occur even when the framing is proper, though, and again, it's part of the nature of VTRs. Before an edit is made, the record VTR locks to the incoming video signal in order to synchronize itself for the edit. There is no way possible, however, for the

A nonframed edit produces a visible "whip" or disturbance in the picture.

VTR to lock up accurately enough to provide perfect horizontal sync; instead, it locks to the vertical sync. If the edit is made with the record VTR lagging or leading the incoming signal by only a bitty half-line, the edit will have a horizontal displacement, and can whip as much as a mis-framed edit. Contrary to popular conceptions, a time base corrector used between the player and the recorder cannot and will not prevent this. It may help, though, since the incoming video will be more stable, thus making it a bit easier for the record machine to lock up more accurately.

When using a time base corrector, be aware that in order to correct the signal's stability, the TBC may have to move the video around a bit to provide an electronically stable signal. The newer FLOATING WINDOW TBCs (units with expanded error correctional capabilities) will often correct wide instabilities, but in doing so, the picture may actually move on the screen, either vertically, horizontally, or both. This can lead to another problem when using an A/B ROLLING (three-machine) editing system.

Any time one dissolve or other transition effect follows another one, it will be necessary for most systems to perform a match-framed edit, as we saw earlier. To review briefly, the procedure would be this: The first scene is started as a cut, coming, for example, from the "A" VTR. The "B" VTR is parked at its preroll point, ready to run with its scene. As the dissolve point nears, the B machine is rolled, brought to speed and synchronized, and the dissolve is then made at the proper point. For

the system to then go directly to another dissolve, a third machine would be required, or very quick cuing of the A machine with it's next scene, and this supposes that the next scene was on the A reel to begin with. Since all of these conditions are rarely met, the normal practice is to end the scene on the B VTR as a cut, with the ending time code stored as the new B edit in point. If a dissolve from the B VTR to the A VTR is then desired, the process is repeated. The scene starts as a match-framed edit from the point where the B machine left off, and a dissolve is made to the scene on the A VTR. This procedure for performing dissolves and wipes involves a fair number of these match-framed edits.

Phasing errors:

The main problem encountered in performing match-frame edits is that the TBC may not lock the video up with the same vertical or horizontal phasing. This results in a shift in the picture on the screen at the match point. This problem is far more common with cassette editing, but can also occur on 1-inch or quad, though its frequency of occurrence and severity are less serious. These glitches are known as H-SHIFTS (Horizontal Shifts) or V-SHIFTS (Vertical Shifts), and again, the only solution in many cases is to make fine adjustments and keep trying until it comes out right. Fortunately, unlike control-track editing, where each new attempt may cut into the previous scene a few frames, time code at least assures that each new attempt comes at exactly the same point.

Color framing errors:

One problem that cassette is immune to, but crops up at times with 1-inch and quad is something called COLOR FRAMING. It's only partially good news for cassette users, as the reason it doesn't crop up with cassette is that the color system on cassette is so technically sloppy that they don't record framed color in the first place, and are thus not subject to color framing errors.

The NTSC system alternates the phase of the color signal by 180 degrees every other frame. If one attempts to make a match-framed edit, and the color framing is off between the record VTR and the incoming video, the result will be a shift in the color or a horizontal shift in the picture (called an H-SHIFT) that can be quite noticeable. It can actually happen with any edit, but with a change in the picture it's much less objectionable even though it's still wrong.

Since the TBCs on all 1-inch and quad systems are tied to HOUSE SYNC (a centralized sync generator), the record VTR must be properly color framed, and once the framing is set by doing a test edit, the system should retain proper color framing for the duration of that editing session. H-shifts can be a problem, and when the 1-inch facilities were first in operation, these were a very common and often a time-consuming hassle. New framing circuits and machine modifications, though, have greatly reduced their incidence, and it's now possible to get through an entire editing session without having the problem.

Audio accuracy problems:

One of the banes of the editor's existence with regard to editing the audio portion of the show is the lack of precision with which a SMPTE system is able to edit audio. Consider that the RESOLUTION capability of a time code system is basically the frame rate of 30 frames per second. Turned around, this means that the best accuracy possible is $\frac{1}{30}$ of a second. Although this may seem like sufficient accuracy, the fact is that, especially when cutting dialog, a thirtieth of a second is an awfully long time, and the inability to place an edit within the "fences" that surround each frame can make life very difficult. There are a number of proposals floating around that would encourage the editing equipment manufacturers to come up with a solution, and several production houses have devised or are working on their own in-house solutions. FIELD-RATE (60 Hz) resolution would help considerably, and even better would be an INFINITE range of edit point selection for audio-only edits. For the time being, though, the industry in general will have to content itself to bitch, holler, and wait.

Earlier in this section I mentioned that the very term "auto assemble" is often a cause for mirth among post-house staffs, and one of the reasons involves the way some of the computers handle the EDL (Editing Decision List). Although most systems currently on the market now include solutions for the problem, there are a good number of the more sophisticated systems around that arrange the edit decision list in the computer's memory not in order of the edit (or EVENT) number, but rather in terms of ascending time code. This can cause an interesting problem, in that when auto-assembling a list, it is quite possible for the system to first perform a video-only edit (such as a cutaway), and *then* the edit the cutaway was supposed to cover. As I said, the newer systems and MODS (modifications) of older systems have addressed this problem, but it would be a good thing to check if you're going to do an auto assembly. If the system does this, you'll have to have someone there during the auto assembly who knows what is supposed to happen in the program, which, as we saw earlier, is a good idea anyway.

How To Cope With Editing Disasters

Perhaps the most devastating experience one can have during an on-line edit is watching a machine eat one of the tapes. If the tape that gets digested is the edited master, the feeling produced will be a decidedly sinking one, although this is where a clean EDL can save the day. When the tape is an original master, though, a show can be ruined, and can lead the producer to contemplate murder, suicide, or both.

The best protection against this occurrence is, again, care in handling the tape. If a tape has been shipped, it may be wise to rack it up and run it in fast forward all the way to the end, and then back again, to repack the tape. Any tape that has been allowed to get cold should be slowly brought to room temperature prior to use. Careful cleaning of the entire tape path before each editing session can also help protect the tape and is important in any event.

When such a catastrophe occurs with an edited master (it almost always happens when the production is nearly or completely finished), one possible solution is to dub down a generation as much of the edited master as possible, replacing from the originals just the parts that were damaged. The edit decision list will help in doing this, since it will give you the precise cut points at which to patch in the replacement material.

Something you'll run into on occasion is DROP-OUTS (oxide that flakes off the tape) in the control track that cause instability or loss of lock when the tape is played back. There is no way to protect against this, and unlike the video portion, there are no DROPOUT COMPENSATORS (DOCs) for the control track. I have found that some VTRs are more forgiving than others, and if careful tweaking and adjustment of both the machine and the TBC fail to provide a good playback, switching to a different VTR may help. Sometimes the tape will play properly under local (manual) machine control, but not under computer control, and in these instances there are two solutions available:

1. either perform the edit manually, or

2. dub down a generation to a worktape, and take the scene from there.

One problem that can crop up in time code editing is that of NONSYNC CODE. Remember—the time code must be precisely referenced to the video signal, and if it's not, the system will have trouble locking up for the edit. The symptom will be a section of tape that plays back just fine until you try to make an edit, at which time the tape will appear to be mistracking severely. In such cases, most systems will abort the attempt at making an edit. What's happening is that the computer is forcing the tape to lock by time code, but the video tracking is too far off, and the system won't make the edit.

There are two possible solutions:

1. Some systems provide for nonsync code by allowing the system to initially sync to code, and then switch to simple control track sync, ignoring the time code. This lets the edit be made despite the bad code.

2. The second solution, which will be employed with systems that don't allow for the above solution, is to re-code the bad sections, laying down new code in its place. This is normally done by JAM-SYNCING new code—SLAVING the time code generator to the old code, then unlocking it once it's running, and insert editing the new code onto the cue channel.

Color Correction

Just as film can be color corrected, so can video, and the more complete editing houses offer color correctors as part of the system. The color corrector permits individual control of nine separate elements. It breaks the video down into the red, green, and blue components, and provides separate correction of black level, white level, and GAMMA (midrange) for each of the colors. Using it allows one to virtually tear the color apart and build it back up, and can save an otherwise seriously misbalanced tape. When using these, there are a couple of techniques that can help.

If the scene being corrected has something in it that can serve as a white reference, then correction is aided by the use of a waveform monitor set for horizontal rate FLAT display (not the IEEE roll-off). The procedure is to adjust for the thinnest possible line on the waveform display in the white portion, in effect doing the same thing the camera's original white balance was supposed to. A vectorscope can also be used, adjusting the signal for a dead-center white vector. In correcting flesh tones, one clue that I can provide, though a full explanation would take too much space, is to work with the blue gamma. (Mystical advice—"Work with the blue gamma, my children, and you'll find the secret of good flesh tones!") Actually, the basic reason can be simply stated. Most color correction problems are related to improper white balance to the color temperature of the light during shooting. Such problems are most noticeable in flesh tones, and are most easily corrected by adding or subtracting blue in the mid ranges—using the blue gamma control.

Proper operation of a color corrector requires both a solid understanding of color, light, and the NTSC system, and a fair amount of practice. A color corrector can be rather dangerous in the wrong hands, and if you're not sure what you're doing, find someone who is.

262

The Psychology of Editing

There are dozens of other types of problems that can crop up during post-production, and some that can invent themselves for particular occasions. If you're just getting started, it might be wise to consider bringing in an experienced editor to help with the first few programs, watching and asking questions as the productions are put together.

Along with directing, editing is my personal favorite part of the production process, and as I've already mentioned, I find many similarities between the two jobs. Editing drives some people up the wall, and I have one friend who often turns his shows over to me to cut, since he basically goes nuts in the painstaking environment of the editing room. As for myself, it appeals to the craftsman in me.

People who have been involved with film production often have a hard time getting used to video editing. Ad agency folks in particular are often used to the comparatively quick process of rough cutting a film, and find on-line video editing to be a classic bore. Once a film workprint has been approved, it goes away to a lab, and a few days later, they see an ANSWER PRINT (a first color-corrected print for them to approve). They'll protest at having to spend eight hours in a video editing suite to cut a couple of thirty-second spots. They often forget that in video, they'll walk out at the end of the day with a copy ready to be aired, without having to wait two or three days for an answer print, and days beyong that for RELEASE PRINTS (final prints).

Of course, it's all a matter of subjective time. Eight hours in an editing suite that results in a finished product *seems* longer than four hours one day, two hours a few days later, and another hour or so a few days after that. Their point is quite valid in some respects, since it's about equivalent to them sitting in the film lab watching the work being done—something no client would even consider.

This brings me to the last point I wish to make with regard to editing problems. Another part of the editor's job is to please the client. The rule holds just as true in an in-house facility that deals with "in-house clients" as it does for post-house staff and freelance editors. In other words, in addition to being an artist and a technician, a good editor must have some of the skills of a behavioral psychologist and a therapist, and at all times, an even temper. If the client knows little about the process of editing—or even worse, just enough to be dangerous—the editor must add the skills of instructor to the above.

It's no wonder that really good editors—those who combine all the skills involved in editing—are in heavy demand and can make very good salaries.

CHAPTER 20

Special Effects —
Adding Visual Impact

The term SPECIAL EFFECTS covers a lot of ground, and has a somewhat different meaning in television than it does in film. Before we get into the subject as applied in television, let's define the term as it is used in film.

In film, a special effect generally is considered to be something that happens in front of the camera. A chair breaking over someone's head during a barroom brawl, an exploding car, the mechanical shark in *Jaws*, or the giant hand of *King Kong*—these are examples of film special effects. They include the use of stunt people as often as they do mechanical objects. The fundamental idea is to make something happen that would normally be impossible, or to dummy up a scene that would be too diffi-

cult or dangerous to actually set up for real. Film special effects people are experts at rigging, making miniatures, handling explosives, etc. Perhaps a more precise definition would be to call these MECHANICAL EFFECTS.

In television these effects are also called special effects, but the situation is confused a bit by the fact that we also use the same term to describe what film people would call OPTICAL EFFECTS. These are effects that are done in the lab in film, or at the switcher during shooting or editing in video. Our subject in this section will be the ELECTRONIC EFFECTS, as they might more appropriately be called, rather than the mechanical effects, as defined earlier.

We will actually consider two different types, or applications, of special effects as used in video. The first would involve scene transitions or the introduction of new visual elements into a scene in a manner that, shall we say, "lets the effect hang out." Examples would include a wipe or key, a chromakey insert, a split-screen, etc. In some cases, such as in keying a person's name into the lower third of the picture, these effects are utilitarian and strictly functional, and would rarely be thought of as true special effects. As applied in programs such as sports, news, commercials, and industrial/educational productions, however, effects are often used for their inherent visual sparkle, in place of a simple cut or dissolve.

The second form of special effect would relate more closely to the film optical effect. In essence, these would be effects designed to create some screen "magic," where the whole idea is that the effect itself *doesn't* show.

Examples here would include using chromakey to place an actor into a miniature set, "magical" appearances and disappearances, and others of this genre. We'll come back to these.

The use of a special effect as a scene transition deserves careful consideration. In the majority of cases, most of the transitions used in a program would normally best be simple cuts. Transitions other than cuts should be employed for a particular reason—to indicate a change of time or place, in which case a dissolve might be the best choice—or as part of definitely established artistic elements. If you were doing a show mimicking the style of early silent films, for instance, this might be a reason to use a variety of wipes, as was much the fashion at the time.

If effects are designed into a show as part of the overall look and style employed, their use may be quite appropriate. Dance sequences,

Special effects.

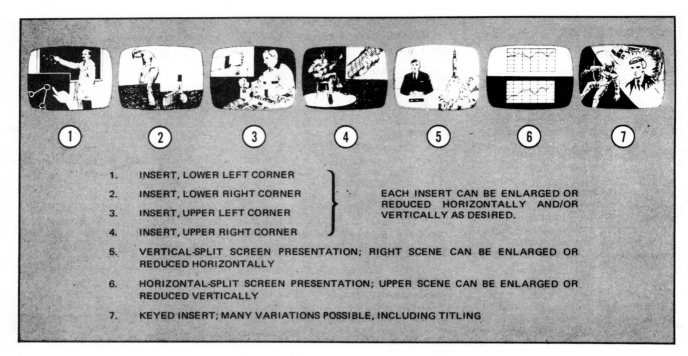

1. INSERT, LOWER LEFT CORNER	
2. INSERT, LOWER RIGHT CORNER	EACH INSERT CAN BE ENLARGED OR REDUCED HORIZONTALLY AND/OR VERTICALLY AS DESIRED.
3. INSERT, UPPER LEFT CORNER	
4. INSERT, UPPER RIGHT CORNER	

5. VERTICAL-SPLIT SCREEN PRESENTATION; RIGHT SCENE CAN BE ENLARGED OR REDUCED HORIZONTALLY

6. HORIZONTAL-SPLIT SCREEN PRESENTATION; UPPER SCENE CAN BE ENLARGED OR REDUCED VERTICALLY

7. KEYED INSERT; MANY VARIATIONS POSSIBLE, INCLUDING TITLING

Typical wipe patterns generated by SEG.

for example, might benefit tremendously from effects such as slow motion, still frames, and other eye-catching effects. Some examples from programs done in the late seventies would include the exquisite first *Ben Vereen Special,* the *Joffery Ballet Special* which was part of the *Dance in America* series, and several of the television works by choreographer Twyla Tharp. Rock groups are also finding some marvelous applications for special effects in their "video albums"—mainly promotional tapes that are run on many of the rock shows. Michael Nesmith and Todd Rundgren, for example, have employed some highly innovative techniques in various of their video pieces.

For most programs, though, the best rule of thumb is to let the program itself suggest the effects, and to make sparing use of anything fancy. Effects for their own sake rarely add to a program, as they get old awfully fast, and not only can bore the viewer, but can distract the viewer's attention.

Going back a few paragraphs to one of our examples, sports producers and directors have in recent years increasingly employed a variety of special effects in ways that are quite appropriate to the nature of their programs. Slow motion has nearly revolutionized sports pro-

grams, and it would be hard to imagine a football game today that didn't include SLO-MO instant replays. DIGITAL EFFECTS such as flips, freezes, spins, and squeezes enhance the pacing and the overall look of sports shows. Because sports programs fall into the category of pure entertainment, adding all sorts of "razzle-dazzle" through the use of special effects is quite appropriate.

The key word with regard to effects is "appropriate." If your program is a musical variety show, there may be places where a soft wipe or two or some digital effects could fit in nicely—again, offering some visual variety to transitions. On the other hand, when producing a serious corporate program on, say, the legal aspects of securities transactions, the chances are that the use of snazzy, showy effects would require greater discretion.

One possible use of effects in such a program would be the technique known as TIME COMPRESSION, which, in simpler words, is program condensation. If a program involves shooting a long presentation by a company expert that originally lasted four hours, it's unlikely that a verbatim tape of the entire presentation would constitute good programming. It would be probable that a condensed version of selected important points would be

266

a more effective way to spread the message on tape. Here, and especially if it was a single-camera shoot, some wipe transitions could serve a dual function that would make their use appropriate.

Since it is usually desirable to avoid jump cuts, the use of a wipe can "soften" the effect of a cut. For instance, a lapse of time could be indicated by a CLOCK WIPE, where the new material is revealed as if by the swiftly moving hand of a clock. This creates a smooth transition while at the same time openly informing the viewer that an edit had been made.

News interviews that must be edited often use a dissolve rather than a cutaway, which can be nothing more than good journalism: it tells the viewer that the material has been edited, rather than hiding the edit with a cutaway of the interviewer or another shot. Of course, if the interview is of an entertainment nature rather than a hard news interview—a celebrity, for instance—this may not be at all necessary, and a cutaway would be used to make the program flow more smoothly.

Special effects in these cases are essentially a technique of editing, whether done at the switcher during the original taping, or during post-production. The best editing, as we saw earlier, is that of which the viewer is completely unaware. More often than not, a special effect makes the viewer aware in no uncertain terms that "reality" has been altered, so when using one, it's important that you have this in mind. In those instances where effects are appropriate, especially where they are used primarily to add some visual pizzazz to a show, keep in mind the fact that the effects your viewers see on the air—on the news, during football games, in the Academy Awards show, and other shows like these—are done with some very extensive and expensive equipment. The networks spend millions on gadgets to produce new and exciting effects for these shows, and the viewer, who really doesn't care *how* they are done, has become accustomed to a high level of technical sophistication. Coming at the viewer with effects that attempt to provide the same results but that fall short, is a sure method of making the show look amateurish. In this respect, it might be wiser to take the view that "if you can't do it

right, then don't do it at all." There is rarely a need to apologize for simplicity, because it usually works well. The number of beautifully produced films and television programs that have been done with nothing more than cuts, dissolves, and fades by far outweighs those that made extensive use of fancy effects.

As to the "magical" effects that can make the impossible happen through the wonders of technology, television has some distinct advantages over film, and some balancing disadvantages as well.

Effects done in video offer the great advantage of being viewable during and immediately after execution, allowing for adjustment until the desired results are achieved. Film, of course, has to go back and forth to the lab, and changes can be time-consuming and potentially expensive. In general, though, film effects tended to look better than the same effects done on tape. This was partly due to the constraints imposed by the state of the art in video equipment, and partly because of the long experience and proven techniques employed in film.

Chromakeys and Mattes

Early CHROMAKEYERS, for example (and virtually all current ENCODED KEYERS), could not and cannot match the quality of well done matte work done in film. RGB CHROMAKEYERS (which work with the three separate color signals, as opposed to ENCODED KEYERS, which work with the composite color signal) provide far better results. The best of these such as the ULTI-MATTE, can virtually match the best results possible in film. As they improve in quality, however, they also become much more critical in terms of setup and operation, and do not lend themselves to quick and easy use by the uninitiated.

The ULTIMATTE represents an excellent example of this criticality of operation. In essence, the Ultimatte is nothing more than a special type of chromakeyer also known as a LUMINANCE CHROMAKEYER. Like all chromakeyers, it uses a backdrop color to key a foreground object over a background video signal. The Ultimatte requires that the camera

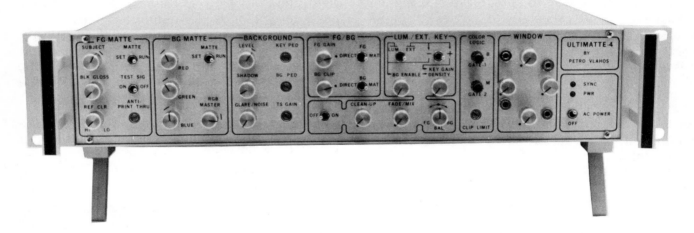

Ultimatte.

shooting the foreground object against the color backdrop (usually blue, as with normal chromakey) provide RGB outputs, meaning that a separate signal will be provided for each of the three colors—red, green, and blue. The NTSC color encoding process reduces the resolution of each of the three color signals, making encoded signals unacceptable for such a sensitive device.

The Ultimatte uses the blue channel signal to first define the area that will be DROPPED OUT (made invisible to the camera) and replaced with background video. It then removes the blue part of the signal, and mixes the remaining foreground image into the background image. It is so sensitive that it can key shadows into the background picture, "see" the background through a glass in the foreground, or key the smoke from a cigarette into the background. In order to do this, it also requires that the blue field behind the foreground object be lit almost perfectly evenly. The Ultimatte can't tell a dark area in the blue field that is the result of uneven lighting from a shadow, and will key both just as readily.

Proper use of the Ultimatte and similar units requires expert lighting and precise operation. Another point is worth noting with regard to the realism of effects done with these units. While it is possible to "see" a background image through a drinking glass filled with water with the proper intensity as defined by the transparency of the glass, there is a subtle flaw in the illusion that can give the trick away. If you actually saw the background

through the glass, the glass itself and water in it would act as a lens to distort anything seen through it. With the Ultimatte and other luminance chromakeyers, however, there will be no image distortion. Often the viewer will not be able to define what seems wrong with the picture, but will sense that something is amiss all the same. This is a factor common to many types of special effects, and one that must be kept in mind when designing them.

Since video effects can be accomplished more quickly than those done in film, it follows that they can also be done at a lower cost, given the proviso that the person in charge knows what he or she is doing. Effects that are well planned, and that are designed by someone who understands the capabilities and limitations of the equipment, can be executed with speed and economy, without a sacrifice in quality. The equipment that is required to do a proper job, though, is expensive, both to rent and to buy. If you're paying for studio time with these high-priced gadgets and must spend time experimenting, the damage to your budget can be considerable.

Some of the more spectacular effects available can often be created without a lot of fancy, high-priced equipment. Careful planning can produce methods of achieving effects that can save money while also improving the visual quality of the results. For instance, if a script calls for a character to magically appear in a scene, such as the transporter used in *Star Trek*, there are a number of possible ways to make this happen. One method would be to use chromakey, and dissolve the chromakey of the actor into the scene to do the effect, then editing to a different angle with the actor actually in the scene. Although this might sound like the simplest method of achieving the effect, it actually would be one of the most difficult ways of making the effect appear seamless and natural.

A major problem with chromakey (one that is demonstrated by innumerable commercials done all over the country by local car dealers) is that unless it's done with extreme care, it looks just plain shoddy. Even with a shadow chromakeyer, in order for two scenes to blend together well, all the individual elements of both scenes must be precisely matched. The camera's perspective, the focal length of the lens, and the angle, color, and quality of the light must all match between foreground and background or the key will be easily detectable as such. Furthermore, any movement by the foreground camera would have to be matched by a corresponding movement of the background camera. Although there are systems available that use computers to accomplish just this task—the MAGICAM being one—these are not everyday items, and you must take your production to their studio and pay the rather high costs of using them.

Getting back to our example, there's a much simpler and less expensive method of making a character appear that would actually result in much better visual quality. It's one of the oldest techniques used in movie making, and involves a matched dissolve of the scene, with the first take shot without the actor, and the second take shot with the actor. If the camera stays locked in position, a dissolve from the first take to the second will result in the actor's "materialization" into the scene. This is essentially how the *Star Trek* transportations were accomplished in the original TV version. To add some visual spice to the effect, sparkles were added in the shape of the actors, accomplished by sprinkling aluminum dust under strong lighting, with the film then run backwards so that the sparkles moved upwards.

The old film art of MATTE PAINTING (or GLASS PAINTING) can also be applied to video, often with other media taking the place of a painting. If you want to have a company spokesman appear to be walking outside your Australian plant, but the boss won't spring for a location shoot, some videotaped footage of the plant's exterior (or in a pinch, a slide), can provide the backdrop. A relatively small set is built in your studio to match the area of the background scene in which you want the spokesman to appear. By surrounding the talent with a soft wipe from the studio picture to the background picture, and with careful adjustment of lighting, video levels, and color, and precise matching of the camera angle to the angle of the background perspective, he'll appear to be standing on location "down under." Likewise, a fantasy setting can be created by an artist, and the same method used to place the talent in an "impossible" location—a direct use of the matte painting technique. The term GLASS PAINTING comes from the fact that a scene is painted on glass, leaving a clear area through which actors can be shot. The edges of these clear areas are carefully matched to the parts of the set behind it that show through. This is a mechanical analog of the electronic technique we've been examining.

Animation

Animation is another area of special effects that has traditionally fallen in the domain of film, but is possible to achieve on a practical basis in video. It has long been possible to accurately edit one frame at a time with videotape, which fulfills the basic requirement for animation. The problem with performing animation on tape, however, is the tremendous amount of wear to which the tape is subjected. Even with the new 1-inch formats, the VTR necessarily must spend a great deal of time in standby mode—with heads spinning and thus scrubbing the tape. Animation onto ¾-inch cassette is especially rigorous for both machine and tape. The magnetic record/playback videodisc units that have been used in sports and other instant-replay applications, on the other hand, are well suited for video animation. Relatively low-cost models are now available priced in the neighborhood of $15,000–$20,000, though the image quality at this price level is rather modest.

As is always the case, of course, there are trade-offs to video animation. Again, one major advantage to working in video is the ability to view the results as you proceed. If a movement or element in the scene is wrong, it can be evaluated and corrected immediately. In film, the results won't be known until the film has been processed and the moment for correction is long past. For straightforward frame-by-frame animation, this makes video a powerful animation tool.

On the other hand, there are some things that can be accomplished in film animation that are simply impossible in video. Motion

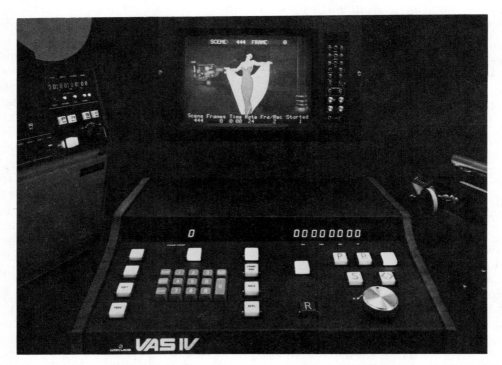

Videodisc record/playback system.

270

graphics, for instance, often require that each frame of film be manipulated in special ways, such as in using a long exposure for each frame and zooming on the graphics while the shutter is open to create a "streak" effect. This is all but impossible in video animation, although there are other ways to electronically create a similar effect.

The new computer graphics systems, such as the Aurora Systems unit, the Quantel 7000, and others extend the possibilities of video animation. The pictures created on these systems exist only in computer memory until they are recorded on tape. Some of these systems are capable of performing the actual animation in the computer, with the signal being recorded on tape in real time.

As of this writing there were no "off-the-shelf" computer animation systems on the market that could fully match the visual quality of cel animation. The few truly comparable computer systems in existence are proprietary ones built at computer animation houses which jealously guard their designs. Some computer animation of this type looks very "computerish," i.e., poor; but the best of them, as exemplified for instance by the system owned by **Information International Inc. (III)**, of Southern California, can provide astonishing capabilities. The time is not far off when computers such as the one at III will be able to create an animated person (the hardest test) that cannot be told from an actor. Current experiments along these lines come very close even now.

There are other special effects that either require the use of film or are better achieved with it. Extreme slow motion is a good example. In video, the Type C 1-inch machines, the **Sony BVU 820** ¾-inch cassette unit, and the previously mentioned disc units can play back video at a slow rate, but the video will always consist of frames shot at a rate of thirty per second. If played back very slowly, the resulting image will perceivably "jump" with each new frame. In normal video applications, there is no way to increase the frame rate during shooting to create a subsequent slow motion effect during playback. With film, that is precisely the technique used to create smooth, fluid slow motion. The film camera is run at high frame rate (called OVERCRANKING), and

Computer generated graphics.

271

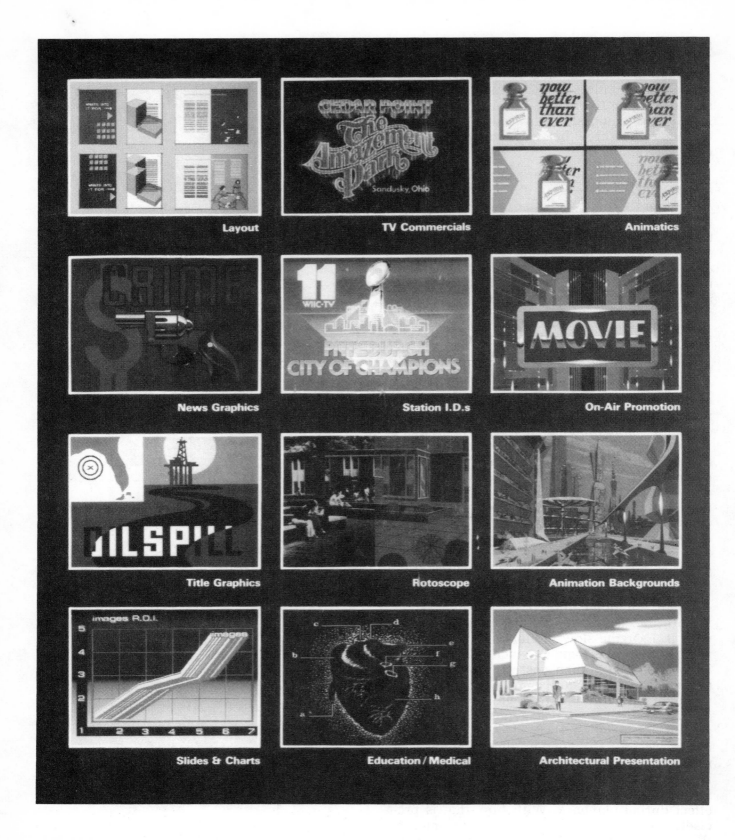

Computer graphics—"IMAGES" System
(Computer Graphics Lab Inc.—New York Institute of Technology) —examples of styles.

272

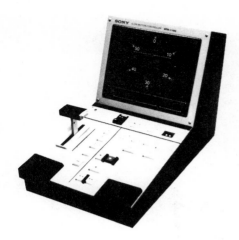
Sony slow motion controller.

the film is then played at normal projection speeds. If the shooting speed was 72 frames per second, for instance, and the projection speed was the standard 24 frames per second, the result would be motion on the screen at one-third the normal rate.

Special effects are one of the most complicated and specialized areas of production, regardless of the medium used. They offer an easy and possibly expensive way to get into trouble. It should come as no surprise that the people who specialize in creating them not only command good money, but can become stars in their own right. People like Douglass Trumbull *(2001)*, John Dykstra *(Star Wars)*, Peter Ellenshaw *(The Black Hole)*, and Ray Harryhousen *(Sinbad)* have become legends for their ability to create images that turn fantasy into reality. These abilities required years of study and practice.

The recent resurgence of big, splashy special effects—given its greatest impetus by the tremendous popularity of *Star Wars*—has brought them to the attention of producers and directors working in every level and area of production. The effects used in *Star Wars* and its brethren, however, were made possible by some of the most incredible computer-assisted equipment ever designed. Lots of money, really vast sums, were spent on these, and the average television producer (for that matter, virtually any television producer) must accept the fact that while the "trickle-down" effect will someday make many of these techniques available, in the foreseeable future these will remain out of the reach of television production budgets.

The key to success with special effects is to not simply throw them into a program for good measure, but rather, to design them into a program where they will add to the show and support its basic objectives. A light and sparing hand applied with a sense of balance can create stunning effects that can either be seamless and totally real to the viewer, or can dazzle the viewer—as the producer wishes. To reiterate a continuing theme, the basic objective should normally be a smoothly flowing program that makes it easy and natural for the viewer to become involved and immersed.

CHAPTER 21

Other Equipment

We've examined the basic equipment involved in production such as cameras and VTRs and some of the ancillary gear such as grip and lighting equipment that are used in production and post-production. This section will focus on some of the other types of equipment not already covered that fill particular gaps in the television chain.

The highly technical nature of television production often scares people away, or at least presents a formidable obstacle to understanding the production process. This situation is exacerbated by the constant process of change that brings increasing complexity to the higher levels of production gear. There's a dichotomy here, since at the lower end, television equipment becomes ever simpler, while at the top end, the exact opposite is true.

Those whose only desire is to make simple tapes using the most basic of systems, that will go on further than a monitor or receiver or two, may never encounter the more esoteric pieces of television equipment. As production ambitions escalate, however, the need for at least a background knowledge of the various BLACK BOXES becomes more acute. Before we get into the real, "hardcore" black boxes, let's first take a moment to look at one of the basic pieces of television equipment.

Switchers

The simplest switcher is a device that has two input connectors and one output connector, and a lever, button, or switch that permits the user to select which of the two input signals is to be sent to the output. There are, in fact, several units available that meet just those specifications that are designed to allow switching between two portable cameras in the field.

Most switchers, however, go beyond the basic requirements, and provide additional capabilities such as dissolves, wipes, and keys besides simple switching back and forth.

The use of a switcher implies that more than one signal source is involved, and in most cases this would be two or more cameras. By pressing the appropriate button, the user can select one of the cameras, sending its signal to a recorder or transmitter. With the use of one or more levers, arms, or slide-controls, the user can also mix two or more signals in various ways, performing a smooth transition from one source to another, at the rate at which the control is moved. Most such transitions, again,

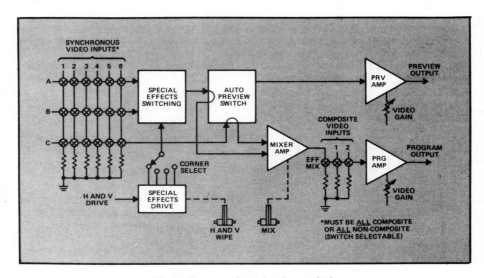

Block diagram of production switcher.

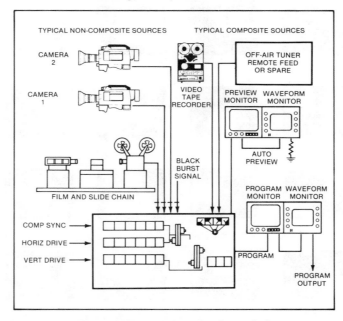

Typical installation of production switcher.

would consist of dissolves and wipes. Since these are generally called SPECIAL EFFECTS, switchers with these capabilities built into them are often called SPECIAL EFFECTS GENERATORS (SEGs). In the broadcast environment where switchers are bought by specifying optional modules, the SEG is often a separately ordered part of the overall switcher. Whereas in the lower end, the switcher is more commonly sold as an off-the-shelf item, and includes whatever capabilities its price permits.

It's important to keep in mind that for any transition between two signal sources to be visually smooth, the two must be in perfect synchronization. This permits the switcher to actually make the switch (in the case of a cut) during the vertical interval, so that the switching point is not seen. All production switchers are thus of a type known as VERTICAL INTERVAL SWITCHERS. Some of the lower-level switchers incorporate a sync generator from which sync signals can be distributed to the cameras, whereas none of the higher-level equipment does.

A very simple switcher might provide three inputs, all of which are fed to two BUSSES (switching banks). By selecting source number 1, for instance, on the "A" buss, and source number 2, on the "B" buss, the user can dissolve or wipe from signal one to signal two by operating the FADER from buss "A" to buss "B".

As the sophistication of the switcher grows, the capabilities are expanded, although the basic theory remains the same. Some of the additional features might include a wider selection of wipe patterns, and on the more expensive designs, these will include what are known as ROTARY and MATRIX wipes that offer more esoteric transitions. ROTARY WIPES involve a wipe transition line that pivots around an axis, rather than one that simply moves evenly across the screen. MATRIX WIPES may involve any number of custom wipe patterns, such as stars, checkerboards, or even a company logo, as is possible with custom-designed wipes. Another very useful feature that will be added is the capability to RE-ENTER effects. This generally means that there will be more than one set (or BANK) of busses, and that the effect set up on one bank can be fed to a second bank, where other effects may be added. This would allow one, for example, to dissolve from a SPLIT SCREEN (a wipe stopped part way) to a key over a different background. Some switchers are designed so that these capabilities are actuated through multifunction logic, with a single set of controls performing a variety or

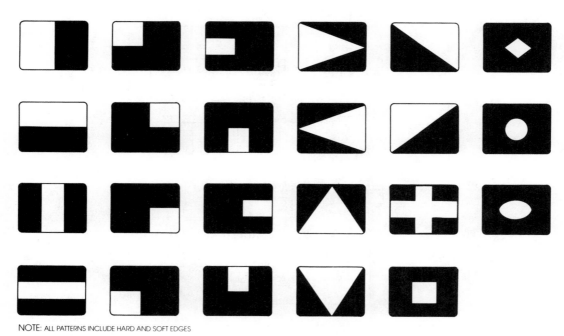

NOTE: ALL PATTERNS INCLUDE HARD AND SOFT EDGES

Basic wipe/effect pattern.

276

combination of functions. This, however, usually results in some constraints on flexibility.

A full-scale production switcher, as found in major stations, production houses, and corporate and educational facilities, will have as many as four MIX/EFFECTS BANKS, three of which may be re-entered into the next bank, and each of which would be provided with full key and wipe capabilities in addition to the basic dissolve capability. Also provided would be a DOWNSTREAM KEYER, which is an additional keyer that can key an insert (such as a person's name and title) over the final output of the switcher without regard to what the main mix/effects banks are doing. The downstream keyer usually also provides a MASTER FADE-TO-BLACK control, which will fade the final output of the switcher to black, again, without regard for any other settings upstream.

"DOWNSTREAM KEYER"

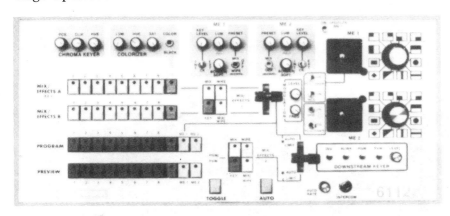

Crosspoint Latch.

American Data.

277

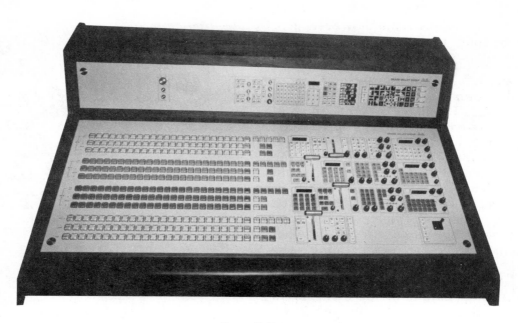

Grass Valley.

Edit console/switcher/control room.

278

Virtually every studio of any size will be equipped with some sort of switcher, since this is where the bulk of multicamera production is done. However, there are many remote vehicles that have switchers onboard, ranging from simple field-oriented designs to the most sophisticated of units. There are even battery-operated systems, some of which are built into suitcase-sized packages along with an audio mixer, a set of monitors, and a sync generator.

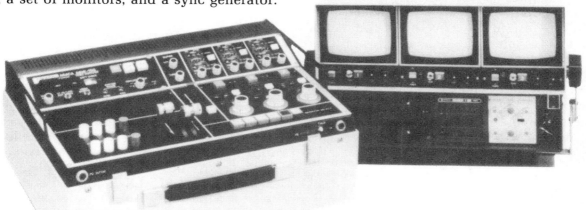

Portable switcher.

Inside mobile van.

Recent switcher designs are more and more frequently offering the ability to program the switcher operation, which is then activated at the touch of a button. This feature ranges from the ability to perform an AUTO-TAKE, which is nothing more than a switcher-controlled dissolve or wipe, the speed of which is set with a knob, all the way to a computer memory that allows the user to program the switcher with a series of complex effects on any number of effects banks, all of which will then be executed in the desired sequence upon command. At the most sophisticated level, this allows effects to be performed routinely and easily that would be far more involved than any human being could manage in real time, or that would require more hands on the switcher than there would be room for people to crowd around it.

Switcher use is by no means confined to multicamera production, as all of the computer editing systems that offer A/B-rolling capability will employ some sort of switcher. The more sophisticated of these will use switchers that could and may double as live production switchers. In post-production, the editing computer normally controls at least one mix/effects bank, and in some cases, more than one.

Prices for switchers cover a very broad range. The simplest portable switchers can be had for as little as $500, while the top-of-the-line models with memory and multiple mix/effects banks can run as high as $200,000 or more.

The first step in learning to use a switcher is to learn the logic of the particular manufacturer's design. Odd as it may seem, some of the larger and seemingly more complicated switchers may actually be easier to learn to use, since the logic will be quite straight forward. On the smaller level, the design may include some rather complex logic in order to squeeze the maximum in capabilities into a small package. The second step is to practice, practice, practice. There's a direct analogy here with touch typing, except that in switcher operation—especially in a live production—if you have to stop and look or figure out how to do something, by the time you have, it's probably too late.

Time Base Correctors

As we discussed when examining videotape recorders, the stability, or TIME BASE, of the signal played back by any VTR is by nature inaccurate, and will need correction before it can be broadcast. Simple tape-to-tape editing or duplication can be accomplished without time base correction, due to the ingenious techniques worked out to handle the color portion of the signal, and also due to the forgiving nature of today's monitors and receivers. In doing so, however, the errors in the playback signal will be recorded into the second-generation tape, to be further multiplied when it is subsequently played back.

The original VTR design, the quad, was inherently stable enough so that correcting time base errors was a relatively simple procedure. Since the errors were relatively small, they could be corrected by electronically switching DELAY LINES (circuits that basically run the video through a longer path, thus delaying it for a short time) in and out, and the signal thus processed could then meet the FCC specs for broadcasting. The FCC specs are very stringent with regard to stability, as they were designed with the early television receivers in mind. As anyone who watched much TV in the late forties and early fifties will testify, simply getting the picture to hold was an accomplishment of major proportions, and the vertical and horizontal hold knobs were not only prominently on the front of the set, as opposed to their position on the rear of today's sets (or absence altogether), but they were used, and used a lot.

Television receiver circuitry improved over the years, of course, and by the time the small-format VTRs such as the ½-inch reel-to-reel and ¾-inch cassettes appeared on the scene, most of the receivers being built would display their signals with few problems. The FCC specs for broadcast, though, had not changed, and the new helical formats simply didn't have the stability to meet broadcast requirements.

Along came a company known as **Consolidated Video Systems (CVS),** which is known as **Harris Video Systems (HVS),** following an acquisition in 1979. Consolidated Video Systems, which started out with an unsuccessful attempt at creating a high-speed tape duplication process, shook the broadcast world at the 1973 NAB exhibit with a digital time base corrector that could take the signal from a helical VTR and bring it up to broadcast specs insofar as stability was concerned. The original model, the **CVS 500,** won them an EMMY for technical achievement, and opened the door for electronic news gathering and field production.

In simple terms, a digital TBC works by using a computer-type memory to store picture information as it comes in from the VTR. It reads in a number of lines at the unstable rate, breaks the signal down into a series of digital bits, stores it for a brief time, then reconstructs the signal and reads it back out at a stable rate. If necessary, it drops a few bits, or repeats some to add to the signal.

I've put all this into as layman-like language as possible, so don't get too excited if it makes sense, for the process is actually considerably more complicated. Suffice it to say that it all works, and that digital time base correction was virtually a dream come true for the entire industry.

There are presently a large variety of TBCs available, with a wide range of price tags and using a number of different technologies. In the bargain basement are various types of "semi-TBCs," commonly known as SKEW CORRECTORS, that don't bring the signal up to full broadcast spec, but that do help with dubbing, editing, and cable transmission. Units at this level can be found in the $2000–$3500 price range.

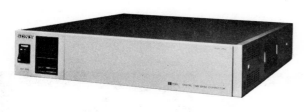

Time base correctors.

Moving up a floor brings us to the true broadcast TBCs, which can put your 1-inch, ¾-inch, or ½-inch VTR on the air, and which will satisfy the basic requirements for A/B-roll editing. These generally fall into the $6000 to $20,000 price range. On the top floor, with other expensive adult toys, are the FRAMESTORE SYNCHRONIZERS, which perform essentially the same function, but which store one entire frame of video at a time. Prices start at roughly $15,000 and move upwards. The original primary function of framestores is to fully synchronize any two separate and independent signals from any source, and as such, they serve as what might be called "super TBCs." There are, however, some interesting possibilities that present themselves once a full frame of video can be stored, and that led to one of the more recent of a long list of crazes to hit the television industry.

Digital Effects

Once you've got a frame of video stored in memory, there are a number of things you can do with it. You would, of course, correct it to meet FCC specs and then send it back out on its way, but as long as you've got it tucked away in there, why not do something interesting with it before you let it go? This is a ques-

tion that was addressed almost immediately by the companies that build these devices.

The picture stored in a framestore consists of a string of BINARY CODES—basically a mathematical representation of the picture. By fiddling around with the equations that are used to send the picture back out, you could cause it to go out backwards, say, or upside down, or both. Taking it a step further, you could compress it, expand it, flip it, rotate it, and generally torture it until you were satisfied. Add a bit more circuitry, and you can do this with not just a single frame, but with a real time video signal. Add still more circuitry, and you can do it to several signals at once. It's true that you'll delay the signal a bit with all this manipulation, but usually not enough to notice, and if necessary, a simple delay line in the audio path can match the video delay, leaving the audience none the wiser.

Digital effects have opened new possibilities in video, and have made both possible and easy many effects that were previously possible only in film, with it's expensive and time consuming optical techniques.

While the first few of these units provided results that were decidedly on the rough side, and some digital effects still are readily identifiable as such since they have a somewhat mechanical quality about them compared to film effects, the latest systems now offer truly optical-quality results. Furthermore, the state of the art is moving at such a pace that the system you buy today will probably be obsolete next month, with the introduction of a newer and better design.

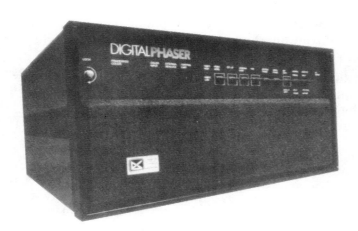

Digital Framestore Synchronizer.

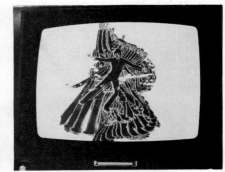

Framestore sequence.

Presently, digital effects units are nothing if not expensive (ranging from about $50,000 to well over $100,000—remember, they are at heart essentially the Rolls Royces of time base correctors, which are expensive devices themselves). The rate of technological improvement, however, virtually assures that within a few years the basic circuits required to store a complete frame of video will consist of a few chips that will cost less than dinner and a movie. Prototype consumer receivers with such circuits built in for the home viewer to play with have already been demonstrated.

With the welter of digital and other circuits and magic boxes available, it might appear that the worse possible signal could be marched through the right black box, and come out on the other side sparkling like clean laundry. Insofar as time base stability is concerned, this is almost true. There does come a point, though, when signals are simply too far gone to be corrected. The devices mentioned so far correct only the time base errors, and have no effect on the visual quality of the picture's content other than a slight inevitable degradation which accompanies any and all forms of signal processing. We are not talking here about aesthetics, such as the camera operator's ability, but rather about the technical quality of the picture, with regard to such things as noise in the video or the chroma. Correcting these requires the use of different types of black boxes.

Image Enhancers and Noise Reducers

Earlier, we examined image enhancers as they are provided in cameras, and the same basic techniques can be applied to video signals coming off tape. These circuits look for transitions in the signal from light-to-dark areas, or vice versa, and assume that any such transition represents an edge of something within the picture. To create what appears to be a "sharper" picture, these edges are enhanced by exaggerating the transition. As already mentioned, over-enhancement, or several generations of enhancement on top of enhancement, can end up giving results that look like cartoon drawings, and for this reason enhancers are best used with restraint. If a little bit of enhancement is thrown in during shooting, and a bit during editing, the results may be very good indeed.

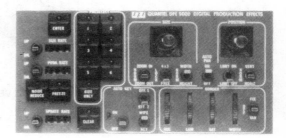

Quantel keyboard.

Quantel effects system.

283

Compression and positioning

Variable aspect ratio

Posterization/solarization

Mosaic

DME 1

Vertical and horizontal flip and tumble

Auto pan and tilt

Split

Hall of mirrors

DME 2

Dual channel compression

Independent control of size and positioning

Simultaneous manipulation of variable aspect ratio in two channels *(rotating cube)*

NEC DVE System digital effects.

NEC DVE control panel.

Enhancers are more appropriately used with tape when the format is cassette, since a high-band recorder will normally need much less assistance. In high-band formats, a slight amount of camera enhancement is usually all that's necessary.

Color-under cassette recording, however, loses so much chroma resolution to begin with that enhancement can be of help. Some time base correctors include enhancement circuitry in their basic design, or offer enhancers as options to the basic unit. The Yves Faroudja Image System mentioned earlier can help the picture quality of heterodyne recorders considerably, and in combination with a good TBC, provides excellent results.

Unfortunately, enhancers look for and work with information that's basically in the high-frequency ranges, and this is precisely where most of the objectionable noise in a signal lives. This creates the call for another black box called a NOISE REDUCER which, again, most often goes to bat for cassettes, though not exclusively so.

The simplest approach to noise reduction would be to put a filter in the signal path that would strip off any high frequency portions of the signal. Since that's where most of the visible noise is, the net effect would be to sacrifice a bit of resolution in order to get a cleaner-looking signal. Having done that, the signal could then be sent to an enhancer to crank back in some artificial resolution. Aside from the fact that such an exercise would be akin to the "rubber glove solution to the leaky pen,"

there is a more sophisticated solution, and it is the one used in most cases.

The noise reducer examines each line of the signal, and compares it to the next line. Any high-frequency SPIKE in the waveform that is not there on the previous or the following line is assumed to be noise, and is removed. In a sense, these operate along much the same principles as a DROPOUT COMPENSATOR—which senses a dropout on the tape and fills in the missing information with corresponding parts of the signal from the previous line—only faster. Some image enhancers compare the two fields of each frame in their search for noise. With the aid of logic that can recognize movement within the picture, anything that looks like noise appearing in field two that wasn't there in field one is assumed to be noise, and is removed.

As with any such signal processing equipment, it is necessary to keep in mind the fact that what's basically happening is that we're asking a mess of wire, silicon, and other unconscious materials to make judgments for us, and that the electronics are bound to make mistakes and have quirks. The best method for achieving a clean, sharp signal is to record it that way in the first place, and employ handling practices downstream that don't require the use of anything more than time base correction.

It's possible nowadays to improve the quality of a signal, and in the right circumstances the above-described circuits can be of immense help. They still, however, do not substitute for proper, quality recording techniques.

Yves Faroudja Image System.

285

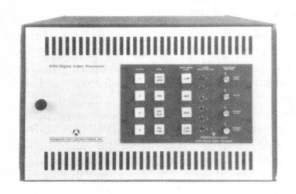

Digital Noise reducers/signal processors.

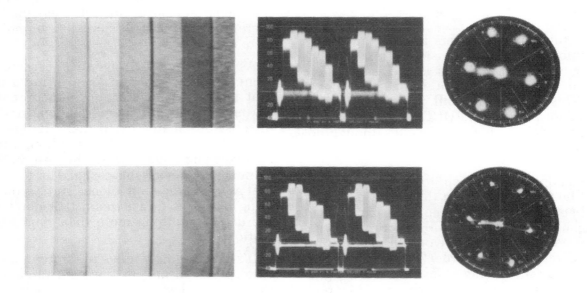

Example of noise reduction.

Part 4

Other Important Considerations

CHAPTER 22

Distribution

Producing a video program is, when you get right down to it, only a first step—a means to an end. Programming does no good if it's not seen by anyone, and some method of distribution is thus necessary to complete the process. The term "distribution" itself works on two levels, economic and logistic on one hand, and technical on the other.

In more basic terms, the first level concerns what could best be described as marketing, since even in those instances where a program is distributed free of charge, someone must be "sold" on the value of the program. The second level involves the mechanical means by which a program will be distributed. This section will examine both levels of distribution,

starting at the top with the oldest, most firmly entrenched and most difficult method of distribution to employ: Network television.

Network Distribution

In terms of over-the-air broadcast networks, there are only three and a half systems in existence. These are the AMERICAN BROADCAST COMPANY (ABC), the COLUMBIA BROADCASTING SYSTEM (CBS), and the NATIONAL BROADCASTING COMPANY (NBC). The "half" network is the PUBLIC BROADCASTING SYSTEM (PBS). I call it a "half" network because it does not have the rigid schedule structure of the three commercial networks, and thus loses some of the advantages of a network operation while attaining some advantages in other areas that help compensate. More on this later.

The basic realities of the commercial networks are that unless they're already buying programming from you, your chances of selling them anything are *extremely* slim. Doing so is not totally impossible, and over the past few years there have been perhaps one or two programs each year that have been purchased from producers outside the normal group of established sources.

For the most part, however, the networks commission programs such as series, specials, and movies rather than solicit them. Documentaries are almost without exception produced by the networks' own news departments. This policy stems mainly from the networks' position on liability. They must take responsibility for the content of any such programs they broadcast, and are very wary of doing so in the case of material they themselves did not produce. There have been rare exceptions in recent years, such as with *The Police Tapes,* which ABC aired and which was done by independent producers, but that was a case of an exception that proves the rule.

In the area of entertainment programs, specials and movies, the commercial networks keep turning to a limited number of major production companies (mostly based in the Los Angeles area) that have provided them with programming for years. These include such companies as *Lorimar, Universal Television,* Norman Lear's *T.A.T.* and *Tandem Productions, QM Productions,* and *M.T.M.,* just to cite a few examples.

Why do the networks keep buying from a relatively small handful of companies? The reason is actually rather simple, if you stop to consider basic human nature and the way programs are developed and purchased.

Let's say you've come up with what you believe is the most innovative concept for a TV series ever developed. You write a treatment and outline the basic plots for 26 episodes, and you take it to the head of program development for one of the commercial networks. He looks at it, tells you he really loves it, that you're a genius, says thanks for bring-

ing it to us, and don't call us, we'll call you. If you ever hear from him again, it'll likely be in the form of a letter saying that while your concept is undoubtedly an outstanding one, it doesn't meet the network's needs at present, and enclosed will be the copy you had provided them. Why? It's simple: If someone at one of the networks were to buy a program from you and it failed, his very job would be in jeopardy. He bought a show from an unproven source, it flopped, and he'd soon be pursuing a new career.

If, on the other hand, the same executive had bought the same exact show from Garry Marshall (*Happy Days, Laverne & Shirley,* et al) and it flopped, all he has to answer to his bosses is "Well, gee, I figured since it was Garry's show, it had to be a hit. Who would have thought that Garry would come up with a loser?" Case dismissed. The moral is that it's a lot better idea to buy from a known quantity than from an unknown one, regardless of the merits of the program itself.

This system certainly would not seem to be the best way for the networks to find new, innovative, and high-quality programming, but it is a sad fact of life. Until you have a good reputation and a track record of successes behind you, the chances of selling to the commercial networks are very, very slim.

This brings us to the "half" network—PBS. Individual PBS affiliate stations can take programs distributed by satellite from PBS and air them whenever they wish. This permits each station to establish its own schedule, and may help them to fit the needs of their local community, but it makes it very difficult for PBS to wage an effective national promotional campaign for its shows. Programs offered on PBS stations have a tendency to play hide and seek at times. The ability to reach a large percentage of the viewing audience, already hampered by the lower ratings on public television, is further hindered by the inability to splash the program across the entire country in a single time slot, as is the case with the commercial networks.

Overall, however, the chances for an independent producer of getting a program on PBS are somewhat better than with their profit-making brethren. The Public Broadcasting System, through the Corporation for Public Broadcasting (CPB), actively solicits program proposals from independent producers, and helps fund productions once they have been selected.

Access to airtime on local PBS stations is also much better, and a well-produced documentary dealing with a matter of local or national interest may well catch the interest of the local PBS affiliate. If the program is one that would be worthy of national exposure, there is also a mechanism in place to allow for national distribution.

PBS was the first network to establish a full satellite distribution network. Not only do stations receive their programming from PBS via satellite, they can also use the satellite to offer programming to other PBS stations. This two-way system is highly flexible, and represents a commendable use of state-of-the-art technology by the PBS system.

A major question regarding PBS will be the way it will be affected by loss of revenues in the budget-tightening era of the Reagan administration. This administration would like to shift the burden to the private sector, and only time will tell if its strategy is valid.

Syndication

The roles and the power of the traditional commercial networks are already in the process of diminishing, and one of the factors working to bring this about is independent program SYNDICATION. Syndication is by no means new, but the power and nature of syndication has been evolving fairly rapidly in recent years, and the trend is likely to continue.

Syndicators in the past occupied themselves primarily with packaging movies, old network series, and game shows for sale to individual

PBS Satellite distribution system.

stations or station groups. They got their biggest boost when the FCC mandated the "Prime Time Access Hour" from 7:00 to 8:00 P.M. as a reserve for local programming. The FCC's intent was to encourage programs of community interest, but what happened in most communities was that the stations bought syndicated game shows to be STRIPPED in that period. STRIPPING means running the same show in the same time slot every weekday evening.

In the past few years, however, the syndicators, and in some cases, the sponsors themselves, discovered that they could set up their own "instant networks," even for a single program. Operation Prime Time, which has distributed several movies and mini-series to independent stations across the country, is one such example.

Your chances of having a program distributed by a syndicator are probably better than your chances would be in dealing with a network. A syndicator may agree to show your program to various program directors and try to sell it as widely as possible, with no guarantees to you. This places most of the risk on your shoulders, for if you were to spend, say, $75,000 producing a program, and a syndicator only sells it in two small markets for a total of $600, you're out of pocket a sizeable sum and even more after the syndicator takes its share of the gross. Actually, the chances of such a situation coming to pass are slim, for most of the larger syndicators normally spend a fair amount of money promoting a program or series, and won't take on a program they don't feel fairly confident about.

The big annual event in program syndication is the convention of the National Association of Television Programming Executives (NATPE), where all of the major syndicators and station programming directors meet each year to buy and sell their programs. Traditionally, most of the action takes place in the hospitality suites that are awash with liquor, hors d'oeuvres, and fetching young women. This is where most of the syndicated programs for the year will be bought. There is a certain perennial sales effort conducted by representatives who call on the stations, but the proportion is small compared to the amount of business conducted at the annual NATPE. If you want to

sell your show through syndication, your chances are best if it's on display at NATPE.

There are three basic financial structures in syndication, though there are hundreds of permutations and combinations that fall between these categories. The three basic types of syndication deals are: OUTRIGHT SALE, BARTER, and BROKER.

OUTRIGHT SALE is just what it sounds like. A syndicator offers a program for sale to a station, at a set price for a set number of airings. The price is determined by the size of the station's market, the popularity of the program, and the precedent prices fetched by the same show in other markets and by similar shows in that market. Prices are sometimes determined by bidding between stations. A series of minor importance sold in a small market might bring only $50.00 per episode, while a major series, possibly earlier episodes of a series still on the networks, such as M*A*S*H or Happy Days, might bring as much as $50,000 or more per episode in a major market.

In the BARTER system, the syndicator gives the program to the station in exchange for a specified number of commercial spots, usually within the program, but occasionally on other programs—a practice known as TIME BANKING. The station pays no cash for the program, and the syndicator makes its (and the producer's) money by selling the advertising time directly to sponsors.

In BROKERING, the syndicator actually buys air time on a station, and sells all of the commercial spots within the program. The station receives cash for their time, acting as a conduit, and the syndicator and producer make their money on the difference between the advertising revenues received and the costs of production and airtime.

As mentioned earlier, there are various other methods of syndication that can be worked out, though most will have at their foundation one of these three basic structures. Syndication takes substantially more work than would a straight sale to one of the networks, and syndicators usually take a fairly healthy percentage of the gross profit for their efforts—approaching and sometimes more than 50 percent. With these economic realities, it is apparent that success in syndication depends on reaching a large number of stations. A very successful program, such as a hit network series now in syndication, might be sold to 200 stations or more. While there are no hard rules, since each program or series is different and costs of production vary, in general it would probably be hard to break even with fewer than about 25 stations in moderately large markets airing a program.

Although there are hundreds of small and/or regional syndicators, the large national syndicators get most of the business, and their names are familiar from the closing credits of various programs. They include companies such as *Four Star Entertainment, MCA TV, Metromedia, Paramount TV Distribution, JWT Syndications, Worldvision Enterprises, Viacom,* and other giants of the industry.

Cable Distribution

Cable distribution operates at three basic levels that are in many ways similar to the levels of broadcast television. They are:

1. Nationally distributed pay cable.
2. Nationally or regionally distributed free cable.
3. Local cable operators.

It should be noted, however, that the cable industry is in a state of flux, and that many of the distinctions are very blurry. For instance, a cable "network" may have a strong subscriber base in two or three widely separated areas of the country, and no subscribers in other places.

The nationally distributed pay cable operations are best exemplified by the two biggest such operations: HOME BOX OFFICE and SHOWTIME. The number of competing pay cable operations increases literally monthly, and the next few years will see numerous new operations started, along with a certain amount of shake-out of current operators.

The pay cable operators are in essence new forms of television networks, with the difference being that they are distributed by satellite and over coaxial cable rather than over broadcast television stations; they charge viewers directly for their programs instead of running paid advertising. Whereas they started out fill-ing their schedules mainly with recent movie releases, most are now producing or purchasing original programming in addition to sports. Many are also becoming involved in series programming as well.

Trying to sell a program to pay cable is a lot like trying to sell to one of the commercial networks. The pay operators may be a bit more open to new ideas and producers, but they still prefer to buy from established and proven sources. For the most part, they're interested in flashy specials with big name entertainers, and if topless showgirls can be worked into the show, then so much the better. Pay TV still sells to a certain extent on its novelty value, and the chance to see recent box office blockbusters, R-rated movies, and Las Vegas-style entertainment has prompted a great many people to sign up. Pay cable executives sometimes privately admit that this is probably a temporary state of affairs, and that eventually they will need more substantive programming, but that's the situation in the early '80s. Recent plans for cultural pay-cable systems provide a ray of hope, though the industry is holding its collective breath while it waits to see how many people will pay a monthly fee for culture.

At the next level are what could be called CABLE SYNDICATORS, who distribute programs to cable operators for showing as an added, no-extra-cost service. An example would be the MODERN SATELLITE NETWORK, a consumer-oriented operation which distributes a daily schedule of programming that reaches more than 4 million potential viewers over roughly 500 cable systems. Many of the programs they offer are what are known as SPONSORED programs, meaning that the production costs have been covered by a company or organization that wants to get its message across in the format of a program. These operations sell commercial time, and in essence could be viewed as alternative or mini-networks.

Finally, local cable originators produce their own programming, usually a mix of public affairs and local entertainment. It is often possible to gain access to time on a local cable channel either for free or at very modest cost. This can provide a very inexpensive way to have your program seen, albeit by an often limited audience.

In the preceding discussion, I've used the word "sell" in discussing program distribution. Actually, in most cases, the last thing you want to do is sell your program outright. In reality, programs normally are "licensed," meaning that the network, station, or cable operator buys the right to exhibit the program a specified number of times. The actual ownership of the program is not transferred.

Selling a program, regardless of the outlet, is a difficult proposition for those who are new to the game. The program or series that is successfully sold based only on a written concept or proposal is a very rare bird. The chances improve considerably if you can find the money to actually produce a program or a pilot, as you then have something concrete to offer. In the case of a single program such as a special or documentary, the program has a chance to sell itself based on merits that are readily apparent. There is an obvious risk, of course, in taking this route. If no one buys the program, you're stuck with what could be a rather expensive white elephant.

The methods of distribution that have been discussed are for the most part the traditional ones. In the past few years, new methods of distribution have opened themselves up, with the home videocassette systems providing the major mechanism. The following, then, represent new technical methods of distribution, and may or may not represent marketing challenges, depending upon the application.

Videocassette Distribution

Long before the first consumer videocassette machine was ever sold for home use, business, industry, and education had seized on and begun to exploit the inherent advantages of videocassette distribution. Its benefits made it a nearly ideal carrier of messages for institutional users: It was simple to use. The picture quality was excellent. It could be cost-effective even in single quantities. Even the relatively large ¾-inch U-Matic cassettes were small enough that they could easily and inexpensively be mailed across the country.

The introduction of the ½-inch Beta and VHS formats only served to further facilitate the use of cassettes for institutional users, being smaller and cheaper while providing picture quality that was actually equal to or better than the original U-Matic cassettes.

As was the case with the originally intended market for U-Matic, the ½-inch formats were aimed at the home user. Unlike the ¾-inch format, however, the ½-inch formats succeeded in establishing a home market, and finding a videocassette recorder in the average home is no longer the miracle it would have been considered only a short while ago. As a friend noted, "When my mother went to Sears and bought a videocassette recorder, I knew the 'video revolution' had finally arrived!"

In the time since the introduction of the home formats, a healthy market for programming has developed, which would indicate good prospects for independent producers

with programming to distribute. It would be instructive, however, to examine the types of programming that are being successfully distributed on a national level. It turns out that the mass market has been for the same types of programs that helped establish pay cable: movies, and a large percentage of X-rated films. For the large part, the public taste seems to be for the same things that have helped the networks to flourish: escape and titillation.

The major problem facing the independent producer is not distributing cassettes themselves; that is basically a detail, and programs can be duplicated and mailed or shipped out either by the producer himself or by companies that provide those services. The problem, rather, is one of promotion. It does no good to have a great or important program available if nobody knows about it.

Overall, however, self-distribution of programming on videocassettes is a possible operation, and some producers have succeeded to varying degrees.

The most appropriate area for cassette distribution is in special-interest programming. Cassettes are virtually a custom made medium for limited-scale distribution, and here is where they are providing tremendous value for independent producers. Programs on such diverse subjects as cooking, sports, health, and social and political matters such as alternative energy and nuclear power can be targeted at select audiences on a very economical basis. At its simplest form, anyone with a camera, a recorder, a means of making copies, and a mailing list can go into the business of producing and distributing programming. This is a demonstration of the latent power of videocassettes at its best.

As the number of units sold for consumer use grows, this market will become ever larger. At the same time, it is worth noting that as more and more producers and organizations exploit the technology, there is bound to be an increase in market fragmentation. Nonetheless, the prospects can only continue to improve as we, the society, learn how to gain access to the body of material available. Program exchanges and directories will take increasingly larger roles in helping to connect producers with their audiences.

Videodisc Distribution

Now we come to the dark horse. Videodiscs have been promised for more than a decade, and only recently actually made their debut. At face value, they could seem to be the ideal distribution medium. In quantity, they are much cheaper to produce than cassette copies of a program; they are lighter and thus cheaper to mail; their image quality is potentially better than that of cassettes, and the players are nominally less expensive than videocassette machines.

It's fairly early in the game to be calling the outcome, but there are some serious questions that must be raised about the three currently available disc formats—the Laser Videodisc Format (LVD) called *Laservision* (MCA/Philips), the Capacitance Electronic Disc (CED) made by RCA, and the hybrid Video High Density (VHD) system made by JVC. First, videodisc distribution is economical only on a relatively large scale. Unlike cassettes, videodiscs go through a mastering process, whereupon they can then be stamped out like audio records. Whereas it's economically feasible to make a single copy of a program on tape, it would be prohibitively expensive to do so on disc. The mastering process is expensive—to use the parlance, there are heavy FRONT END costs. Once the master is made, the stamping is where the cost savings start to accrue. The more copies you stamp, the lower the cost per copy becomes. Videodiscs are thus by definition a large scale proposition.

In the institutional sector, the lines are fairly clear-cut. For users with massive distribution networks, such as Ford and GM, IBM, the Bell System, and others with a need to send out thousands of copies of training, sales, and other programs, discs are a perfect solution. The educational market can also take full advantage of disc technology, with programs being sent to thousands of schools across the country at greatly reduced costs. These are areas where there is a definite need for the program material, and the job is already being done with more expensive technology. Disc will serve to reduce costs and make more wide-spread distribution possible.

In the home market, however, the question is one of whether there will ever be a suffi-

JVC VHD System

Magnavox Optical System

RCA "Selectavision"
CED System.

ciently large market for programs on disc. I personally have long had doubts about this, and early sales figures seem to bear out these doubts.

The success of videodiscs rests on several assumptions, all of which must turn out to be correct if the whole structure is to work. First, enough people must be convinced that a videodisc player represents a good enough investment of discretionary income (their entertainment budget) that they will buy one instead of or in addition to a videocassette machine. Here, there are several factors working against this assumption. The first and foremost is that there are three different formats—none compatible with the others—from which to choose. If the consumer were to choose a format that lost the battle with the other formats, the machine ends up being nothing more than an expensive paperweight. With the videocassette systems, there were only two choices (Beta/VHS), and even if one of these were to become virtually obsolete, the machines could still serve their primary purpose of recording programs for later viewing.

This leads to another factor working against discs, the fact that they're playback-only devices. The consumer is faced with the classic chicken/egg dilemma. Why buy a disc player when there isn't a large variety of pro-

grams, while the manufacturers at their end must produce large numbers of programs without a consumer base to buy them, at least during the early stages. The fact that there are three formats only compounds this, since the manufacturers collectively must provide hundreds of titles in each of the three formats without knowing ahead of time which ones will sell.

This leads to what I see as the primary problem facing videodiscs. Based on ten years of personal experience with home video, I don't believe the present videodisc formats make sense for consumer entertainment distribution. There are several reasons behind my theory.

First, the discs themselves are expensive. This statement would seem to fly in the face of the whole theory of videodiscs, and raises an immediate response: programs on videodisc are priced at about half the cost of the same program on cassette, and cassettes have been selling very well. Discs should therefore do even better.

The answer is that it's true that cassettes have been selling relatively well. There is a core group of what might be called "home video freaks" who support the cassette programming industry, and who have accounted

296

for most of these sales. One factor that should be considered, however, is that many of those cassettes were not *sold* to the consumer, but rather, *rented*. Across the country, there are thousands of Home Video stores doing a brisk business renting cassettes out for from $1.00–$10.00 for one or two days. The nationwide Fotomat chain is one of the leaders in this business.

videocassettes will be able to compete on this level in the forseeable future.

Then comes the question of the ability to watch films as many times as you wish. Here is where I suspect the rosy predictions for discs are based on a fundamental error. Starting in 1972, I began to collect a video library, using the newly developed ¾-inch cassettes. I

There is nothing that would prevent these outlets from renting videodiscs, of course, but the major distributors are uneasy about the whole question of rentals, since it's virtually impossible for them to keep track of rentals, and thus the royalties they may be losing to unreported rentals. This problem, of course, is also a factor in cassette rentals.

The videodisc business is predicated on the theory that consumers will be willing to pay an average of $25.00 to have their own copy of a film (less in the case of nonentertainment programs) for their library to view as often as they wish. The industry points out that $25.00 could be less than the cost of taking a family of four to the movies. There are two problems with this theory, however.

First is the inappropriate comparison of viewing a movie on disc and watching it in a theatre. The two are completely different experiences. The movie studios and theatre operators are well aware of this, and are working to improve the movie-house experience with 70-mm prints, Dolby multichannel stereo, and other lures to bring the public in. Many people turn a trip to the movie theatre into an event, even an outing, and neither videodiscs nor

could be considered something of a video freak myself, especially since the cost of saving a two-four film back then approached $60.00 for tape stock alone, as opposed to today's cost of as low as $7.50. My own motivation came from two directions: First, I was in the business, and all of my equipment could be justified for business use; second, having video equipment in my home was a source of awesome novelty, and until about 1975, when Sony introduced the Betamax, I was literally "the first on my block," if not the first in town. I gave several parties structured as "video festivals," complete with cartoons, short subjects, and a feature film.

What I discovered over a period of several years was that once I had watched a newly acquired film, about the only time I'd watch it again was when showing it to friends. The finest film in the world gets old after two or three viewings. Films and other video programs are not at all like audio records, as the videodisc promoters would like to believe. Music can be appreciated in a number of ways. You may sit down and seriously listen to a new record, devoting your full attention to it. You also may play it as background while doing other things.

In short, it's not at all unusual to play a record many, many times, and the level of sales of replacement records for ones that have been worn out through repeated playings might be surprising. Films and other video programs do not share this versatility of use. You either watch a program, or you don't, and running a movie while reading, visiting with friends, or tinkering in the workshop doesn't make a whole lot of sense. At least, not at 25 bucks a crack for the program. For "background video," there's lots of material available for free over the air that will do just fine.

With regard to my own video library, as the '70s wore on and more and more friends bought their own VCRs, the novelty wore off. In looking at my library of several hundred titles built up over the years, there are very few I've watched in recent years, and at times I wonder to myself why I'm keeping them.

There's another element to drop into my theory of the home video market, and that is the availability of virtually the same program material on pay TV. The penetration of pay TV in its various forms is increasing at a rate that astounds even its most fervent supporters. In addition to pay cable, we now have STV (Sub-

scription TV, meaning the broadcasting of a scrambled signal over-the-air), MDS (Multipoint Distribution Service, which sends programs into homes via microwave), and before long, we'll have DBS (Direct Broadcast Satellite, whereby viewers receive programs directly from space).

The cost factors involved make these forms of entertainment distribution a phenomenal bargain for the home viewer. For the $25.00 cost of a single movie on videodisc, pay TV will deliver a month-long schedule of as many as 10 new recently released films. The films are shown repeatedly during the month at various times, giving the viewer a chance to see them more than once if they wish. For those favorite films, a $10.00–$15.00 videocassette can record it for addition to the library.

In talking with other videophiles, I've found that the major entertainment purposes for which I use my videocassette machines are fairly typical: I record something using a timer when I'm not home; I record a program that conflicts with something else I want to watch; and very, very occasionally these days, I record something to add to my collection. Most tapes are viewed once, maybe twice, and then

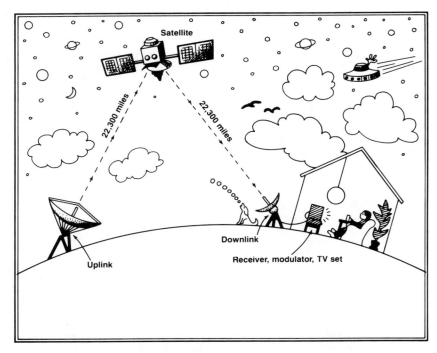

Direct broadcast satellite system.

298

recycled. This is where videocassettes, in combination with a pay TV service, outshine videodiscs in economic terms, and why I think that, along with the other factors cited above, the current videodisc formats will have a very difficult time succeeding.

There's one last factor, another "dark horse" that will soon appear to administer what I suspect will be the fatal blow to the current videodisc formats. Notice that in all this discussion of discs, I've been using the term *current* formats. The major deficiency of the MCA/Philips, RCA, and JVC formats is their inability to record. They can only play back programs, making them dependent on a ready supply of programs that the public wants to see, and at a reasonable price.

What is soon to appear is a new system that will let the consumer enjoy the cost and other benefits of disc along with the flexibility of videocassettes: A record/playback videodisc system.

Various such systems are under development, and most of the major manufacturers are working on them. For example, JVC is working on a home disc recorder/player, which raises some interesting questions regarding the future they envision for the VHD system.

One highly promising system I've recently seen demonstrated is being developed by the McDonnell-Douglas Electronics Co. Their system (called **MDEC**) has roots going back to the early '70s, and has passed through many hands and several companies during that period. The MDEC disc operates on optical principles, as does the MCA/Philips disc, but there the similarity ends.

The MDEC disc is a photographic one, and the basic media is nothing more than standard lithographic film. The discs are very inexpensive (under $5.00 for the material cost of the master), and copies, costing a few dollars each, are made by simple contact-printing techniques. The discs are rugged and flexible, and can be rolled up and mailed in a standard mailing tube. The picture produced by the early model I was recently shown was excellent, and the first players, which will be aimed at the institutional market, are scheduled to be priced at somewhere in the range of $3500—about the same as the similar models from MCA. The player does not use a laser to read the disc, as does the MCA/Philips system, but instead, uses a standard low-wattage light bulb. The potential is clearly there for a low cost consumer player. Eventually, a consumer recorder/player is envisioned, whereby the home user will be able to record programs with a materials cost of a few dollars.

McDonnell-Douglas has a ways to go before such a consumer unit is ready to market, but with the number of companies working on their similar systems and given the rate of developments in the field, the chances are excellent that some such system will be available within the next few years. So what's the bottom line on discs? For those institutions

The MDEC videodisc system.

with a captive audience and the ability to establish one particular format as the standard, the current disc systems can serve well. Interactive videodisc training using a microcomputer, to control the player and lead the student through a course of instruction, is an especially good application of videodisc technology.

For the broad consumer market, however, I have grave doubts about the existing systems' chances for success. Certainly a fair number of players will be sold, but it will come as a great surprise if enough are sold to justify the tremendous development costs that have accrued. Considering the new technology waiting in the wings to replace them, I would view the current disc formats as being a premature introduction of a product before the technology has been fully developed. If I'm right, it will be a shame, since a lot of money will be lost by both the companies involved, and by the consumer, who, once again, will have served as guinea pigs for market testing.

CHAPTER 23

Coming Attractions — Equipment of the Future

Now it's time for some crystal ball-gazing, as we peer into the murky depths of the future to try and predict the directions video technology is likely to take. What follows is based on the extension of present technological possibilities, and on established trends within the equipment industry.

Perhaps the best path over which to tiptoe through the gizmos is the one taken by the video signal, so we'll start with the prospects for camera development.

CCD Cameras

The path here is fairly clear. Eventually, cameras will do away with the last of the tubes—the vidicons, Plumbicons, Saticons, and gizmacheecons—and become completely solid-state devices, the way nature intended them to be. Cameras employing imaging chips known as CHARGE-COUPLED DEVICES (CCDs) have been around since the early seventies, and a number of black and white units of this design are already being sold, primarily for surveillance purposes. In the NAB (National Association of Broadcasters) exhibits of recent years, RCA has demonstrated an improved version of their developmental color CCD camera, and the picture, though grainy and containing some flaws, is still impressive.

The CCD cameras offer some potentially attractive benefits. They can be made extremely light sensitive (some of the original development work was done for the military, while working on designs for "starlight scopes"); can handle an enormous contrast range; are potentially immune to image lag and burn-in; draw minute quantities of power; are very compact; and if produced in quantity at a HIGH YIELD RATE (low number of defective chips—one of the major obstacles presently in their path), could be nearly as cheap as bottle caps.

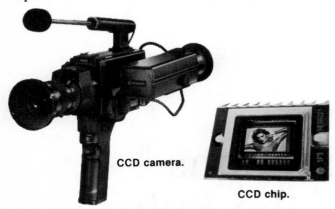

CCD camera.

CCD chip.

The CCD cameras can be made so small that their size and low weight actually become a hindrance. A certain amount of mass is needed for smooth camerawork, and one can envision cameras the size of cigarette packs that are built into dummy cases with weights to make them manageable.

This problem would be alleviated with designs that combine the camera with a video-

tape recorder in a self-contained package, and developments in this area are well under way. The 1981 NAB show in Las Vegas saw the first unveiling of three such units. Sony demonstrated a unit that combines a single-tube color camera with a recorder that uses standard Betamax tapes, albeit with a new recording technique. Their unit provides up to 20 minutes of recording time on a standard L-500 cassette (which normally provides one hour when used on their industrial Betamax machines, and two or three hours in home units). Panasonic and RCA, meanwhile, showed their

Sony Betacam system.

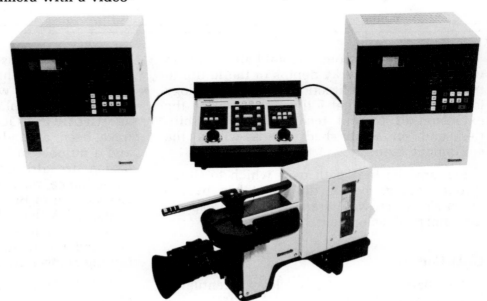

Panasonic "Hawkeye" system.

302

versions of the same basic design, using VHS tapes—also in a new recording format with a 20 minute capacity. The RCA and Panasonic designs, which are mutually compatible, employ three camera tubes, and weigh in at roughly 22 pounds for the total package. The Sony system is a bit lighter at about 15 pounds, mainly as a result of its single-tube design. Sony will also market a three-tube unit.

All three units employ a new recording system that provides a higher signal quality than the standard ¾-inch format. The RCA and Panasonic units are accompanied by a new editing system, while Sony provide a player that can be incorporated into existing editing systems.

CV-One.

ally represent a significant reduction below current camera-only units. At that time, the portability and ease of operation of video systems will finally make origination on video tape a simpler proposition than originating on film in virtually all circumstances. The remaining reasons for shooting on film, mainly the use of 35-mm film for motion picture production, a result of its currently superior resolution, will then be challenged in the next step of the evolution of technology, as we shall see a bit further on in this section.

As to recording technology, videotape is eventually doomed. Using a narrow ribbon of magnetically coated material to record signals is one of the least elegant means available to perform the assigned task. It is, however, also the simplest method, and, in practical terms, the easiest one to manage, where recording and playback are required. Tape may be doomed in the long run, but it still has a healthy stretch ahead of it before it hits the dusty trail.

Audio cassette | Compact video cassette | Beta cassette | VHS cassette | U-matic cassette

Videocassette tape size comparison.

Although these competing systems have received considerable attention, a system with possibly even more promise has since been shown by Bosch. Their proposed format uses ¼-inch tape to provide broadcast quality pictures, reducing size and tape consumption even further.

The trend towards all-in-one packages will certainly continue, and the chances are excellent that by 1985 most ENG work and a good deal of EFP work will be done with these systems. Once CCD camera technology is ready to supplant the tubes in existing systems, the size and weight of the total package could eventu-

In the past few years, helical formats have stolen the thunder from quad, and this trend will certainly continue. New helical formats such as those discussed previously will continue to be introduced, and will reduce the cost and size of VTRs while improving the picture quality.

Digital Video

In the broadcast market, the currently fashionable battle-cry seems to be "Digital or Die!" which would appear to be in step with the growing application of digital techniques in

303

Interactive video.

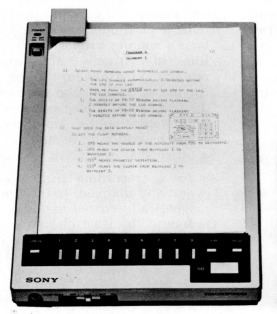

Sony Videoresponder

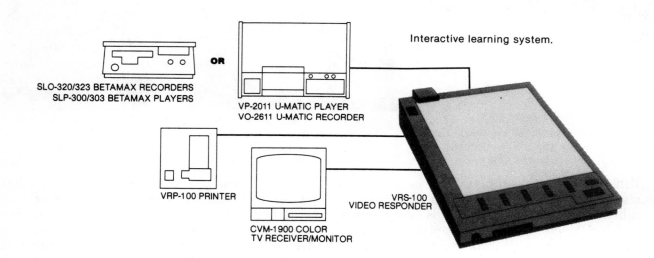

Interactive learning system.

SLO-320/323 BETAMAX RECORDERS
SLP-300/303 BETAMAX PLAYERS

OR

VP-2011 U-MATIC PLAYER
VO-2611 U-MATIC RECORDER

VRP-100 PRINTER

CVM-1900 COLOR
TV RECEIVER/MONITOR

VRS-100
VIDEO RESPONDER

other areas of signal processing. Digital recording would have much to recommend it, since the essentially simple nature of DIGITAL ENCODING (any particular bit is either "on" or "off"—there is little room for doubt) can make it virtually immune to noise or multigenerational degradation.

Indeed, three of the major VTR manufacturers, Ampex, Sony, and Bosch, have demonstrated Digital Video Recorders (DVRs), all of which were based on present analog machines. These machines have demonstrated incredible picture quality with virtually no picture degradation even after dozens of generations. The major manufacturers, however, have been very cautious about making any predictions regarding marketing dates, and have stressed heavily that the units shown were "feasibility studies" only, or words to that effect.

There are three major factors acting to delay the introduction of digital video recorders, the first being that there are some formidable technical problems remaining to be solved. Digital recording requires the use of much higher frequencies than does analog recording, and though it's not impossible, the consensus among the manufacturers seems to be that digital recording for its own sake is not enough—that any such new format must offer broadcasters substantial improvements, either in size, quality, or cost, and ideally in all three areas.

The second factor is an old and familiar need: standardization. The switch to digital recording offers an opportunity to develop a multinational standard that would allow for fairly easy conversion of material between NTSC, PAL, and SECAM. The subject of standardization also touches on the compatibility of other digital units, including switchers, time base correctors and digital effects units, transmission systems and other types of equipment. A set of standards that will allow each of the various pieces of equipment to TALK to each other in a common LANGUAGE is the overall goal of study groups within SMPTE and the EBU (European Broadcast Union, the European counterpart of SMPTE). In all likelihood, there will be several different though compatible digital standards established, which would include a high resolution COMPONENT system (which will record the red, green, and blue signals separately), along with several lower-resolution systems for such applications as ENG.

The third factor is that analog recording has come nowhere near its inherent limitations. In terms of signal quality, the current top level of recorders is capable of results that are better than our present system of transmission, yet even better performance is possible, even within the constraints of analog design, as the new ½-inch systems described earlier demonstrate. The application of METAL-PARTICLE tape technology, new processing circuits and other innovations assures that analog recording will have a place in video production for a long time to come. Combine this with the fact that the major manufacturers only recently spent rather vast sums of money on the development and production of the 1-inch format machines. These sums must be amortized over a fairly long time so it's not surprising that the industry is not pursuing digital recording on a crash-program basis. This is probably fortunate in the long run, since the companies and study groups involved have the luxury of being able to take their time with the development of digital standards. This has encouraged a thoughtful approach to the problem, which should eventually result in better formats and standards than might otherwise have been the case. Taking these factors into consideration, an educated estimate would put the introduction of the first commercially available digital recorders at sometime between 1984–1986.

One more factor that must be considered is that by the time digital standards have been worked out, developments in other areas may well have made digital video*tape* recording obsolete before it gets off the ground. One possibility is a high-quality, record/playback videodisc system.

In the previous chapter we discussed the economics and marketing of consumer disc systems. Let's now take a moment to examine the technology of the systems.

Videodisc Systems

The MCA/Philips/Magnavox group was first on the market with their laser-based optical disc system, only about five years behind their target date, and suffering enormous supply and quality control problems. Then RCA introduced their own videodisc system, which is incompatible with the optical systems, offers far fewer bells and whistles, and uses (believe it or not!) a *mechanical stylus* like a common phonograph record. Although the RCA technology is less elegant than laser disc systems, it is mechanically simple and cheap. (Can you spot the key word in that last sentence?) The Zenith Corporation has announced their licensing of the RCA design, marking the first time these two domestic industry leaders have agreed to cooperate in such a manner, thus giving the RCA system tremendous marketing clout.

Meanwhile, General Electric has announced their agreement with JVC to manufacture and market the third disc system, known as VHD (Video High Density). This one is also mechanical, but offers many of the features of the optical systems such as still frame, slow-motion, and stereo sound while promising cost and complexity benefits similar to the RCA system.

For broadcast-quality production, videodisc technology could offer some very attractive benefits. The advantages of a highband disc recorder/player matching current 1-inch tape quality would fall into two primary areas. (The McDonnell-Douglas system mentioned in the previous chapter does not, and is not intended to meet these specifications.) The first advantage would be the cost of the recording

medium. Disc storage is far more efficient on a basis of storage density per square foot of material, and with a one-hour reel of 1-inch tape costing roughly $75.00 minimum, the prospects for disc recording are exciting. The second major advantage would come in editing, where the random-access quality of discs would speed the editing process considerably. Thus, the possibility of a videodisc production format would provide major benefits, and should not be ruled out.

In the end, though, videotape and videodisc machines will go the way of all machines that wiggle, squiggle, and spin. In science fiction novels, the ultimate machines have no moving parts, and this is how recorders will someday be. The constant reduction in size and storage density of solid state circuits virtually assures that one day in the not-too-distant future, video programming will be stored in MEMORY CHIPS (essentially consisting of ultra-miniaturized multiple frame stores that will be able to store entire programs); thus giving you the opportunity to carry one (if not several) episodes of *The Gong Show* around in your shirt pocket (for historical purposes, of course).

High Definition Television (HDTV)

And on what will you watch those episodes? Why, a wall-sized TV screen, of course. This particular prediction is one that I won't

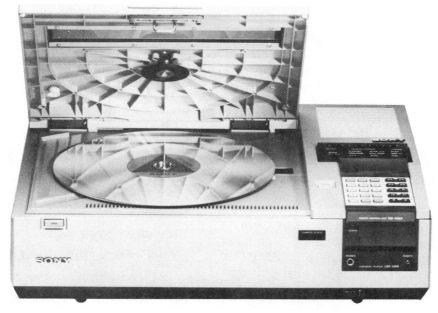

Laser/optical system.

spend much time on. We've been hearing about flat, wall-sized screens that hang in the living room like a picture (and that can display fine art, a Picasso, a Van Gogh, a Vermeers, or even a Keane, when it's not otherwise occupied) for years now, since at least the 1930s. Every so often a manufacturer lets someone in to see their murky 5-inch square developmental model, and predicts it'll be ready "within five years or so." It will come, in its own time, but I wouldn't recommend holding your breath.

One of the main problems to be dealt with first is the rather low performance capabilities of the NTSC system. Take the best possible NTSC signal and blow it up to wall-screen proportions, and you've got a nice, big, fuzzy picture. The 525 lines with a 300-line or so limit on horizontal resolution just doesn't make it if you want to view on a grand scale. The problems involved in increasing the line rate and resolution are in no way technical because it's done all the time in closed-circuit systems, and could be transmitted today with no real problem. The barriers, rather, are economic in nature. A switch to a high-resolution system could instantly make obsolete every television receiver in the country—the total number estimated being somewhere over 100 million, not to mention the facilities of the nearly 1000 television stations in the United States. And this does not begin to take the world market into consideration.

The problem is similar to the one that led to the development of the NTSC compromise-color system itself. No one wants to be the first to tell the public they'll have to go out and buy new sets. The probable solution that will eventually introduce a better system (for one will certainly be needed) is likely to be found in a gradual transition; perhaps using new sources such as direct satellite-to-home transmission, with new sets that can receive signals on either the old NTSC system or the new RGP (Real Good Pictures) system.

At the 1981 Winter SMPTE conference in San Francisco, NHK, the Japanese broadcasting company, demonstrated a high resolution television system that provided 1125 scanning lines at 60 fields per second. Their system employed a three-tube camera and a specially designed monitor with an aspect ratio of 5:3.

The pictures shown on the monitor (and on a specially modified video projector) were stunning in their clarity. It was more like looking at 35mm slides projected on a small screen.

The NHK demonstration did not include a video recorder, but Sony has since demonstrated a high resolution system which they call HDVS (High Definition Video System). Based on the NHK system, it incorporates a video recorder capable of recording the 30 MHz signal the system produces, along with a time base corrector and other necessary system components.

This system does what had long been thought to be all but impossible—it approaches the resolution capabilities of 35mm film. It offers the promise of allowing film producers to do their original production and post-production on videotape, saving time and money, and enhancing creative control. After post-production, the movie could be transferred to 35-mm film for release, while the eventual goal is to distribute directly by satellite to theatres equipped with high resolution video projectors.

Other forces are moving in the direction of high resolution television as well. For instance, IBM has been working on a system that would provide an effective 1050-line resolution vertically with a similar doubling of horizontal resolution, yet which requires no more bandwidth than standard NTSC signals. Their system, which would also be fully compatible with current NTSC television receivers, works by transmitting one high resolution frame every four standard frames, shifting the picture up, down, left, and right by a half picture element with each succeeding frame. The net result would be high resolution pictures when viewed on new receivers equipped to decode them, and a normal picture on existing receivers. This system would get around the problems of limited spectrum space on the television broadcast bands, and make the change-over easier and less of a shock economically to the entire industry and the public. In the long run, however, the chances are that a system along the lines of the NHK/Sony developments will eventually replace existing standards.

Just so that I don't disappoint the fringe ele-

Sony High Definition video system.

HDVS Future Applications

**High Definition
TV Broadcasting System**

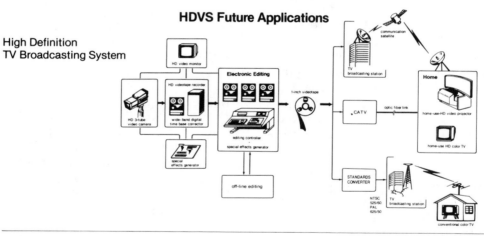

**Cinema Production Using
High Definition Video System**

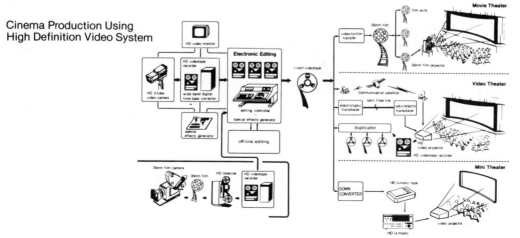

ments, yes, 3-D television is being worked on, and yes, it will be toyed with over the next few years, and yes, holography will probably be applied in some form or other to television, and yes, maybe someday our grandchildren or great-grandchildren will be able to have their own equivalent of Johnny Carson right there in their own living room, just as life-like as you please. But come, we stray from our purpose in this wondering at the distant future. What's likely to happen in our own lifetimes, specifically, within the next few years?

Here's how I'd call it:

- CCD cameras of a broadcast quality with built-in VTRs—by 1984.

- Broadcast-quality, highband VTRs the size of today's ½-inch cassette portables, with a one-hour capacity—by 1984/85.

- Record/playback videodiscs, of whatever design—by 1984.

- Top-quality highband videodisc-based editing systems (an editor's dream)—by 1985.

- True flat-panel, probably solid-state, color wall-sized receivers—by 1987.

- Small, black and white, flat panel displays for video or data display (to fit in a briefcase, wallet, or wristwatch)—by 1983/84.

- Across-the-board quality network programming—1984. (I believe that, as a result of the growing moral decay in the world, the network programming executives will suddenly see the light, and will resolve to offer nothing but the finest programming, even if it does result in lower ratings. After all, it's only money.)

The challenge, dear reader, is to spot the spurious prediction in the batch above. You get three tries.

Video Information Systems

There's a lot of noise currently being made about the various information transmission systems such as VIEWDATA, TELETEXT, and the like, and a number of various methods and techniques being studied. Some use the vertical interval portion of a broadcast transmission to carry data, while others use the telephone lines. As in other areas, since everybody has his/her own idea (which is obviously better than everybody else's), there'll be intense struggles and huge amounts of money involved before any one system becomes a true standard. Again, the technology is moving too rapidly for any single approach to make sense right now. The result is likely to be a large number of competing systems, all operating at the same time, meaning that just as you can't send your Beta home tapes to your Uncle Nelson, cause he has a VHS, the chances are that your friend across town will have a data transmission system different from yours, and trading recipes will still be best done with a postcard.

The consumer video revolution has begun, and it's hard to see anything holding it back now. The synthesis of a communications system that will combine television, personal computers, fibre-optic two-way cable, and probably the nationwide telephone system, has already begun. It's impossible to predict what effects all this will have on our lives, but it's a safe bet that this technological evolution is imbued with the potential to change the entire structure of society. It won't happen all at once, of course, but over a period of time—we're in for some very interesting changes.

Those of us working with television today will have ringside seats from which to watch the show.

Video Information Transmission Systems.

Teletext system—examples.

CHAPTER 24

Getting Started in Video

The person approaching television for the first time is presented with quite a challenge. Those with previous experience in film production will at least have some creative techniques and the fundamental theories of moving imagery and content design to bring along, but those who are starting from scratch will have a clean slate, ready to be filled.

Even those who have worked or played with the simplest video equipment such as the black and white portapaks or home video taping systems will find that broadcast quality production represents a quantum leap, in terms of technical and aesthetic demands. Learning to cope with and understand the various elements—technical, creative, and admin-

istrative—takes time, and there is little substitute for experience. It's a process of building knowledge, rather than acquiring it all of a sudden. The more you learn about television, the more you find there is still left to learn.

This is one of the fascinating things about television, from the other side of the screen. It never stands still. The constant changes and improvements in the equipment and its application assure that today's expert will again be a student tomorrow.

Another factor to consider is that there are a lot of places one can start when jumping into video, and various entrances lead along various paths. The student interested in engineering matters would obviously take a different route than someone pursuing the disciplines of program design.

There's a good argument, however, for a basic background in the technical operation of television regardless of the area in which one wishes to work. Creative-type people certainly need not become qualified engineers, but a basic understanding of how television works will help in at least two important ways: it allows one to establish a more realistic approach when designing a program, and it prevents one from being totally in the dark as to why something doesn't turn out as expected.

how to thread a VTR and adjust for skew, but that was about the extent of my knowledge. Fortunately, I had been making films for years, so I at least had an idea of what to do with the stuff once I got it to work.

My first step was to unpack all the equipment and read the instruction books. It was an "Alice in Wonderland" experience, discovering that when I fed a signal to a VTR, and punched the "Edit" button, the damned thing actually made an edit! It seemed much easier than working in film (which just goes to show how little I knew), and it was love at first sight.

The more I learned about production tech-

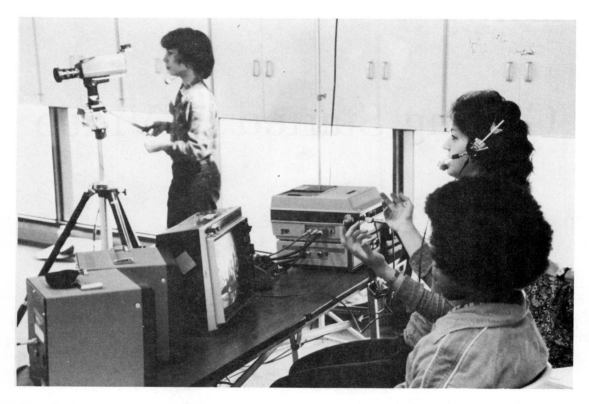

Information Sources and Conferences

When I first began my career in television production, I was put in charge of a brand-new one-man department, provided with a batch of shiny new (black and white) equipment, and given the charge to do something with it. Well . . . .

I had played around once or twice with a little video equipment, meaning that I knew where the power switches were, and knew

niques, though, the more I realized that there were giant hills to climb. I'd put together some little tapes, a few of which weren't too awfully bad, and then I'd watch some of the stuff on the networks, and I'd notice quite a difference—even discounting the fact that my shows were in black and white. I resolved to learn as much as I could about the technical side of television, so that once I had a firm background, I could get on with the business of actually producing the stuff without having to constantly guess at what was happening with the equipment. I wanted to know how to achieve the results I was after, without either having to describe them to somebody else, or rely totally on someone else's experience and judgment as to whether something could be done, or how to do it. A pilot, after all, should know enough about his aircraft so that its condition, operation, and capabilities are second nature.

If a camera went down in the field, I didn't want the engineer to tell me that the "razencrats forsnell is giving us anticipatory overshoot," and have me swallow it. I wanted to know what was going on.

and the intricacies of the overall television system were wholly different matters. It was a very confusing field, yet I didn't have the time or the patience to spend two or four years in school to study the medium.

Coming from the "bottom up" may not be the most elegant way to learn television production, but I benefited from a happy circumstance of timing. As soon as the brand new videocassette system was introduced by Sony, I was able to obtain the machines and while I fiddled with them at the "industrial" level, the broadcast folks started fiddling with them as well. Since the new equipment violated nearly all of their technical rules, they had only a

So I read the instruction books, and produced some simple tapes, and at least got the equipment I had to do what I wanted. I also started reading. Everything in sight.

I quickly found that virtually all of the books available dealt almost exclusively with the traditional broadcast studio environment and were of little help to me. The books also seemed to be almost universally ten years out of date. I found that the explanations of the basic workings of black and white television were pretty simple in theory, but that color,

slight advantage over people like me; after all, they had years of established practice and prejudice to overcome. I saw a strong analogy between film production and the new, lightweight, portable cassette gear, and reacted with the proverbial "Ahh!"

Again, I read. I read every television magazine I could get my hands on, and every piece of sales literature published. These were up-to-the-minute sources of information, and though much of what they contained made little or no sense, I read them anyway. Over a period of time—if only by osmosis—little bits and pieces of knowledge and understanding began to creep in. Each new bit of data filled in a chunk of the puzzle, and slowly the picture began to flesh itself out.

At the same time, I joined one of the professional associations, ITVA, which then stood for International Industrial Television Association (the "Industrial" was later dropped), which put me in touch with a large number of very helpful people, many of whom had been down the same road before me. To a great extent, they were willing to share their knowledge and experience. My membership in the association, and the information it provided me were major contributory factors in helping to learn more about the medium. Another beneficial group was SMPTE, though much of what they discussed was at the time way over my head. Again, I found the members of the local chapter more than willing to help a newcomer.

If there was any one factor that was of greatest importance, though, it was one that comes from within, and with which anyone can arm themselves in their battle to understand the medium: a driving desire to learn.

After about a year of total immersion, which included extensive readings and, most important, picking people's brains for the realities of video, I was able at least to speak pidgin television. The shadowy mysteries of television techniques and practices began to take on some detail.

For someone just now starting out in the field, the sources of information have now multiplied tremendously. There are a number of excellent books now available; a year-long schedule of video shows, seminars, and workshops is being offered; and the number of magazines in the field has more than doubled.

The seminars and workshops offered at the various video shows and conferences can be of tremendous value to the beginner. The yearly ITVA *International Conferences* alone provide some of the most comprehensive of these, at virtually every level of competence. But such commercially produced events as the various *Video Expos*, done by Knowledge Industry Publications and scattered across the continent and the calendar, and the *Annual Los Angeles Professional Videoshow,* produced by Tepfer Publishing, also offer a menu of workshops that can be of great value.

The books and periodicals listed in the bibliography provide substantial amounts of information, and a well-stocked selection of such resources is an important part of a beginner's learning process, and ends up becoming a valuable reference library. A recommendation I would strongly make in this area would be to read "over your head." Formulating the right questions is every bit as important as finding the answers, for without the questions, the

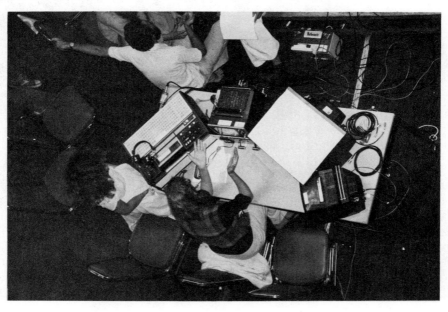

answers are unlikely to come.

For those starting from scratch who want to learn the basics of television, there is always the academic route, but supplementation with some or all of the resources mentioned above will be of substantial benefit, and will complement classroom and textbook knowledge. As valuable as formal training in television may be, it is by no means the only route available.

All of these suggestions, however, are merely aids to learning, and, though helpful, cannot stand on their own as means to the end of learning television production. The best way, and ultimately the *only* way, to learn television production is to *DO IT!*

The best and soundest path to proficiency in video production is through what is nothing more nor less than traditional apprenticeship. By signing on as a gopher or production assistant, one can learn more about production in a single project than in months of study, with the additional benefit that accrues from hands-on experience. Even on an individual level, getting your hands on some basic equipment and actually producing tapes provides experience and understanding for which there is no substitute. Since we learn from mistakes, the more mistakes one makes in early productions, the more one learns. Of course, it's wise to make these mistakes on "practice" productions, rather than on ones with a serious purpose or done in a business environment.

Tackling television requires a two-pronged approach. At the same time one learns the technical aspects, one should also be building an understanding of creative and aesthetic techniques. Again, the sources of information mentioned before will help, but some of the best preparation for production would include study of the programming available over the air. You needn't approve of or like the content of the programming, and in some ways it can pay to study just those programs that you *don't* like—something put them on the air, and keeps enough viewers tuned in to keep them there.

It often amazes me how many people within the business profess total avoidance of television viewing. On the other hand, it sometimes strikes me as being ironic that after 12 hours of watching monitors during shooting or editing, I am likely to go home and relax with some wine and an old movie. Maybe there's something wrong with me. (Actually, I'm more

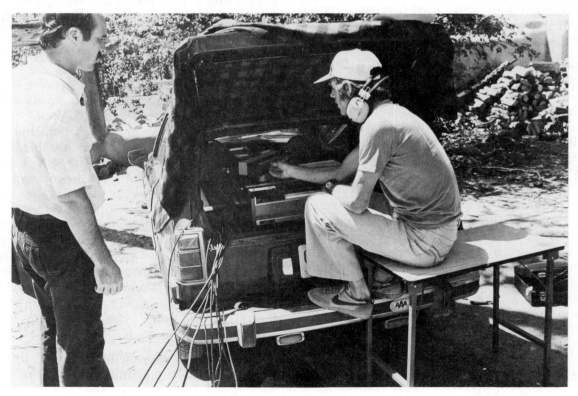

likely to watch the day's rushes, or the results of the edit.) The late Marshall McLuhan told us that "the medium *is* the message," and in many ways he was right on target, but at the same time, it's possible in individual circumstances to find exceptions that prove the rule. There's some fine programming available on television (and though it sounds almost gratuitous to say that a lot of it's on PBS, I will), and a fashionable avoidance of television denies one access to some excellent and thought-provoking material. (It's also amusing to find people who "almost never watch TV" asking "Say, did you happen to catch *Love Boat* the other night? I never watch it, of course, but I happened to be changing channels, and . . .".)

If you want to make television that reaches the masses, you'll have to couch your programming in a form that has a chance of getting on the air. If, on the other hand, you are more concerned about personal self-expression and video experimentation and don't necessarily care about reaching the masses, then by all means, do whatever you want.

If you need to use television for business or education, then you're involved in perhaps the purest use of the medium, and certainly its most serious and powerful application. Getting off on the right foot here is of utmost importance, and it would be good to seek some professional help and/or advice in getting started.

Companies that want to establish a television operation would probably do well to hire a consultant at the very least or, even better, a full-time media professional, to get the tape rolling. When small-format tape first became available, an awful lot of systems ended up in the storage room after the poor folks in the training department suffered abysmal failures in their unguided attempts to produce training or other programs. In part, the manufacturers must take part of the blame. At a manufacturers' panel at the 1979 ITVA Conference in Dallas, a member in the audience asked a representative of one of the "big three" Japanese manufacturers to justify their ads aimed at management which stated that their system was so simple that a camera, recorder, and monitor were all that were needed to create boffo training tapes. To paraphrase the accuser: "We've spent years convincing management that good, effective television requires a strong commitment in terms of equipment and trained personnel, and then you guys come along and tell them that any damn fool with $2000 worth of equipment can make effective television as easy as making toast!" The accusation brought heavy applause from the rest of the audience, and an embarrassed promise from the rep to "talk with New York." The next day we were informed that the ads in question would be withdrawn from all publications, and replaced with something a bit more realistic.

"Write if You Find Work!"

The single question I am most often asked by students of television is one that could easily be predicted: "How can I get a job in the industry?" With roughly 30,000 broadcast graduates leaving colleges and universities annually to chase after perhaps 10,000 jobs (probably an optimistic estimate), the field is extremely competitive, to say the very least.

I see the problem from both ends. As a part-time college instructor of television production, I want to help my students find work, while as a producer/director with a production company to run, I have a continuing need for qualified personnel. Speaking from the latter viewpoint, there are three things that impress me about a prospective employee: attitude, knowledge, and experience. Let me expand a bit on these.

The bulk of my staff and crew people are professionals I have come to know over the years, and whose performance I can count on. Because of this, the positions I normally need to fill for a production from outside the core group are generally on the entry level. In terms of attitude, what I look for is someone who's serious about the work, is professional about it, knows when to keep quiet, and who is willing to do the most menial tasks in order to be on the set. In exchange, I find time to answer their questions, and make an effort to involve them in as many phases of production as possible. I also pay them a decent wage. I view these beginners somewhat as apprentices, and figure that the more I can show them, the more valuable they become.

In terms of knowledge, I look for people with a broad basic understanding of the production process, both on a technical and a creative level. Just as the fellow who usually lights my productions can easily take over for an ailing cameraman and do an excellent job of it, I look for production assistants who have an understanding of the various aspects of production, and who could pinch-hit in several areas. Emergency situations are often where big breaks come.

In terms of experience, I look for people who have been involved in production previously—ideally in the "real world" of professional production. Resumes filled with academic experience do little for me—I know exactly how much school production experience is worth on average. I have hired some of my past students for productions, and some of them have wildly exceeded my fondest expectations, but there are also those who managed to pass my course, but whom, I am sorry to say, could never hold down a job in production.

The one thing that most impresses me when interviewing a job applicant is the same tool I use to sell my services to clients and programming outlets: A demo tape. This is the *Catch-22* item that is admittedly a difficult one for most beginners to tackle. You need a demo reel to get work, but you have to first find work to build a reel. This is where persistence and dedication bring us back full circle to attitude. If you're really serious about finding a job in the business, you have to be able to demonstrate your abilities. And if it comes right down to it, you may have to finance or otherwise finagle your own demo reel.

Demo Reel Specifications

A demo reel should contain as wide a variety of production styles and techniques as possible. Single camera, multicamera, documentary, music, interviews—any and all types of productions.

A demo reel should be short. Ideally, it should run about 5 minutes, and normally no more than 10. A key factor is to leave the viewer (prospective employer) wanting to see more, rather than wondering when it's going to end. Also—and this will become important if your prospective employer becomes interested—it should be honest. If the position you filled was that of production assistant in charge of morning coffee, be very sure that you clearly state so when showing the reel. There's nothing wrong with a low-level position, as it gives you the chance to observe and learn, but inflating your role for personal gain will seriously damage your chances.

Lastly, there is a fundamental rule that is violated with a regularity that never ceases to amaze me: if the work doesn't meet your highest standards, *don't show it!* It absolutely astounds me how often someone comes in with a demo reel that is embarrassing in its amateurishness. What makes it even worse is having them apologize or offer explanations while it's running. If the only thing you have to show that you're truly proud of is a single 30-second public service announcement you did for your local library, then let that serve as your demo reel.

The Job Market

As mentioned earlier, the job market in television production is highly competitive. There are really only two "major-major" production centers in the United States—Los Angeles and New York. In addition, there are several secondary centers, including Chicago, San Francisco, Dallas, and Miami. Beyond that, there are smaller production centers scattered around the country, and hundreds of lonely production companies, often where you'd least expect them to be. There are the three major networks, all of which operate almost totally out of Los Angeles and New York. There are also roughly 1000 television stations, including VHF and UHF, and commercial and public outlets. There are countless cable systems as well. All of these are potential employers. Keep in mind the fact that in many areas, station employment is done through one of the various unions, and that union entrance restrictions vary considerably.

In the major centers, the vast number of positions that need to be filled provides a large number of opportunities for the beginner. Keep in mind, however, that these areas draw job applicants the way circuses draw children. The secondary centers are perhaps the toughest nuts to crack, since the turnover is lower in numbers. The stations and cable operators are an unanswerable question, as they vary from one community to the next, as well as with their local economies. Suffice it to say that while landing a job with a network or with a station or production house is not impossible, it is not the easiest challenge facing someone who is new to the business.

One method that has provided a route to employment for many has been to start off with a station or production company in a smaller town, gaining experience and credit along the way. In very small operations, the chances for a wider range of assignments are better than at a large, compartmentalized organization. An entry level position can more quickly lead to something with more challenge and responsibility. After working your way up at a small operation and building up a good demo reel, you then are better equipped to tackle a larger market. You have something tangible to offer.

There are two major alternatives to the above markets, however, and they bear consideration by those who hope to make a career in production. The first is much easier than the second, but both offer satisfactions of their own. The are: PRIVATE TELEVISION, and INDEPENDENT PRODUCTION.

PRIVATE TELEVISION is the adopted moniker of the corporate, industrial, and educational segment of the industry. In terms of the amount of programming produced, it is several times larger than all of the entertainment segments combined, and continues to grow. Private television facilities range from simple one-person operations using a portapak to huge, network-grade facilities with large in-house production staffs and crews. Probably the best way to approach these operations is by becoming involved with and obtaining the membership rosters of the major associations they belong to: ITVA, ASTD, etc. After a decade of expansion, there is currently a minor retrenchment taking place, but the job prospects for a beginner are still fairly good.

Independent Production

INDEPENDENT PRODUCTION is a far greater challenge, yet can also offer far greater rewards. It basically entails the creation of a job for yourself where none existed. Independent production can take two basic forms: production of programs on contract for clients called FREELANCING, or production of programs independently for distribution.

The factors that offer the main advantages also offer the main drawbacks: you're your own boss, which can be very satisfying, but you also end up with all the headaches of any small business operator. You can possibly make a great deal more money than in a regular job, but you can also wind up losing your shirt.

Independent production does not require that you go out and purchase a lot of expensive equipment, a subject we'll deal with in the next section. If you know production, how to put together a budget, and how to round up the equipment and crew you'll need, you can serve as an independent producer. What your client will be buying is a combination of your creative and administrative abilities. The only caveat here should be obvious: you'd better know what you're doing.

The most precious possession an independent producer has is his or her reputation. Aside from Los Angeles and New York (and even there to a certain extent) it's amazing how tightly knit even the larger markets are, and the people involved in the production industry tend to know each other. It takes years to build up a good reputation, and a single incident can damage or destroy it. As in any small industry, the people involved love gossip, and a single complaint by a client, even an unjustified one, can reverberate around town until everybody's heard it, leaving you with *Mud* for a name.

If you come across a job that you'd just love to do, but that you know is beyond your scope, don't try it on your own. In such a situation there are two choices open: the first is to simply tell the prospective client that you don't think you're equipped to do justice to their project, and, ideally, suggest someone who is. At the very least, they'll appreciate your honesty, and perhaps keep you in mind for something simpler at a later date. The second alternative is possibly even better. Take the job on, and bring in some outside help to work with you on it. In this manner, you keep the client and expand your capabilities at the same time by learning from your "consultant." It goes without saying that the person you bring in must subscribe to a certain standard of ethics with regard to client stealing.

Ethics is the name of the tune. You either leave a trail of satisfied clients and good experiences behind you, in which case your stock will rise, or you leave the opposite, in which case you might consider moving to a new town. In the latter case, you'll eventually run out of new towns.

I won't spend too much time on the business aspects, but there is one basic rule worth mentioning that should be drummed into the brain of all beginning independent producers: never be afraid to turn down business that's not profitable. It's terribly easy to be so eager for work that you underbid a job, or agree to take less than you are worth. One of the old saws of business deals with the fallacy of "losing money on each deal, but making it up in volume."

The thing that many independent producers fail to realize is that production is a business first, and a creative or technical proposition second. Production involves much more accounting, paperwork, logistics, and client coddling than it does lights, cameras, and action. The skills and tasks are essentially the same as in any small business, with the commodity offered being either a service, as in the case of a freelance producer, or a product, in the case of an independent producer of programs.

Setting Rates

This is a two-fold question for the independent producer: what does one charge for one's services, and what does one expect to pay for crew people?

With regard to producers and directors, there are no hard and firm rules. In the big-time network entertainment field, the producer usually owns a percentage of the program, in addition to receiving a five-figure salary per show. The DGA (Director's Guild of America) directors also receive salaries in the low five figures for a program. In the private television markets, of course, such amounts are unheard of. A producer of an industrial or educational program might make anywhere from $500 to $5000 for a half-hour show, depending in part on how good they are at the business dealings. Directors sometimes work for a flat fee, but just as often work at a day rate. Outside of entertainment programming and national commercials, directors' rates range from as low as $150/day to as much as $1000 per day, depending greatly on their "market value," something not always related to how good they are. It's simple: a director with a hot reputation commands more pay than an unknown. Commercial directors working on local spots would generally fall into a $150–$1000 range, while directors working on national commercials will earn from $1000–$7500 per day. Keep in mind that these figures are awfully general, and should not be taken as gospel, nor as models, without research into individual circumstances.

In terms of crew members, the figures listed below must also be used only as a rough reference, since they vary widely from one section of the country to another and with the skills of the personnel involved. They are based on the rates paid in a medium-sized market (San Francisco), and do not take any union scales into account. Outside of L.A./N.Y., you should be able to find good crew people within the ranges shown below.

NOMINAL CREW RATES: (As of late 1981)
- Asst. Dir.: $250–500/Day
- Prod. Mgr.: $150–250/Day
- Tech. Dir.: $150–250/Day
- Camera: $100–300/Day
- Gaffer: $125–250/Day
- Audio Engineer: $150–250/Day
- Grips: $75–200/Day
- Prod. Assts.: $75–150/Day

It is certainly possible to shop around and put together an entire crew at a flat $50.00/day/person rate, and it is also possible to locate people to fill a crew where the minimum day rate for the lowest position is $250/day. It all depends, again, on the market, the people, and the level of competence you're after.

In Summary

There are many people who hoped for a career in broadcast television production having spent four years in a broadcasting school, who wound up completely disillusioned by the job market, and who gave up their search. This brings us back to the matter of perseverance. If you really and truly want a job in the field, and if you learn the fundamentals, and are willing to put in hard work, the chances are that eventually you'll find a way into the industry. If you become discouraged and quit trying, then I'd suggest you really weren't all that dedicated to the field to begin with, and perhaps you will find that your time would be better spent in a related or different area of personal endeavor.

CHAPTER 25

Equipment — Own or Rent

The decision on the question of owning versus renting should be based on two primary factors:

1. The amount of use to which the equipment will be put.
2. The capabilities of the people who will be asked to run it.

Although the situations will differ between a business or educational application and an independent producer, many of the same criteria can be applied. We'll start by examining the decision from the business user's point of view.

Incidentally, in this discussion, we'll consider buying and leasing to be basically equivalent. Leasing offers the benefits of requiring a smaller amount of money up-front, and the ability to write payments off as an expense rather than a capital expenditure. But since the interest rates on which the lease will inevitably be based are the same as a straight loan, and since there will always be some cost involved in the lease itself, leasing is usually more expensive in the long run. Straight purchase usually requires either the total amount in cash, or a large down payment plus financing charges; but the interest and depreciation deductions and the investment tax credit will make a purchase cheaper in the end.

Though it would normally be wise to start slowly, some organizations may become sold on video, and immediately decide to make a commitment to a facility and staff. This can be dangerous business, since the equipment alone does no good if there isn't a competent staff to back it up. Such staffs don't appear out of nowhere, and training people who are already with the company takes time. Normally this situation would call for bringing someone onboard who has experience to guide the process of setting up and making programs.

The whole idea of establishing an in-house facility is worth some careful study and consideration. All too often, management is drawn by the glamour of having their own TV studio, and many of the salesmen who push video equipment will be all too eager to extol the benefits and effectiveness of television, without taking time to explain the difficulty involved in using it properly.

One of the dangers inherent in making a major equipment purchase is that of obsolescence ("planned" or otherwise) that will always be a factor in the purchase of gear. The video manufacturers often seem to have a disdain for logic in designing and marketing their wares, and it's very easy to get stuck with obsolete equipment if decisions are not based on sound judgment.

This has never been demonstrated so well as it has in the consumer video circus. For instance, to anyone in their right mind, it would be obvious that in the billion-dollar videodisc sweepstakes, the entire industry (not to mention the consumers) would, in the long run, benefit from the establishment of a single standard. Has such a standard been established? Of course not. There is not one standard, but three major standards at the time of this writing, with additional ones waiting in the wings.

Actually, there is a certain amount of reason behind the seeming madness of the "format wars."

One of the problems with establishing a standard is that it has the immediate effect of freezing development. The government, both in the United States and elsewhere, frowns on standardization, partly for this reason, but mainly for reasons having to do with restraint of trade, collusion, and matters relating to the laws prohibiting the formation of cartels. It's a dilemma: on the one hand, the consumer benefits from the advances that new technology and product development produces, yet in order to win these gains, a lot of people have to lose by committing to quickly obsolete designs.

In the professional markets, the buyers are generally far better informed, and are thus better able to make judgments regarding capital investment. The average consumer, though, who is just now being introduced to the plethora of competing designs, is usually ill-equipped to make sound decisions, and often ends up getting burned. Few consumers can take the factors of amortization and equipment replacement into consideration. For instance, in the early 1970s those who bought the Cartrivision system—the home tape format that was ahead of its time and behind technologically—learned a bitter lesson.

From the manufacturer's viewpoint, it's a matter of balancing a moderately sized piece of a large pie against a gamble for a huge piece of a perhaps slightly smaller pie. It almost seems to be a matter of pride with the industry leaders to be the ones to establish a standard, rather than license someone else's design, and each of them is convinced that his or hers is the best answer. It's an old premise: invent a better mousetrap, and wait for the knocks on the door.

The upshot of all this is that the newest, shiniest, and very bestest equipment will be made obsolete by a newer, shinier, and even bester model, perhaps even before the maker can start regular shipments.

Beyond the question of obsolescence, though, is the question of appropriate technology. The classic industrial television setup until recently has involved the establishment of a studio, along with all the paraphernalia that goes with it. More and more companies are now finding that the new breed of ENG and EFP equipment and the production techniques for which they were designed make much more sense overall. So even when the decision is made to purchase equipment, there's the further complication of making the right choices regarding the type of equipment.

There's the primary question, however, still to be answered. Is it wiser to own or rent?

There is a unilateral answer available, once some conditions are established. First, if you or your company are asking the question in the first place, then the answer is the one that would also be most appropriate for any company just getting started: *rent*.

If you've been involved in television production for a while using rented equipment, you'll probably know when the time has come to buy. Companies have accountants and planners, and other people who take joy in shuffling numbers around, and when the numbers all indicate that money could be saved by making the capital investment, they're more than likely to start suggesting that a call to the video dealership might be in order. In this case, it might then be time to play devil's advocate, and challenge their assumptions. This can, of course, be very, very difficult.

Television equipment, to many people, is a lot like an exotic sports car. Aside from practical considerations, such as availability and reliability of maintenance, there's something about equipment that causes people within the industry to *want* it. Any corporate television or media manager who wouldn't prefer to have a nice inventory of equipment on hand just isn't right in the head, and this is true even if getting a lot of equipment isn't a good idea. It relates to a well-known tendency called "empire building," and any manager knows quite well that the more people and assets you have under you, the more your own position is enhanced.

But consider a prototypical company that made a major commitment to television production in 1976. For their several hundred thousand dollars, they got three studio cameras with 1-inch Plumbicon® tubes, two heterodyne color one-inch VTRs, a switcher, a character generator, a bunch of lighting instruments, a slide chain, and were able to convert two meeting rooms into a studio with a ten-foot ceiling.

Today, they're stuck with cameras of old design, that tend to lag and lose registration; their VTRs that were only manufactured for a year before the new one-inch highband models came out (the manufacturer had to get rid of a bunch of old transports and came out with the "improved" model the company bought) are obsolete; their switcher is incapable of expansion at any reasonable cost; and their character generator provides graphic quality they now find embarrassing. Furthermore, most of their programs now call for production in the field, and their studio cameras are simply unsuited for such work. As a result, they do a few shows from the studio, but for the bulk of their work, they end up renting both a mini-cam setup and editing facilities, since they can't get capital funds for new equipment until the old stuff has been fully amortized.

Given the directions taken by production styles and techniques over recent years, I personally would question the value of even considering a fully equipped in-house studio, unless the company involved is both very large, and has ongoing requirements for programs that lend themselves to studio production.

The new minicams offer the best possible versatility, as they can be taken into the field on battery power, or equipped with a larger viewfinder and plugged into a remote control for studio-type work. As a result they are likely to be the best choice for any in-house operation today.

Those companies that do not have heavy requirements for production may be better off doing all of their work with rented equipment. Aside from the total avoidance of capital expenditure, there are some attractive benefits to be gained by renting equipment. One of them is the fact that it's possible, when renting, to enjoy a wide choice of different types of equipment. By building a file of what's available from the various rental and production houses in the area, you can choose exactly the right equipment for each project. Also, when equipment is rented, it's more likely to be the latest and best available. The rental houses and production companies have little choice but to turn their equipment over fairly often in order to stay competitive. Since they also tend to get more than average use out of their gear than the typical in-house facility, they can spread the cost over a larger number of productions done for clients. The result is that even after figuring in their profit, the cost of rental can be equal to or even less than the cost of purchase, even without taking the other advantages mentioned into account.

Many companies have successfully compromised, and established some basic equipment to take care of simple needs, while going outside for more esoteric items. One area of investment that is perhaps a bit safer in the long run than cameras and other production equipment is a basic post-production setup. Most independent production companies who offer both production and post-production packages figure to make their real money in the post-production end. Furnishing production facilities is rarely a highly profitable venture, and those companies that do consider it to be such are made conspicuous by some rather high rate cards.

It may thus be both expeditious and cost effective to rent production facilities, which again, can be matched to the precise needs of each production, and establish an in-house post-production facility, at least for basic editing.

The problem here, of course, is that full post facilities, especially complete and high quality systems, are a very expensive proposition. Although some of the larger corporations have indeed built extremely well-equipped operations, with all the capabilities one could hope to find at any station or independent production house, they also make extensive use of them. They also are among the pioneers in business use of television—companies with a long history of growth in the understanding and use of television as a business tool.

For individuals and the independent producers of television, the question is more likely resolved with the decision to rent. Consider that a basic single-camera package (specifying a three-tube camera of acceptable quality) with a portable cassette recorder, accessories, and a simple cuts-only editing system, would start in the neighborhood of $40,000. The same package, with a top-grade camera, a one-inch deck, a well-equipped van, and the same cassette editing would run about $200,000. For a full one-inch editing system by itself, you could start at maybe $300,000 to $400,000, but to really do it right, be ready to sign a check for a million or more.

The pain of renting as an independent is the pain felt by renters everywhere: start to do enough of it, and the records show all those dollars sailing away that could have gone towards purchase. Especially for certain types of work, such as documentaries, there's a lot to be said for owning at least a basic production package, and here, it still depends on the nature of your business.

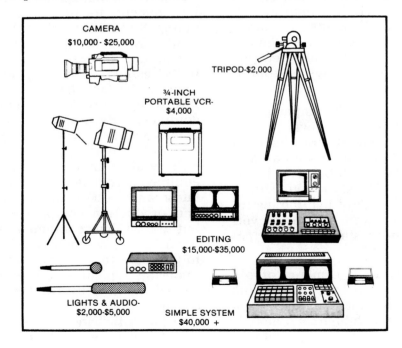

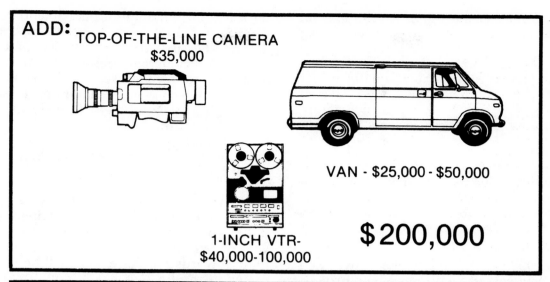

ADD: TOP-OF-THE-LINE CAMERA
$35,000

VAN - $25,000 - $50,000

1-INCH VTR-
$40,000-100,000

$200,000

1-INCH EDITING SYSTEM
$300,000 TO $1,000,000

If you expect to operate as an independent program producer, and can afford to purchase a package, then doing so may be an appropriate course of action. If you want to get into the equipment rental business, the question has, of course, already been decided. It's the person in between, one who provides independent production services, who is faced with the biggest quandry.

This is a position I can strongly sympathize with myself, since that type of work makes up a large chunk of my business. The standards to which I work would require a substantial investment in broadcast equipment, and unfortunate as it may be, I was not born into a wealthy family. I am not being facetious—it's quite amazing how high the percentage is of facilities that have been financed with family, or similarly acquired money. It almost seems to be a tradition within the industry.

The rule of thumb I've always quoted has been to defer thoughts of purchase until an

325

examination of at least a year's worth of rental records shows that purchase would have been considerably less expensive. Extreme caution must be exercised, however, and I can name several companies that went down the tubes because they based their projections on past trends, and went into hock for heavy equipment purchases just in time to hit a slump or recession.

Personally, I operated for nearly four years making exclusive use of rented equipment. In the process, I built a strong and valued relationship with a particular production house, and have found the relationship to be a very satisfactory one.

Early in 1980, I finally broke down and bought a basic cassette editing system, primarily to do rough-cuts of shows, but also to have a system around that I could play with, and use to put together tapes that are not being paid for by a client. Eventually, I'll pick up a mid-range camera, so that I can work on documentaries and other projects ON SPEC, though

with the current state of flux in camera design and price, I'm in no rush to buy one. I'm anticipating the arrival on the scene of the new solid-state cameras, while also keeping my eyes open for a good used three-tube camera at a reasonable price. Meanwhile, I can rent state-of-the-art equipment from local sources, and enjoy all the benefits of a full engineering staff, careful maintenance, and much lower bank payments than would be the case had I bought a camera.

As the price of video equipment comes down, and the performance obtained for each dollar spent increases, the question of buying versus renting will begin to lean more and more towards purchase, and will be that much easier to resolve.

Meanwhile, the decision should be based primarily on volume of use. Renting equipment on a regular basis is obviously expensive, but is relatively safe, while buying equipment can be cheaper, but also carries higher risks.

CHAPTER 26

Video Gestalt —
Putting It All Together

One night, after a long but pleasant day of shooting on a show for a client, one of the client's staff and I went out for a drink. The shooting had gone well, and everyone involved was enjoying the work on the project. After a while, the conversation turned to the feelings one experiences when immersed in production. She asked me what my theory was to account for the special nature of production work.

I responded that I thought two factors were involved. Since I've always taken special pleasure in watching a crew perform—quite literally choreographed as carefully and gracefully as any ballet, if it's done right—I said that my first guess would be that production work

tends to bind people together, and that the feeling of camaraderie that develops is probably what makes production work so satisfying. My second guess was that one basic aspect of production work is that it's piecework; that it has a definite beginning, middle, and end; that it provides an opportunity to watch a project go from an idea to a completed production, and that this in itself was a very satisfying process. Unlike many other areas of endeavor, where the job is much the same from one day to the next, production work, by its very nature (especially for an independent, who moves from one project to the next) provides a variety, and a sense of accomplishment that would be very similar to that felt by a fine carpenter, or an artist, or an architect. A sense of craftsmanship.

She considered this, and agreed that all of this was true, but that she had a pet theory that went beyond those factors. She had studied the human mind extensively and had earned a Ph.D in psychology. Her premise was that television production is one of the few types of work that requires one to use both hemispheres of the brain simultaneously: the left half, governing physical control and mental acuity, and the right half, governing creative and aesthetic processes. There's a lot of physical activity and coordination required in production, while at the same time one must constantly be considering the creative elements of the program. She suspected that these dual demands gave one a thorough workout, leaving one with a mental "rosy glow" that is essentially the equivalent of the physical glow one has after a good day of hard work. It's basically a form of exhaustion, but it's a very healthy and satisfying one.

The more I think about that conversation, the more I think that we were both completely right. Television production, if not unique, is a very special and unusual field of personal endeavor.

Throughout the preceding pages, we've examined the disciplines involved in each of the various aspects of production, but it's appropriate to tie them all together here. Though each of the jobs involved has an individual emphasis and a special set of requirements, to a certain extent they all share the same set of demands and require similar attitudes and abilities.

This is the GESTALT of the production process, the interweaving of the parts so that they fit together perfectly and complement each other. Each separate piece of the puzzle means little until it is fitted in with the others. Individual staff and crew members see only their own "tree," whereas the producer and director must not only examine each of the "trees," but also be able to gain the distance necessary to see the "forest."

In achieving this gestalt, there are three fundamental areas of concern, with which the team, both individually and collectively, must deal.

There's *the management aspect*—the special purview of the producer, but also important for each of the department heads, and on down the line. Even the beginning production assistant will have a specified set of duties, and will have to exercise some creative administration in order to get the job done efficiently. Part of the key to successful management is to delegate authority and responsibility, and to encourage initiative among the members of the crew. This not only results in a more efficient operation, but allows the members of the staff and crew to grow in their positions.

There's *the technical side,* which demands the attention of the crew members directly responsible, but also of the director and other staff. With the thousands of details involved in even relatively simple productions, and the synergistic way in which everything has to fit together, it's more than just helpful to have everyone keeping an eye out for the little details that can slip by—it's necessary.

The engineering factors are obviously of tremendous importance. Unless the equipment is properly maintained, connected, and adjusted, the results simply cannot reach the levels to which we all should be striving. It takes a special sort of person to give the attention and care to equipment that it deserves. The engineers rarely receive adequate credit for their work, since we often don't think of them until something breaks down, but without them, we wouldn't be in business in the first place.

One of the things that amazed and delighted me about Charles Bensinger's **THE VIDEO GUIDE** is a wonderful statement he makes in the chapter on *Maintenance and Troubleshooting* that many people might find hard to swallow, yet which I know without doubt to be true. Picking him up in midstream: "Even so-called inanimate matter such as electronic circuits and pieces of metal and plastic are all made up of atoms and molecules that must bind together in certain absolute patterns. A kind of INTERNAL INTELLIGENCE and energy is necessary to maintain this pattern...."

"The internal intelligence of VTRs and cameras will definitely respond to highly negative or positive emotional fields generated by people. Like organic matter such as plants, animals, or people, a video system will respond well to those operators who approach it with care and love. An overly frustrated or negative person will pass those personal frustrations onto the equipment and 'strange' failures will inevitably result. This is why equipment 'works' for certain people and 'doesn't work' for others. It happens every time . . . ."

As I said, there are those who would find this hard to accept, yet Charlie's right—it happens every time. I edited a network show, working with the director, on which the producer was under terrific financial and scheduling pressure. Every time he came into the editing room, the equipment stopped working properly, and as soon as he would leave, everything would go back to normal. I wouldn't have believed it, except that I had seen this happen too many times before to not believe. After one very tense and trying half-hour period of trying to make a *single* edit with the producer in the room, when the system simply wouldn't work, I took a a gamble and leaned over to whisper to the director. I said: "Look, L . . . is tired—why don't you see if you can get him to go home." She nodded, and I think had some notion of what I was thinking. She succeeded in sending the producer off, and we waited until we knew he was out of the building. Once I new he was out the door, and without changing anything on the console, I hit the "record" button. The edit went down perfectly. I promise you—the phenomenon is real.

Finally, there're *the creative aspects*. Again, everyone involved in a production should be encouraged to offer suggestions, though in the proper context and at an appropriate place and time, to help make the production better. Though there are such things as single-handed productions, it's very difficult to achieve any kind of real quality by one's self, and the results usually suffer. The interplay of the people involved, and the synthesis of a program from all the varied elements that go into it can make a program more than the sum of the parts. The creative process starts with the original concept, and carries through to the final edit; it should rarely be locked firmly in place until the last fade to black is made.

Working in television is a continual process of learning, and the discoveries that come daily, weekly, and yearly are, perhaps, the most fascinating things about it. It's akin to mountain climbing, with the difference that there is no peak. The joy is in the constant improvement and refinement, with the various rewarding plateaus that each completed program provides.

People outside the industry commonly think of television and film production as a glamorous, exciting field, where everyone makes scads of money and goes to fancy parties every other night. There's irony in the fact that at certain times, in certain circumstances, there's a certain amount of truth to this perception. The irony is provided by the fact that these instances happen to about five percent of the people in the business, about five percent of the time. The glamour is there, but it takes a different form than is popularly supposed; the work is exciting, although more often in the same way that archeology is exciting; there's money to be made, although very few ever really hit it big; and the fancy parties, though there are such, are confined for the most part to Los Angeles/Hollywood and New York.

The popular perception of television production relates almost totally to entertainment, yet the vast bulk of television today is done for business and educational users. In this field, the glamour is personal: it's the feeling you get when you walk into the studio in the morning, before anyone else has shown up, and as you leaf through the script, you envision how the show will look when it's done. *That's* the real glamour—the knowledge that a good number of hours, days, or weeks later, after a lot of hard work, there'll be a program with a life of its own, that serves the purpose for which it was designed. That's the exciting part of television production!

It's not a career for someone looking for an easy job. Universally, the hours are long, and are filled with scores of details that can become awfully tedious. It requires a highly professional attitude on everyone's part to keep the spirits up after 17 takes on a simple scene.

If all the jobs are done well, and the show comes out the way it should, none of the hard work will show on the screen. The program will look as if it had been effortlessly done,

and the audience will find it difficult if not impossible to understand why a ten minute show took two days to shoot and 75 hours to edit, or how a 30 second commercial could possibly require a crew of 13 people working for three days to make. The pleasures are private, mainly to be shared within and among the crew. Others will look at the show, and say "That's nice," or, if you're fortunate enough to have a script with universal appeal, and a competent team that has produced a truly fine show, you may succeed in touching the audience deeply. They'll never know, though, how much work was involved in getting the program on the screen.

When television people gather, the conversation nearly always turns to shop talk. It's a subject that is usually completely lost on people outside the industry, and at a gathering of people from diverse fields, once you've mentioned that you work in television (and get the inevitable "Oh? What station?"), you've said about all you can. My pet one-liner, when asked what I do, is: "Well, right now I'm a television director, but what I really want to do is sell insurance." It usually gets a chuckle, and, if I'm lucky, steers the conversation to a new subject. God help them if it doesn't, because the fact that I truly love the business

virtually ensures that if they succeed in getting me going, they'll pay for their error by being literally bored to tears.

A friend of mine, an artist and art teacher, once explained why any piece of work actually takes twice as much time as the actual execution entails. Once a project is completed, it then takes an equal amount of time to sit and study it, analyze it, and criticize it (and if all has worked out well, grin at it for a while). A true artist and craftsman is never completely satisfied with the results obtained, and will constantly be looking for ways to improve on the next project. I have never seen such a thing as a flawless production, and though I strongly suspect that there can be no such animal, I hope my suspicion is correct, for if there ever was one that turned out perfectly, it'd be time to quit, and move on to something else. The chances are that I'd never be able to top it. As I say, in reality, I suspect this is one danger from which we're all quite safe.

What I've tried to do with this book, beyond simply offering some hopefully useful information, is to present a concept of *attitude*—of the approach and philosophy required for successful production. A friend, to whom I described the outline and objectives while the book was

in progress, said: "It sounds like it could be called *Zen and the Art of Television Production.*" That is almost exactly what I had in mind. The working title, and the title that I will always apply to it personally, is the title of this last section: *Video Gestalt.*

As I've said, television production is hard work, and creating material for this extremely powerful medium is a serious business. At the same time, it's important to keep in mind the fact that if you're doing it right, the work is fun. When you drag yourself away from a marathon editing session with the tape in your hand, tired, bleary-eyed, and wondering if it was all worth it, all you'll have to do to answer the question is sit down, unwind for a short while, and watch the results of the labors. Then you'll know if it was worth it.

When asked by Barbara Walters during a recent interview how he'd like to be remembered, Laurence Olivier reflected for a moment, and then answered with simple eloquence:

"I would like to be remembered as a dili-gent—workman."
(Walters: "So prosaic?")
(Pause) "I think a poet's a workman. I think
        Shakespeare was a workman.
        I think God's a workman.
        I don't think there's anything better
        than a workman."

Part 5
Appendices

APPENDIX A

Production Checklist

The following lists of items are divided into the three basic areas of Pre-Production, Production, and Post-Production. Please note that many areas overlap, and that precise division is impossible. The best way to use this checklist is as a prompting device for matters that will need attention.

Pre-Production

- Producer and Staff
  - Script approvals
  - Production design
  - Script breakdown (Director)
  - Budget approvals
  - Staff and crew selections/assignments
- Insurance
- Music clearances
- Facilities selection
- Lighting design
- Shot sheets for camera operators
- Shot list (film-style shoots)
- Talent
  - Casting
  - Contracts and clearances
  - Wardrobe and fittings
  - Release forms
  - Makeup
  - Welfare worker for children
- Location Scouting
  - Power
  - Parking

- Permits
- Location fees
- Bathroom facilities
- Overnight accommodations
- Telephone
- First Aid/Hospital location .
- Noise problems
- Cable runs/Dolly runs
- Floorplans
- Weather forecasts
- Lighting (sunrise/set times, windows, etc.)
- Viewing facilities
- Security

Production

- Personnel
  - Call sheets and crew lists
  - W-4 forms
  - Time sheets
  - Production reports
- Facilities and Equipment
  - Facilities request
  - Equipment list
  - Rentals (pickup & return)
  - Grip equipment and/or truck
  - Lighting equipment
  - Tape stock
- General
  - Props

- Sets and construction
- Meals, drinks, tables, and chairs
- Petty cash
- Accounting forms
- Checkbook
- Credit card
- Transportation (vehicles)
- Maps

Post-Production

- Off-line
  - Scheduling/booking
  - Worktapes/window dubs
  - Tape logs and notes
  - Audio/video XFRs
- On-line
  - Scheduling/booking
  - Off-line EDL
  - Technical evaluation of masters
  - Graphics
  - Audio/video XFRs
  - B-rolls and worktapes
  - Submasters
  - Black and Coded stock (drop or non-drop frame)
  - Sweetening
  - Protection master
  - Duplication
  - Trafficking/distribution
  - Vaulting/disposition of tapes

APPENDIX B

Production File Contents

The following list is given as an example of the paperwork generated during the various phases of production. It is based on an actual production done in 1981, and represents the permanent record of the event, as stored in the author's files.

The production was an entertainment program that entailed a multicamera taping with both a live switched recording and an isolated camera, along with two days of location single-camera shooting. The mastering format was 1-inch Type C. It involved talent, a full crew, off-line control track editing on ¾-inch cassette, and on-line editing of the 1-inch masters using a CMX 340X system. The total budget for the production was roughly $35,000. As much as possible, the file is listed in the order in which the contents were generated.

(Note—the production in question was unscripted. The files for scripted programs would include the various drafts and revisions of the scripts, plus breakdowns and shot lists, in addition to the items shown below.)

Items generated during pre-production and production:

- Notes from initial client contact—nature and tentative format of show. Phone numbers. Tentative budget.

- Tentative crew list, including day rates, phone numbers. Checkoffs as crew members were booked.

- Initial facilities list. Sources and rates for equipment. Phone numbers. Several questions noted to ask engineers.

- Notes on financial arrangements and terms. Notes on tentative budget.

- Director's notes on production style, camera placements, recording style, necessary cutaways.

- Tentative shooting dates to be cleared with all concerned.

- Notes on direct and immediate costs, and on deferred costs.

- Location scouting notes: Power not adequate. Determine generator parking area, measure cable runs to lights and equipment. Gaffer's estimation of number of instruments. Tentative design of lighting plot. Further notes on camera placements—platforms will have to be built.

- Audio track assignments, equipment layout, and interconnection.

- Copy of certificate of insurance sent to rental houses. Copy of liability coverage policy sent to city permit office.

- Copy of order for videotape stock.

- Notes on conversation with producers—change audience between shows? Date of performer's appearance on Tomorrow Show? Publicity and ticket sales.

- Notes from conversation with police department and city traffic survey on parking permits.

- Notes on set rentals.

- Bids for generator and lighting equipment rentals.

- Bids for wireless microphone rental.

- Copy of signed production contract.

- Notes on locations for remote segments.

- Copy of city park/recreation requirements for location shooting on city property.

- Wording for audience notice of taping to be placed near entrance—serves as general release.

- Wardrobe for talent—meeting to make selections.

- Makeup requirements for talent—test shades.

- Names for guest list, from crew and talent.

- Tentative schedule for main shooting day.

- Note to rent "No Parking" signs.

- Final camera placement layout.

- Final lighting plot.

- Final budget.

- Shooting plan for cameras.

- Notes on opening title sequence design.

- Tentative credits list.

- Correspondence on music clearance.

- Want list of expendables, adapters, cables, etc.

- Final shooting schedule for distribution to crew and talent.

- Final crew and contact list for distribution to crew and talent.

- Staging checklist—items to be taken to shoot.

- Vehicle list and parking assignments.

- Lunch and dinner order sheets.

- Copies of receipts for petty cash expenditures.

- Copies of all invoices from suppliers.

- Copies of AFTRA member report forms, Pension & Welfare forms, tax forms.

- Printout of in-progress Budget Tracker report (cost accounting).

Items generated prior to and during post-production:

- Tape logs with assistant director's notes.

- Log of cutaway material by type, shot length, and description.

- Paper edit decision list from first rough cut of program.

- Notes on changes from first viewing.

- Paper EDL of revised edit of program.

- Revised EDL with full notes, ready for use during on-line edit.

- Camera art used on-line—titles.

- Staging checklist for on-line edit.

- Time budget (ideal schedule) for on-line edit.

- List of cassette copies to be made from edited master.

- Final list of credits, with character generator page numbers noted.

- Computer EDL of opening title sequence.

- Computer EDL of main body of program (five copies, generated at various stages of completion).

- Computer EDL of closing credits sequence.

- Paper punch tapes of EDLs (in edited master tape box).

Items generated after completion of post-production:

- Copies of remaining invoices.

- Printout of final Budget Tracker report (cost accounting).

- Invitation list for premiere showing.

- Copies of promotional material.

- Newsletter to crew members on progress since taping.

- Copies of air date announcements.

- Copies of publicity releases, and articles as published.

- Copy of TV Guide listing, critics' reviews, etc.

APPENDIX C

Computer Use and Application

Production management is an obviously important part of the overall process of any video project, yet it often receives less attention than do the more glamorous parts of the job. Many independent and freelance people, for instance, quickly learn (and sometimes to their surprise) that the "business side of the business" is actually as important as the creative and technical matters—if, that is, ·there is the presumed desire to *stay* in business for any length of time.

Production, by its nature, involves a substantial amount of paperwork. Much of this concerns the forms that are used during the course of the production such as call sheets, tape logs, talent releases, etc., but there is often an avalanche of paperwork having to do with the business and financial aspects of production as well. As *Appendix B* demonstrated, productions seem to thrive on paperwork, and by the end of a production, there can be hundreds of sheets of paper that will have been generated. Getting a handle on the paperwork is crucial, to avoid getting bogged down either during or after production.

Late in 1979, I did some work on a PBS show that dealt with computers and children. The kids today, starting in grade school in many instances, are learning about computers right along with history and math. What's more, they're taking to it with astonishing ease and facility. In many cases, after a short while, they are turning around and teaching their teachers about the machines. Everyone has heard about computer LANGUAGES, and these are precisely what are involved: Computers are programmed in specific languages, of which there are many available, and as with any foreign language, children seem naturally to be quicker to learn than we older folks.

Though I'd been curious about microcomputers for some time, and had long planned to look into them, that show prompted me to act. Having read several articles on the subject in general magazines, and in consultation with some friends and associates who knew about these beasts, I wound up with an Apple® II* microcomputer system. Things have not been the same since.

The Hardware

First, for the computer wizards out there, I'll describe my system in the proper terminology (having a need to show off my new knowledge), and then I'll backtrack and explain in lay terms what the gibberish means.

The system I chose consists of an **Apple® II** with 48K RAM, Applesoft floating point BASIC in firmware, two minifloppy disk drives, and a **Centronics 730** dot-matrix printer with the Apple **Parallel Interface Card.** The CRT is a 17-inch black and white television converted to monitor use. The next additions to the system will be an 80-character display board, a **D.C. Hayes Modem,** and a letter-quality daisywheel printer.

If you're like I was at the end of 1979, about the only words in the above paragraph that make sense are the ones about the TV set converted to monitor use.

To begin with, the Apple II is a self-contained microcomputer. It incorporates the computer (essentially a model 6502 microprocessor chip), some memory, a keyboard, and a bunch of built-in functions and capabilities, in a package just slightly larger than a portable typewriter. It is quite possible to do things with nothing more than the basic Apple II and a monitor of some sort, but the real power and

flexibility of a computer become available when some options are added.

The 48K RAM indicates that there are (roughly) 48,000 BYTES (or characters) of solid-state, Random-Access Memory (RAM) built into the device. The minimum with an Apple is 16K. A 16K memory would be enough to run some simple games, but for serious applications, the larger the memory, the better, and 48K is the basic maximum available with the Apple II. There is a Language Card available that adds the capabilities of a language called PASCAL, and which increases the effective memory to 64K, but it is best used by advanced programmers who are ready to graduate from BASIC.

This subject of the language is something that can be initially confusing. A computer doesn't "know" anything at all until you tell it something. Its sole capability is to push numbers around (in the form of binary, or off/on BITS) according to the instructions it is given. Since the computer speaks BINARY (a sample instruction might be: "10011010," with thousands of such instructions in a single program), and we out here speak English, the computer languages have been developed to eliminate the need for people who use computers to have to enter instructions directly in this binary code. To do so would not only be tedious in the extreme, but since errors are not obvious, could easily drive one nuts.

The first step, therefore, is to give the machine a means of taking instructions that are recognizable to humans and convert them to OBJECT CODE which is the on/off numbers such as 10110 . . . that the computer uses. The most common of these languages for use in microcomputers is the aforementioned BASIC, which stands for "Beginner's All-purpose Symbolic Instruction Code." Unfortunately, just as there are several incompatible ½-inch videotape formats, there are dialects of BASIC, many of which are not mutually compatible. A BASIC program written for the Apple, for instance, will not run on a Radio Shack® TRS-80®* Although the programs will look somewhat similar when read on a printout of the program itself, the computer would stop at the

---

*Apple is a registered trademark of Apple Computer, Inc.

*Radio Shack and TRS-80 are registered trademarks of Tandy Corp.

first instruction that differed from what it expected.

This is one of the first things that must be learned about computers. They are *absolutely* literal. A single comma misplaced in a long and complex program can cause the entire program to CRASH.

Once the language has been loaded into the computer, it is then ready to receive instructions. These are the proverbial PROGRAMS we hear about, and they can range from a few lines to pages upon pages of instructions. Put simply, a program written in BASIC is a series of numbered lines, each line telling the computer to do something. The computer executes these lines in numerical order, pushing around DATA, or information, that the program requests and deals with. For example, a line taken at random from one of our programs reads:

1670 IF F = 0 THEN PRINT N$: GOTO 1685

Translating this into human talk, line number 1670 of the program tells the computer that if "F" (a variable, which would be a number that was earlier assigned the name "F") is equal to 0, then print the string variable (words and/or numbers) called "N$" (also earlier assigned). The colon separates a subsequent instruction that tells the computer to go to line number 1685 after execution, *if* the foregoing conditions were met. In other words, if "F" turned out to be equal to "3", then the computer would *not* print the value of N$, and would *not* go to line number 1685. Instead, as soon as it evaluated the value of "F" to be other than 0, it would go immediately to the next larger line number (which in the program used as our example, happens to be 1675), where it would execute that instruction.

The Apple we use has two BASIC languages available. The "basic BASIC" is called INTE-GER BASIC, and as its name implies, it handles only integer numbers. (Remembering your grammer school math, this means that fractions or decimals are a no-no.) Integer BASIC is a rather limited language, and has some problems when it comes to business or scientific applications, but it does have the advantage of being very fast. The programs we have

developed, however, have been written in an enhanced BASIC, known by the trade name of APPLESOFT, which will handle numbers of any size, and has some additional functions built into the language.

The MINIFLOPPY DISK mentioned is the description of a 5-¼-inch magnetic disk, contained in a protective jacket, that is used to store programs and data or text files. Since everything in the computer goes away when it is turned off, some method of saving information is necessary. The cheapest method is to record information on cassette tape, but it's also very slow and cumbersome. The disk system is quicker, packs a large amount of data into a small package, and provides random access to any information on the disk. It is a practical necessity for any serious use of the computer. Though a single disk can suffice, adding a second drive eliminates much changing of disks while shuffling information around.

The printer mentioned is a dot-matrix type, giving the advantages of speed and low cost, along with the disadvantages of limited print quality. The original manuscript of this book, for example, was generated on this printer, and reading it requires a page or so to get used to the type style. We will soon be adding a type of printer that uses a character wheel to type on the page about the way a standard typewriter does. While the print quality is far superior, as indicated, such printers are slower, as well as being more expensive (roughly $2000 to $3000, compared with under $1000 for a dot-matrix design).

The other additions will be a circuit board that will expand the video display of the Apple from its standard of 40 characters per line (upper case only) to 80 per line, upper and lower case (most useful for word processing). Also, the MODEM mentioned (D.C. Hayes being the trade name) will let our computer talk over telephone lines with other computers.

Altogether, our initial system investment was about $3,500, and by the time we've added our planned bells and whistles, we'll have perhaps $7000 to $8000 invested. Apple has since introduced a big brother called the Apple III, intended for business users. It should be obvi-

The editor's APPLE II word processing system.

ous that we are into the world of computers, and I should mention that the Apple II can be stretched fairly far in applications before its capabilities are exhausted.

A word also, before we move on to applications, on the Apple versus other computers. The Apple II was our choice, and we have been very satisfied with it. It has proven to be easy to use, easy to learn, and as reliable as a granite curbstone. This is not to denigrate its competitors, however. There are dozens of systems available, offering a range from simpler than the Apple to far more powerful, and a shortage of choice is not a problem in looking at computers. When considering a purchase, though, there are a number of factors to be weighed. Make sure that service is available, and that there is a good selection of prewritten software (programs) that can be run as soon as the computer is hooked up. If you're a true beginner, I would strongly recommend buying your system from a local dealer who will help you get started. We bought our system from a

local computer chain, and the staff there were of tremendous help, even letting us in while closed for their week-long end-of-year inventory to answer questions and iron out some minor bugs in the printer interface.

The main thing is to not be frightened of computers. They may seem formidable, but once learned, they can turn out to be almost friendly and certainly very useful devices. How useful? Well, let's examine now some of the ways we've put our computer to work for us.

Computer Applications

The first and justifying reason for the purchase of our computer was word processing. I had this book to write, and knew that a word processing system would speed the process. Beyond the book, the word processing capabilities could also be applied to writing scripts, proposals, letters, etc.

Along with the hardware, I thus bought a word-processing program called *EasyWriter* written specifically for the Apple. It turns the Apple into a formidable word processor, though it does take a few days to become accustomed to. Unlike a dedicated WORD PROCESSOR (a computer built to do just that one job), there are some initially awkward requirements for using the system. For instance, in order to capitalize, it is necessary to first hit a key labeled "ESCAPE." It's not as bad as it sounds, though, and within a day or so, the whole thing becomes second-nature.

There were some pleasant surprises in actually using the system once I got into the work. First, though I had anticipated that the work would go faster, I hadn't been prepared for how much faster it would be. My best guess is that the system has speeded the whole project, overall, by a factor of three or better.

To begin with, the actual typing is faster. Since there's nothing mechanical going on, nor carriage returns happening, the pace is set by how fast a typist one is. In that respect, the system encourages increasing speed.

When it comes time for revisions and editing, however, the real power of the system becomes apparent. Rather than laboriously retyping passages and pages, one simply scrolls through the text to the section that needs work, and deletes, adds, and changes on the screen at will. A paragraph or section can be moved elsewhere, removed, or stored away for insertion at a later point, with the result that revising work becomes an easy and fast process instead of a chore. As such, the computer is an aid to the creative process as well as a mechanical tool.

The benefits have carried over now beyond the writing phase. My editor, Charles Bensinger of Video-Info Publications, has picked up a similar system, and used it to edit my copy. The entire book is contained on six minifloppy disks, copies of which we shuttle back and forth. All final revisions are made in the computer. Once the text is ready, we then will enjoy one of the major benefits of the system, as the book will be typeset with the text being fed from the computer directly to the typesetter with no human intervention. This provides us with three advantages: the process goes much faster (with the entire typesetting reduced from days to hours); the cost is reduced considerably in comparison with having the book manually reset; and (one of my favorite aspects) there are no new errors introduced by a typist resetting the book. Since there is a formidable amount of technical jargon contained herein, this is a major attraction. As a result, any typographical errors you find in these pages are directly attributable to me. (Of course, as all writers know, these are all the fault of the editor, as it was Charlie's job to catch them!)

One of the reasons I bought a full computer instead of a dedicated word processor, and put up with some minor inconveniences in word processing applications, was so that when the system was not processing words, it could process other things. The first task, then, was to learn a bit about how computers work, and then find some applications that would help in the business of television production.

Two things immediately became apparent: first, there is very little written material that is of any value for the rank beginner. Most of the books on computers, even those aimed at the beginner, are either so "cutesy" that they tell one nothing, or assume so much knowledge that they quickly leave the reader bewildered. Beyond that, many of the available sources tell *how* to do something, but don't give a clue as to *why* one would want to do it!

The way I finally began to learn about the computer (it requires a nearly completely different frame of mind) was to obtain a bunch of program listings from magazines and books, and begin the tedious process of manually entering them on the keyboard. (Programs are usually loaded from tape or disk.) In doing so, I began to see how programs flow, and slowly began to see the patterns and logic behind programming.

The second thing that quickly became apparent was that there were virtually no prewritten programs available that related directly to television production. Aside from some general accounting and ledger programs (of which there are many), any specialized programs we were to use would have to be written in-house.

The first application I decided to tackle was getting the computer involved in putting together a production budget. My first version of a budgeting program was an unwieldy program that had a limited number of categories, and was limited to a total amount of $32,767 (that being the largest number that Apple's Integer BASIC can handle). It did, however, serve as a starting point, and examining its drawbacks made the next version much more useful.

Though the current version of the budget program is officially called Version 2.0, (integers indicating major revisions, decimals indicating minor changes or adaptions), in reality it would be more like "2.9.9". The program has undergone constant change over a period of more than two years and is now a powerful and speedy aid in budgeting.

The budget program prompts the user to enter information for each and every item that has been written into the program. As this is written, the current program includes 54 above the line categories, while below the line there are 60 production and 20 post production categories. These categories were established by going through the standard budget forms used in the industry, along with all of the budgets and expense records for past productions, and including every item that was deemed important. Once entered, the entire budget can be stored on disk, pulled back off at any time, and any item can be revised. Once revised, the budget can be stored back on disk in place of the original, or separately, under a revision number. The program will display a summary, the entire budget, and the file data (who, what, when, where, etc.); and any or all of the information can be printed out at any time.

Again, we found some unexpected benefits in using the program. We had anticipated that budgeting would go faster, as with word processing, but also found that our budgets ended up being more accurate. Since the system prompts the user on so many items, one could say that the program has the experience of all past productions behind it. It's thus much less likely that an item will be forgotten. Also, as the budget is being put together, it's so easy to revise, polish, and change that the net result is a more accurate and realistic budget—created in a fraction of the time it would take to put one together on paper.

Recently, a companion program has been completed called the Budget Tracker. This program loads a finished and approved budget from disk, and then accepts entry of actual expenses as they begin to come in. The computer keeps track of the expenses for each item, comparing them with the budgeted amount, and shows the balance remaining for each category. If a category goes over budget, the computer gives notice of the fact, indicating where and how much. For in-house productions, it gives instant information on how the budget stands, and for productions done for clients, serves the additional purpose of determining net profit or loss. As with the Budget program, the Tracker program stores records on disk, and prints out both summaries and detail sheets showing budget/expenditure status at any time.

This is the type of application for which computers are best suited. In the two programs above, the computer performs all the mathematics, does so without ever making a mistake (as long as the correct data is entered—the old "garbage in/garbage out" maxim being quite true), and leaves the user free to do "creative budgeting," rather than get all wrapped up in calculator paper. The programs have been written to work in simple English, and require virtually no special training to run. Anyone can sit down at the keyboard and be using the program within minutes. There is no "computerese" to know.

We pressed on, taken with the capabilities of our machine. Other programs were added, each one delving further into the capabilities of the computer as we learned more about the critter. We now generate our call sheets on the computer, which is actually a rather mild advantage over a paper form. In that particular application, the program serves essentially as an electronic form, and the primary benefit is speed.

Simpler, though more useful, is a Rundown program that aids in putting together a show RUNDOWN. Here, the computer keeps a running total of segment times, and allows segments to be mixed, moved, shortened, or lengthened until the program comes out balanced and on time. A press of a button then

```
PRODUCER:
C.B. DE MERDE   - $ 50000

DIRECTOR:
HARRY FLEX    - $ 25000

ASSOC. PROD.:
TRIXIE LA FLAME
45 DAY X $150/DAY = $6750

OFFICE RENT:
PROD. OFFICE
2 MONTH X $750/MONTH = $1500

TELEPHONE:
        - $ 1000

SCRIPT RIGHTS:
        - $ 7500

XEROXES:
        - $ 400
```

```
ABOVE-THE-LINE SUBTOTAL - $  198,600.00

 PRODUCTION SUBTOTAL - $  120,055.00

 POST PROD. SUBTOTAL - $   22,695.00
                          ------------
BELOW-THE-LINE SUBTOTAL - $  142,750.00
                          ------------
        TOTAL BUDGET = $   341,350.00


  <PRESS SPACE BAR TO RETURN TO MENU>
```

A final budget as approved.

```
WHAT NEEDS CHANGING?

1-EXEC.PROD.  18-MISC.OFF.  35-TALENT#10
2-PRODUCER    19-WRITERS    36-EXTRAS
3-DIRECTOR    20-SC.EDITR.  37-STNT/DBLS
4-ASSOC.PROD  21-REWRITE    38-WLFR/TCHR
5-LEGAL       22-SC.RIGHTS  39-OTHR.TAL
6-AS.TO PROD  23-PENS.WGA   40-CAST P/FR
7-PROG.SECT.  24-XEROXES    41-PLW-AFTRA
8-PROD.MGR.   25-MISC.SCR   42-MISC.CAST
9-PR.STAFF#1  26-TALENT #1  43-MUS.RGHTS
10-PR.STAFF#2 27-TALENT #2  44-MUS.ARRGT
11-PR.STAFF#3 28-TALENT #3  45-MUS.PERFM
12-PR.STAFF#4 29-TALENT #4  46-TX-NON PR
13-PR.STAFF#5 30-TALENT #5  47-INSURANCE
14-PENS.DGA   31-TALENT #6  48-CONTINGCY
15-PYRL.TX/FR 32-TALENT #7  49-ACCOUNTNG
16-OFF.RENT   33-TALENT #8  50-OTHER ATL
17-TELEPHONE  34-TALENT #9  51-OTHER ATL

REVISE (#) ? ■
```

The current budget program includes 131 categories.

```
   ###  TRACKER MENU  ###

  G - GET DATA FROM DISK

  S - SAVE RECORD TO DISK

  E - ENTER EXPENDITURES

  D - DISPLAY BUDGET/EXPENSES

  P - PRINT BUDGET/EXPENDITURES

  R - REVISE ORIGINAL BUDGET

  X - MASTER PROGRAM MENU
```

```
"THE HEARTBREAK OF FRECKLES"  #59-12
SECTION    BUDGET      SPENT    BALANCE
-------    ------      -----    -------
ABOVE   198,600.00  93,612.00 104,988.00
PROD.   120,055.00  25,193.00  94,862.00
POST     22,695.00       0.00  22,695.00
        ----------  --------- ----------
TOTALS  341,350.00 118,805.00 222,545.00
----------------------------------------
CATEGORIES OVER BUDGET AS OF 1/23/82:
ABOVE: 4,
PROD: 42,
POST:
```

A budget tracker as it would appear once production bills start to come in and
be paid. Items over budget are so indicated by brackets (< >) in right column.
```
```

prints out as many copies of the rundown as needed. Once again, the computer makes it easy to tinker with a rundown until one is satisfied, and no paper is involved until a printout is asked for.

The most complex program so far is one that promises to eventually save us literally thousands of dollars in on-line editing time.

Presently called *Apple 340,* it is a program designed to generate a paper tape containing a complete edit decision list, ready to be loaded into a computer editing system.

As detailed in the post-production section, my off-line technique involves cassette editing of a window dub of the master material for a program. Until now, the time code information for each edit taken from the SMPTE display in the video was noted on a paper log form with the numbers then entered manually on the on-line editing system's keyboard.

With the use of the *Apple 340* program, the numbers will be entered on the computer keyboard, and at the end of the session, the system will spit out a paper tape of the edit. Since an average editing session might involve perhaps an hour of actually entering the time codes on the on-line keyboard, at current rates the new program could easily save us $200–$300 per production, or more.

The name *Apple 340* is a tip of the hat to both the manufacturer of our computer, and to CMX. The program is patterned after the operation of the CMX 340 editing system, and operates much the same as a 340 with the record

```
        PROGRAM SCHEDULE/RUNDOWN

                CHOICES:

    N - ASSEMBLE NEW PROGRAM LIST
    F - DISK FILING SYSTEM
    P - FILE PRINTING SYSTEM
    D - DISPLAY FILE
    R - REVISE FILE
    X - MASTER PROGRAM MENU
```

```
*SAMPLE PROGRAM RUNDOWN*
SEGMENT #1 -
OPENING TITLES WITH THEME
            LENGTH - :45      TOTAL - 0:45

SEGMENT #2 -
HOST MONOLOG & INTRO SHOW
            LENGTH - 4:15     TOTAL - 5:00

SEGMENT #3 -
COMMERCIAL BREAK # 1
            LENGTH - 2:00     TOTAL - 7:00

SEGMENT #4 -
HOST INTERVIEW FIRST GUEST
            LENGTH - 3:30     TOTAL - 10:30

SEGMENT #5 -
GUEST PERFORMANCE (BELLY DANCING)
            LENGTH - 2:30     TOTAL - 13:00
```

```
        *SAMPLE PROGRAM RUNDOWN*
                        TOTAL SO FAR
                            7:00
    ITEM #4:

[HOST INTERVIEW FIRST GUEST ,

    LENGTH:

    MINUTES: 3    SECONDS: 30


    SEGMENT LENGTH      NEW TOTAL
        3:30              10:30

    IS ABOVE CORRECT? ■
```

The Rundown program allows segments to be moved, or their items or lengths changed, at will.

```
                "APPLE 50 SAMPLE EDIT DISPLAY"
 023
                          IN              OUT
 A / V    REC         01:51:18:14

 DIS

 B>A   ¥A-002        02:14:55:12   02:15:43:20
 030   B-004         04:27:48:16

       AUX

       BLACK

 ▮ 022 02 B C        02:13:25:18 02:13:25:18
                     01:49:48:20 01:49:48:20
   022 04 B D    030 04:26:18:22 04:27:48:16
                     01:49:48:20 01:51:18:14
```

Apple 340 program.

function turned off. No machines are controlled, and hitting "record" simply stores the edit in memory. Like the 340, edits can be opened and changed, and the *Apple 340* program will RIPPLE, or update, the list. Aside from some keyboard differences, though, and some minor changes on the CRT display, one could be working on a CMX 340 as far as the system's reactions are concerned. Any competent computer editor would quickly feel at home on the system. Edit decision lists can be stored on disk (alas, the disks are not compatible with the CMX floppy format, hence the old-fashioned though quite standard paper tape). The paper tape and the printout are indistinguishable from those generated on a CMX or other standard editing system.

We're constantly looking for other applications for the computer, and new ones keep suggesting themselves almost weekly. We recently converted our invoicing to a custom computer program, and will eventually hand over all bookkeeping to the computer.

Overall, the computer has been a tremendous asset for us, and has more than paid for itself in less than a year. Personally, I find that

I enjoy the logic of the machine, and I've become fairly fluent in BASIC. I'm about at the point where I'm ready to tackle ASSEMBLY LANGUAGE and/or PASCAL, Assembly Language being a large step closer to the machine's internal language, while Pascal is a faster and higher-level language than BASIC. In fact, if it weren't for the fact that I love television production so much, I could easily envision myself turning to advanced programming as a business.

Partially, though, I am constrained by the fact that it isn't the computer itself so much that fascinates me as it is what the computer can do for us in practical terms. Since becoming involved, I've met a number of total computer fanatics, some of whom seem completely wrapped up with computers, often to the exclusion of most everything else. I can understand this, but don't share their total depth of interest. To me, computers are a means—not an end.

In the area of microcomputers, the bulk of the software available seems to be games, some of which are extraordinarily complex and quite sophisticated. Personally, I have very little interest in computer games, which sometimes earns me some odd looks if I bring up the fact in a computer store. I ran the Star Trek game that came with the Apple a few times late at night after the work was done and it was time to unwind, but it's a lot like having a videotape of a Star Trek episode: how many times can you watch it?

Our little Apple works for us, and works well. We're considering the possibility of marketing the programs mentioned above, sharing the usefulness of computer applications with other producers and companies. Eventually, we'll apply the computer to camera motion control and to graphics, blending the two into some intriguing animation and motion graphics concepts we've been kicking around. One company in San Francisco, for instance, has an Apple controlling six different movements of an animation camera, and the new Apple III has the ability to support high-resolution NTCS video. These and others are applications of computer technology that will help us do a better job at our business of television production.

One of the points made in the PBS show I mentioned at the beginning of this Appendix, and during the marvelous *Fast Forward* PBS program that came out of Toronto, was that, in the next five years or so, anyone who doesn't understand the basics of computers will be functionally illiterate. Although the new generations of computers will be so easy to use with their packaged software that many people will make daily use of them without knowing what makes them tick, there's a certain validity to the thought. Computers become friendly when the programs they run are designed for the specific applications involved, and for the people who will be using them. Unusual requirements, such as the production environment, make it desirable to either know something about programming, or to have someone around who does.

Beyond all this, though, in addition to being useful, computers can be a lot of fun.

5000 IF SECTION DOES NOT MAKE SENSE, THEN GOTO BEGINNING AND RE-READ
5005 END OF SECTION

APPENDIX D

Other Applications

Teleconferencing

If you've ever participated in a telephone conference call, then you've had an exposure to teleconferencing. The basic definition of the technique is communication between more than two parties at distant locations by electronic means. Increasingly, however, the term is used to indicate an audio/video link between locations.

Teleconferencing does not indicate any particular method of signal transmission, but, rather, the net result—a video and audio connection, without regard for how the signals get from one place to another. The Bell System, for example, offers their Picturephone Meeting Service, which connects a series of specially equipped Bell-owned conference rooms in major cities together via two-way video and audio channels. Users of the service gather at PMS locations in their respective cities, and conduct "face-to-face" meetings by electronic proxy.

In the past few years, however, the term has increasingly come to be understood as indicating the use of satellite signal delivery, and this is where the main action will be in the future. The reason is simple: satellites can deliver voice and picture at a far lower cost than "land lines" (the long-distance wire and microwave system operated by AT&T).

The use of satellites has become a major factor in entertainment, and is becoming ever more important in business uses of television. Pay cable companies such as Home Box Office, Showtime, Warner-Amex, and others owe their successes to the ability to use satellite technology. The distribution of programs by satellite makes their operation feasible; distribution of programming via videotape or AT&T land lines would be prohibitively expensive for these operators. In the past few years they have been joined by a growing number of corporate, educational, and governmental users, who have found that satellites can give them the ability to lash together an "instant network." This permits them to distribute even a single program to all parts of the country simultaneously, and at a reasonable cost.

The basic technology involved is rather elegant. Communications satellites are "parked" in an orbit approximately 22,300 miles above the equator. At that height, their orbits precisely match the earth's rotation, so that they appear stationary with respect to any location. This is called a "geosynchronous orbit." On board each of the satellites are devices called "transponders," that, in the simplest terms, consist of a receiver and a transmitter. Each satellite provides generally either 12 or 24 channels. Some of the major communications satellites include Westars I, II, and III, operated by Western Union; Satcom 1, 2, and 3R (a replacement for the satellite that was literally lost in space in 1980), operated variously by RCA or its leaseholders; and Comstar D2, operated by Comsat General.

On earth, the basic equipment required to use a satellite consists of an UPLINK, or earth station transmitter, and a DOWNLINK, or receiver, also known as a TVRO (Television Receive-Only) unit. The equipment needed to establish an uplink is rather on the expensive side, with the result that most uplinks are operated by major communications companies. On the other hand, the cost of the hardware required to receive satellite programming has been continuously reduced, to the point where it's now possible to buy a TVRO kit for as little as $2500—the type that are sprouting up in affluent back yards across the country. Business communicators are turning to satellite teleconferencing for the most basic of reasons: cost. As an example, if a company has an important message to get out to 20,000 employees at 20 different locations across the country, there are essentially four alternatives:

Option 1. Bring all of the employees to a central location. This would be ruinously expensive, logistically nightmarish, and is thus obviously out of the question.

Option 2. Take the presentation around to all 20 locations. Feasible, but very time-consuming for the executives, and still rather expensive.

Option 3. Produce and distribute a videotape of the presentation. This has been the most common approach, but it has some major drawbacks, in that it does not provide any opportunity for the employees to conduct a dialog with the executives during the presentation, and inevitably entails a delay in producing the program and getting it out to the audience.

Option 4. Hold a satellite teleconference.

Doing the latter can save tens of thousands of dollars compared with either of the first two alternatives, and is more efficient, productive, and not necessarily much more expensive than the third. Increasingly, this is the route being taken.

Applications of satellite teleconferences are still being developed and discovered, but some of the more common already being exploited include:

● Corporate communications
● Management training
● Medical training
● Stockholder meetings
● Sales presentations
● Educational uses

There are a number of companies that provide satellite teleconferencing services for corporate and other users. The common practice is to take a video feed provided by the company's video department (or from hired facilities), and send it via land lines or microwave to an earth station uplink, where it is sent to the satellite. At the receiving end, there are several options. The TVRO stations can be rented for the day, or the local meeting can be held at a facility that has an earth station already in place. One such company is HI-NET (a wholly owned subsidiary of Holiday Inns) that operates 170 satellite receiving stations at hotels across the country.

Two-way video/audio teleconferencing is not unheard of, but is usually not necessary. Instead, the common practice is to provide one-way video and two-way audio, allowing those at the viewing end of a teleconference to participate.

While satellite teleconferencing can, as we've seen, be inexpensive compared with its alternatives, at present it's still cost-effective only on a relatively large scale. Given the costs of hardware, production, satellite time, reception, and display, it's rather unlikely that this will be changing. It's a technique that is currently and will continue to be best applied by large businesses and organizations.

On the other hand, when Direct Broadcast Satellite (DBS) arrives, as mentioned in the chapter on distribution, it may be possible for independent producers to make use of teleconferencing-type technology. Note the word "may" in that sentence. The question of whether or not this happens will hinge on the structure that evolves to administer the available channels. While it's possible that a channel could be rented for a specific length of time on one of these new satellites, the chances are that the channels will be leased by major corporations. The corporations will establish networks that will be as tightly controlled as the current commercial networks. At present, the field is still too new and the stakes much too high to be making predictions with any certainty. The only thing that is certain is that teleconferencing and similar technologies will have a growing impact on the way we live and work.

Interactive Video

One of the major advantages long recognized in using video for training and education has been the student's ability to control the tape, and thus the speed of a lesson. If a sec-

tion of a lesson was not clear, the student could rewind the tape and view the section repeatedly, until it made sense. This is what made ½-inch and ¾-inch videotape such a success in the industrial and educational fields.

In the most basic sense, the term "interactive video" describes any system whereby the viewer interacts with the program material, and manual control of a VTR would squeak by as qualifying under the definition. In practice, however, what the term really signifies is a system that places control of the program material under the direction of some sort of a controller—a program locator, or a computer.

Interactive video can be based either on videotape or video discs. The majority of applications use tape, simply because disc requires high volume to be cost effective. In either case, the results are essentially the same, although each format offers some distinct advantages and disadvantages—matters we'll return to a bit later.

At the basic level, the hardware consists of a videocassette player and a program locator. Examples of the latter would include the Sony model **RX-353 Auto Search Control,** and the **Video-Dex 2040** from **Videodetics.** These units are capable of automatically searching to and playing as many as 60 or more separate program segments. Thus, a lesson booklet written for a program might direct the student to "segment 28", for example. The student merely enters that segment number, and the controller then automatically shuttles the tape to the proper location and plays the segment. With videotape, the controller uses control track pulses to find its way around the tape; whereas with video discs, frame numbers that are encoded on the disc are used.

The real power of interactive video is seen with the application of what has come to be known as CAVI (Computer-Aided Video Instruction). The basic operation is similar to using a program locator, but the added power comes from the computer. In these applications, an entire lesson is written, with the work being shared by the computer and the videotape machine. The lesson exists both as a computer program, and as a program on videotape. The monitor used may at times display information generated by the computer, the

352

playback signal from videotape, or even a combination of the two. In a typical example of a CAVI lesson, for instance, the computer will play a section of a tape, and then stop the playback to ask the student questions. If the questions are answered correctly, the computer then moves on to the next section, plays it, asks new questions, etc. If the question is answered incorrectly, the computer would then either repeat the playback of the program section, or play a remedial section—depending on how the computer and videotape programs were designed—and ask the questions again. This is called "branching," in that each set of responses to questions will cause the computer to react according to the responses, with the possible actions resembling the branches of a tree.

CAVI depends upon the random access capabilities of either tape or disc, and it's here that the disc has some advantages resulting from extremely rapid access time. So far, all interactive video disc systems employ the optical laser disc format, which is ideally suited for CAVI. With the access time of videocassettes limited by tape fast forward and rewind times, the net operating speed will be slower than disc, although careful arrangement of the tape segments and branching, along with care in writing the computer programs, can make this a minor factor. On the plus side for tape is the ability to custom design programs even in single quantity, and to easily change and update programs without having to produce entirely new masters—something that would be an expensive proposition with discs.

The simplest and least expensive CAVI systems use a dedicated computer, and may or may not display information on the screen. The **Video Responder** system and its accessories from Sony do, for instance, while the **RAM Series** systems from **Instructional Industries, Inc.** do not.

More advanced CAVI systems are designed to interface standard microcomputer units, such as those from Apple Computer, Inc., Radio Shack® Division of Tandy Corp. Inc., Atari, etc., with videocassette units in either Beta, VHS, or ¾-inch U-Matic formats. They include an INTERFACE CARD (a printed circuit board with cables attached) that plugs into the computer and connects it to the VCR. They also usually provide some level of SOFTWARE (computer program) support. The hot items these days are what are known as "authoring languages," which permit those who are not computer wizards to write a program for instructional purposes without having to know computer languages such as BASIC, Pascal, etc.

The hardware that has been developed for interactive video is also finding its way into other applications. Sears Roebuck and Company, for instance, now has a complete catalog on videodisc, allowing customers to enter a number on a keypad to see products on a TV screen. Some products are shown as still frames, while others are shown in real-time playback. The same basic design could produce a video magazine that could combine still-frame "pages" of copy with real-time playback for pieces that warrant moving pictures.

Computer-Aided Video Instruction is already having a major impact on education and training, and that impact will continue to grow. It permits students to learn at their own pace, and in some ways provides an electronic form of individual attention that a flesh-and-blood teacher may not be able to give. Although they will not replace human teachers in the foreseeable future, they present a powerful tool that can help teachers do their job more efficiently and effectively.

Since the hardware now exists to control a VCR with a computer, it would also be rather simple to devise a computer program that could turn almost any microcomputer into a fairly powerful control track editor. Scenes could be logged and given an identifying name, and the decision list capabilities could approach those of a full-scale computer editor. Even SMPTE code could conceivably be used. Will the day come when an Apple II will replace a CMX 340X? It's not likely, but microcomputers like the Apple could quite possibly take the place of control track editing units.

APPENDIX E

Manufacturers' Addresses

AMERICAN DATA
401 Wynn Dr.
Huntsville, AL 35805

AMPEX CORP
401 Broadway
Redwood City, CA 94063

AMTEL SYSTEMS, INC.
29-16 Connell Ct.
Toronto, Ontario, Canada M8Z 517

ANTON BAUER
66 Center St.
Shelton, CT 06484

ANVIL CASES, INC.
P.O. Box 888
Rosemead, CA 91770

ARRIFLEX CORP.
500 Rt. 303
Blauvelt, NY 10913

ARVIN/ECHO
485 E. Middlefield Rd.
Mountainview, CA 94043

ASACA
1277 Rand Rd.
Des Plaines, IL 60016

BARCO VIDEO SYSTEMS
Rohde & Schwarz
14 Gloria Lane
Fairfield, NJ 07006

BTX
12 Huron Dr.
Natick, MA 01760

CHYRON CORP
265 Spagnoli
Melville, NY 11747

CINE 60, Inc.
630 9th Ave.
New York, NY 10036

CINEMA PRODUCTS
2307 Granville Ave.
Los Angeles, CA 90025

CMX (ORROX CORP)
3303 Scott Blvd.
Santa Clara, CA 95050

COLORTRAN
1015 Chestnut St.
Burbank, CA 91502

COMPREHENSIVE VIDEO SUPPLY
148 Veterans Dr.
Northvale, NJ 07647

COMPUTER GRAPHIC LAB.
Chrysler Bldg. 59th Floor
405 Lexington Ave.
New York, NY 10174

CONVERGENCE CORPORATION
1641 McGraw
Irvine, CA 92714

CROSSPOINT LATCH CORP.
316 Broad St.
Summit, NJ 07901

DATATRON, INC.
2942 Dow Ave.
Tustin, CA 92680

DIGITAL VIDEO SYSTEMS, INC.
716 Gordon Baker Rd.
Toronto, Ontario, Canada M2H 3B4

DYNAIR ELECTRONICS
5275 Market St.
San Diego, CA 92114

FAROUDJA LABORATORIES
946 Benicia Ave.
Sunnyvale, CA 94086

FERNSEH
Robert Bosch Corporation
6300 Arizona Circle
Los Angeles, CA 90045

GRASS VALLEY GROUP, INC.
PO Box 1114
Grass Valley, CA 95945

HITACHI DENSHI AMERICA, LTD.
175 Crossways Park
Woodbury, NY 11797

HME
6151 Fairmont Ave.
San Diego, CA 92120

IKEGAMI ELECTRONICS
37 Brook Ave.
Maywood, NJ 07607

JVC
41 Slater Dr.
Elmwood Park, NJ 07407

KANGAROO PRODUCTS
9190 Manor Dr.
La Mesa, CA 92041

LOWEL-LIGHT MFG, INC.
475 Tenth Ave.
New York, NY 10018

LYON LAMB
8255 Beverly Blvd.
Los Angeles, CA 90048

MICROTIME, INC.
1280 Blue Hills Ave.
Bloomfield, CT 06002

MOLE RICHARDSON
937 N. Sycamore Ave.
Hollywood, CA 90038

NEC AMERICA, INC.
130 Martin Lane
Elkgrove Village, IL 60007

O'CONNOR ENGINEERING LABS
10 Kalmus Dr.
Costa Mesa, CA 92626

PANASONIC CO.
One Panasonic Way
Sesaucus, NY 07094

PORTA BRACE (K & H PRODUCTS)
Box 246
North Bennington, VT 05257

MCI QUANTEL
P.O. Box 10057
Palo Alto, CA 94303

RANK CINTEL
20 Bushes Lane
Elmwood Park, NJ 07407

RCA
Building 2-2A
Camden, NJ 08102

RECORTEC, INC.
475 Ellis St.
Mountain View, CA 94043

SENNHEISER ELECTRONICS
10 W. 37th St.
New York, NY 10018

SHARP ELECTRONICS CORP.
10 Sharp Plaza
Paramus, NJ 07652

SHURE BROTHERS INC.
222 Hartrey Ave.
Evanston, IL 60204

SONY CORP.
9 W. 57th St.
New York, New York 10019

TEKTRONIX, INC.
PO Box 500
Beaverton, OR 97077

THERMODYNE INTERNATIONAL
12600 Yukon Ave.
Hawthorne, CA 90250

THOMSON-CSF, Inc.
37 Brown House Rd.
Stamford, CT 06902

3-M
223 5N-01 Mag A/V
St. Paul, MN 55144

TOSHIBA AMERICA, INC.
292 Gibraltar Dr.
Sunnyvale, CA 94086

VIDEOMEDIA, INC.
250 N. Wolfe Rd.
Sunnyvale, CA 94086

Glossary

A/B ROLLING—In video editing, indicates two VTRs playing two source tapes, to allow for dissolves, wipes, etc., between them.

A.D.—Assistant Director, Art Director.

A.D.R.—(Automatic Dialog Replacement)—A system used in looping (replacing) actors' dialog.

A.F.M.—American Federation of Musicians, a union.

A.F.T.R.A.—American Federation of Television and Radio Artists, a union.

A.G.C.—(Automatic Gain Control) A circuit that automatically adjusts input levels, either for audio or video.

A.P.—Associate Producer, Assistant Producer.

A.P.L.—Average Picture Level.

A.S.C.A.P.—American Society of Composers, Authors and Publishers, a music licensing organization.

A.S.T.D.—American Society of Training Directors.

A.T.A.S.—Academy of Television Arts and Sciences.

A.T.R.—Audio Tape Recorder.

ABOVE THE LINE—A section of a budget dealing with the creative and artistic personnel and items.

ACADEMY LEADER—Film leader that features countdown numbers to aid in cuing the film prior to use. Also called SMPTE leader.

ACE—A 1000-watt fresnel light.

ACTION AXIS—An imaginery line drawn between two actors or along a line of motion as an aid in establishing continuity of screen direction.

ADDITIVE COLOR—The system of colored light, as used in television, where the basic color primaries are added to make white.

AMBIENCE—The natural background sounds found everywhere, which are part of the recorded audio.

ANALOG—Describes an electrical signal that is continuously variable in strength.

ANIMATIC—Limited animation, consisting of artwork shot and edited to serve as a videotaped storyboard. Commonly used for producing test commercials.

ANIMATION—The recording of one to several frames at a time, changing or moving artwork or models, etc., between frames, to create the appearance of movement upon playback.

APERTURE—The variable opening in a lens used to control the amount of light to be passed to the focal plane. Also called the IRIS.

APPLE BOX—One of several sizes of sturdy wooden boxes ranging from about 2 inches to 8 inches in height, used to support equipment and set elements, along with numerous other uses.

ARC—Movement of a camera in an arcing, or circular movement, usually around the subject.

ARC LIGHT—A high-intensity light that uses a carbon arc for illumination.

ASPECT RATIO—The ratio of height to width—in television, 3:4.

ASSEMBLE EDIT—An edit wherein all existing signals on a tape (if any) are replaced with new signals.

ATTENUATE—To reduce the strength of a signal.

AUDIO—The sound portion of a program.

AUDITION—1. To try out for a part as talent. 2. To preview or listen to a sound before using it in a production.

AUTO ASSEMBLE—An operation in which a computer performs editing unaided, working from a previously prepared edit decision list.

AUTO IRIS—Automatic Iris, a system that automatically adjusts the aperature of a lens according to the brightness of the scene being shot.

AUTOMATIC BEAM CONTROL—A circuit that provides dynamic control of the beam in a camera pickup tube to reducing lag and comet tailing. Also called Auto Beam Optimization, and known as A.B.C. or A.B.O.

B.M.I.—Broadcast Music Incorporated, a music licensing organization.

B-ROLL—A duplicate copy of original footage made to permit A/B roll editing.

BABY—A small fresnel lighting instrument, generally 750–1000 watts.

BACK LIGHT—A light placed over and behind a subject to help define the subject from the background.

BACKGROUND LIGHT—A light used to light the background.

BACKTIME—To determine the starting time of an element (such as a musical piece) by subtracting its length from the program time at which it should end.

BANDING—A picture abberation (on TV screen) consisting of a series of horizontal lines sometimes seen upon playback of a tape in a segmented format, such as quad.

BARNDOORS—Metal flaps mounted on lighting instruments, used to control the spread of light.

BARS (See Colorbars.)

BARTER—A system of financial arrangements used in program syndication, where use of the program by a station is traded for commercial spots within the program.

BATTEN—Pipes on which lighting instruments are hung.

BEAM—The electron beam inside a camera pickup tube, and inside a receiver or monitor picture tube.

BELOW THE LINE—A section of a budget dealing with the technical elements and crew.

BETA (Betamax)—The ½-inch videocassette system developed by Sony for consumer and industrial use.

BIAS LIGHT—Small lights built into a camera or contained within its pickup tubes, directed at the tubes' targets to help reduce image lag.

BINARY—A system of counting using a series of on/off, or 1/0 pulses.

BIT—A single binary pulse.

BLACK BOX—The generic slang term for pieces of electronic equipment with no moving parts—usually referring to signal processing equipment.

BLACK LEVEL—The electrical signal level defined as representing black in a picture—usually set at 7.5 IEEE units.

BLANKING—The portions of the video signal during which both the camera and receiver complete a line (horizontal blanking) or a field (vertical blanking), and retrace to begin the next scan.

BLOCKING—The placement and movement of both talent and camera positions prior to and during production.

BOOM—1. A device used to raise a camera above normal tripod range. (See Crane.) 2. A device used to extend a microphone near talent.

BOOMING—The act of raising or lowering the camera prior to or during a take.

BRIGHTNESS—1. The measure of how bright an object appears. 2. The overall level of brightness to which a monitor or receiver is adjusted.

BROAD—Generic term for several types of lights, often open-faced quartz lights, that provide a large, wide source of illumination.

BROKER—A system of financial arrangements in program syndication, where air time is purchased from a station, and the producer or his agents sell commercial time within the program.

BRUTE—A high-powered lighting instrument.

BUMP—1. To transfer, or dub, from one tape or channel to another. 2. To alter the synchronization of tapes by one or more frames during editing.

BURKE—A test of audience reaction to a commercial, often a test commercial.

BURN—Noun: A flaw in a camera pickup tube caused by extended exposure to a bright light source. Verb: To "burn a take" is to re-record over it when it has been determined to be worthless.

BURST—(See Color Burst.)

BUS (Alternate: BUSS)—A row of buttons on a switcher representing the various input signals.

BYTE—A digital "word," made up of a group of bits usually comprised of either 8 or 16 bits.

C-47—A common crew slang term for a spring-type clothespin.

C-MOUNT—A threaded lens mount used on some film and video cameras.

C-STAND—A stand used to hold lighting and other equipment.

C.C.D. (Charge Coupled Device)—Integrated circuits, one variety of which can be used in place of pickup tubes in camera imaging.

C.C.U.—Camera Control Unit.

C.G.—(See Character Generator.)

C.R.T. (Cathode Ray Tube)—A vacuum tube containing an electron gun that is aimed at a screen coated with phosphors that glow when struck by electrons. Used for TV picture tubes, waveform, and vector displays.

C.U.—Closeup.

CALL SHEET—A sheet listing call times (times due on the set) for cast and crew, usually issued daily for the next day's work.

CAM LINK HEAD—A camera mounting head that uses cams to provide counterbalance for medium to large cameras.

CAMEO LIGHTING—Lighting the subject in front of a completely black background.

CAMERA CONTROL UNIT (CCU)—Controls that allow a camera to be adjusted from a remote location, usually the control room or production truck.

CANS—Slang term for headphones.

CAPSTAN—The rotating shaft that, in concert with a pinch roller, pulls tape through a VTR or ATR.

CAPSTAN SERVO—A circuit that precisely controls the rotating speed of the capstan.

CARDIOID MICROPHONE—A microphone with a heart-shaped pickup pattern.

CARTRIDGE (Cart)—An endless-loop tape enclosed in a plastic shell, used in radio and television broadcasting.

CATTLE CALL—Slang term for an open audition, usually widely publicized.

CELS—Sheets of acetate, commonly used in animation and preparing graphics.

CHARACTER GENERATOR—An electronic typewriter that creates letters and other graphic elements in the form of a video signal for use in production.

CHEAT—Repositioning talent, an object, or the camera to improve a shot.

CHROMAKEY—A method of shooting an object or person against a solid colored background, whereby the background is electronically replaced by another video signal.

CHROMINANCE—The color portion of a composite video signal.

CLIP—1. The control that determines at what brightness level a signal will be keyed. 2. The process of compressing a brightness level, usually when it would otherwise be unacceptably high.

COLOR BLACK—A black signal containing full sync, color burst, and a black level of 7.5 IEEE units. Also known as Crystal Black.

COLOR BURST—A sample of the color subcarrier that is inserted into the horizontal blanking interval at the start of each line of video.

COLOR TEMPERATURE—The mix of various colors contained in "white" light, generally referring to the amounts of red and blue, measured in degrees Kelvin.

COLOR UNDER—The heterodyne color process used in videocassette recorders, whereby the 3.58 MHz color frequency is converted down to a lower frequency, and then reconstructed upon playback.

COLORBARS—A standard color test signal containing samples of the primary and secondary colors in television, plus black and (usually) white.

COMET TAILING—Streaking in the picture created by movement of a bright object, and having the appearance of a comet tail.

COMP—Short for an actor's Composite, a sheet containing several photographs of the actor in various clothing and moods.

COMPOSITE VIDEO—The full video signal, including sync, colorburst, and picture information.

COMPOSITION—The art and science of creating pictures that are pleasing and/or effective, as necessary.

COMPRESSION—In audio, the practice of reducing the dynamic range of sound, sometimes for expansion at a later point (a transmission technique), and sometimes to boost the entire audio level of commercials to an annoyingly high (and attention-getting) level.

CONFORMING—Performing final editing using an off-line edited master as a guide. (see Auto Assembly.)

CONTINGENCY—A budget category that, with luck, will cover unexpected costs.

CONTINUITY—The flow of action, sound, etc., from one scene or shot to the next.

CONTRAST—The ratio of bright to dark areas within a picture.

CONTROL TRACK—The "electronic sprocket holes" recorded on videotape to guide the heads during playback.

COOKIE—(See Cucalorus.)

CRAB DOLLY—A camera support on which all wheels can be steered, allowing it to be moved in various directions while maintaining its orientation to the subject.

CRADLE HEAD—A camera mounting head designed for medium to large cameras.

CRANE—A device that allows a range of camera height from very low to very high.

CRASH CART—A cart that holds a VTR, batteries, monitor, and/or other accessories, allowing for very quick transport and setup.

CRASH EDIT—An edit that is electronically unstable, such as one made by using the pause control on a VTR, or using a noncapstan servoed VTR.

CRAWL—In graphics, information moving horizontally through the picture, usually at the bottom.

CRYSTAL BLACK (See Color Black.)

CUCALORUS—A metal or glass disc containing a pattern that is inserted into an ellipsoidal light to project that pattern, as onto a curtain.

CUE—1. A signal given to talent by the floor director to take or end some action. 2. The act of positioning tape or film so that it is ready to be used (as in a live show, or during editing).

CUE CARD—A card with performer's lines printed on it, held or placed near the camera for the performer to read.

CUT—1. An instantaneous transition from one picture to another. 2. To stop the tape and all action, such as after a take. 3. A section of a tape or a record.

CUTAWAY—A shot that can serve to cover an edit, such as one of an interviewer, or of an item being discussed.

CYCLORAMA (CYC)—A continuous surface that presents an unbroken background. Curtains are commonly used as Cycs, while the term "hard cyc" describes two or more smooth walls with rounded corners and coved bases that blend with the floor.

D.A. (Distribution Amplifier)—An audio or video amplifier that accepts a single input signal, and provides several identical output signals, usually in multiples of four.

dB (See Decibel).

D.B.S. (Direct Broadcast Satellite)—A distribution system whereby satellite broadcasts are received in the home by a small dish antenna.

D.G.A.—Director's Guild of America, a union.

D.O.C.—Drop Out Compensator, a circuit that minimizes the visual effect of tape dropouts.

D.P.—Director of Photography.

D.V.E.—Digital Video Effects (also the tradename for the digital effects units marketed by NEC and The Grass Valley Group).

D.V.R.—Digital Video Recorder.

DAILIES—Quickly made copies of the day's work made for the director and others to view either that evening or the next day.

DEADPOT—In audio, to play a source with the mixer's potentiometer turned down until the source is needed. Usually done when backtiming an audio source.

DECIBEL—A unit of measure applied to both sound and electrical signals, based on a logarithmic scale.

DEMO REEL—A videotape containing samples of a person's or company's work. Also called a Demo Tape, Sample Reel, etc.

DEPTH OF FIELD—The range (in distance from the lens) that will be acceptably sharp. Varies with distance, focal length of the lens, and aperature.

DEUCE—A 2000-watt lighting instrument, usually a fresnel type.

DICHROIC MIRROR—A mirror that transmits light of one color, and reflects light of all other colors. Used in low-priced color cameras.

DIFFUSION FILTER—A filter that diffuses light, creating a fog-like effect.

DIGITAL—A system whereby a continuously variable (analog) signal is broken down and encoded into discrete binary bits that represent a mathematical model of the original signal.

DIGITAL EFFECTS—Effects, such as picture compression, rotation, reversal, etc., performed with a digital effects system.

DIRECT COLOR—A recording system whereby the color subcarrier signal is recorded directly without conversion to a lower frequency, as opposed to heterodyne color. Requires a recorder with high bandwidth capabilities.

DISSOLVE—The gradual fading out of one signal simultaneous with the fading in of another signal.

DIVERSITY ANTENNA—A multiple-antenna receiving system used with wireless microphones.

DOLLY—Noun: A camera support mounted on wheels to allow smooth movement. Verb: The act of moving the camera towards or away from the subject.

DOWNSTREAM KEYER—A keyer that acts on the final signal of a switcher, after all other mix/effects banks. Usually also provides a master fade-to-black of the final switcher output.

DROP FRAME—A type of SMPTE time code designed to match clock time exactly. Two frames of code are dropped every minute on the minute except the tenth minute, to correct for the fact that color frames occur at a rate of 29.97 per second, rather than an exact 30 frames per second. (See Nondrop Frame.)

DROPOUT—A patch of missing oxide on a videotape, seen as a white speck or streak in the picture.

DUB—Noun: A copy of a tape. Verb: To copy a tape, or to add new audio to an existing tape.

E TO E—Electronics To Electronics, meaning that the incoming signal is passed directly through a device without being affected (usually as with a VTR).

E.B.U.—European Broadcasting Union, the European equivalent of SMPTE.

E.C.U.—Extreme Closeup.

E.D.L.—Edit Decision List, the list of edits prepared during off-line editing prior to on-line editing.

E.I.A.J.—Electronic Industries Association of Japan, an industry body that devised the original ½-inch open reel tape format standards.

E.F.P. (Electronic Field Production)—The practice of applying film-style production techniques (commonly single-camera) to videotape production.

E.F.X.—Short for Effects.

E.N.G. (Electronic News Gathering)—The technique of using video equipment in place of 16mm film equipment for news production. Generally describes a package of a battery-operated camera and VTR used by a small crew that can move, setup, and shoot quickly.

EDGE NUMBERS—Numbers either pre-exposed or printed along the edge of film to aid in locating a scene during editing, and for synchronizing picture and sound.

ELLIPSOIDAL—A type of focusing lighting instrument that produces a hard light with distinct edges. Also called a Leko.

ENCODER—A circuit that combines the primary red, green, and blue signals into a composite color video signal.

EQUALIZATION—In audio, the balancing of various frequencies to create a more pleasing sound, by attenuating or boosting specific frequencies within the sound. In video, has several meanings, mainly related to correcting errors of signal nonlinearity over a transmission path, and adjustments to match the performance of various playback heads on a VTR.

EQUALIZER—In audio, a device that performs equalization.

ESSENTIAL AREA—The area in the center of a picture that will be seen on virtually all receivers, regardless of possible poor adjustment.

ESTABLISHING SHOT—A shot showing an overall view of a location, used to establish the location and/or characters to be involved. Usually a wide shot, to help familiarize the viewer with the scene.

EVENT (Editing)—In most computer editing systems, defines an action or sequence of actions performed by the computer in a single pass of the record VTR's tape.

F-STOP—The number that corresponds to the opening of a lens' aperture, and, thus, how much light is passed through the lens. The larger the opening, the smaller the F-stop number, and vice versa.

F.C.C.—Federal Communications Commission, the governing body for radio and television broadcasting.

FADE—The gradual increase or decrease of a video signal from or to black (video), or from or to silence (audio).

FADER—A lever, arm, slider, or knob that accomplishes fades.

FAX—Short for Facilities.

FEEDBACK—The phenomenon created when the output of an audio or video device is fed back to the input, creating an endless loop of the signal. In audio, usually creates a howling sound. In video, can be used for certain visual effects.

FIELD—One-half of a television frame, consisting of 262½-lines, produced at a rate of 59.94 Hz (color), or 60 Hz (black and white).

FILL LIGHT—A light used to fill in the strong shadows created by the use of a key light.

FILM CHAIN—Generically, a system combining a film projector with a television camera, used to transmit films or record them on videotape.

FILM STYLE—Refers to single-camera videotape production done scene by scene, and often out of sequence, as is done in motion picture production.

FISHPOLE—A lightweight, hand-held microphone boom.

FLAG—A dark, usually rectangular, panel used to block light, and usually made of a wire frame with black cloth stretched over it.

FLARE—A reduction of contrast and/or streaks appearing in a picture, caused by a bright light source in or near the scene being shot. Light entering the lens is reflected and scattered by the various elements and interior surfaces in the lens.

FLAT—An element used in studio set construction, traditionally made of a wooden frame with muslin stretched over it. Several flats can be combined to serve as walls, scenery, etc.

FLIP—A digital video effect whereby the picture is reversed, either prior to or during a shot.

FLUID HEAD—A tripod head on which a camera is mounted, that uses a viscous fluid controlled by a valve, to provide variable degrees of resistance to movement, thus smoothing camera moves.

FOAMCORE—A lightweight, easily cut material comprised of two sheets of smooth cardboard with a layer of foam sandwiched in between them. Commonly available in ³⁄₁₆-inch and 1-inch thicknesses.

FOCAL LENGTH—In a lens, the distance from the optical nodal point (where all light rays converge) to the focal plane (where the image is formed). A telephoto lens has a long focal length (e.g., 200mm), whereas a wide angle lens has a short focal length (e.g., 6mm). A zoom lens has a variable focal length.

FOLEY—Background sounds added during audio sweetening to heighten realism, consisting of footsteps, door slams, voices, etc.

FOLLOW SPOT—A high intensity lighting instrument designed to focus a tight beam of light and project it over a long distance. Usually used in theatres during stage productions, and to simulate the look of same.

FONT—A full set of letters and symbols of one size and all in the style of an individual typeface. Also sometimes used as shorthand slang for Character Generator.

FOOTCANDLE—A basic measure of light intensity, corresponding to the amount of light produced by one international standard candle at a distance of one foot. Equal to one lumen per square foot.

409 (Editing)—The tradename of a computer program designed for "listing cleaning," that will go through an edit decision list and eliminate any overcut edits by shortening them to match the in point of the next edit.

FRAME—A complete television picture, comprised of 525 lines, made up of two fields, produced at a rate of 29.97 Hz (color), or 30 Hz (black & white).

FRAMESTORE—A digital device designed to store and display a single television frame as a "freeze frame." A Framestore Synchronizer uses the same basic technology to accept a nonsynchronous signal and synchronize it with a second signal, such as "house sync."

FREEZE FRAME—Stopping the motion of a scene and displaying one frame for an extended period. (A field freeze displays a single field as a frame.)

FRESNEL LENS—A lens with its optical characteristics determined by a series of concentric circular planes, serving to reduce thickness compared with a normal lens. Fresnel lighting instruments allow light to be focused either in a wide (flood) or a narrow (spot) beam.

FRICTION HEAD—A tripod head on which a camera is mounted that depends upon friction to hold the camera position. Used in still photography, but poorly suited to film and video work.

GAFFER—The technician in charge of placement and rigging of all lighting instruments.

GAFFER GRIP—A clamp used to hold lights and other lightweight pieces of lighting equipment.

GAFFER's TAPE—A cloth-backed adhesive tape measuring 2 inches wide that can be used to hold virtually anything to anything. Removes from virtually all surfaces without leaving a mark. Can be wrapped around shiny metal objects to eliminate reflections. Has hundreds of other uses. Vaguely similar to common duct tape, but does not bleed "goo" after a while, and is INFINITELY superior. One of the miracles of modern production.

GAMMA—The characteristics of the response curve of a camera's pickup tube and electronics from black to peak white.

GAIN—The amount of amplification of a signal, usually accomplished at the input stage with a preamplifier featuring a variable control, such as a potentiometer.

GEARED HEAD—A tripod head on which a camera is mounted that controls camera movement with rack-and-pinion-type geared cranks. Useful for very precise control of panning and tilting.

GEL—Translucent sheets, usually colored, used to filter light. Originally made of gelatin (hence, "gel") but now usually made of plastic.

GENNY—Short for generator (electrical).

GENERATION—Distance from the original tape, in terms of how many times the material has been copied. The original is "first generation," a copy of it is "second generation," a copy of that copy is "third generation," etc.

GENLOCK—A system whereby the internal sync generator in a device (such as a camera) locks onto and synchronizes itself with an incoming signal.

GESTALT—The way in which each of the individual parts of a whole work together in such a manner that the resulting system could not function if one or more of the parts were eliminated. As used in this book, it describes the way all of the people and technology involved in production work together to create results that would be impossible if were it not for the collaborative effort.

GLITCH—A slang term for a visual disturbance in a video signal.

GOFER—Slang term for a production assistant, derived from the commonly heard command "Go for . . . (coffee, supplies, etc.)." Alternately spelled Gopher.

GRAPHICS—In general, printed material, and artwork seen on the screen.

GRIP—1. A person on the crew who handles equipment during setup, production, and strike. 2. Equipment normally handled by grips.

H.D.T.V.—High Definition Television. Describes several new systems under development that will someday provide much higher picture quality.

H.M.I. (Halogen-Metal-Iodide)—A type of lamp for use in lighting instruments that is highly efficient and low in heat output. An HMI light is usually daylight balanced (nominally 5500 K).

HARD LIGHT—Spectral light with a point source that casts a clearly defined shadow.

HEAD DRUM—The rotating drum used in VTRs that holds the video recording and playback heads.

HEADROOM (Video)—The room that should be left between the top of a person's head and the top of the frame when composing a shot. (Audio) The amount of available gain boost remaining before distortion is encountered.

HELICAL—Literally describing a helix, as in the tape path around the head drum of all but quad VTRs. Generally refers to all helical VTRs.

HERTZ (Hz)—Cycles per second.

HETERODYNE—The conversion of one frequency to another frequency, as used in the color system of videocassette recorders. (See Color Under.)

HIGH BAND—A videotape recording system that employs an FM signal deviation of 7–10 MHz for recording. Generally, a high-quality VTR. (See Direct Color.)

HORIZONTAL SYNC—The synchronizing pulses used to define each line of a television picture, occurring at a rate of approximately 15,734 Hz (color), and 15,750 Hz (black and white).

HOT SWITCHING—Slang term for live switching between multiple cameras to a single VTR during production in real time.

HUE—Color tone (red, blue, yellow, etc.).

HUM—Interference in a video or audio signal, often at the 60 Hz power line frequency.

I.A.T.S.E.—International Alliance of Theatrical Stage Employees, a union.

I.B.E.W.—International Brotherhood of Electrical Workers, a union.

I.E.E.E.—Institute of Electrical and Electronics Engineers, Inc., a professional organization.

I.F.B.—(Interruptible Feedback)—A system that allows the director to break into a program audio feed to talent.

I.O. (Image Orthicon)—An early and now obsolete type of camera pickup tube.

I.P.S.—Inches Per Second.

I.T.V.A.—International Television Association. A professional television organization.

IMAGE ENHANCER—An electronic device that enhances the apparent sharpness of a video signal by exaggerating transitions between light and dark areas in a scene.

IMPEDANCE—Resistance to the flow of an electrical current.

IN THE CAN—Originally, a film term, meaning that a program or segment has been completed.

INSERT EDIT—An edit in which existing control track is used as a reference, and video and audio signals may be recorded separately, or in any combination.

IRIS (See Aperture.)

ISO (ISOLATED)— Describes the technique during multiple-camera taping of recording the signal from each camera on a separate VTR.

JAM-SYNC—The process of synchronizing a time code generator with the code being played back on a tape, and then performing an insert edit of time code from the generator onto the tape. Usually done to extend code on the tape, or to replace bad code—in either case without disturbing the continuous count of code numbers.

JITTER—A picture abberation seen as small, fast, vertical, or horizontal shifting of a picture or part of a picture.

JUMP CUT—Any cut that visually jars or disturbs the viewer.

JUNIOR—A fresnel lighting instrument.

KELVIN—The scale by which the color temperature of light is measured.

KEY—An effect in which a circuit uses bright portions of a signal to perform electronic switching between that signal and another (internal keying), or between two other signals (external keying). (See Matte.)

KEY LIGHT—The main source of illumination, normally angled to provide shadow detail.

KEYSTONING—Perspective distortion caused by shooting a flat object, such as camera artwork, at other than a perpendicular angle.

KINESCOPE—A film shot from a television monitor. The original method of preserving video productions prior to the invention of videotape.

L.D.—Lighting Director, Lighting Designer.

L.S.—Long Shot.

LAG—The retention of an image by a camera pickup tube after the camera has been moved. Somewhat similar to Comet Tailing.

LAVALIER—A type of microphone that can be hung on a cord around talent's neck, or clipped onto clothing.

LEKO—Ellipsoidal spotlight.

LEVEL—The strength of a signal.

LIMBO LIGHTING—Lighting the subject in front of an evenly lit, indistinct, and therefore infinite-appearing background.

LIMITER—A circuit used in audio that prevents the signal level from exceeding a preset limit—usually 0 VU.

LINE—1. The high-level input to an audio mixer is also called a "line level input." 2. The main program monitor in a studio is also called a "line monitor." 3. A line generically is any signal path. 4. "The Line" is also used in

camera blocking (see Action Axis). 5. Budgets are commonly divided into above and below the line sections.

LIP SYNC—Commonly done in music taping, where performers mime to playback of pre-recorded music. Also denotes proper synchronization of video and audio.

LIST MANAGEMENT—In computer editing, the process of using the computer to rearrange edits, "clean" the list, etc.

LIVE—A program that is transmitted as it happens, with no delay.

LOCATION—Any place other than a studio used as a production setting.

LOG—A list of scenes and takes, prepared either during or after production, in preparation for editing.

LOW-CON (Low Contrast Filter)—A filter on a camera lens used to reduce contrast.

LOOKING SPACE—Space in front of talent, between them and the other side of the frame.

LOOPING—A technique used when dialog must be replaced by talent. A scene is repeated continuously so that actors can practice lip syncing to the picture. Once they are ready, the dialog is recorded.

LOW BAND—A video recording system using relatively low FM carrier frequencies, as in videocassette systems. Denotes lower quality than high band recording.

LUMEN—(See Footcandle.)

LUMINANCE—The brightness of an object determines its luminance value.

M.D.S.—(MULTIPOINT DISTRIBUTION SYSTEM)—The transmission of television programs over microwave links, usually to several receivers. Used in industrial and educational broadcasting, and in some areas for home pay-TV distribution.

M.O.S.—Slang term for silent shooting. From the bastardized German "Mit Out Sprechen"—without talking. (The correct German phrase would be "Ohne Sprechen.")

M.S.—Medium Shot.

MAGICAM®—The trademarked name for a computer-controlled system that slaves two cameras together. One camera shoots a miniature set while the other shoots actors or objects against a blue screen, for insertion electronically or photographically into the miniature background. All movements at the master camera are duplicated in scale at the slave camera.

MARKS—Places marked on the floor, usually with tape, to indicate talent and camera positions.

MASTER—Master tape is the original tape shot during production. An Edited Master is the tape onto which a program has been edited during on-line editing.

MASTER SHOT—The shot that will serve as the basic scene, and into which all cutaways and closeups will be inserted during editing. Often a wide shot showing all characters and action in the scene.

MATTE—A key in which the area being inserted into a background signal is electronically filled in with a solid color. Most titles and credits are matted in. Also called a Matte Key.

MICROPHONICS—A picture abberation appearing generally as dark horizontal bars running up or down the screen, caused by extremely loud noises near the camera. Created when the wire mesh inside the pickup tubes vibrate sympathetically with the sound.

MIKE—Short for microphone. Sometimes spelled mic.

MIX/EFFECTS BANK—The section of a switcher that performs dissolves, wipes, keys, etc.

MIXER—A device that allows various audio sources to be combined and mixed together, with their relative levels being adjusted.

MONITOR—In video, denotes a picture tube and associated circuitry, but without tuner or audio sections. In audio, is another name for a speaker.

MONOCHROME—Black and white.

MORTICE—An effect wherein a picture is compressed and surrounded by a black or colored border. Often done at the end of commercials to permit graphics to be matted into the border.

MULTIPLEXER—A device that uses a system of mirrors and/or prisms to allow a variety of slide and film projectors to feed a single camera in a Film Chain.

N.A.B.—National Association of Broadcasters, a trade association.

N.A.B.E.T.—National Association of Broadcast Employees and Technicians, a union.

N.D. FILTER—Neutral Density filter, a grey filter that reduces light intensity without affecting color.

N.G.—Short for No Good (as for indicating a bad take).

N.T.S.C.—National Television Standards Committee, the committee that established the color transmission system used in the U.S. and some other countries. Also used to indicate the system itself.

NEEDLE DROP—A unit of measure in determining payment for use of musical pieces in programs. Each time a piece of music is used in a production (in other words, each time the "needle drops" on the record), a fixed charge is assessed.

NI-CAD—Short for Nickle-cadmium, a type of battery.

NOISE—In video, a visual aberration that appears as very fine white specks (snow), and that increases over multiple generations. In audio, usually heard as hiss. Undesirable in all cases.

NONDROP FRAME—A type of SMPTE time code that runs in continuously ascending numbers, even though it will not exactly match actual elapsed time. (See Drop Frame.)

NONSEGMENTED—Those videotape formats that record a full field with each pass of the head are called nonsegmented formats.

OFF-LINE—Preliminary, or test editing, usually done on a low-cost editing system using videocassette worktapes. Performed to allow editing decisions to be made, and to gain necessary approvals prior to performing the final edit.

OMNIDIRECTIONAL—Describes a microphone that picks up sounds from all directions.

ON-LINE—Final editing, using the original master tapes to produce a finished program ready for distribution. Usually preceded by off-line editing, but in some cases programs go directly to the on-line editing stage. Usually associated with high-quality computer editing systems.

OPTICALS—A film term denoting visual effects produced optically, either in the camera or (more commonly) in the lab. These effects are done electronically in video.

OVERCRANKING—A film technique whereby the camera is run at a higher than normal speed to produce slow motion when the film is subsequently projected at normal speed.

OXIDE—The iron oxide coating on audio and video tape that magnetically stores information (pictures and sounds).

P.A.—Production Assistant.

P.A.L.—(PHASE ALTERNATION by LINE)— The color television system developed in Germany, and used by many European and other countries.

P.L. (PRIVATE LINE)—An intercom system used by crew members to communicate with each other during production.

P.O.V.—A Point of View, or subjective shot.

PACING—The apparent flow and rhythm of a program as perceived by the audience.

PAN—Camera movement on a horizontal axis from a stationary position.

PANTOGRAPH—A scissor-type extensible device used to hang lighting instruments from battens, allowing their height to be adjusted.

PAPER EDIT—A list of edits made in preparation for editing, made while viewing original material, but without actually making any edits. Normally makes use of SMPTE time code numbers.

PAPER TAPE—A 1-inch-wide tape made of paper, used to store an edit decision list in the form of a series of small holes that can be used at a later time to load the list back into a computer editing system. Also called a Punch Tape.

PATCH PANEL—A panel equipped with rows of input and output connectors, allowing signals to be routed with the use of Patch Cords. Used for Audio, Video, and Lighting.

PEAK WHITE—The brightest level of the video signal, normally set no higher than 100 IEEE units.

PEDESTAL—1. The level of the video signal representing black, normally set at 7.5 IEEE units. 2. A rigid camera mount normally used in studio production, and mounted on steerable wheels to provide smooth movement. 3. Director's command to a camera operator to raise or lower camera during production.

PHASE—The timing relationship between two signals, commonly but not necessarily of the same frequency.

PHOTOMATIC—A limited animation done on videotape, using photographs as artwork, to serve as a video storyboard. Commonly used to produce test commercials. Similar to an animatic.

PING-PONG—To transfer audio from one channel of a tape to another. If program audio has been recorded on the channel normally assigned to time code, the audio will be ping-ponged to another channel so that time code can then be recorded on the proper channel.

PLUMBICON®—The tradename for a type of camera pickup tube that employs lead monoxide as the light-sensitive element.

POLECAT—A spring-loaded pole that can be braced between floor and ceiling to hold lights, set elements, etc.

PULSE CROSS DISPLAY—A special test display of a video signal that offsets both horizontal and vertical blanking intervals so that they cross at the center of the screen, and are thus visible.

PORTAPAK—A portable, battery-operated, camera/recorder system.

POST-PRODUCTION—The editing process.

PRACTICAL LIGHTS—Lights that are part of a set and are also used for scene illumination.

PRE-PRODUCTION—The process leading up to and preparing for production.

PREROLL—The length of tape time ahead of an edit point to which tapes are cued prior to performing an edit. Necessary to allow tape speed to stabilize before the edit is made.

PREVIEW BUS—A row of buttons on a switcher that permits a signal or an effect to be viewed on the preview monitor prior to being selected on the program bus.

PRIME LENS—A lens with a fixed focal length.

PRISM OPTICS—In a three-tube color camera, a compact, rugged, and efficient optical system that splits the incoming light into the component red-green-blue portions to be picked up by the tubes. Found in higher quality cameras.

PROC AMP (Processing Amplifier)—A unit designed to correct levels of a video signal, and to either reshape or replace sync pulses with new pulses.

PRODUCTION—The process of physically creating a program.

PROGRAM BUS—A row of buttons on a switcher that sends a signal out on the program line, either to a transmitter, or to a VTR.

PROMPTER (See Teleprompter.)

PROPS—Short for Properties. Objects used either in decorating a set (set props), or held and used by talent (hand props).

PROTECTION MASTER—A copy (dub) of a master tape, usually made immediately once the master has been recorded. Used as a backup in the event the master is damaged, and normally is stored in a safe place.

QUAD (QUADRAPLEX)—The original videotape format, using 2-inch tape, and employing four record/playback heads in a transverse scanning pattern.

QUAD SPLIT—A special effect wherein four pictures are combined on the screen, one in each corner.

QUANTEL—Tradename for a digital video effects unit made by MCI Quantel.

QUARTZ LIGHT—A high intensity bulb with a constant color temperature used in lighting instruments.

R.F.—Radio Frequency.

R.F. MICROPHONE—(See Wireless Microphone.)

R.G.B.—Red, green, and blue; the primaries in color television.

RS-170A—The EIA (Electronic Industries Association) standard for color television signals.

RACK FOCUS—To shift focus during a shot, either between two subjects at different distances from the camera, or as an effect.

RASTER—The scanned area making up the active portion of a video signal.

RE-ENTRY—The capability of larger switchers to re-enter an effect set up on one mix/effects bank into a second mix/effects bank for further manipulation. Larger switchers may offer double, triple, or even quadruple re-entry.

REACTION SHOT—A shot of one or more people reacting to some action or dialog.

REAL TIME—Denotes the actual time over which events transpire. A program done in real time is one that has not been edited.

RECEIVER—In television, a receiver is a television set that includes a tuner and an audio amplifier and speaker. It is capable of receiving broadcast radio frequency signals, as opposed to a monitor, which accepts a composite video signal only.

REGISTRATION—The process of physically and electronically aligning the three tubes in a color camera so that the pictures they form are exactly superimposed on one another.

RELEASE—A signed agreement giving a producer the right to reproduce the likeness of a person, place, or thing in a program. A talent release is signed by a performer or actor, while a property release is signed by the property owner.

RELEASE PRINT—A film term denoting a color corrected print of a completed film made for distribution. The video counterpart would be a dub made from an edited master tape for distribution.

REMOTE—Indicates production done on location, rather than in a studio.

RESOLUTION—The measurement of the amount of fine detail reproduced by a video system.

REVERB—Short for Reverberation, an electronic sound effect similar to echo, used to create a fuller sound, or to duplicate the ambience of a room.

REVERSAL FILM—Film that produces a positive image when developed, rather than a negative image.

RIDING LEVELS—Carefully adjusting audio or video levels during production.

RIPPLE (Editing)—An action performed by a computer editing system. If the length of an edit in an existing edit decision list is changed, the computer can change the record starting times of all edits that follow the altered one to correct the list. A fairly advanced technique that is part of what is known as "list management."

RISER—A platform, usually about a foot high, used to raise seated performers to camera eye level.

ROLL (Title)—In graphics, information moving vertically on the screen, usually from bottom to top, as with credits at the end of a program.

ROLLING—"Tape is rolling" means that the VTR has been started and tape is moving.

ROUGH CUT—A tentative, preliminary edit of a program. Corresponds to off-line editing.

RUNDOWN—A succinct program schedule, giving brief descriptions of segments along with precise segment times and total program running time.

RUNTHROUGH—A rehearsal of a production.

RUSHES (See Dailies.)

S.E.C.A.M. (SYSTEME ELECTRONIQUE POUR COULEUR AVEC MEMORIE)—The color television system developed in France, and used there and in most of the communist-block countries and a few other areas, including parts of Africa.

S.A.G.—Screen Actors Guild, a union.

S.E.G.—Screen Extras Guild, a union.

S.E.G. (SPECIAL EFFECTS GENERATOR)—A section of a switcher that provides the capability of performing wipes of various patterns. At the smaller levels of all-in-one, off-the-shelf switchers, sometimes used to indicate the entire switcher.

S.M.P.T.E.—Society of Motion Picture and Television Engineers, a professional associa-tion. (Usually called by the shorthand name pronounced "Simptee.")

SMPTE TIME CODE—A frame numbering system developed by SMPTE that assigns a number to each frame of video. Divided into hours, minutes, seconds, and frames (e.g., 01:42:13:26). Used primarily in computer editing.

S.O.T.—Sound On Tape.

S.T.V.—Subscription Television, a system of over-the-air pay TV employing a scrambled signal that requires a decoder box to be received.

SAFE ACTION—An area comprising about 90 percent of the television raster that is likely to be seen on the majority of receivers, regardless of misadjustment, and in which it is therefore safe to include action.

SAFE TITLE—An area comprising about 80 percent of the television raster that is likely to be seen on virtually all receivers, regardless of misadjustment, and in which it is therefore safe to include printed information.

SATICON®—The tradename for a type of camera pickup tube that employs a selenium/arsenic/tellurium compound as the light-sensitive element.

SATURATION—The measure of the amount of color relative to the luminance level in a picture or portion thereof.

SCANNER—The assembly comprised of the video head drum and heads.

SCANNING—1. The process of moving an electron beam horizontally and vertically to create or reproduce television pictures. 2. The process of moving a video head across videotape to record or reproduce pictures.

SCRATCH DUB—A "quick and dirty" copy of a master tape, or a copy made during production (usually on a low-cost cassette format) simultaneous with recording on the master tape. Often used as dailies in video production.

SCRIM—1. A wire mesh screen that can be inserted into a holder in front of a light to cut the light's intensity. 2. Fiberglass material used to cut light intensity (see Tough Spun). 3. Diaphanous cloth used in stage and studio production that appears opaque when lit from the front, and transparent when the front light is turned off and objects behind it are lit.

SEAMLESS—Shorthand for Seamless Background Paper. Paper available in wide rolls and in various colors for use as a backdrop.

SEGMENTED—Those videotape formats that record less than a full picture with each pass of the head are called segmented formats. Includes quad and the Type B 1-inch format.

SEGUE—A smooth and seamless transition from one musical piece to another with no space in between. Also has commonly come to mean any smooth transition.

SERVO—Any of various systems comprised of a variable-speed motor and the associated electronics that control its speed.

SETUP LEVEL (See Black Level.)

SHADING—The adjustment of a camera to produce the desired picture quality both prior to and during production.

SHADOW KEYER—A chromakey unit sensitive enough that it will key shadows of foreground objects.

SHADOW MASK MONITOR—A color monitor with an internal mask directly behind the screen containing thousands of small holes that regulate which color phosphor dots the red, green, and blue beams are allowed to strike. Until the introduction of the Sony Trinitron tube, which employs an aperture grill, all color receivers and monitors were shadow mask designs.

SHINY BOARD—Common term for lighting reflector.

SHOT LIST—A list of shots compiled from a script breakdown, normally used in single-camera, film-style production.

SHOT SHEET—A list of a camera operator's shots for a program, usually affixed to the rear of the camera for reference.

SHOTGUN MICROPHONE—A highly directional microphone, used to pick up sound over a distance, or to isolate sounds in noisy areas.

SIGNAL-TO-NOISE RATIO (S/N)—The amount of video or audio noise mixed in with the basic signal.

SILK—A translucent cloth (made of silk) stretched over a frame that can be positioned overhead to cut the intensity of direct sunlight when shooting outdoors.

SKEW—1. Errors in tape playback caused by improper tape tension, and seen as a curve or hook at the top of the picture. 2. The control on a VTR that corrects skew errors.

SLATE—A board containing the pertinent information about a shot, recorded on tape or film at the start of each take.

SLIDE CHAIN—Generically, a system combining a slide projector with a television camera, used to transmit slides or record them on tape.

SNAKE—A multiconductor cable containing several lines with individual connectors at either end. Used mainly in running audio lines.

SNORKLE—An optical system that mounts a lens at the end of a long tube to allow shots to be taken in very small, tight spaces. Looks like an upside-down periscope attached to a camera.

SOFT LIGHT—1. Light that has a diffused source. 2. A lighting instrument that produces soft light.

SOFT WIPE—A wipe effect from one image to another that has a soft, diffused edge.

SPECS—Short for Specifications.

SPEED—The call given by a tape operator once the tape has been rolling for enough time that all servos are locked and the VTR has reached a stable speed, and (usually) that there is enough preroll time for use in editing.

SPLIT EDIT—An edit where the video and audio edits are made at different points, one preceding the other.

SPLIT FOCUS—The practice of focusing at a point between two objects at different distances from the camera, allowing depth of field to keep both acceptably sharp. In cases of extreme difference in distance, a "split-field filter" can be used which will compensate for the difference.

SPLIT SCREEN—A wipe between two signals stopped part way, with the two scenes separated along a horizontal or vertical line.

SPREADER—A device on which the legs of a tripod are placed to keep them from spreading on a smooth surface.

SQUEEZOOM®—Tradename for a digital video effects unit marketed by Vital Industries.

STAGING—A term describing the act of assembling all equipment, props, etc., in an area prior to loading into trucks for a location shoot. The area used is called the "Staging Area."

STAR FILTER—A filter with a series of finely etched lines that can be placed on a camera lens. Any spectral lights or reflections within the scene will create a starburst effect. Generally available in four, six, and eight-point star patterns.

STEADICAM®—Tradename for a camera stabilization system marketed by Cinema Products.

STILL STORE—One of several types of devices that store still frame pictures for use in production. Most such units store video frames on computer-type disk drives, either in analog or digital form, allowing for extremely fast access times.

STOP DOWN—To decrease the opening of the lens aperture, reducing the amount of light transmitted (moving to a higher F-stop number).

STORYBOARD—A series of panels of pictures (usually sketches) designed to show how a production will look. Comic books are essentially storyboards.

STRIKE—The process of dismantling and packing away equipment and/or studio set elements after a production.

STRIPE—Most commonly, the process of recording SMPTE time code on a previously recorded tape.

STRIPE FILTER—A special filter used in single-tube color cameras to separate the red, green, and blue signals from white light.

SUBCARRIER—The two 3.58 MHz color difference signals used in color television.

SUBMASTER—A tape used as an intermediate source in editing, created from the original master. For instance, when multiple effects are needed that are beyond the switcher's capabilities, a submaster is created with the first "layer" of effects, and then used as a source, at which point the additional effects are added.

SUBTRACTIVE COLOR—The system of colored pigments, where the basic color primaries combine to make black.

SUPER—Short for Superimposition. Correctly used, indicates a dissolve stopped half way through. Also commonly used to indicate a key, such as a person's name, matted in over the video.

SWEETENING—The process of audio post-production, at which time problems in the audio are corrected, and sound effects are added, etc.

SWISH PAN—An extremely fast pan of the camera, producing a blurred image.

SWITCHER—A device with a series of input selectors that permit one of various inputs to be sent out on the program line.

SYNC—Short for synchronization. 1. Pulses contained within a composite video signal to provide a synchronization reference for equipment. Also a separate signal that can be fed to various pieces of equipment. 2. Indicates synchronization between picture and sound. 3. Sound recorded on a separate audio tape, but synchronized with videotape or film shot simultaneously.

SYNC GENERATOR—A device that generates synchronizing pulses.

SYNOPSIS—A brief outline of the plot or subject matter of a program.

T-STOP—Similar to F-stops, but corrected to take into account the transmission factor of the lens, thus providing a more accurate indication of the amount of light actually transmitted.

T.D.—Technical Director.

T.V.R.O. (TELEVISION RECEIVE ONLY)—A satellite earth station that can receive signals, but not transmit them.

TAIL SLATE—Slate information recorded at the end of a take rather than at the beginning. Usually indicated as such by being shot upside down.

TAKE—Verb: The director's command to select a video source. Noun: An individual shot, scene, or segment of a program.

TALENT—Generic term for people who appear or are heard in a program.

TALLY LIGHT—A light (usually red) on the front of a camera that indicates it is in use. There is also usually a tally light in or near the viewfinder to let the operator know when that camera is "on," and on the camera's monitor in the control room.

TARGET—The faceplate of a camera pickup tube, where the electron beam scans the image.

TELECINE—(See Film Chain.)

TELEPHOTO LENS—A lens with a long focal length.

TELEPROMPTER—A device mounted on the front of a camera that projects copy on a semireflective mirror placed directly in front of the lens to permit talent to read lines while appearing to look at the camera.

TELEVISION—A system that allows people to see things at a great distance without the use of a crystal ball. Discovered by Milton Berle in a men's room in the Catskills in late 1946.

THREE POINT LIGHTING—A basic standard lighting technique employing Key, Fill, and Back lights.

TILT—Camera movement on a vertical axis from a stationary position.

TIME BASE CORRECTOR (TBC)—A device that corrects time base stability errors (errors in the rate at which the signal is coming) during tape playback.

TIME CODE (See SMPTE time code.)

TONE (TEST TONE)—A constant audio frequency signal recorded at the start of a tape at 0 VU to provide a reference for later use, such as in post-production.

TOUGH SPUN—Common term for a heat-resistant, fiberglass, cloth-like material used to diffuse light.

TREATMENT—A complete description of a program, including characters, locations, and intended audience.

TRACE—(Editing) A computer program that compiles several generations of rough (off-line) edit decision lists into a single EDL ready to use for auto assembly.

TRACK—1. The section of tape on which a signal is recorded. 2. The sound portion of a film or video program. 3. Pipes or boards on which a dolly moves, generally used on location.

TRACKING—1. A shot in which the camera moves along with performers who are walking, driving, etc. 2. The adjustment of the positioning of video heads during playback of a tape so that the heads reproduce the strongest possible signal.

TRAFFICKING—The distribution of a completed program on tape to various destinations. The duties performed by the trafficking department are analogous with those of a shipping department.

TRIPOD—A camera mounting device with three legs.

TRUCK—The act of moving the camera from side to side on wheels relative to the shot being taken.

TYPE C—The SMPTE standard for the 1-inch nonsegmented helical videotape recording format.

U-MATIC—The tradename for the ¾-inch videocassette system originally developed by Sony. Now established as the ANSI (American National Standards Institute) Type E videotape format.

ULTIMATTE®—The tradename of a very high quality special effects system similar in application to a chromakeyer.

UNDER FIVE—An actor with fewer than five lines, paid at a lower rate.

UNDERCRANKING—A film technique whereby the camera is run at a lower than normal speed to produce fast motion when the film is subsequently projected at normal speed. At ranges near or below one frame per second, is considered to be time-lapse cinemaphotography.

UNDERSCAN—Reducing the height and width of the video picture so that the edges, and thus portions of blanking, can be observed.

UNIDIRECTIONAL—A microphone which picks up sound mainly from one direction.

UP CUT—In editing, to cut back into the end of the previous scene, often by mistake. In general, to cut short.

V.C.R.—Video Cassette Recorder.

V.H.S. (VIDEO HOME SYSTEM)—The ½-inch videocassette format developed by JVC for consumer and industrial use.

V.O.—Short for Voice Over (narration—the speaker is not seen).

V.T.R.—Video Tape Recorder.

V.U. METER—Short for Volume Unit meter. A meter used to monitor audio levels.

VECTORSCOPE—A special oscilloscope used in television to monitor color reproduction.

VERTICAL INTERVAL—Synonymous with vertical blanking. Also indicates a type of switcher or editor that will only make a cut during the vertical interval.

VERTICAL SYNC—The synchronizing pulses used to define the end of one television field and the start of the next, occurring at a rate of approx. 59.94 Hz (color), and 60 Hz (black & white).

VIDEO—1. The visual portion of a television program. 2. Colloquially, has several meanings: (a) Synonymous with television. (b) All television other than broadcast television. (c) As a description for a program, as in "I just finished a video." (as opposed to " . . . a film."). This latter term is awkward and distasteful (" . . . a tape" or " . . . a program" is much preferred).

VIDEOCASSETTE—A plastic shell containing two reels and a given length of videotape.

VIDEODISC—One of several technologies whereby programs are stored on a flat disk, similarly to an audio record.

VIDICON—A type of camera pickup tube now rarely used, but which provided the basis for current pickup tube technologies.

VIGNETTING—A darkening at the corners of a picture, usually caused by improper matching of lens to camera. Often called "portholing."

W.G.A.—Writer's Guild of America, a union.

WAVEFORM MONITOR—A special oscilloscope used in television to evaluate various aspects of a video signal, including levels, blanking, *et al*.

WEDGE—1. Wedge-shaped pieces of wood used as shims in adjusting platforms, dolly track, etc. 2. A portion of a test pattern used to measure resolution.

WHITE BALANCE—The adjustment of the red, green, and blue channels in a color camera to produce the correct balance (and thus white) when shooting a flat white field.

WILD SOUND—Sound that is not synchronized with the video, such as sound recorded on a separate audio recorder.

WINDOW DUB—A copy of a time-coded videotape with a visual display of the numbers keyed into the picture.

WIPE—A transition from one scene to another wherein the new scene is revealed by a moving line or pattern.

WIRELESS MICROPHONE—A microphone that uses a radio transmitter and receiver to eliminate the need for a wire connecting the mike to the mixer or recorder.

WORKPRINT—A copy of a videotape (usually a master tape), usually made on a videocassette for off-line editing. Workprints are often made as window dubs for computer editing.

WRITING SPEED—The speed of a recording head relative to the tape.

X.L.R.—A three-pin balanced audio connector used on all professional equipment. Also called a Cannon-type connector.

Z—Electronic shorthand for IMPEDANCE.

ZEBRA PATTERN—A pattern of stripes superimposed over areas that exceed a specified brightness level (usually 100 IEEE units) in the viewfinders of some cameras.

ZOOM—Noun: A lens with a variable focal length. Verb: The act of varying the focal length of a zoom lens.

Bibliography

The Book of Movie Photography, by David Cheshire, Alfred A. Knopf, New York, 1979. A profusely illustrated and very well done book on film techniques, much of which applies to video. Designed for the novice filmmaker.

The Cool Fire, by Bob Shanks, Norton, New York, 1976. An outstanding overview of the television industry, covering production techniques, and with special attention to the business aspects.

ENG/EFP/EPP Handbook, C. Robert Paulson, Principal Author, Broadband Information Services, New York, 1981. An excellent technical reference book covering the equipment used in electronic news gathering and field production equipment.

The Five C's of Cinematography, by Joseph Mascelli, Cine/Graphic Publications, Hollywood, 1965. A marvelous treatise on the aesthetics of filmmaking, easily applicable to television production.

Four Arguments for the Elimination of Television, by Jerry Mander, William Morrow and Co., New York, 1978. This book should be required reading for all those who work in television production, despite the ultimate recommendation made. Well written, well researched, and well thought-out.

The Handbook of Private Television, Nathan Sambul, editor, McGraw/Hill Book Company, New York, 1982. Twenty-seven contributing authors examine the nature, uses, techniques, and management of "private," or nonbroadcast, television, as employed by business, government, medicine, etc. A comprehensive overview of video designed for the media manager.

The Hollywood Guide to Film Budgeting and Script Breakdown, by Danford Chamness, D. Chamness & Assoc., Toluca Lake, CA, 1977. A really comprehensive guide to how scripts are broken down and budgets estimated by the professionals. Includes detailed examples.

How to Make Good Pictures, Eastman Kodak Co., Rochester, NY. This little book, designed for amateur photographers, has all sorts of nifty ideas that can be applied to television production. Covers the basics of lenses and optics, and basic composition.

The Independent Filmmaker's Guide, by Michael Wiese, Michael Wiese Film Productions, Sausalito, CA, 1981. "How to finance, produce and distribute your short and documentary films," written by a producer who's done it.

Independent Video, by Ken Marsh, Straight Arrow Press, San Francisco, CA, 1973. An introduction to the basic operation of the television system, written for nontechnical people.

Lighting for Location Motion Pictures, by Alan J. Ritsko, Van Nostrand Reinhold Co., New York, 1979. Although focusing on location work, also an excellent work on lighting in general.

Making Films Your Business, by Mollie Gregory, Schocken Books, New York, 1979. A comprehensive guide to proposing, funding, budgeting, and distributing independent work. Written for filmmakers, but can be applied to video production.

Sight Sound Motion, by Herb Zettl, Wadsworth Publishing, Belmont, CA, 1973. A fine textbook for students of the aesthetics of television production.

Sound Recording, by John Eargle, Van Nostrand Reinhold, New York, 1976. An in-depth study of audio recording equipment and techniques.

The Technique of Television Production, by Gerald Millerson, Hastings House, New York, 1974. An overview of studio production practices. First published in 1961, now in 9th revised edition.

Tektronix Books: *Television Waveform Processing Circuits, Television Systems*—both by Gerald A. Eastman, Tektronix, Inc., Beaverton, OR, 1969. Two fine technical reference books on television circuits and signal processing.

Television Production, by Alan Wurtzel, McGraw-Hill Book Company, New York, 1979. An outstanding textbook concentrating on studio production equipment and techniques.

The Video Guide, Third Edition, by Charles Bensinger, Howard W. Sams & Co., Inc., Indianapolis, IN, 1982. An excellent introduction to small-format videotape equipment and its use.

Writing for Television and Radio, by Robert Hilliard, Hastings House, New York, 1976. Covers the basics of scriptwriting, including samples of various formats.

PERIODICALS

American Cinematographer (monthly)
P.O. Box 2230
Hollywood, CA 90028

Published by the American Society of Cinematographers (ASC). An excellent magazine covering the feature film industry. Increasing coverage of video. Lots of "behind the scenes at—" and "on location with—," etc. Useful info on grip, lighting, various other areas of production.

American Film (10 issues/year)
P.O. Box 966
Farmingdale, NY 11737

Published by the nonprofit American Film Institute. Written mainly for the general public (members of the AFI). General-interest, nontechnical articles on film and TV's impact on society, obscure new directors, etc.

Audio-Visual Communications (monthly)
Media Horizons
475 Park Ave. S.
New York, NY 10016

Coverage mainly of slide/tape and "multi-media." Some coverage of video. Aimed at corporate in-house media production. Well written and edited.

BM/E—Broadcast Management/Engineering (monthly)
Broadband Information Services, Inc.
295 Madison Ave.
New York, NY 10017

An excellent technical and management magazine. Examines new technology, products and techniques. Heavily oriented toward station management and engineering staffs. Covers radio and TV.

BACK STAGE (weekly)
Back Stage Publications
165 West 46th St.
New York, NY 10036

Back Stage is the weekly newspaper for the film and tape production industry. Emphasis on commercials and industrials. Lots of "who's doing what." Special sections on regional activities. Relatively little "how to." Aimed at production professionals, network people, and ad agencies. Essential for those in the entertainment and commercial production areas of the business.

Broadcast Communications (monthly)
Globecom Publishing Ltd.
4121 West 83rd St. Suite 132
Prairie Village, KS 66208

A very well-done general magazine on broadcast technology. Oriented toward station management—emphasis on TV, but also covers radio. Not overly technical.

Broadcast Engineering (monthly)
Intertec Publishing Corp.
P.O. Box 12901
Overland Park, KS 66212

A hard-core engineering magazine featuring deeply technical report on radio and TV technology. Good coverage of trade shows and new products.

Broadcasting (weekly)
Broadcast Publications, Inc.
1735 DeSales St., N.W.
Washington, D.C. 20036

Put together primarily for television management in the areas of programming, advertising sales, and station management. Covers both TV and radio. In publication since 1930.

CableVision (weekly)
Titsch Publishing, Inc.
2500 Curtis St.
Denver, CO 80205

Designed to cover the business, production and technical aspects of cable programming, with emphasis on pay-cable. Very well done.

Commercials Monthly
470 S. San Vincente Blvd., Suite 103
Los Angeles, CA 90028

Aimed mainly at producers, directors (and especially), casting directors and talent. Concentrates on location, talent (lots of agency ads with head shots), with some coverage of production and companies.

EITV—Educational & Industrial Television (monthly)
C.S. Tepfer Publishing Co., Inc.
51 Sugar Hollow Rd.
Danbury, CT 06810

The granddaddy of nonbroadcast television magazines. Sometimes arthritic, but occasionally very useful articles. Frequent "how-tos" and company profiles. Aimed at corporate television producers and schools. Excellent for those starting out in video.

Filmmaker's Monthly (monthly)
P.O. Box 115
Ward Hill, MA 01830

A pleasant little magazine aimed at "professionals and semiprofessionals working in film and videotape in studios, independent production houses, university film departments, TV stations, and corporations" (their description). Has been around for a long time, occasionally has something of interest. Sometimes runs in-depth "how-tos" on various subjects.

Home Video (monthly)
P.O. Box 2651
Boulder, CO 80322

Published by the same people as "Videography" for the home market. Fair quality. Some decent articles, but tends to fall flat. Feeling that it's put out mainly to cash in on the home video craze.

Millimeter (monthly)
12 E. 46th St.
New York, NY 10017

Millimeter is the *Back Stage* of the magazine field. Covers commercials, TV, and feature films. Frequent "special subject" issues. Personality profiles, state-of-the-art, state-of-the-business, new products, etc. A must for those in the business who need to know what's happening. Few real "how-tos" or technical information. Heavy on "what's going on" columns. Aimed at production professionals and ad agencies.

On Location (monthly)
6464 Sunset Blvd. Suite 570
Hollywood, CA 90028

A handsomely produced magazine covering film and tape production. Covers features, series, specials, and commercials. Less emphasis on business matters than Millimeter. Occasional glimpses of "how-to" sneak through. Mainly articles—columns somewhat on the weak side. Aimed at the production professional.

Shooting Commercials (monthly)
PTN Publishing Corp.
101 Crossways Park West
Weoodbury, NY 11797

As the name implies, covers the commercial production business. Recently changed hands for the second time in as many years, with new publisher doing excellent job of upgrading.

60 Seconds (monthly)
6610 West Sixth St.
Los Angeles, CA 90048

In-depth coverage of the commercial production scene. "Short Takes" department gives synopsis of commercials currently in or just completing production. Good feature articles. Established in 1981, looking good.

Video (monthly)
Reese Publishing Co., Inc.
P.O. Box 1118
Dover, NJ 07801

A surprisingly well-done consumer video magazine. Excellent equipment tests, product and software reviews, and fairly well-written articles on equipment and its use. Sometimes frustrating for video professional due to lowered aim.

Video Review (monthly)
P.O. Box 919
Farmingdale, NY 11737

Ties with "Video" for top place in the consumer video market. Well-executed equipment tests, good articles, and very comprehensive series of program reviews. Some excellent features. Relatively new, and coming on strong.

Video Systems (monthly)
Intertec Publishing Corp.
P.O. Box 12912
Overland Park, KS 66212

Aimed at managers of production facilities, both broadcast and nonbroadcast. Recently redesigned and expanded in size and scope. "Theme" issues focus on specific subject areas. Greatly improved, and worthwhile.

Video User (monthly)
Knowledge Industry Publications
2 Corporate Park Dr.
White Plains, NY 10604

From the people who put on the Video Expos. Lots of recycled press releases along with some reporting and articles. Notorious for inaccuracies and poor proofreading. Has improved somewhat in terms of content, and is overall worthwhile.

Videography (monthly)
475 Park Ave. So.
New York, NY 10016

A generally entertaining all-purpose magazine aimed at nonbroadcast TV, independents, and video artists. Very few technical or "how-to" articles. Lots of interviews, industry gossip, occasional facilities and equipment surveys. Strong on columns which range from excellent to fair.

Videoplay (bi-monthly)
C.S. Tepfer Publishing Co., Inc.
51 Sugar Hollow Rd.
Danbury, CT 06810

Another consumer video magazine. Decent tests, reviews, and reports. Lots of "what's new" in products and programs.

Videowriter (bi-monthly)
J. M. Bade & Associates
P.O. Box 2410
Glen Ellyn, IL 60137

Established at the start of 1981, this falls between a newsletter and a magazine. Aimed at scriptwriters in video, film, and multi-image (slide/tape) production for business. Very ambitious, does a good job.

INDEX

382

IF YOU'RE IN THE VIDEO BUSINESS...

And have a line of video products you need to sell, Sams can help you do it with your own AV/Video catalog.

It's neither difficult nor expensive to have a catalog produced with your name on the outside and your product lines on the inside, and it definitely makes you look good while it helps you sell.

Call 800-428-3696 or 317-298-5566 and ask the Sams Sales Manager for full details.

Many thanks for your interest in this Sams Book about the world of Video. Here are a few more Sams Video Books we think you'll like:

You can usually find these Sams Books at better bookstores and electronic distributors nationwide.

If you can't find what you need, call Sams at 800-428-3696 toll-free or 317-298-5566, and charge it to your MasterCard or Visa account. Prices subject to change without notice. In Canada, contact Lenbrook Industries Ltd., Scarborough, Ontario.

For a free catalog of all Sams Books available, write P.O. Box 7092, Indianapolis, IN 46206.

THE HOME VIDEO HANDBOOK (3rd Edition)

Easily the nation's most popular, most respected book on the subject of home video recording! Shows you how to simply and successfully enjoy your home TV camera, videocassette recorder, videodisc system, large-screen TV projector, home satellite TV receiver, and all their accessories. Tells you how to hook everything up to make it do what you want it to do, how to buy the best equipment for your needs, how to make your equipment pay for itself, and more! By Charles Bensinger. 352 pages, 5½ x 8½, soft. ISBN 0-672-22052-0. © 1982.
Ask for No. 22052 . . . .**$12.95**

THE VIDEO GUIDE (3rd Edition)

If your work involves a hands-on understanding of video production hardware, this is your book. Tells you about standard and state-of-the-art videotape and VCR units for studio or portable use, industrial and broadcast cameras, videodiscs, editing systems, lenses, and accessories, and how they work. Then it shows you how and when to use each one, and how to set up, operate, maintain, trouble-shoot, and repair it. A classic reference guide for video professionals and ideal for those just learning, too. By Charles Bensinger. 264 pages, 8½ x 11, soft. ISBN 0-672-22051-2. © 1983.
Ask for No. 22051 . . . .**$18.95**

THE VIDEO PRODUCTION GUIDE

Helps you professionally handle all or any part of the video production process. Contains user-friendly, real-world coverage of pre-production planning, creativity and organization, people handling, single- and multicamera studio or on-location production, direction techniques, editing, special effects, and distribution of the finished production. Ideal for use by working or aspiring producer/directors, and by schools, broadcasters, CATV, and general industry. By Lon McQuillin, edited by Charles Bensinger. 352 pages, 8½ x 11, soft. ISBN 0-672-22053-9. © 1982.
Ask for No. 22053 . . . .**$28.95**

CABLE TELEVISION (2nd Edition)

Designed for the engineer or technician who wants to improve his knowledge of cable television. Helps you examine each component in a cable system separately and in relation to the system as a whole. Discusses component testing, troubleshooting, noise reduction, and system failure. Contains valuable information concerning fiber optics and communications satellites. By John Cunningham. 392 pages, 5½ x 8½, soft. ISBN 0-672-21755-4. © 1980.
Ask for No. 21755 . . . .**$13.95**

THE SATELLITE TV HANDBOOK

An easily read, amazing book that tells you what satellite TV is all about! Shows you how to legally and privately cut your cable TV costs in half, see TV shows that may be blacked out in your city, pick up live, unedited network TV shows that include the bloopers, start a mini-cable system in your apartment or condo complex, plug into video-supplied college courses, business news, children's networks, and much more! Also covers buying or building and aiming your own satellite antenna, and includes a guide to all programs available on the satellites, channel by channel. By Anthony T. Easton.
Ask for No. 22055

BASICS OF AUDIO AND VISUAL SYSTEMS DESIGN

Valuable, NAVA-sanctioned information for designers and installers of commercial, audience-oriented AV systems, and especially for newcomers to this field of AV. Gives you a full background in fundamental system design concepts and procedures, updated with current technology. Covers image format, screen size and performance, front vs. rear projection, projector output, audio, use of mirrors, and more. By Raymond Wadsworth. 128 pages, 8½ x 11, soft. ISBN 0-672-22038-5. © 1983.
Ask for No. 22038 . . . .**$15.95**